DECODING THE DIGITAL CHURCH

Rhetoric, Culture, and Social Critique

DECODING THE DIGITAL CHURCH

EVANGELICAL STORYTELLING *and the* ELECTION *of* DONALD J. TRUMP

STEPHANIE A. MARTIN

THE UNIVERSITY OF ALABAMA PRESS
Tuscaloosa

The University of Alabama Press
Tuscaloosa, Alabama 35487-0380
uapress.ua.edu

Typeface: Adobe Caslon Pro

Cover design: Lori Lynch

Cataloging-in-Publication data is available from the Library of Congress.
ISBN: 978-0-8173-2084-3
E-ISBN: 978-0-8173-9341-0

To my parents

Contents

	Acknowledgments	ix
	Introduction	1
ONE	Evangelicals and the Continuous Reawakening to the Greatest Story Ever Told	23
TWO	Digital Rhetorical Ethnography: Going to Church in My Pajamas	38
THREE	America Is (Still) Great	54
FOUR	Don't Worry, Be Happy—But God Wants You to Vote	74
FIVE	Do Unto Others?	104
SIX	#MeToo Goes to Church	147
	Conclusion	165
	Appendix A. Rhetorical Sample of Sermons from the Great Recession and Recovery	177
	Appendix B. Rhetorical Sample of Sermons from the Presidential Campaign of 2016	189
	Notes	193
	Bibliography	235
	Index	255

Acknowledgments

Saint Augustine, in *The Confessions*, wrote that love "has the hands to help others." Throughout the writing of this book, I have been loved beyond measure, both directly and indirectly. Various academic communities have enriched my thinking about rhetoric, communication, political theory, and conservative social movements. I am forever indebted to to the departments of Communication and Sociology at the University of California, San Diego and, in particular, John Evans, Isaac Martin, Gary Fields, Valerie Hartouni, and Robert Horwitz. Robert and Val's presence in my life and work has been especially significant. Whatever abilities I have as a scholar and writer owe much to them. They are simply the best. At UCSD, I was constantly made smarter by my fellow graduate students, most notably Lauren Berliner, Erin Cory, Laurel Friedman, Katrina Hoch, Kate Levitt, Carl McKinney, Reece Peck, and Emily York, among many others. Our La Jolla community is second to none. I am grateful every day for how it formed me then and continues to influence me now.

I can imagine no better place to have continued the research for this book on the relationship between conservative evangelicalism and the American public sphere than I have found at Southern Methodist University and my division of Corporate Communication & Public Affairs. The support and goodwill of this community have been constantly present, especially from Sandy Duhé, Rita Kirk, Owen Lynch, Maria Dixon Hall, LaShonda Eaddy, Cara Jacocks, Amber Benson, and Christopher Salinas. Chris, in particular, spent long lunches with me working through the rhetorical theories and arguments that I present in this book. His generosity made me smarter and his friendship makes working at SMU fun and rewarding. He is a gift. Jared

Schroeder, as a colleague down the hall, shared drafts and encouragement. His camaraderie and friendship never failed. Rebecca Hewitt laughed at my jokes, offered encouraging hugs, and kept the snack cabinet full. Dean Sam Holland provided important funding, including a crucial sabbatical leave.

In the field more generally, I have been supported and encouraged by a number of senior scholars who generously gave their time and advice. Special thanks go to Rod Hart, Mary Stuckey, Jennifer Mercieca, Julia Azari, and John Murphy. The team at the University of Alabama Press have been professional and terrific, especially Dan Waterman, Joanna Jacobs, and series editor John Lucaites, who saw potential in this project from the beginning. The advice and attention of two anonymous peer reviewers sharpened my argument and writing immeasurably.

In life, sometimes a friend appears when one least expects but most has a need. For me, that friend is Allison Prasch. Allison has been so many things to me during the years I have worked on this book. She has taught me important theoretical concepts, championed my efforts, listened to my doubts, and maintained confidence when my own wore thin. She read every draft of every chapter, and then kindly did it again, always offering useful suggestions. My debt to her is matched only by my gratitude. She is the definition of a true friend.

And then there are those who have simply been there with laughter or babysitting or some other personal offering that made life better over the years. Big thanks to xtine burrough and Paul Martin Lester, for all the reasons they know. Stefanie Barraco Zmich never failed to send texts that kept me smiling and knowing there was life beyond my office. Father Matthew Burdette of St. Thomas's Church in Fort Washington, Pennsylvania, was a trusted friend. He talked through ideas and gave valuable support. Tracy Watson Campbell is a hero. Her presence exists on every page of this book, as it crosses every page of my life. My parents, Richard and Joyce Martin, get special credit for always doing whatever I asked, from babysitting, to reading drafts, to helping keep my house in order. The book is dedicated to them, for all they have always done. I am blessed with two brothers who are more than family; they are friends. I would choose them to be my people, and that's saying a lot. Their wives are even better. My partner, Francisco Aragón, is the one who makes life possible. His love and support are the indelible grace that give my life meaning. Our sons, Niles and Tate, are joy, pure and simple. Their laughter is a celestial song.

Of course, I worry that I've forgotten someone who deserves mention. If I have, you know who you are, and I do thank you. I could not have finished this work without so many people in my professional and personal life who believed these questions were worth asking and answering, and who helped me and encouraged me along the way. I share my success with gratitude. All the mistakes are mine.

DECODING THE DIGITAL CHURCH

Introduction

On November 8, 2016, Donald Trump was elected the forty-fifth president of the United States. The following Sunday, John Ortberg, senior pastor of Menlo Church, just outside San Francisco, stood to address his congregation.[1] The support of conservative Protestants like those who attend Menlo Church had been essential to Trump's win. Eighty-one percent of self-identified white evangelicals across the United States voted for the GOP standardbearer.[2] Trump lost in California, however, including in San Mateo County, where Menlo Church is located.[3] Trump's popularity with evangelicals across the nation but relatively poor showing in the neighborhoods nearby may have left Ortberg feeling somewhat awkward. He was in the middle of preaching a sermon series called "House of Cards" about the election and about how true Christians might respond to turbulent political seasons. In earlier messages, he had suggested that the contest between Hillary Clinton and Donald Trump was vitriolic, messy, and painful to watch. Even so, he had encouraged his congregants to vote for one or the other and to be kind to those who chose differently. He told his listeners that God was ultimately not very worried about the American presidency. "Presidents come and go," he said. "Elections get won and lost. Political parties ebb and flow. Governments rise and fall. But the government of God is the one that matters, and it will be ruled over by Jesus Christ, the crucified carpenter of Nazareth. He is the King of Kings and the Lord of Lords, and of his government, there will be no end."[4]

In the days and weeks following Trump's election, people across the political spectrum were upset—maybe even more so than usual. Newspapers ran stories about friendships broken over voting disputes. The *Washington*

Post ran a piece about a grandmother who unfriended her granddaughter on Facebook because they disagreed about the election, rights to reproductive freedom, and—ultimately—which of the two was behaving more judgmentally toward the other's views.[5] In his postelection sermon, Ortberg acknowledged the national strife, but said unity could still be achieved. Unlike so many who presumed that because the large majority of conservative, white evangelicals had voted for Trump, he necessarily enjoyed strong and universal support among all such believers, Ortberg gestured to the possibility of diffidence, dissension, and anger, even inside his own church. "Part of what's unusual about this is . . . there's this sense that there's a division in our midst, like we want to come together, but there could be people in this church . . . there might be people in this pew . . . who voted the wrong way [*audience laughter*]."[6]

I watched Ortberg's sermon on my computer screen as part of an ongoing project studying the language and narratives of contemporary American evangelicalism as it relates to political and economic issues. I aimed to understand how American megachurch pastors deploy and circulate this language to their congregations as well as to a larger audience online. My interest in the narratives of these online churches was part personal and part professional. For more than twenty years, I have been watching, talking with, and befriending conservative evangelical Christians while studying their public rhetoric. For a short time, the fascination was part of my own faith journey. During my undergraduate years, I attended a conservative evangelical church. But the personalized gospel story these believers proclaim did not ultimately resonate with me. Even so, I have always admired the steadfast faith commitment of born-again Christians. I have puzzled over the way my personal experiences with these believers have differed from how scholars and popular writers typically frame their thinking and behaviors. For the most part, the white evangelicals I know, though socially and politically conservative, are not nearly as intolerant and prone to knee-jerk reactions as the stereotypes of them often conjure. Most really do try to live their lives being faithful to their spouses, providing good examples for their children, and remaining open-hearted toward their neighbors. While many conservative Christians struggle with the idea of abortion and refuse to accept it as a reproductive right that all women should have, and many disagree with the US Supreme Court's ruling that affirmed marriage equality, these believers would not deny friendship to a woman who terminated her pregnancy or refuse neighborly hospitality to a gay couple who live down the street.

However, even as I have personally liked my own evangelical friends, I have shared the confusion of other scholars and public intellectuals about the ongoing political rhetoric and electoral actions (votes) of this group. Beginning with Thomas Frank's 2004 book, *What's the Matter with Kansas?*, the question has circulated as to why so many highly religious but not wealthy voters should strongly support the Republican Party and its platform of low taxes and business deregulation instead of backing the Democrats, who agitate on behalf of the middle class, the marginalized, and the working poor.[7] Frank reasoned that evangelical believers privilege social issues at election time, and so subordinate other political priorities in order to escalate values questions in the public sphere. They vote for GOP candidates who campaign on promises to pass abortion restrictions, crack down on Hollywood for promoting promiscuity and violence, and defend "traditional" families; and they cast these votes at any cost to any constituency. The problem with this strategy, Frank and others argue, is that it ultimately fails. After Republican candidates become Republican officeholders, they forget all about those values issues their evangelical base holds dear, preferring to use their actual governing time passing tax cuts, deregulating business, and eliminating the social safety net.[8] In this view, it is a classic bait and switch.[9] To pull it off, the GOP has usually depended on running a candidate at the top who presents at least some semblance of virtue. The conundrum now is how so many of these believers could have overlooked Donald Trump's well-documented and constantly publicized character deficiencies to vote for him anyway.

As it turns out, the pastors whose rhetoric I studied were very bothered by Trump's lack of virtue. Like John Ortberg, many of them worried about the divisive nature of the 2016 election and acknowledged the possibility that their own congregants might feel alienated from Trump's candidacy—along with Hillary Clinton's—and hence from the democratic process itself. In this book, I will introduce you to pastors like Ortberg and, more particularly, their worldviews with regard to politics, economics, and elections as revealed through the sermons they give.[10] In the pages that follow, I invite you to come with me to listen to some of the messages these pastors deliver from the pulpits and stages of the megachurches they lead across the United States. I pay special attention to their thoughts about the Great Recession and the campaign leading up to the election of Donald Trump. To be clear, this is not primarily a book about the Great Recession or President Trump himself. Instead, these are the historical moments I interpret as a means for understanding how the political language and narratives of conservative evangelicals take shape. I have used megachurches on the internet as my avenue into conservative Protestantism because doing so allowed me to attend more than one church at a time, and to visit congregations that attract a lot of people and so manifest cultural and rhetorical resonance.[11] The approach is imperfect—not everyone likes a large church, for example, and plenty of churches do not have flashy websites with sermons available for easy online viewing—but it did give me a way to hear more stories than I could have had I done the research by attending services physically, in person. Using megachurches also allowed me to be systematic in my approach.[12] I refer to my hybrid research methodology as "digital rhetorical ethnography." I combined the resources of the digital church with rhetorical criticism to go deep inside conservative evangelicalism in America, at least as it exists on the internet. I will further explain how digital rhetorical ethnography works in chapter 2, "Digital Rhetorical Ethnography: Going to Church in My Pajamas." Very briefly, to practice digital rhetorical ethnography I immersed myself in the online church as American megachurches have curated it, both individually and across the internet, in order to participate in specific kinds of sermons about national politics and economics.[13] I watched and listened deeply. For example, the homily by Kevin Myers of 12Stone Church near Atlanta (which I detail in chapter 5) was one that I watched seven times. I made a complete transcript of Myers's words, of which I read all or part more times than I can count. And I took extensive notes about both his delivery and his language use almost every time I interacted with his sermon. I did this in part because I was behaving as a digital ethnographer: I was joining the online church and so I had to spend time there. And I also did this because I was behaving as a rhetorical critic: I had come to the church to hear the sermons so I could analyze homiletic arguments about politics and economics, whether these arguments were explicit or implicit.

In this book, I will inveigh against understanding conservative evangelicals in the United States as obsessed with social values in the American political sphere. When Frank and others have framed born-again Christians as electorally transactional, which is to say, willing to hand power to sometimes contemptible candidates to achieve desired political ends, they miss the point. I suggest that these Christians' votes are better understood as the natural outgrowth of a storytelling logic that sees culture as both irrevocably lost *and* as having been better in times before. This logic also positions evangelicals as the rightful heirs and so natural defenders of the values of the truest Americans: those who founded the country and knew best what they intended for the future. Such a "founders' rhetoric," I will show, underscores white, conservative Protestant claims to truth and in defense of traditional culture. When pastors at America's largest conservative Protestant churches talk about electoral questions or the American public sphere, the constituent of foremost concern is always the nation itself. Defending the country and maintaining its presumed status as the "exceptional" land always comes before any person or group, no matter how marginalized or at-risk. However, as I will discuss further, pastors rhetorically tempered this worry over the nation during the campaign between Trump and Clinton. While many ministers in their 2016 election-themed sermons still advanced a hope that the United States would remain a strong country with traditional values, they also conceded that this might not happen, no matter who prevailed in the campaign. As a remedy, pastors encouraged their hearers to remember that their primary citizenship is in heaven and that God's divine plans are always preeminent over temporary circumstances, including questions of who lives in the White House or who prevails on election day.

Readers may ask, "What is meant by the term 'conservative white evangelical'?" This fundamental question is also one of the most difficult to answer. There is no easy way to define "conservative evangelicalism" in the United States, let alone enumerate precisely who counts as a "conservative evangelical" or a "conservative Protestant." Throughout this book, I will use these two terms interchangeably, along with a third term, "born-again Christian." In using these terms, I have in mind a person who *self-identifies* as a follower of Jesus, believes confessing faith in Him is entirely necessary and sufficient for salvation, affirms the Bible text as authoritative guidance for their life and describes it as infallible (perhaps literal) in its original form, and who embraces the Great Commission as the believer's foremost call.[14] Key to this definition is self-identification—those who say they are evangelicals count as evangelicals. Evangelicalism, that is, qualifies as an imagined community that coheres through constitutive rhetoric.

Indeed, when pollsters like Pew or Gallup query respondents about religious affiliation, they rely entirely on self-identification. When writers like Thomas Frank—or myself—write about evangelical voters, the community we have in mind is also self-identified. It is imagined. The 81 percent of evangelicals who voted for Trump do not attend the same church, live in the same town, or necessarily share the same statement of faith. Their community is created intangibly from both the outside and the inside. Benedict Anderson has written about how it takes imagination for nations to cohere. It takes imagination for subcultures to cohere, as well, and this imagination depends on shared meaning. I developed this project from the suspicion that self-identified evangelicals find shared meaning through symbols and stories, what James Boyd White first termed "constitutive rhetoric." Communities continuously make and remake themselves through words and language, which means that "we constitute ourselves as individuals, as communities, and as cultures, whenever we speak."[15] We create families, communities, and worlds in our minds—together, through language—before we materially create them and are able to inhabit them in lived space. Moreover, as Charles Taylor made evident, shared imaginaries and shared histories are the essential threads that link communities together.[16] In chapter 2 I will more fully describe evangelicalism as an imagined community built in constitutive rhetoric. For now, the idea is simply that evangelicalism is an exceptionally creative and fluid movement that defies easy definition or description, as the volume of scholarly and popular writing about the religion make plain. While surveys and percentages reveal something about outcomes, the sermons I have catalogued expose the texture of how believers interpret their faith when it comes to political and economic issues.

"But are they all white?" While not all evangelical Christians are white (the audiences who heard the sermons I studied likely included some people who identified as nonwhite), the subculture is not very racially diverse. Thus, I write with mostly white Americans (which is to say, US citizens of European descent) in mind. The Pew Research Center's 2014 "Religious Landscape Study" found that just over one-quarter of Americans identify as evangelical Protestants. Of those, more than three-quarters (83 percent) identify themselves as white, 8 percent as Latino, 4 percent as Black, and 1 percent as Asian. Politically, just over half (55 percent) of evangelical Protestants also identify themselves as conservative, just over one-quarter (27 percent) as moderate, but just more than one-tenth (13 percent) as liberal (6 percent decline to identify).[17] For churches to be included in my study, I required that they list on their publicly available statements of faith, within the first three items, a declaration that the Bible is the authoritative word of God, inspired, and infallible. Such scriptural affirmation, I found, is common at evangelical churches with white pastors and white congregations but not at those led by Black clergy. A detailed description of my criteria for selection in this project is provided in chapter 2.

Rhetoric and Worldview

This book is my attempt to bring together years of knowing conservative Protestants and—especially—listening online to their sermonic rhetoric as it applies to public problems. I have also included some limited analysis of conversation as it exists on social media such as Twitter, Instagram, and

Facebook. My intention is to make plain *how* evangelicals develop and then deploy their worldview, especially through the public rhetoric of their pastors. I propose that pastors likely influence the worldviews of their congregant-hearers, because pastors are important members of the subculture and community. As well, their rhetoric is suggestive, though certainly not determinative, for what other born-again believers might say about politics.[18] This book does not take up the question of *why* so many of these Christians believe or vote as they do. Instead, in these pages I invite readers to experience the homiletic reality of evangelicals, to see *how* it takes shape and how it may influence the personal, social, and political commitments of believers. I want to make clear from the outset that I make no apologies for the very real effects these commitments may have. Sometimes conservative Protestants deploy rhetoric that signals intolerance and even hate for certain other groups, such as the American poor, minority populations, feminists, and others. To me, this is wrong. And when these believers help elect individuals who enact policies that make life more difficult for vulnerable populations, this often feels both hurtful and confusing. My aim in writing this book is not to explain why these believers think these kinds of arguments are good or "Christian," or why these believers may ultimately support candidates whom progressives find intolerable. Rather, my aim is to reveal how these arguments take shape and to show how their formation is often softer, and in some ways more insidious, than the over-the-top framing of evangelical discourse that more typically appears in popular media.

It was Aristotle who first defined rhetoric as the "faculty of observing in any given case the available means of persuasion."[19] This essential definition points to my reason for emphasizing *how* over *why*. To state the matter bluntly: why does anyone do anything? Questions of why may well be interesting, but they can often be answered only speculatively, even judgmentally. Rhetoric and rhetorical criticism, in contrast, reveal the structures of arguments, the nuts and bolts. By asking how, and then deeply unpacking the homiletic economic and political rhetoric of some of America's most important evangelical churches, we can reveal the texture of that discourse. Moreover, asking how—and staying with Aristotle's definition—is about *seeing*. Seeing is, for the critic, the essence of ascertaining the rhetorical act, because rhetors—in this case, pastors—seek out and then leverage their available means of persuasion.[20] And so I examine in these pages how some influential pastors—who have built and now lead very large churches—craft sermons using persuasive means that emphasize longstanding narrative concepts including the Protestant work ethic, American exceptionalism, personal responsibility, living in the world but not of it, and more. Deploying these homiletic storytelling warrants, in turn, allows the pastors to develop arguments that sometimes create false equivalencies or to transpose theological concepts with transcendent timing into material moments that are happening now. I heard such rhetoric repeatedly during my study, most especially when it came to the 2016 presidential campaign between Clinton and Trump.

For an example, let us return to the series of sermons about the 2016 election that John Ortberg gave at Menlo Church. The pastor began by creating rhetorical identification with his audience about the special character of American democracy—its superior nature, in fact—while also acknowledging discomfort with the 2016 candidate slate:

> When I was quite small, my parents got me a little book called *Being an American Can Be Fun*. It was all about how democracy works. I thought that was so cool . . . The first time I was ever [in Washington, DC,] to see the Capitol Building and think about the great speeches that have been given, to go to the Lincoln Monument and stand there with that great statue of Lincoln seated on that chair, and to read the words to the Gettysburg Address and the second inaugural address was an intensely moving thing to me.
>
> I've just always loved that part of our history and our life. But I have to tell you that I am genuinely looking forward to when this election is going to be over. Is anybody else experiencing anything like that? An article online from *Time* magazine said . . . that therapists are saying that the level of anxiety in our nation is going up because of this election.[21]

Ortberg's words resonate. Scholars of political science and political rhetoric, not to mention average citizens, celebrate Lincoln's second inaugural address as an exemplary text from an exemplary president.[22] Americans are a proud people; evangelicals are especially so. The bitter contest between Clinton and Trump challenged this patriotism. In the compendium of sermons I studied, I often heard pastors like Ortberg urge their hearers to vote despite their dyspeptic feelings toward the candidates or politics in general. The civic duty to participate remained. "Let's all be involved," Ortberg said. "Politicians can be good. They can be bad . . . Welcome to the human race. [But] government was ordained by God. It's a good thing to seek to govern as best we can. To be involved politically is a really good thing."[23]

Claims like this one by Ortberg point to a crucial tension that many pastors were trying to help their congregants resolve in the lead-up to the presidential election of 2016. On the one hand, there was the vitality of American democracy. Its vibrancy comes from citizens, those people willing to participate despite—or even because of—ongoing imperfections.[24] On the other hand, for conservative evangelicals, the vitality of American democracy is not the vitality of life. For them, such a vitality reaches beyond one's experience on earth; it goes all the way to heaven. "If I find in myself a desire which no experience in this world can satisfy," wrote author and lay theologian C. S. Lewis in *Mere Christianity*, "the most probable explanation is that I was made for another world."[25] Evangelicals sometimes describe the feeling Lewis identified as a calling to be "in" the world but not "of" it.[26] I describe this central tension as an evangelical rhetoric of "active-passivism." It asks the faithful to participate in politics while also remaining separate from its worst tendencies —to "straddle the line between secular accommodation and religious distinction," as Christine Gardner has written.[27] Particularly during the 2016 campaign, this rhetoric affirmed civic participation as a duty *and* exempted true believers from accountability for the votes they cast, including those for a norm-breaking candidate like Donald Trump.

The Rhetoric of Active-Passivism

Donald Trump broke the mold for Republican presidents (and presidential nominees) who had previously earned widespread evangelical support at the ballot box. For example, where Ronald Reagan could speak lyrically about values and the shining city on the hill, Donald Trump was often inarticulate and garbled. Or where George W. Bush had self-identified as a born-again Christian, Donald Trump had never been an active churchgoer, and when he did attend services, he usually chose congregations affiliated with the prosperity gospel instead of with conservative evangelicalism. Before the 2016 election at least sixteen women had accused Trump of sexual misconduct and even assault. By the summer of 2019, the number had risen to eighteen.[28]

Moreover, it was not a foregone conclusion in 2016 that white, conservative Protestants would support Trump in large numbers. Instead, there was fracturing in the movement over his candidacy. Some urged their fellow believers to abstain from voting or to choose a third-party option such as Gary Johnson of the Libertarian Party, Evan McMullin of the Better for America Group, or even Jill Stein of the Green Party.[29] Others—including Russell Moore, president of the Ethics and Religious Liberty Commission of the Southern Baptist Convention—announced that the election had made them "hate" the word "evangelical" and that they had begun to eschew it.[30]

Several months after the 2016 election, I received an email from a pastor with whom I had long since lost touch. He knew, from following my career online, that I study evangelicals and politics, and he wondered how I was doing. "Just to let you know," he told me in closing, "I've disclaimed the name evangelical for myself. I still believe the Bible and in Jesus and all, but when 80 percent of the 'evangelicals' in the U.S. voted for Trump, I knew I was no longer one of THEM, whoever they are." With this sentence, my friend tried to draw a distinction. He wanted to continue to be associated with what he thinks are the positive aspects of the faith, including Christ's love and saving grace, the pursuit of moral character, and a spirit of welcoming friend and foe alike. But at the same time he wanted to distance himself from the more incendiary things evangelicals had seemed to embrace in the election—or at least had shown themselves to be willing to put up with in order to win. These included Trump's disrespect for women, his use of disparaging language about refugees and people of color, and his broken marriages.[31] In short, while it is true that the large majority of self-identifying conservative, white evangelicals ultimately cast ballots for Trump, focusing on the hard fact of their votes obfuscates the complexity of the movement and how we might understand the mostly shared political worldview of so many of the subculture's adherents.

I cannot write this clearly enough: In my study, I did not hear pastors endorse, or even, for the most part, advocate for, either Donald Trump or Republicans in general. I also did not witness invectives against Hillary Clinton or Democrats. Rather, the pastors I heard seemed at pains to speak in appealing tones in their sermons about the election and to avoid incendiary topics. I encountered very few diatribes against abortion, feminism, a gay social agenda, or "Hollywood filth." This does not mean that the ministers who spoke affirmed liberal political values or have come to support reproductive freedom, women's liberation, marriage equality, or the culture industry. Instead, hostility toward such a progressive agenda was implied through homiletic storylines that framed the main characters in the election—Clinton and Trump—as unlikeable but peripheral to what the pastors wanted to emphasize in their messages. Many ministers created a community of minds with their congregations by talking about how glad they would be when the campaign was over because it had become tiresome and had debased American politics and the American democratic system. But even though the public sphere had become depraved, pastors still called on their audiences to vote. Casting a ballot was their basic duty as citizens and believers. Doing so honored those soldiers who had died to protect freedom and democracy, including the voting franchise.

For those who were worried about not having a good choice in either Clinton or Trump, pastors reminded their audiences to remember God's providence. God is always in control, they said, even during campaign seasons, and even when the presidential candidates are dreadful. To develop this idea, ministers relied on the rhetoric of active-passivism. Echoing C. S. Lewis, pastors encouraged their audiences to embrace the idea that they were dual citizens—residents of heaven first and of the United States second. This meant that no matter what happened in the election, they were always already protected and safe as occupants of the Kingdom of God. The call to be active was the call to vote as a civic duty—to participate as citizens and to choose one candidate or the other. But that was it. Beyond this simple democratic act, pastors stressed passivism—including, somewhat strangely, divesting oneself of interest in the election's ultimate outcome. Whatever the result of a vote—even if it were in support of (and so helped to elect) a nonnormative and potentially harmful candidate like Trump—God had ordained that result, and so God would make of it whatever He chose. Because God could be trusted, true Christians should trust Him, full stop. In any event, good or bad, the Bible-believing evangelical could be sure God maintained divine control and would protect His subject in love. By rhetorically emphasizing trust—and this is a key point—pastors exempted believers from responsibility for any bad effects their votes might cause, either to the nation or to marginalized, at-risk constituencies.[32]

The rhetoric of active-passivism is suggestive beyond the election of Donald Trump, however. Rather, it marks a discursive shift. The pastors of the nation's largest churches have begun to leave out of their political narratives those hot-button issues—the values rhetoric—that outsiders imagine takes up so much of the conversation inside these institutions, and that is often used by elite conservative evangelicals when they talk about politics.[33] This is surprising because the popular media's framing of Bible-believing Christians typically situates them as concerned primarily with the rhetoric of the so-called culture wars.[34] However, that the discourse inside churches may less heavily emphasize opposition to abortion or gay marriage, among other issues, does not necessarily mean that these issues have lost salience or that these voters are open to persuasion absent a new conversation from a trusted interlocutor such as a pastor. Instead, I argue, this conversation is now submerged under active-passivism, and this act of submersion was particularly evident during the homilies I studied in the lead-up to the 2016 election. By focusing on God's will and sovereignty, ministers were able to discharge guilt hearers might have felt about voting for Trump, thus giving them permission to cast a ballot they might have been feeling bad or worried about. To show how this works, I will draw links between ministerial rhetoric and literatures in political science, particularly new studies about partisan identity. In systems of identity-based democracy, partisans understand themselves in contrast to those they are against. Elections are not about ideas so much as they are about winning, while also ensuring that the other side never has a chance to win. The United States is now this kind of system. Faced with a candidate like Trump, what conservative Protestant voters needed were warrants that let them do what they already wanted to do—vote for the GOP. The rhetoric of active-passivism provided exactly that.[35]

Stories as Rhetoric

I first became interested in deeply learning the stories of evangelicalism in the United States in the aftermath of the 2008 election of Barack Obama. His election coincided with the Great Recession, which threw into at least temporary doubt popular backing for free markets and financial deregulation—commonly called neoliberalism among academics and political elites. British journalist Paul Mason wrote that the crisis meant that "neoliberalism is over: as an ideology, as an economic model. Get used to it and move on."[36] But even as the Obama administration was using precious political capital during its early months in office to pass a stimulus package that government and academic economists said was essential to staving off a cataclysmic depression on par with that of the 1930s, a populist rebellion known as the Tea Party emerged as a counterweight on behalf of citizens who were angry about federal bank bailouts and individual financial recklessness alike. White, conservative Protestants made up a disproportionately high percentage of Tea Party members, as compared to their share of the general population. Sociologists Theda Skocpol and Vanessa Williamson estimated that about 40 percent of Tea Party constituents also identified as born-again Christians, while only 26 percent of Americans in general so identified.[37]

As a demographic matter, American conservative Protestants tend to be middle-class to lower-middle class, although megachurch members are somewhat wealthier.[38] This suggested to me that perhaps the events of the 2008 financial crash might upset their longstanding support for GOP politics and policies. Maybe, I thought, Thomas Frank's prediction that pocketbook matters would prevail over values questions at the ballot box would finally come true. The emergence and success of the Tea Party indicated otherwise. In the 2010 midterms, the Democrats suffered historic losses in both the Senate and the House. The newly elected members of Congress—many of whom aligned themselves with the ideology of the Tea Party—took legislative positions that emphasized the ameliorative power of the free market. Economic conservatism retained its policy-making hold and—just as relevant to me, a student of language and stories—its rhetorical influence across the public sphere.[39]

In response to the elections of 2008 and 2010, I began to follow evangelicalism much more closely. My decision was born of my long interest in deep understanding—in investigating the "turtles all the way down," as Clifford Geertz once wrote. The turtles of evangelicalism are an especially rich system of stories for understanding the American political landscape.[40]

Among the best ways for investigating the turtles is finding and hearing the stories of a people or a subculture. This theory, first applied to the fields of rhetoric and communication by Walter Fisher, is as intuitive as it is straightforward.[41] Stories are more persuasive than arguments, it says. The best communication happens by way of personal and collective account. So, while people are sometimes rational actors, as has been argued since the Enlightenment, humans also often behave according to "good reasons." These good reasons, wrote Fisher, emanate from experience and culture by way of a "set of stories which must be chosen among [in order] to live the good life." These stories are also made and remade "in a process of continual recreation."[42] Such stories are not limitless; rather, as the sermons I describe will show, they come as types. For example, in the United States and for conservative Protestants, there are heroic stories about the nation's Christian founding, tragic stories about a culture gone to waste, comic stories about individual ineptitude, and so on. Fisher referred to his theory of good reasons as the "narrative paradigm." Of course, not everyone was immediately convinced by Fisher's hypothesis. Some said it unnecessarily bifurcated between reason and story, and so situated them as opposites, as though humans can only use one lens or the other to understand their lives, at any given time. Others suggested the paradigm was too loose. While Fisher emphasized the value of narrative and story in human life, he was not entirely clear definitionally about what counted as narrative, story, topic, argument, and so on.[43] His paradigm was both too hard and too easy to use. Even so, Fisher's theory made plain how narrative fosters effective human communication. Good stories are exceptionally persuasive.

One of the first scholars to successfully apply Fisher's paradigm was William Lewis. In an essay that explained what made Ronald Reagan an especially masterful storyteller, Lewis emphasized how truth is something humans ascertain through shared experiences—events and occurrences that happen to us in common, sometimes at the same time, and sometimes not. "Since narrative makes sense of experience," he wrote, "the sense that is made will be grounded in the presuppositions of those who accept the narrative, and those presuppositions are common sense. Persuasive narratives, then, both express and assume a knowledge that is shared by the community."[44] The pastors I studied leveraged the common sense of the evangelical community to give meaningful sermons about political and economic topics. To do this, they sometimes assumed particular Bible knowledge—stories about Jesus and the tax collectors, for example, or stories about God's creation of the world in Genesis. Other times, the knowledge was about shared value systems, such as a belief that children are always better off when their parents are married in opposite-gender relationships, or that the US military is a venerable institution whose service members (including leadership) always merit admiration and respect.

To explain how common sense functions, Lewis drew explicitly on Geertz and his notion that what communities define as truth is largely a function of cultural rules and expectations. Ethnography is literally the study of culture. It happens when researchers venture beyond their own lives and worlds to join the communities they study. This joining necessarily means learning another's language, symbols, and systems of interpretation. It requires studying rhetoric.[45] For more than half a century, scholars in rhetoric, anthropology, and performance studies, among others, have worked across the borderlands of their fields to do studies revealing how the world is more plural, less predictable, and far more playful than the harder, more rational social sciences often suggest.[46] In the introduction to *Text + Field: Innovations in Rhetorical Method*, Sara L. McKinnon and her co-authors reviewed a shift in rhetorical studies from a method that privileged standalone texts and tried to emphasize (the presumed possibility of) objectivity, to one that embraced the subjectivity of the reader and critic and acknowledged that texts—all texts—emerge from some *place*. As some rhetoricians became critics who moved away from the archive and into the field, a new way of doing research developed. "The field," McKinnon and her colleagues wrote, is the "nexus where rhetoric is produced, where it is enacted, where it circulates, and, consequently, where it is audienced."[47] Such a field has come to include in situ investigations of the Vietnam War Memorial, and of Jerry Falwell Sr.'s leadership at Thomas Road Baptist Church; activist participation against breast cancer awareness; in-depth interviewing of teenagers and young adults who took sexual purity pledges; study of the deliberations and activities of public school boards; an exploration of an empty lot in Chicago that became a literal site of and for democratic discourse and negotiation; an examination of the online vernacular of "digital Jesus" during the days of the early internet; and more.[48]

It is to this rich set of studies and scholarship that I offer this book. In the pages that follow, I introduce you to some of what I heard in some of America's largest conservative evangelical churches during the time of the Tea Party and campaign between Donald Trump and Hillary Clinton, along with a small cast of characters who helped to craft the tales. In so doing, my hope is that readers will be able to briefly join a community that may be foreign to them and come away with a new understanding of the sometimes mystifying subculture that is evangelicalism in the United States in the early twenty-first century. The stories I have catalogued here—which begin in the early years of the Obama presidency and the crisis of the Great Recession and run through the early years of the presidency of Donald Trump—are filled with plotlines that emphasize American exceptionalism, individual resilience, and a culture gone to waste. Where popular media and the popular imagination have often foregrounded those pastors, churches, and evangelical outreach efforts that are most outrageous or come closest to transgressing social and political norms, I only infrequently heard any of the "fire and brimstone" approach that outsiders may imagine.[49] Over the course of eight years I studied hundreds of sermons posted online by megachurches across the country about social topics like gay rights, political topics like America's place in the world, and economic topics like tithing or why the recession had occurred.[50] In those sermons, pastors typically used language that was both conciliatory and winsome. Few ministers spoke of these topics in terms that presumed absolute knowledge. Rather, most sought to craft stories that worked to illustrate their own subjectivity as citizens and Christians, in order to build a bridge of understanding with their congregant-listeners. They created an American narrative of personal and national faith that situated the country as providentially blessed but also in need of believers willing to take more seriously their duty to live out their sacred calls.

A Brief Word about Terminology

In describing the narratives and stories of white, conservative evangelicals in the United States during the years 2010–18, I write from my perspective as a rhetorical critic. I make frequent use of the terms "rhetoric," "narrative," and "story," each of which has a distinct meaning. For the most part, I use these terms in the following ways:

Rhetoric: I use "rhetoric" to refer to speech that includes modes of proof and symbolic meaning-making from a speaker to an audience—what Aristotle termed "the available means of persuasion." In addition, and following Roland Barthes, I argue that rhetoric can be—and often is—a social practice that is related to language. Those with power, including clergy, decide how words are used and what words mean. To be somewhat reductive, there is no reason swear words are intrinsically worse than non–swear words, except that we have socially decided that they are. This is power at work in rhetoric. In the sermons I analyze here, pastors similarly use rhetoric and rhetorical techniques to emphasize certain Bible words by going back to a presumed original Greek or Hebrew meaning. Moreover, the very fact of pastoral speech—including the continuing truth that men still dominate the pulpits of white, conservative evangelicalism—contributes to the ways its power works through rhetoric.[51]

Narrative: I use the term "narrative" to refer to those things pastors talk about as having a set and readily understood plot or sequence, and that happen over time. To understand a narrative, a hearer must conceive of a past, a present, and a future. For conservative evangelical audiences, this connection between time and narrative may be especially poignant. As Paul Ricoeur argued, humans tend to understand the future as it relates to the past; a sense of regret may become heightened over time, for example, or a person may come to value what's left of her life as she watches her children grow and experience life for themselves, including first days of school, trips to the waterpark, first loves, graduations, and more. Making sense of these kinds of experiences, however, requires the development of narratives, what Ricoeur called "emplotment." Through emplotment, humans tie unrelated events into united wholes, and establish connections between moments that may be actually unrelated. This, for example, is the logic that gives life to the American proverb that "everything happens for a reason." Such a reason is available, Ricoeur might argue, because a narrative can be created to explain it. Finally, and perhaps especially for conservative evangelicals, narratives almost always have a moral component, including moral responsibility. There are right ways to act and wrong ways to act; better choices and worse choices; should-haves and could-haves. These moral components will be clearly present in the sermonic narratives I present in this book.[52]

Story: A story is smaller than a narrative, and stories are also the component parts of narratives. A pastor might tell a story as a way to demonstrate the "bigger truth" of a larger narrative. For example, many of the pastors in my study talked about the United States as a nation that was founded originally with traditional values that were rooted in the Bible. This is a narrative. To illustrate this narrative, they might tell a story about the faith of a particular founder and his affinity for prayer or scripture reading. This is a story. The story only makes sense when grounded in a narrative, even if—and this is key—that narrative is assumed as understood by an audience, rather than explicitly stated. Although there is a difference between "narrative" and "story," they go together and intermingle. For this reason, I do not always clearly distinguish between the two, and readers may sometimes find I use the two terms interchangeably.

Outline of the Book

This study seeks to situate the narratives and stories of white conservative Protestants at center stage. Of course, many have traversed this terrain before, and have done so in a way that makes plain that religious messaging is a particularly salient form of political communication, especially in the United States.[53] My approach is different in that I seek not only to describe the contours of the narratives, but also to explain something about the feel of the communities in which these narratives take shape. This blended technique is what I have already identified as "digital rhetorical ethnography." Over the course of almost eight years, I committed to "deeply hang out"—to use Clifford Geertz's term—inside the digital church of conservative evangelicalism as it is curated by American megachurches, in order to systematically study its culture, architecture, and online structure.[54] By doing this, I was able to draw some conclusions about the customs, habits, and systems of belief of the faith communities I found.

My approach was not wholly ethnographic, in that I never formally joined any particular conservative Protestant church. But my immersion was real. I drew my conclusions from having spent hundreds of hours listening to contemporary texts online, watching videos, and sometimes interacting with the pastors and technicians who maintained the websites of the churches I studied. I had to learn to navigate the digital spaces of America's megachurches—to become one of the "many who are watching from all over the country and the world," as pastors often say at the beginning of their talks. To obtain transcripts, I almost always had to make them myself. I attended megachurches, in person, in southern California; Boise, Idaho; Dallas, Texas; and Fargo, North Dakota. For more than three years, I listened to every sermon, political or nonpolitical, delivered at San Clemente Presbyterian Church in San Clemente, California. At the time I followed SC Pres, as it is colloquially known, the church stipulated on its website that it was "a church of evangelical conviction," and its pastors preached directly through (not only from) a Bible passage each week. As such, during the time I followed its services, SC Pres adhered doctrinally and culturally more closely to conservative Protestantism than to mainline Protestantism. I will explain this distinction more fully in chapter 1.

In short, as I studied contemporary conservative evangelical rhetoric and tried to learn its narratives, I also immersed myself in its community. I came to know both how it sounded and how it felt. This has made my approach unique. Where others have focused primarily on the words and speeches of movement leaders, I include the words of less well-known, nonelite pastors and speakers (though the familiar voices of the leaders do appear as well).[55] In chapter 1, I discuss the history of conservative Protestantism in the United States. Even so, I suggest that it is a mistake to overemphasize the role of the historical record in understanding how born-again Christians conceptualize their worldview. While it is important to take account of how evangelicals have situated themselves in the American landscape and how they have responded to some of the most vexing problems and questions of the day, ultimately what the movement rests upon is its understanding of truth. This is both the beginning and the necessary end of the evangelical faith. For evangelicals, history exists outside of truth and is an extension of its continual manifestation in the life of the believer. Indeed, as this book makes plain, because conservative Protestants believe so absolutely in truth, and also believe they have particular access to this truth through faith and the words of the Bible, the stories they tell emphasize plotlines of American providence and exceptionalism, as well as a disdain for broken culture. For Bible-believing Christians, to suffer in the United States is very nearly an absurdity, because there is always already a better life available—God's salvation through Christ—even as there is no need to worry about this life because one's true citizenship is always in heaven.

In chapter 2 I explain more fully the technique of digital rhetorical ethnography. This technique joins a thick description of the digital church with rhetorical criticism in order to unpack the narratives and storytelling logics of contemporary conservative Protestantism in the United States today.

Chapter 3 takes as its point of departure the election of Barack Obama in 2008 and the Great Recession that marked his time in office. Bible-believing Protestants have long been stalwart defenders of free market capitalism and its importance to the American way of life. However, some evangelicals experienced momentary dissonance during the early part of the recession, between their idealized sense of what they imagine the United States is supposed to be, and the extant market realities that were happening then. Scholars generally frame American exceptionalism as something the United States gives to the world—the purported "city upon a hill" whose good works and moral values engender providential blessing. During the recession, however, pastors emptied exceptionalism of the idea that the country's foremost international role is as an archetype or example for others to follow. Instead, the emphasis fell on notions of presumed bounty. Pastors told stories that situated individual failure as something people allowed to happen through their ungodly habits and bad acts. Taken in mass, these individual failures resulted in recession. Widespread struggle was not the heart of the exceptional nation. Even in hardship, widespread prosperity remained the norm. Neither could the system be to blame. It was structurally sound, so long as people used it humbly and well. To make these stories cohere, ministers insisted that true suffering and deprivation was something that happened outside the United States. There—usually in the developing world—true Christians would find true need. Even in crisis, the country's exceptional nature still held.

In chapter 4, I turn to the sermons told near the end of the 2016 campaign. White, conservative Protestants were never great fans of Barack Obama, and many were glad to turn the page on his two-term presidency.[56] However, pastors avoided strident sermons about how to vote or what issues were most important in the homilies they gave about the election. Instead, they focused on themes of surrender, reassurance, and resolve. I suggest that this lack of overt political clamoring arose in part from the declining importance of the culture wars in American discourse. When the US Supreme Court affirmed marriage equality in 2015, many pundits presumed these battles were over, and the progressive side had won. My interpretation is different. In the sermons given in the weeks just before and just after Trump's election, many pastors emphasized the benefits of citizenship in the United States, making plain again the evangelical idealization of American exceptionalism. The plotline was subtly complicated, however. Most ministers continued to venerate the United States in their election narratives. But they also said that believers already also lived in heaven. Thus, while pastors across megachurch pulpits urged their congregants to vote, they also reminded their audiences that God already sat on the throne as the perfect moral leader, no matter which candidate one supported in the election. He alone was the example worth following. All candidates fall short of His standard.

This logic attenuated Donald Trump's perceived character shortcomings—and, it is worth pointing out, Hillary Clinton's as well. Ministers were trying to defuse tension from the public sphere. However, as political rhetoric, the pastors' words more likely benefited Trump and the GOP, for two reasons. The first is negative partisanship. While many voters, including conservative evangelicals, may refuse party affiliation, they do tend to align themselves against a side they do not like. Under this theory, while a person on the Left may feel disillusioned with Democrats and so refuse to formally join the party, such an individual may well hate Republicans and always vote against them.[57] Likewise, even evangelicals who may have been dispirited with the failure of the GOP in the culture wars or disappointed about the candidacy of Trump, were still conditioned to despise Democrats, and particularly Hillary Clinton.[58] There is nothing in an argument from pastors about God being the ultimate leader, or one's true citizenship being in heaven, that might move a believer from a vote for Trump to a vote for Clinton, especially if such a voter was predisposed to negative feelings toward the Democratic candidate.

Second, and even more powerfully, the narratives I heard told in the weeks leading up to the election framed culture in perilous terms. However, unlike in traditional culture-war rhetoric, which calls on evangelicals to restore values and defend tradition, at this point pastors talked about how the external world had become broken beyond repair. The only hope was Jesus. Life's most vexing problems would never find solutions through politics. Individual conversion was the only real source of hope. Such a message always works against progressive politics, because it encourages complacency. The concern for "saving American culture" could be subordinated to the decision to turn one's eyes toward heaven instead. At most, pastors encouraged individual acts of service that aimed to help individual people, particularly when those acts were meant as introductions to Jesus. Politics was not presented as a means for help, especially not in the form of collective action or programs of social justice.

In chapter 5, I offer a close reading of four sermons given during the closing weeks of the 2016 presidential campaign, at three conservative Protestant megachurches. These analyses show how pastors developed the rhetoric of active-passivism across homilies and issues. Writing from my perspective as a rhetorical critic, I begin with a sermon that was, from my vantage point, the least political and most urgent in its call to believers to keep their hope in heaven rather than in the election. Next, I analyze two sermons that were given about politics, and show how the pastor (Kevin Myers, senior pastor of 12Stone Church in Lawrenceville, Georgia) repeatedly insisted his intent was not to "be political," even as he spoke at length about race and also mentioned issues like the morality of the national debt, the federal deficit, abortion, marriage equality, and more. The final sermon is clear in its call to activism, and most stereotypical in its dismissal of political liberalism. While the pastor in this case (Ed Young, senior pastor of Fellowship Church, which has locations in Texas, Oklahoma, and Florida) did not disparage Democrats by party, he did mock big government, frame social safety net programs as rife with fraud, and speak of being gay as a feeling rather than an identity.

In chapter 6, I take up a possible site of rupture in the evangelical discourse. Even as megachurch pastors, almost exclusively white men, forwarded the surprisingly unified narrative of active-passivism during the years of my study, some conservative evangelical women have begun to object. In the aftermath of the release of the *Access Hollywood* tape in October 2016, in which Trump was heard bragging about kissing and otherwise assaulting women against their will, some conservative Protestant women—writers, bloggers, and speakers—resisted the male leaders of their movement who tried to give the GOP nominee a pass, or said his behavior was no worse than Bill Clinton's. These male leaders also urged their fellow evangelicals to continue supporting the New York businessman in his bid for the presidency. In this chapter, I analyze the rhetoric of dissent against these leaders, especially that of the prolific Bible-study writer Beth Moore. I argue that this new conversation constitutes a discursive ambiguity that opens new avenues of future opposition. Moore used her position of authority to question old ways of thinking, including longstanding beliefs in patriarchy and female submission. She also condemned the idea that political tradeoffs—like voting for Trump despite his abusive behavior—were always worth the cost. The question, going forward, is whether this new conversation will have any noticeable, or lasting, effect, or whether its interlocutors will be silenced instead or expelled from the movement.

The book concludes with a look ahead, not for the presidency so much as for conservative evangelicalism itself and what it means to the United States. When Alexis de Tocqueville studied American democracy in the nineteenth century and wondered what made it exceptional then—which meant, to him, its status as the first of its kind and its ability to flourish and survive where other nations had floundered and failed—he pointed to the nation's Protestant traditions. He called them the "first" US "political institutions" and said they enabled citizens to harness the tyranny of the majority, tempered their impulses toward too much individualism, and protected against democratic despotism.[59] It is easy to point to today's conservative evangelicals and see only the worst that religion has to offer democracy and wish them out of the public sphere. But they are unlikely to go. The stories I offer here provide insight into the conservative Protestant worldview and reveal how evangelical Christians use narratives as a way to reconcile their political commitments with their faith. This, in turn, may return some of Toqueville's hopefulness about religion to our public conversation. Maybe it really can be, once again, something that holds democracy together, rather than tears it apart.

1

Evangelicals and the Continuous Reawakening to the Greatest Story Ever Told

On September 11, 2016, Dan Kellogg, pastor of Gold Creek Community Church in Mill Creek, Washington, just north of Seattle, took the stage in front of his auditorium-style congregation. Wearing worn jeans and a red T-shirt with the words "Life Is Better Together" printed on the front, Kellogg seemed casual and at ease, ready to engage in friendly banter or, perhaps, a music performance of some kind, rather than to give a formal sermon. The room around him was darkened. A small wooden stool and matching lectern were clearly visible onstage, along with several audio speakers. Behind him was a screen large enough to show a Hollywood blockbuster, on which several oversized digital icons of smartphones appeared. Instructions on the screen encouraged audience members to "Open the GC (Gold Creek) Message App" and vote for one of several options for which sermon they would most like to hear. The possibilities included messages about marijuana use, Black Lives Matter, transgenderism, and the choice that ultimately won: "How Would Jesus Vote?"[1]

The setup for that Sunday's sermon was as notable for its technological savvy as any such message could have been in 2016. Kellogg and his team of pastors meant to engage those who attended in a "live" process of choosing their sermon experience. Bars appeared next to possible topics that slowly grew as votes came in. But the topic that audience members eventually picked—a sermon that imagined how Jesus might choose between Hillary Clinton and Donald Trump—was on the minds of more people than just those gathered in Mill Creek, Washington, that September morning. It was a question that vexed conservative evangelicals throughout the 2016 election cycle. However, its significance was not entirely new. Going back to at least 2004 and the presidential contest between George W. Bush and John Kerry, scholars and pundits alike had similarly been preoccupied. These thinkers have wondered why conservative Protestants should, in election after election, and by wide margins, choose the Republican Party over the Democratic Party, despite the GOP's failure actually to outlaw abortion, defend the heteronormative family from further erosion, or stop the encroachment of "Hollywood values," in general. Shouldn't evangelical voters give up and cast ballots in their own economic best interest instead?

Thomas Frank posed this query in his 2004 book, *What's the Matter with Kansas?* Frank never asked directly about how Jesus might vote. Instead, he accused his fellow Kansans of engaging in electoral "derangement" that privileged values issues over economic fairness.[2] In other words, and as Frank might have written had he wished to put it so plainly: Why is a party that seems to be against poor people supported by so many, well, poor people? And, again, why don't those poor people seem to care about others like themselves? Isn't that supposed to be the Christian way?

Since 2004, others have asked similar questions or suggested reasons why Democrats have struggled with heartland voters, or why they have had little success in winning over evangelical Protestants, while Republicans have continued to receive the lion's share of their votes.[3] Beginning with the 1980 election and the rise of the so-called Reagan Democrats, the GOP has had a solid base of conservative, white voters whose "parents had been the backbone of Franklin D. Roosevelt's [New Deal] coalition."[4] A large portion of this working- and middle-class base has been comprised of white evangelicals, particularly in the South.[5] Many observers have argued that stagflation, the oil embargo, and growing unemployment soured these voters on the Keynesian economic policies that had ruled the American public sphere from the time of the Great Depression, and opened the door to new voices, new politics, and so new kinds of voting priorities.[6] Evangelical historian Randall Balmer argues that in the 1970s, American culture was "ripe" for an evangelical political-cultural surge to the Right.[7] "After the Watergate scandal, the ignominy of Vietnam, and the implosion of the counterculture, Americans were ready to hear . . . a message that cloaked itself in a very simple morality, one that appropriated the language of Christian values," he writes.[8] By this way of thinking, not only were the structures and favored policies of the nation's politics undergoing change, but so were the controlling narratives. These narratives richly inform our political imaginations, for better and for worse. Indeed, they are as important as material interests for motivating voters. Good stories that are widely shared give each of us a means to understand our own lives, our communities, and the lives of other people, too.

Conservative Protestant believers in the United States have long told stories about politics, faith, and elections, and how the three intertwine. In the weeks leading up to the presidential vote of 2016, pastors at many of the nation's largest churches spoke to their congregations with these narratives in mind. At Gold Creek Community Church, Dan Kellogg reminded his audience of the story of the nation's beginning and the faith of the founders. The point of this origin story was that authentic Christians should stay positive despite the temptation to become cynical, given the dire choices before them in the election. "I love the thought that our founding fathers, when they founded this great nation, had a deep faith in them that deeply influenced the way this nation was formed," Kellogg said. "Because they allowed their faith to inform their political views, it affected the decisions they made . . . That is the most important thing you can do. Once you are on His side, you go to Him and you allow Him to influence your political views." This "founders' rhetoric" typifies evangelical storytelling about the United States. It situates the conservative Protestant narrative and conservative Protestant truth at the center of the American story, from the beginning. The narrative claims that those men who led the Revolution and who wrote the founding documents were not only Christians, but conservative evangelicals, who intended for the United States to be a nation with God at the center of the public sphere. This story was especially resonant during recession-era sermons (see chapter 3). However, it also appeared in messages given during the 2016 campaign.

The logic of this founders' rhetoric, however, does more than center the collective evangelical story at the center of the American experience. By making it the preeminent narrative of what it means to belong in the United States, because the story claims that the founders actually made the country in a particular kind of Christian way, pastors are able, through a kind of narrative magic, to make the conservative Protestant story, even at the individual level, more true or genuine than other kinds of stories. White evangelicals are thus able to frame themselves as those Americans with a rightful, and so first, claim to the nation's benefits. This creates a necessary tension for people outside the subculture, as opposed to those within it. Berkeley sociologist Arlie Russell Hochschild described this tension well, although in a somewhat problematic way, in her 2016 book *Strangers in Their Own Land*. Like Thomas Frank twelve years before, Hochschild was vexed by the political conservatism of most white evangelical voters. While he had studied Kansas, she went to Louisiana. But rather than describe the "Tea Party friends" she made there as "deranged," Hochschild used her ten visits to Louisiana to conjure for them a "deep story" to understand their lives. This deep story imagined a scene where good and righteous people were waiting in line for years, even decades, for their turn and their success, and were becoming frustrated by the wait. Why was it taking so long? they wondered. They were trying hard. They understood that work was part of the deal. But with enough hard work, the American Dream should be within reach: a home of their own, a secure retirement, a small weekend home where they could go fishing. Perhaps a little bit of extra money to help the kids go to college. But it seemed that they had begun to stand still in the line. Maybe they had started going backward. Other, less deserving folks—people of color, feminists, the Obamas, and even the endangered brown pelican—were cutting ahead. A process that was fair in generations past was not fair anymore. It was time to fight back.

In Hochschild's telling, the story was familiar, yet also deeply passive. Her Tea Party friends felt this story to be true. Because they felt its truth, it informed their conservative politics. But the story was also something she herself imagined, as an ethnographer and a sociologist. After she spent time in Louisiana, she retreated to her office in Berkeley to come up with the narrative, and then she returned to those same people in Louisiana "to check whether the deep story resonate[d] with them."[9] But the fact that she had to conjure the story herself is the heart of the problem with it. Most people order their lives according to *narratives they live by* as structured *by the lives they have lived*. Hochschild's deep story, while compelling, is a work of fiction. No one is actually standing in line. No one is actually taking unfair cuts. So even though her interviewees affirmed the resonance of her narrative, her account also depended on never challenging some of its darker impulses. *Decoding the Digital Church* will give readers the chance to hear some of the narratives and stories that white, conservative Protestants have created for themselves, as told and heard in their churches. I invite you to sit in the digital pews along with me. This does not necessarily make the narratives I catalogue less imagined than is Hochschild's deep story. However, I suggest that taking account of evangelicals' own stories as told in their own language returns important agency and responsibility to the group being studied.[10]

Nonetheless, there is good reason why Hochschild sought to make sense of Louisiana conservatives through narrative, imagined though it might have been. As Walter Fisher made plain, narration may well be the dominant form of human communication. Moreover, assumptions—what Fisher called "good reasons"—undergird the narratives we forward. Believable stories hold up. Audiences require both narrative fidelity (the story being told must ring true to lived reality) and narrative probability (the story must be coherent and not full of impossible-to-be-true details).[11] But this is not all. Good narratives are not standalone stories, like children's books that need never be part of a larger canon, but only pleasing enough to settle a wakeful toddler for sleep. Rather, a good narrative is internally consistent and joins well with "the larger discourse of which it is only a part."[12] I will develop this idea more fully in chapter 2, when I discuss Blaise Pascal's notion of the *esprit de finesse*. Pascal posits this as a kind of gut knowledge that most of us have about the world. We make judgments about whether to believe stories based on our experiences, the stories we've lived, and the stories we've heard before. I will return to Pascal's theory of the *esprit de finesse* throughout this book.[13]

When it comes to political stories, the question is whether one's sense of, or requirement for, truth tends toward the rigid or the forgiving. Recent research in political science suggests that partisans—a term that increasingly describes almost everyone—think about politics and political issues using motivated reasoning. With motivated reasoning, individuals seek to explain their choices in ways that are consonant either with what they already believe is the case or with what they want to believe is the case, rather than with what is actually true or actually happening.[14] In terms of political narrative, and building on Fisher's theory, we might say that audiences listen to decide not whether a story is true in all its parts, but rather if a story is *true enough*. In contemporary politics, true enough means that a story matches a predetermined worldview. To this, we can add William Lewis's contribution that great political storytellers are able to marshal national myths in the service of imposing order on a chaotic world.[15] Such larger-than-life stories also work as moral arguments in the crafting of a shared moral imagination. Indeed, Fisher held that narrative functioned best for advancing moral claims and moral arguments. Storytelling worked better in this realm than practices of formal rhetoric.[16] Moral arguments are those having to do with right and wrong, as well as the higher notions of life: truth, justice, freedom, and so on.

Pascal's theory of the *esprit de finesse* and Fisher's theory of narrative are both useful for understanding the nature of storytelling in politics. Each shows how stories do the important work of sewing together the rhetorical quilt that tells the people of a nation its stories. In the United States, these include stories of origin, of war, of peace, of prosperity, of freedom, of responsibility, and more. These stories infuse culture with "common sense." It is in this infusion that ethnography and rhetoric meet. Stories are told in communities. To draw together the theories of Clifford Geertz and Walter Fisher—as Lewis first did—social narratives are not only, or even mostly, the work of elite speakers, even politicians. Instead, these stories emerge from "the received wisdom" of the group. They belong to everyone. They do not require special degrees or pedigree for understanding. To join their *esprit* is simply to recognize their tune, to affiliate with the sense that holds them to the common.[17] Pastors are expert at singing these songs.

I turn now to the history that informs the narratives that conservative evangelicals in the United States most deeply rely on for their shared understanding of both who the country is and what they contend it is supposed to be going forward. For while national myths and moral arguments represent common sense, they also represent contested claims. Not all Americans share the same stories or highlight the same histories to the same degree. For example, conservative Protestants stress the theme of American exceptionalism more than is true of citizens who identify as politically progressive. Evangelicals also emphasize this exceptionalism with a kind of "always-ness" and essential providence that more secular citizens find problematic.

The stories I introduce here represent the narrative threads that informed the recession-era and Trump-era sermons that I listened to during my digital rhetorical ethnography. The pastors who spoke did not develop their sermons and the accounts that supported them out of whole cloth. Rather, as Bakhtinian dialogism insists, no conversation ever begins afresh, but rather joins in on a longstanding exchange made up over time and already existing in culture and artifacts.[18] These are the stories of American conservative Protestantism from the founding, even as they are also only just happening in the now.

A (Very Brief) History of American Evangelicalism

Above all, conservative evangelical Protestantism is a religious tradition. As I noted in my introduction, attempting to write about "evangelicals" or even "conservative evangelicals" is fraught with confusion and difficulty, because there is little consensus about what the social movement (the tradition) means. In this study, I have adopted—for better or worse—Randall Balmer's three-part definition of evangelicals: an evangelical (1) reads the Bible as God's authoritative word; (2) believes in the essential nature of conversion as the means for going to heaven; and (3) recognizes the call of Jesus in the Great Commission to save the world for Christ.[19] But to call conservative Protestantism a tradition is to recognize its imprint across history. Although my focus is primarily on the rhetoric and stories of Bible-believers through the Great Recession and election of Donald Trump, their influence matters because they have long been relevant to American culture. Similarly, my main focus is those evangelicals who are white, which is to say of European descent, as these are the believers who tend to most closely identify with the stories I detail and who attend the churches I study.

In the late 1960s, scholars who were not necessarily also born-again believers began to identify evangelicalism as a defining influence in the United States. William McLoughlin wrote in 1968 that "the story of American Evangelicalism is the story of America itself in the years 1800 to 1900."[20] More recently, Frances FitzGerald described this same century as a time of "evangelical hegemony." It was when these believers "dominated all cultural institutions, including the public schools and the universities. In this period there was no real distinction between religion and politics."[21] When contemporary conservative Protestants talk about the nation's Christian underpinnings, and insist that the nation has drifted from its roots, this is what they mean. Understanding the rhetorical power of American evangelicals today requires acknowledging its historical clout, and conceding that though it has diminished, it retains an important role in shaping public culture and public life.[22] Bible-believing Christians are present and make arguments in the public sphere. They always have. Moreover, they expect these arguments to carry weight and, they hope, eventually to carry the day.

Returning for a moment to the definition of a conservative evangelical believer, there is more to consider than the three essential beliefs I have highlighted here. Christian Smith has described evangelicals as inhabiting an oppositional subculture that sees itself as able to "thrive" because [it is] "embattled." To be "saved" is to turn from being "secular" and so leave the larger group. Smith argues that contemporary conservative evangelicals flourish as a result of this "distinction, engagement, tension, [and] conflict with secular society."[23] Born-again Protestants see themselves as set apart from other Americans, but also as the rightful descendants of the truest Americans. This simple, yet complex, tension lies at the heart of their narratives. The pastors I listened to over the course of my digital rhetorical ethnography encouraged their listeners to live lives of tradition and to defend the country as it once was, while at the same time they reminded these same listeners that their true homes are in heaven, and so this world—including the United States—can never be home.

While Protestantism, in general, and evangelical Protestantism, in particular, may well be threaded into the narrative fabric of the United States, the two began to unravel into separate camps in the decades following the Civil War. The rifts that appeared then feel relevant now, largely because they have never been fully resolved. Today, however, they appear as a division between the secular and sacred worlds. At first, they represented division between believers themselves. George Marsden, among others, has exhaustively detailed how the twin forces of scientific discovery and the industrial revolution required response. The more easily adaptable clergy were able to make peace with the upheavals that emerged then, and so found ways to blend the words of the Bible, the call of their faith, and the cultural shifts. These so-called liberals came to populate mainline churches that were especially prevalent in the Northeast and were especially powerful in American Christianity through the 1960s.[24] Conservatives, on the contrary, abhorred such adaptation. For them, the authority of the Bible always came first. It could never be retrofitted for a modern world. Rather, the world belonged to God, and His purposes never altered. Many of these believers lived in the South. Until the 1925 Scopes trial (*The State of Tennessee v. John Thomas Scopes*, on the teaching of evolution in state-funded schools), the debate was largely over whether any accommodation between true faith and secular society was possible. After the trial ended, and despite the fact the fundamentalists had won (Scopes was found guilty and fined, though the verdict was overturned on a technicality), evangelical Protestants supposedly disappeared from public view until the late 1970s. The story goes that they reemerged with Jerry Falwell Sr. and his Moral Majority.

I shall return to the claim of their disappearance, but first I offer an abbreviated history of conservative evangelical social and cultural activism, and how it became more traditionalist than progressive in emphasis. The mid-nineteenth century, a period often called the Second Great Awakening, saw born-again believers become socially and culturally active, and interested in causes like temperance and abolition.[25] In the aftermath of the Civil War, Christians of all stripes aimed for social and structural reform, and believed that saving individual souls was related to saving the whole of society. Para-church groups like the Salvation Army were formed during these years. Preachers like Charles Finney gained fame for delivering electrifying sermons against wealth, and agitating against the poverty, disease, and filth that were endemic to industrial slums. Finney called believers to intervene and engage their faith for the public good.[26] However, as progressive as this message was, it also pointed to the coming change in discourse. Finney emphasized how all individuals had "the liberty of power and choice," a kind of spiritual democracy that made everyone capable of controlling their own lives as well as their spiritual destinies.[27] This rhetoric of personal responsibility still resonates across conservative evangelicalism today. As the nineteenth century came to a close, debates had already begun over who faced poverty and what kinds of individual responses were required for overcoming suffering. As happens now, these disputes took on religious connotations, despite some secularization of charity work. Michael Katz has detailed how the poor were spoken of as being either "worthy" or "undeserving," a bifurcation that persists with often racialized overtones.[28]

In the early twentieth century, socially and progressively motivated believers advanced the Social Gospel. The Social Gospel was a progressive movement that descended from the earlier view that saving individuals and saving society went together. This theology taught that Christians had a literal obligation to work to instantiate God's kingdom in the world, as Jesus taught in the Lord's Prayer: "Thy kingdom come / Thy will be done / On earth as it is in heaven." According to this teaching, Jesus's preordained second coming would remain forestalled until the world had been set right. The duty of believers was to do good works and intervene against injustice. This required continual engagement with secular culture. Christians were to be in the world, living up close to even the most irreligious of souls, trying to make things better, and acting under the belief that real progress both could be and was, indeed, being made.

For conservatives, the all-out worldly engagement suggested by the Social Gospel was anathema. These believers took a different view of Jesus's second coming and believed that society would worsen inexorably, whether Christians intervened or not. For these believers, moral decay was inevitable, even necessary, as explained to them by the influential British Bible teacher John Nelson Darby and made popular in the *Scofield Reference Bible* (1909; rev. ed., 1917) edited by American theologian Cyrus I. Scofield. Darby insisted that humankind would continue through a series of dispensations until Jesus Christ returned to begin a thousand-year reign. After this, He would defeat Satan in the battle of Armageddon. The job of the church was to prepare Christ's people for His return, and to win souls for heaven. It was not to save society from anything, because this was an impossible task. The chasm between this view and that of the Social Gospel could not have been starker. While it overstates the case to say that every conservative Protestant of the early twentieth century went to bed at night looking out the window hoping to see Jesus returning, the skepticism toward social activism that took root then among these believers has never abated.[29]

In the early twentieth century, conservative evangelicals subtly changed their critique of capitalism. Rather than worry about the sin, slums, and disease that had dominated their discourse during the years of the Second Great Awakening, they began to fret over how the system was changing from one based largely on the production of capital goods to one that privileged credit, consumption, and quick self-gratification. People across income levels suddenly found themselves able to buy more and more expensive goods, increasing living standards for almost everyone. However, the value of delayed gratification lost some of its appeal, as being in debt was no longer something that only happened to those who were desperately poor or undeniably immoral. Consumer goods furthered this undermining. They made instant pleasure accessible to more people, and slowly equivalized human "wants" with human "needs."[30] People stopped thinking of their labor as a way to discern whether they had received God's grace or as a way to show others evidence of their Christian character. They believed their work should be mostly about amassing weath and acquiring status. Conservative evangelicals still decry this diminution of the Protestant work ethic. Consumer culture and consumer values represent worldly temptations. They are the site and the fruit of sin. Fundamentalists—the term generally used for traditionalist, conservative believers by 1920—devoutly insisted that true Christians had to separate from this culture to remain pure.[31]

The bitter proceedings of the Scopes trial in 1925 only intensified these impulses toward separation. The trial, among the most famous of the twentieth century, pitted fundamentalists and modernists against each other. The matter had to do with a Tennessee law banning the teaching of evolution in public schools. Although the trial's protagonist, John T. Scopes, came out on the losing side—he was convicted of teaching Darwin's theory and levied a small fine—conservative Protestants faltered in the more important battle for public opinion. Media portrayed them as backward and beyond social redemption. The trial "is genuinely fabulous," wrote H. L. Mencken, in his role as a reporter for the *Baltimore Sun*. "I have enough material stored up to last me 20 years."[32]

In the aftermath of the Scopes trial, conservative Protestantism, especially in its most ardent and literal form, receded from view. Its adherents turned inward and created a network of Christian schools, universities, magazines, para-church organizations, and more. The purpose of these institutions was to create a national subculture that was especially robust in the South, where believers could co-affiliate to do business, teach one another's children, create media, and so on, free from the influence and pressure of secular culture.[33]

Billy Graham Takes Evangelicalism Mainstream

Recent scholarship has challenged the notion that conservative evangelical Protestants ever really disappeared from secular society. This challenge highlights how Bible-believing Christians in the United States have never ceded their claim that the country, across all culture, belongs first to them and needs protection from those who might fail to defend traditional values. The activity of rejoining—or noticeably reappearing in—society began during World War II. In 1942, J. Elwin Wright and Harold Ockenga formed the National Association of Evangelicals (NAE) as a response to both the more separatist American Council of Christian Churches (ACCC) and the more liberal Federal Council of Churches (FCC). It was a first step that would be followed later that decade by the beginning of the ministry of Billy Graham. Graham's emergence was something of a wonder. Frances FitzGerald writes that he was "a powerful preacher who could hold an audience rapt with an intake of breath. To those who met him he seemed a nice young man, friendly, open, and sincere. But where his crowds came from puzzled many a Protestant minister."[34]

After all, Prohibition—which conservative Protestants had backed—had deterred many Americans from both church attendance and Christianity itself, as had the fallout from the Scopes trial. The troubles of the Great Depression led many to question their faith, rather than draw them to church. Yet Graham, who had originally planned to go to Harvard's Divinity School, instead joined Youth for Christ founder Torrey Johnson in a movement to convert culture.[35] He would leverage his skills as a preacher, the enthusiasm of youth, and the fervor of the war's aftermath to take evangelicalism mainstream. He was helped by men who included Harold Ockenga, Charles Fuller, and Carl Henry. These men would become "titanic" figures within conservative Protestantism, and are now remembered for their efforts to modernize the faith.[36] Their movement became known as neo-evangelicalism. Conservative, capitalist, and resolutely anticommunist—Graham, for instance, once described the Garden of Eden as a paradise "in which there were no union dues, no labor leaders, no snakes, no disease"—neo-evangelical leaders also reminded believers of their duty to offer compassion and care to the needy among them.[37] Graham, Ockenga, Fuller, and Henry created seminaries, most prominently Fuller Theological Seminary and Gordon-Conwell Theological Seminary, as counterpoints to the perceived doctrinal liberalism of mainline Protestantism and its then dominant Union Theological Seminary. Graham also founded the magazine *Christianity Today*, among conservative evangelicalism's most influential periodicals.[38] Along with church issues, it covers news and politics. During the 2016 campaign, the magazine published stories like those in the mainstream media about the "newly" discovered white rural poor and the character defects of Donald Trump.[39] But with the exception of its anticommunist strain of language in the early years, the NAE—at first—steered mostly clear of politics. Together with his partners, Graham was much keener to reestablish conservative evangelicalism as part of American life, and to present it as a positive force.

This reestablishment required coming to terms with some aspects of modernity, accommodations for which the public preacher was sometimes criticized.[40] However, his success at mass crusades made him popular, and, soon enough, politicians hoped he would associate with them. So, while most conservative Protestants were actually quite apathetic about politics from the formation of the NAE in 1942 through the 1960s, Graham rubbed elbows with every president from Dwight Eisenhower through Barack Obama. His early political engagement was endorsed, in a way, through Carl Henry's 1947 publication of *The Uneasy Conscience of Modern Fundamentalism*. Henry held that evangelical separation was wrong on two fronts. First, believers who remained separate were relinquishing their duty to act as a moral authority for society. Second, by remaining apart, they were failing to save more souls for Christ.[41] Several decades later, a series of documents would echo Henry's message, including the Chicago Declaration of Evangelical Social Concern (1973), and the Lausanne Covenant (1974).[42] In the period between the publication of *The Uneasy Conscience* and the end of the 1970s, some conservative Protestants also began to grow wary of US Supreme Court decisions they saw as unfavorable and liberalizing of culture. These included *Engel v. Vitale* (1961), which declared prayer in public schools unconstitutional, and the abortion decision in *Roe v. Wade* (1973).[43]

More than anything—and even still—conservative Protestants who want to both engage culture and remain pure from its vices object to what they take to be creeping "secular humanism." This is the lens that best explains the anger that propelled Jerry Falwell Sr.'s rise to prominence with the Moral Majority in 1979, as well as other controversies going forward from there. Falwell and his inner circle of supporters believed most citizens rejected the seeming atheism, amorality, and pro-evolution ideology of the American Left. The legacy of the movement is debatable—there is little doubt of its success at generating lasting name recognition[44]—but its arrival marks the onset of the Christian Right as a force in American politics. From the 1980 election forward, scholars began to measure the voting influence of this group, particularly as it had moved toward supporting Republicans.[45] It is best described as "a broad yet organizationally synergetic movement of moral protest and political action that drew on antiliberal, antifeminist, and antigay sentiments among increasingly discontented and mostly white religious conservatives." However, where neo-evangelicalism had paid at least some attention to the needs of the poor or otherwise ailing, the religious Right more often copied that movement's cultural charisma, but deployed it "in the name of fundamentalist rancor. Controversial government actions . . . galvanized fundamentalists to enter the political fray, inspiring a reactionary and largely unprecedented wave of grassroots activism and church mobilization."[46]

Falwell's Moral Majority was followed by other conservative evangelical groups with similar motives. These included the Religious Roundtable (also founded by Falwell), Concerned Women for America (founded by Beverly LaHaye), the American Family Association (founded by Donald Wildmon), Focus on the Family (founded by James Dobson), and, after some of these organizations foundered, the Christian Coalition of America (founded by Ralph Reed and Pat Robertson). Each of these organizations advanced rhetorics in the public sphere about how the United States was properly constituted as a country of traditional values based in the Protestant work ethic.[47] Through the decades that have passed since the Christian Right first arrived on the American political scene, some critics have contended that these voters have been used or else wasted their time. For all the agitating and politicking they have done, little has changed. Abortion is still legal (though sometimes hard to access, particularly in rural parts of the country).[48] LGBTQ citizens have gained increasing public recognition and rights, including Constitutional protection for marriage equality and against employment discrimination. Prayer is still restricted in public schools.[49]

This argument may be true to a point. It also helps explain why the rhetoric of the religious Right has grown softer over the years, as some of its adherents have grown weary of the strident tone they think has given it a bad public image and strained its ability to convert new believers. But what the argument misses is how the movement's members, from the very beginning, depended not on results but on a clear conviction that they could make a difference. Ronald Reagan's skills as a politician and communicator were especially crucial on this front. Although he did not share the faith, Reagan spoke the language of conservative evangelicalism, and endowed those believers who were especially invested in politics with an "aura" of confidence.[50] He took positions that resonated with religiously conservative voters, as he demonstrated for his fellow Republicans and those who would come after how to successfully knit together religious priorities and GOP talking points. Reagan blasted IRS efforts aimed at forcing reforms in religious schools. He denounced the Federal Communication Commission for having tried to regulate religious broadcasting. And he promised that the United States would always be a close ally of Israel, an issue that was beginning to emerge as an important one for evangelical voters and that would only increase in saliency over the coming decades.[51] But more than anything, Reagan vowed to protect liberty by shrinking the power of the federal government, while promoting individualism, personal responsibility, and a laissez-faire economic system. He denounced the welfare system because he said it "sanctioned women having children without husbands" and so threatened American family life.[52] The language in his speeches celebrated the power of business for propelling the economy forward, and lauded old-fashioned hard work as necessary for achieving the American dream. His was a vision of tradition and exceptionalism that framed the protest decades of the 1960s and 1970s as antiprogress and full of sin. To go forward was really to go back.

In short, Reagan made his followers believe their side could win elections and then enact (or retract, as the case might be) programs aimed at restoring "traditional values, including a strong Judeo-Christian faith" and work ethic.[53] His presidency marked the beginning of a voting constituency based on language and ideas, as much as on policy. Thus, even though many conservative Protestants felt only lukewarm about the candidacy and election of George H. W. Bush in 1988 (though they still mostly supported him at the ballot box), religious leaders and voters continued to coalesce and mobilize around social and economic issues, and to support Republican candidates.[54] Evangelical preference for the GOP has never wavered since Reagan's election. For those who wonder at this support, or who suggest that the more "Christian" political priority would be ballots cast on behalf of poor or marginalized populations through supporting candidates who promise to shore up the social safety net, the point is that conservative evangelicals do believe they are voting on behalf of a vulnerable constituency: that of America itself.

For Bible-believing Protestants, the foundations of the country are still, and have long been, in peril. The evidence of this runs through their discontent with industrial slums, Billy Graham's crusades calling people to be saved but also to resist communism, and into and beyond the 2016 election when they agreed, at least tacitly, with Donald Trump that the time had come to "Make America Great Again." Conservative Protestants treasure John Winthrop's formulation of the country as a "city on a hill" and—perhaps more than other Americans—pay no heed to the fact that, in his original formulation, Winthrop was speaking as an Englishman to other Englishmen. As an English Puritan and one of the co-founders of the Massachusetts Bay Colony, Winthrop had no conception of himself as an American settling a new land that would one day be a sovereign nation.[55] This idea of a continental constituency—the argument that the country is the only populace that really counts—informs how the pastors of the nation's largest churches develop their homiletic narratives about the United States when it comes to politics, elections, and evangelical voting priorities. By developing narratives grounded in patriotism and American exceptionalism, ministers craft homiletic stories that emphasize abundance over scarcity, and possibility and opportunity over circumstance or misfortune. In the United States, they say, everyone *always already* has the means to succeed and be free, because each citizen is *always already* loved by God, and is *always already* living in the most prosperous nation on earth. Proper politics means maintaining this greatness while defending against erosion or loss. It does not mean promoting progress or change, even when it might be framed for the beneficent good.[56]

2

Digital Rhetorical Ethnography

Going to Church in My Pajamas

It was November 6, 2016, the Sunday before Election Day. At Taylors First Baptist Church in Taylors, South Carolina, people gathered onsite and online for the morning's worship service. As part of its effort to reach all kinds of people, whatever their preference or comfort level, Taylors First Baptist holds several different kinds of services at its site. On this day, there was the traditional service, during which a pastor in a formal suit directed a hymn-filled worship time, joined by a choir of grandmotherly types wearing bright green robes with gold collars. There was also the contemporary service, in which the worship pastor wore only slacks and a button-down shirt, and stood in front of a smaller choir in business-casual clothes. The songs were modern but still easy—a kind of "Yes, Jesus Loves Me," Sunday School vibe, but for adults. And there was the modern service, in which a worship band led the music, complete with drums and electric guitar. All three services featured the same sermon, however. Pastor Paul Jiminez preached from the pulpit in the traditional service, and his sermon was transmitted into the other two spaces. Taylors First also archived the sermon online, where it remained as of 2019, along with hundreds of others.[1] For about forty minutes, Jiminez talked about ways his audience could apply their faith to the election that was to take place the following Tuesday. It was the second in a set of four messages he gave on the topic. The series was called "Culture, Politics and the Church." It aimed to explain how true Bible-believers might think about the campaign and politics, given the nastiness of public discourse and the corrupt quality of modern culture.[2]

Like many other megachurches in the United States, Taylors First Baptist uploads its weekly services to a website. About five months after Jiminez first preached his sermon about the 2016 election, I attended the church online and participated in the November 6 "traditional service." As soon as I clicked "play," the 1923 hymn "Great Is Thy Faithfulness" began filtering through the speakers of my laptop computer. For a moment I considered skipping ahead to the actual (spoken) sermon part of the service. After all, this is the heart of my research. As a rhetorical critic I write as an interpreter of stories. I seek to make meaning, and to make that meaning persuasively. But as the first notes of the hymn emerged through my computer's speakers, I could hardly help but close my eyes and listen. I was transported back to my girlhood and time spent with my paternal grandmother, now deceased, who sometimes used to quietly sing hymns while she went about her day. I could hear her voice along with the choir, and I could see her doing the dishes, making cookies, and reading her morning newspaper. I missed her, and I wondered about her faith. I thought for a moment, too, about the questions I still have about my own. This is how music works: it takes us back in time to days and people and moments we cannot forget, whether or not we wish to remember in that moment when we hear a song, and even when we have work to do.

This is also the experience of digital rhetorical ethnography. I developed this methodology over the course of this project as a way to both experience and interpret the texts with which I was working. I realized early in my research that there was not going to be any archive for me to visit. To hear the stories inherent to contemporary white, conservative Protestantism, I was going to have to find a subset of their churches where I could listen. Furthermore, I wanted to hear certain kinds of stories. Unlike others who have gone into similar spaces, this meant I could not simply seek to participate in only one or two megachurches or clearly delineated evangelical activities or movements.[3] This kind of deep engagement would have allowed me to approach the point of view of some of those who identify as conservative evangelicals, an essential ingredient of ethnography.[4] However, my focus as a critic on narratives about economics, American exceptionalism, the 2008 recession, and the 2016 presidential campaign meant that I could not rely on only one or two churches to supply me with enough sermons. First, pastors only gave the kinds of messages I was looking for occasionally, during the time the events happened, if they did so at all. Second, my scholarly intention was to approach the rhetorical worldview of white, conservative evangelicals across the United States, writ large. I wanted to know if the stories pastors told in California sounded much like the ones pastors told in Florida. I also wanted to know if the stories in California and Florida resembled those being told in Minnesota. Very often, I found that they did.

To hear the stories, I had to find a way to attend church in a lot of places, at once. Enter the digital church. Megachurches across the country have created vibrant online spaces where individuals can find virtual community and join believers in the act of worship.[5] During the eight years I spent logging onto different faith platforms, I was asked many times by colleagues, family, and friends—most of whom are not frequent churchgoers—if it isn't terribly boring to spend so much time alone in my office going to church online? The truth is, for the most part, it is not. There is a reason these bodies have grown so large. The music is usually dynamic and uplifting. The pastors I watched and heard almost always had a magnetic speaking presence that created easy identification with their audiences, including me. Even online, the overall experience was one of being welcomed and wanted, even as a seeker or scholar with questions. Moreover, as Annette Markham so well described in her early depiction of internet ethnography, "to be present in cyberspace is to learn how to be embodied there. To be embodied there is to participate."[6] Over time, I realized that being part of the digital community in the white, conservative evangelical megachurch did not require me to be a believer, or even require me to look or act in a particular way. Indeed, this was precisely the point. Megachurches across the country, with varying statements of faith and different approaches to attracting new members, put their services online to be available to those who would regularly attend but have to miss because they are sick, working, or out of town. They also do it—and this may be the more important reason—in the hope of converting new believers to Christ.[7] Other watchers and hearers of the sermons I found online may well share my skeptical viewing and listening approach, if not my tendency toward scholarly analysis. In fact, there exists the distinct possibility that the rhetors—the pastors—who knew their sermons would go online prepared them with unbelievers like me in mind. Very often, the churches I attended and the messages I engaged with began with preliminary remarks that acknowledged my online status and the possibility of such disbelief. For example, the message by Jud Wilhite that I analyze in chapter 5 opened with a quick hello from one of the church's associate pastors. He did not give his name. He was white, with light brown hair that was neatly parted and combed back. He wore a casual, hooded, denim jacket with sweatshirt sleeves, and he offered a friendly smile. "Thank you so much for joining us today," he said. "If Central [the church's name] has impacted your life in any way send us an email." He then flashed the URL of a website for making financial contributions.[8] Other churches were less formal in their introductions to the online audiences. But many pastors still made mention of those "watching online" in their welcoming remarks to their congregations. I do not mean to suggest that I was exempt from the requirement that I remain always mindful of my own subjectivity, outsiderness, and awareness of my status as an academic. Mindfulness of researcher subjectivity is the hallmark of ethical research, including digital ethnography and rhetorical criticism. Rather, I suggest that this positionality may not have been entirely unanticipated, or at least was not unwelcome, insofar as the pastors whose messages I studied intended for all kinds of people, maybe even scholars of rhetoric, to listen to what they had to say.

What Is Meant by Digital Rhetorical Ethnography?

I described in the introduction how I initially began to follow the narratives and stories of conservative evangelicals during the early days of the Obama administration. I was interested in finding ways to apprehend how born-again Christians were describing the financial crash, economic recession, and recovery that accompanied Obama's election and early days in office. I thought it possible the crisis was so large and destabilizing that it might disrupt the longstanding electoral and rhetorical bond between white evangelicals and the GOP. When this turned out not to be the case, I began to wonder whether considering closely some of the most public narratives available about financial and economic topics would elucidate how these believers understood their faith in the context of the then-emergent ideals of the Tea Party, which had a high population of evangelicals among its constituents.[9]

It was not immediately obvious to me how to find such narratives or who would be telling them. My first instinct was to look for places where evangelical leaders and pastors were joining faith literatures, including the Bible, with business literatures. Using Linda Kintz's notion of rhetorical resonance, I surmised I might be able to find crossover between constituencies—places where ideas and narratives were "linked together by feelings aroused and organized" in similar ways.[10] I decided to look for pastors who were applying "management" or "leadership" texts to help them run their churches. I reasoned that I might be able to identify places where ministers were using business principles to help them guide their flocks, and that these would lead me in a fruitful direction. One of the first pastors I found, Tod Bolsinger, led a church in the southernmost part of Orange County, California. Bolsinger was then writing a blog about church leadership. His writings included musings about many things, including baseball, barbecuing, and running triathlons. But what caught my eye was the list of books he recommended, which ran down the lefthand side of his home page: they were business texts that, he suggested, could help pastors better lead their churches. The list included an autobiography and advice book from restaurateur Danny Meyer; two books by the management guru Jim Collins; and Ori Brafman and Rod Beckstrom's book *The Starfish and the Spider: The Unstoppable Power of Leaderless Organizations* (2006). Bolsinger had even written a series of blog posts about *Starfish*. This book about networked and decentralized business organizations, Bolsinger wrote, "offers a most fascinating set of possibilities for creating healthier, more missional and re-producing churches." Silicon Valley in an evangelical Presbyterian Church, I thought. Resonance.[11]

It did not take long before my interest drifted away from Bolsinger's blog. I am an avid runner and tend to be on the lookout for things to listen to while I train. In the weeks after I began reading his blog posts, I also started downloading his weekly sermons to see if he would mention the books he recommended or use business examples to explain theological concepts. For the most part, Bolsinger did not. However, his preaching was very compelling. I found myself waiting anxiously on Mondays for his Sunday sermons to upload to the church website, so that I could download them to my iPod (it was 2011, after all) to listen to while I ran. I felt like a sixteen-year-old who had discovered a new favorite band and was always on the lookout for another hit single. I would run while listening to the latest homily, and then as soon as I got home I would sit down at my computer and respond to what I had heard.[12]

Bolsinger's church had a large archive of sermons available for listening, and it did not take long before I began to wonder whether other pastors had similar styles or preached on similar topics. I was also not having a lot of success finding other blogs or resources like his that clearly combined management and leadership texts with Bible themes and spiritual insights. But the internet was full of sermons, from all kinds of people. At the same time, I was beginning to realize that what I was doing was weird—listening to homilies while I ran, in my spare time, while doing research looking for online texts combining business and the Bible, and often coming up with little of use. Clearly, my real interest as a scholar was the sermons themselves. I needed to find a better, more formal way to find what I sought. Simply deploying Google searches would be far too random and could lead to results that I knew would be inexact.

A conversation with John Evans, a sociologist of religion at the University of California, San Diego, helped me begin to design the project that has become this book. He directed me to the Hartford Institute for Religious Research and its database of megachurches, which is easy to sort by both state and size. Hartford's archive created the possibility of consistency—no longer would I be forced to search the internet by keyword in the hope of finding a sermon worthy of engagement, or else be limited to studying only pastors whose names I already happened to know. I decided on megachurches because their size gave them natural reach and influence. I also believed such large churches were most likely to have good websites with archived sermons. So I made the decision to focus on megachurches, despite knowing this would eliminate smaller congregations that might privilege different kinds of narratives.[13] To find sermons, I began by randomly sampling sermons from every third church listed in Hartford's "by state" directory, as many megachurches post audio MP3 or video streams of their weekly services. However, this approach quickly became unworkable, as I found that some churches either did not have high-quality websites or else posted only limited numbers of sermons for public access. This meant that I had to become more deliberate in the way I found sermons to include in my project, even as I still tried to pay close attention to achieving good geographical diversity.[14] In the end, I would describe my archive as a carefully culled convenience sample.

It is unusual to think about ethnography, even digital ethnography, and experimental samples in the same study. Although I did not realize it at the time, I was developing a hybrid methodology. I initially intended only to gather texts to hear and analyze. But what I was really beginning to do was leverage networked technology to enter the digital church and experience the sermons I studied live. This fact of my presence in digital space was essential to my research. The project that had begun as a search for resonance across GOP constituencies (wanting to know how pastors borrow language from business executives and business writers, and so reinforce it) had become an investigation of homiletic language about political-economic issues.

Still, as I had been doing earlier in my life, I was investigating what it meant to be a conservative evangelical in the United States. The difference this time was that my questions now were scholarly, not personal. I was not trying to find faith myself. Rather, I was learning to understand how the faith of other people showed up in their narratives and might reinforce their political worldviews. In making explicit the fact that there was always something personal about this project, I join Roxanne Mountford's admission of both wariness and conviction about a similar state of subjectivity in her own work. Mountford noted that many scholars "come to their subject through a profound experience early in life," and suggested this was probably especially true of those who, like me, affiliate with cultural studies.[15] There is a "precarious balance," she wrote, that one must maintain "between reflection and confession . . . since an ethnographer is the primary eyewitness to the story she wants to tell."[16]

During the years I worked on this project, I prioritized precision and reflection as a way to maintain scholarly distance. Still following the example of Mountford, who herself had followed Patricia Bizzell, I endeavored to create an archive that could withstand scrutiny. Mountford argued that "feminist rhetoricians need[ed] to reclaim the word 'empiricism.'" While this book is not explicitly a work of feminist scholarship, I share Mountford's commitment to "rigorously attending to the world around us, listening for insights that are new to us, [and] resisting the temptation to turn our work into self-righteous grandstanding." Applying such rigor required taking breaks from the research from time to time to contemplate my findings, reconsider my arguments, and make sure I was treating the communities I was meeting online with respect and fairness. I had to compile a critical mass of sermons to be sure I had identified patterns, rather than lucky soundbites. I decided not to use the first sermons I heard—I conceived of the project organically and started without really realizing I had started. Because of this, I could not defend my early method or the ways I responded to the first texts I found.

What had begun as scholarship in rhetorical criticism became, right from the start, participatory, a hybrid research project. I modeled my approach to what I eventually termed digital rhetorical ethnography after Aaron Hess, Phaedra Pezzullo, and Dwight Conquergood. These thinkers all urged scholars to carefully join the communities whose stories and language they dared to decipher.[17] There were congruences between the online communities I was studying and the breast cancer survivor groups Pezzullo described in her work, particularly the creation of "copresence."[18] By going online and spending hundreds of hours attending worship services at digital megachurches, I was able to be with tens of thousands of conservative evangelicals in the United States over the course of eight years. As I write that, it sounds absurd, precisely because it is. Nevertheless, this *is* the feeling—the affective experience—of the online megachurch. Among my most important tasks was creating transcripts and detailed notes about a "public discourse that [was] not yet recorded."[19] I paid close attention to how pastors dressed, how churches decorated their stages, and which churches used worship bands and which preferred soloists and individual worship leaders. Every detail was important. Every prayer mattered as potentially significant to this project.

My experience of attending digital megachurches was deeply participatory and deeply visceral. The very nature of being online and present in the digital church drew me into its ambience, including what I imagined was the ambience of the physical church where the sermons actually happened. I learned to navigate the structure of various online communities, to find listings of services and statements of faith, and to read the biographies of pastors. Each of these things required time and increasing levels of familiarity with the environments I encountered. This participation constituted my embodiment into the imagined community of conservative evangelicalism as it exists online in megachurches. These churches were all also material communities with brick-and-mortar buildings, community groups, Bible study groups, and members, many of whom I would see, captured on camera, singing and participating along with me. They appeared as a co-present congregation. And there is no other way to put this: it felt real. When I attended an internet service, I felt materially present in time, even as I was also out of time. I could sing along with the worship if I so chose (I almost never did). The sermons I watched during my study worked in such a way that, as a virtual viewer, I became included in the audience through what was happening onscreen, especially the songs and the homilies. While watching, I felt I was among those actually congregated in the physical pews, sitting in front of the pastor as he spoke, although those in the pews had long since gone home. As Althusser might have explained, the material community *always already* included and interpolated me into the imagined community. In response, I also reimagined the material community right back.[20] Importantly, however, the fact of being online meant that I could attend churches all over the nation. Time-shifting froze the communities in place, as they waited for me to be ready to digitally worship. So where other ethnographers[21] of evangelicalism have had to reorder their lives to join a church or a movement, I was able to "join" the digital church across the evangelical internet while remaining in my own home. The collection of sermons I compiled over eight years, and especially those I collected during the presidential contest between Clinton and Trump, includes messages that happened simultaneously across the United States. On November 6, 2016—the Sunday before the presidential election—I attended services at twenty-one different churches. During the economic recession and recovery era (2008–13) there was no one date that was similarly popular for studying, as the timeframe was longer and not tied to an event like an election. All together, I listened to more than one hundred sermons related to the financial crash, and more than fifty about the 2016 campaign.

But even with all of these similarities and potential advantages, I must acknowledge the following: both Pezzullo and Hess argue that, as a methodology, participant observation should work to disrupt power and trouble hegemonic and mainstream discourses. Hess, in fact, called his method "critical-rhetorical ethnography" for this very reason.[22] And so my borrowing and adding to the methodology of these critical researchers is somewhat out of tune. In studying the stories of white conservative Protestantism via digital rhetorical ethnography, I entered the networked world of one of the most normative institutions in the United States to hear some of its most dominant stories. My purpose is not to advocate the claims or narratives of the disadvantaged. Rather, like Sharon Crowley, my hope is to reveal contemporary born-again homiletic plotlines in the hope of generating new conversations across constituencies.[23] But I also mean to expose some of the tensions and contradictions within evangelical rhetoric to allow those outside of the subculture to understand its arguments. I uncover how, when it comes to politics, framing all conservative Protestant discourse as obsessed with values issues like opposition to abortion or marriage equality elides an important narrative logic. This logic emphasizes God's will alongside meta-stories of American exceptionalism, personal responsibility, and, yes, the importance of embodying a lifestyle of traditional values. In this book, I will thickly describe each of these rhetorical warrants. In so doing, I join my ethnographic approach with rhetorical criticism with the explicit goal of revealing to those outside conservative evangelicalalism how they are situated in the discourse as "not belonging." This exclusion is rhetorically justified within the discourse, not because unbelievers are sinners who cherish the wrong values (for instance, they might be pro-choice), but because the country belongs foremost to conservative Bible-believers who must protect the nation from decline. This claim of ownership and duty is one that is often overlooked. Coming to understand it through these pages will allow those who wish to challenge it—and especially communities who are situated as marginalized within evangelical rhetoric—to formulate counter-stories and counter-claims that are in tune with the original narratives, while also suggesting broad themes of inclusion and rights to self-determination.

Finally, although I did find community online with those tens of thousands attending evangelical megachurches, very often it felt strange to conceive of my time "at" the digital church "as" ethnography, because I was usually in my own office, or at my own kitchen table, using my own computer, surrounded by my own books and coffee cups, and I was physically all by myself. But then I would remember: this is the experience as the designers of the online church intended it. Sociologists who study the online church debate whether making such solitary experiences possible for people is mostly about mission (extending Christianity's reach) or convenience (increasing access).[24] For my purposes, it did not matter. I was in my home, or in my campus office, *and* in the virtual evangelical community. I was participating in the digital church. Moreover, my entry into the digital church influenced the meaning I created through my criticism. I read the texts, and I felt them, too. Even so, the heart of my research involved revealing how "argument is a way of knowing."[25]

It is precisely because my primary way of knowing remains through argument—through rhetoric—that I do not want the "rhetorical" in "digital rhetorical ethnography" to get short shrift. Throughout my research, I was never foremost an evangelical pilgrim, sitting in a digital pew, engaged and wondering about conversion to the faith. My first identity remained that of a rhetorician. This is my primary training. I was always aware of the need to describe deeply the church environments with which I interacted, and I also wanted to acknowledge that my identity as a researcher necessarily limited some of my insight: my immersion in the community was always only in part, even if this immersion was particularly well suited to outsider interaction. My primary interest was always the stories, and I never stopped breaking them apart, seeking interpretive clues, or asking what these clues might suggest about conservative storytelling in the United States, writ large. Further, the digital megachurch was my avenue to the stories, and never the other way around. My first assumption was always that an important way of knowing for the believers in those churches likely had something to do with the stories the pastors were telling and that were so consistent across American geographical spaces and time.

It follows that my descriptions of the online environments are necessarily less rich than my descriptions of the homiletic stories themselves. My analysis emphasizes narrative. Throughout my project, I borrowed one important idea from David Ricci's book *Politics without Stories*.[26] Drawing on a theory by Blaise Pascal, as elucidated by historian Jacques Barzun, Ricci distinguished between two ways of knowing. One is the *esprit de géométrie*—the spirit of geometry, of math, of science. We might think of this as the scientific method, a way of knowing something precisely, or as close as human knowledge can come. This is not rhetoric, not argument as a way of knowing. Rhetoric as collected and repeated through stories creates an *esprit de finesse*—a sense of things. This is a way of knowing that grasps the whole. It is gut knowledge. *Esprit de finesse* is rhetorical resonance—those stories that are true because they have always been so, and that are so because they have always been true.[27] Upon hearing a narrative that relies on *esprit de finesse*, I argue—following Pascal, Barzun, and Ricci—that these stories cannot be said to generate their power through the cumulative effect of their constituent parts. Rather, their sway is the product of their whole. Many conservative evangelical sermons deploy long passages about American exceptionalism, the power of personal responsibility, and the promise of God's sovereignty over the United States as He intends it to be. These are grand ideals, sweeping narrative *esprits* that allow conservative evangelicals to embrace a conservative worldview intact, without stopping to inspect individual warrants or argumentative claims.[28]

Sermons as Rhetoric

The sermons I collected for this book constitute a unique archive. There is no one church, or speaker, who emerged in my research as the quintessential space or voice. Instead, the method of digital rhetorical ethnography works across texts to find the common meaning that underlies the pastors' main argumentative claims, supported with necessary description of the networked environments in which I participated. Because ministerial rhetoric is helpful but not determinative, no pastor, no matter how influential, could ever speak on behalf of every believer about matters of faith, let alone about political inclinations or political worldviews. For this reason, my arguments throughout take account of the history of the movement. Additionally, recent research in political science, particularly having to do with the power of political identity, weak parties but strong partisanship, and negative partisanship, undergird the stories I forward.[29] Because white, conservative Protestants are already primed as Republican voters, it is predictable that their stories favor the GOP. My animating question, however, is not why conservative Protestants are a reliable Republican constituency, or whether or not it is sensible that they should be, but rather to wonder how white, conservative Protestants continuously create and re-create a conservative worldview through their narrative, particularly as these narratives take shape from the front of the nation's largest evangelical churches.

Even so, the question remains, why choose pastors? Writers from Saint Augustine to Max Weber and, more recently, Susan Harding have argued for the role of clergy as influential interlocutors in society.[30] Ministers influence how believers interpret the worlds they inhabit and help to determine the language they use when speaking about this world. Conservative Protestants replicate the language and stories they hear from their clergy. This means that through studying the language of an admittedly small, yet influential group of people, namely, pastors, we can come to understand something about the words and worldviews of a larger constituency—in this case, conservative Protestant believers and voters.

I previously described Pascal's theory of the *esprit de finesse*. This sense of things characterizes what I was trying to hear in the sermons I collected and studied. Sometimes, however, formal rhetorical analysis was needed. Occasionally I turned to Kenneth Burke's theory; more often, I relied on the work of Walter Fisher, or else that of Chaïm Perelman and Lucie Olbrechts-Tyteca as developed in their book, *The New Rhetoric*. Perelman and Olbrechts-Tyteca argued that studies of rhetoric should extend beyond the examination of pure logical reasoning to evaluate questions of values and belief. They further urged that we consider these questions as argumentative propositions about how things might become, rather than as claims about the world as it already is.[31] This approach is well suited to studying evangelical discourse like sermons, because it provides a framework for finding and analyzing the belief and value claims pastors rely on, including those claims that are not immediately obvious. For example, when evangelical megachurch ministers preach, they rely on the authority of scripture. Often unstated but necessary to their homiletic assertions are arguments about why such authority is essential, or what might be the consequences of failing to believe in it.[32] Depending on the Bible underwrites pastoral authority and bulwarks believers from criticism and contrary information. I suggest that this fortification explains how some evangelicals remained rhetorically attached to Trump in 2016, despite his character shortcomings, which were clearly at odds with the values previously espoused by the GOP, most especially including its conservative Protestant members.

Even more germane to this project, Perelman and Olbrechts-Tyteca's theory of argumentation explains two other important things. The first is the role of hierarchy in argument. All audiences rank premises according to the facts and ideals they privilege. Provable truths or scientific data do not necessarily have purchase over values or beliefs. Rather, understanding requires noticing how proofs are deployed with respect to the audience at hand. Returning to the primacy of scripture in the evangelical community, every argument and claim—by definition—sits below this foremost value. For outsiders to the subculture, this can be confusing. For insiders, no other option exists.

Second, and related, Perelman and Olbrechts-Tyteca's theory is audience-dependent. Like Kenneth Burke, who emphasized the role of speaker-hearer identification, Perelman and Olbrechts-Tyteca state that "it is in terms of an audience that argument develops." Speaking to evangelicals requires understanding evangelicals. Pastors necessarily are helped along in this task because they are also members of the community. They have built-in credibility and so capacity to leverage shared values and narratives as persuasive means. As they do this, ministers create and reinforce a "community of minds" with their audience, a shared worldview that allows speakers to forward new arguments and claims.[33] In the sermons I collected, ministers would almost always begin with a shared joke or story, sometimes Bible-related but very often having to do with American history or politics. Once this common ground was firmly established, pastors could advance new ideas and narratives about the relationships between economics, politics, voting, and faith.

But what about narrative as rhetoric? Megachurch pastors sometimes forward formal arguments that require formal rhetorical analysis. However, I more often heard messages based on stories and narrative. As I noted in the introduction, Walter Fisher first proposed a narrative paradigm as a way to understand human communication and human relationships. Fisher also emphasized the role of community in understanding how both argument and persuasion work. Fisher quarreled with the notion that humans are foremost rational actors who behave according to scientific logics or agreed-upon best practices. He stressed the storytelling nature of people. For Fisher, narrative is the emblematic trait of the human condition. Individuals use narrative both as an interpretive framework and to explain what has happened and what is likely to come down the road. The megachurch pastors I studied often blended Bible accounts and American narratives—for example, putting together the parable of the talents (Matthew 25:14–30) with plotlines that emphasize duties to hard work, investment, and saving—to explain contemporary problems and provide a lens for understanding a potential future.[34]

By emphasizing narrative, Fisher was thinking along similar lines to those Perelman and Olbrechts-Tyteca had earlier developed. Both theories of rhetoric emphasize the routine logics behind everyday speech. The mutuality of purpose between these approaches provides another reason I have used their theories together.[35] Fisher, however, blurred the line between argumentation and narrative. He did not distinguish between formal proofs and telling a story that resonates from beginning to end.[36] Instead, narratives provide individuals with a reliable means for assessing behavior, deciding between right and wrong, and choosing among competing beliefs. Stories are the building blocks of narratives. They are smaller and furnish essential data points for individuals to assess whether new claims—new stories—merit inclusion into the community's narrative canon.

The majority of the megachurch pastors I heard were master storytellers.

Very few built arguments deliberatively. Rather, in their sermons they depended on shared narratives and repeated storylines. Most prominent were those that stressed a "founders' rhetoric" and insisted that the nation was created and formed from the beginning to belong to the God of the Bible, and that the United States would prosper so long as its citizens remained committed to this idea. Also notable were those that supported the rhetoric of active-passivism that was especially evident during the campaign of 2016.

In my research, I was deliberate in sermon selection to make sure I mostly watched messages that were likely to be about the topics I was trying to study—American economics, nationhood, and politics from a conservative evangelical point of view. I identified these kinds of sermons based on their titles or on the Bible passages that were listed next to the sermon title. I only included sermons from churches that publicly affirmed, in an easily identifiable way (usually found in their statements of faith), a belief that the text of the Bible is inspired by God and so always authoritative. Indeed, the vast majority of the churches I studied used language that declared the Bible to be the "infallible Word of God, and the supreme and final authority on all matters upon which it teaches," or something very similar to this.[37] I chose this as my key selection criterion because, as Robert Putnam and David Campbell wrote in their book, *American Grace*, the doctrine of biblical authority represents "the very bedrock of evangelical theory."[38] A small number of churches were eliminated from my study because I could find no such statement of faith. Even so, this selection criterion ultimately created more inclusivity than it did exclusion. Doctrinally strict churches like McLean Bible Church, Vienna, Virginia (near Washington, DC), affirm a belief in the infallibility of scripture alongside seeker-friendly congregations like Southcast Christian Church, Louisville, Kentucky, and Saddleback Church, Lake Forest, California. Pastors of all three of these churches—Lon Solomon (now pastor emeritus of McLean Bible Church), Dave Stone (now retired from Southeast Christian Church), and Rick Warren (founder and senior pastor of Saddleback Church)—are featured in chapter 3. Thus, by having a relatively low threshold for a church—and so its leader—to be included in this study, I was able to go widely into the megachurches of conservative evangelicalism in the United States. This makes the uniformity of the narratives I found all the more surprising.

Conclusion

Digital rhetorical ethnography is a practice that allows for both immersion and careful textual examination. I developed and refined this methodology over the course of the research that led to this book. I intended to do more than go inside the virtual communities of American evangelical megachurches in the United States. I also wanted to understand and decode their narratives about economics and politics in the early twenty-first century. The analyses I present extend the work of scholars including Susan Harding, R. Marie Griffith, Roxanne Mountford, Robert Glenn Howard, Omri Elisha, Jonathan Edwards, and Christine Gardner, among others. Each of these writers elucidated how words, symbols, rituals, and the very communities—both online and offline—of conservative evangelicalism in the contemporary United States have created a vibrant and fluid religious movement. Many outsiders also conceive of this evangelicalism as a necessarily, and overtly, political movement. Others resist such characterization. Digital rhetorical ethnography allowed me, as a researcher, to investigate the nuances and realities of this tension.

Inherent to this tension is the very nature of what Dwight Conquergood referred to as "meaning-making."[39] Meaning, like beauty, is in the eye of the beholder. Humans continuously construct and decode meaning, with good and bad effects, to good and bad outcomes. Earlier in this chapter I noted the essential influences of Aaron Hess and Phaedra Pezzullo to my work, and to my understanding of how the kinds of meanings Conquergood wrote about become negotiated in twenty-first-century communities. Their in situ examinations of activists make evident how rhetoric is always bound to a specific time and a specific place, even as rhetoric is also always ephemeral and dynamic. As Candace Rai explained of her own rhetorical sitework, "rhetorical ethnograph[ies] . . . provide a good vantage point for observing rhetoric-in-action because they demand the sustained inhabitation . . . of a researcher, who must go to the places where rhetorics are produced and circulate."[40] The benefit of digital rhetorical ethnography is the ease of access to the field Rai describes. The vastness of cyberspace means a researcher can go both wide and deep. Even so, the sermons I studied only made sense in the contexts—the pulpits and stages—in which they were preached. At the same time, these homilies were also part of a larger and longstanding conversation, what I call in these pages an *esprit de finesse*. Digital rhetorical ethnography grasps both the local dialect and the culture, even as it also listens for a longitudinal tune. As I discovered over the course of this project, while the methodology is not perfect, its advantage is in its reach.

Returning now to the sermon with which I began this chapter, at First Baptist Church in Taylors, South Carolina, Paul Jiminez developed his message around several key themes. He called the election in 2016 a "major,

major time for choosing," and so endowed the race with national importance, as was typical of pastors throughout my study. Jiminez then encouraged his audience to engage with politics as servants of God. He said true believers should try to "live honorably in submission" to government leaders. Next, the pastor exhorted his congregation to vote with the commandment in mind that they should "love their neighbor as they loved them[selves]." Doing so meant considering the Bible and noticing where it spoke directly about contemporary political issues, and where it was silent. As examples, the pastor said scripture was clear about the sanctity of life, about marriage and family, and about how God cared deeply for the poor. He said God would judge those nations who abused their power against weaker countries. In closing, Jiminez reminded his audience that no matter who won the election, God was in control and would work things together for good.[41]

Jiminez's sermon was exact in its formulation of the rhetoric of active-passivism as I will demonstrate it in chapters 4 and 5. Vote and rest easy, pastors said. Over and over again, whether I was visiting a traditional service online and being reminded of my grandmother or taking in a more seeker-friendly virtual space with a hipster vibe, megachurch pastors across the nation told similar stories.

These stories, made digitally accessible to me and countless others, form the basis of this book's analysis. Importantly, however, these stories are much more than simple narratives. In fact, they reveal the powerful undercurrents of evangelical political thinking. By going to church in my pajamas, I entered their inner sanctum to participate, for a time, as one of them.

3

America Is (Still) Great

In April 2009, Jon Meacham wrote an essay for *Newsweek* detailing the "end of Christian America."[1] In this piece, Meacham wrote of changing demographic patterns and how the Northeastern United States had become less religiously affiliated than the Northwest, which had long been the nation's least-churched region. He described an email conversation he had about this turn with Albert Mohler Jr., president of Southern Baptist Theological Seminary. "A remarkable culture-shift has taken place around us," Mohler wrote to Meacham. "The most basic contours of American culture have been radically altered. The so-called Judeo-Christian consensus of the last millennium has given way to a post-modern, post-Christian, post-Western cultural crisis which threatens the very heart of our culture."[2]

For Mohler, this shrinking Christian influence meant the nation had begun to tell a new story about itself, one without God at its center. Only months earlier President Barack Obama had moved into the White House. While neither Mohler nor Meacham mentioned Obama's election as part of their evidence, there is little doubt that his presidential win represented a progressive hope for a new multiculturalism that would embrace a multiplicity of American narratives.[3] Important to Obama's win had been a coalition of voters that included a rising population of individuals who claimed no religious affiliation. These were the citizens Meacham had highlighted in describing the purported decline of Christian America.

Only days after Meacham's *Newsweek* article appeared, Rick Warren, pastor at Saddleback Church in Orange County, California, appeared on the syndicated radio program hosted by Hugh Hewitt, a conservative talk show host and political commentator. Near the beginning of their conversation, Hewitt asked Warren about Meacham's article. Warren began with the premise that of the two religions that were growing in the world—Islam and Christianity—Islam was growing through births, while Christianity was growing through conversions. He said that he had travelled to 162 countries across the globe. Outside of America, he continued, Christianity was doing fine. Turning his attention to the United States, Warren said the nation had reached a "stage" where it needed to decide "a number of major factors. One of them is will America return to the historic roots, Christian roots, that are foundational for every one of our institutions."[4]

This statement placed Warren's understanding of US history as in line with that of Mohler. However, where Mohler felt despondent over demographic changes, Warren was hopeful. He first urged that "faith" was always better than "secularism" because the lack of belief created a vacuum that required filling. He then argued that the financial and housing crisis that coincided with Obama's presidential election were drawing people to church. Three days later, on Good Friday, Warren returned to Hewitt's studio to finish their conversation. This time, the two focused even more on the nation's economic crisis. Again, Warren presented the financial collapse in a positive frame. "I think that this recession is actually a good thing," he said. "If you know anything about American history or Church history . . . revivals are often in the seedbed of recession . . . when things are bad, they're good for the Church . . . the good news actually gets better when the bad news gets worse."[5]

In fact, Warren continued, there was risk in overstating how bad things were during the recession, because Americans, in general, struggle with suffering. The key to surviving hardship, the pastor counseled, is "to look at what is left, not just what you've lost. Life is really two, it's a yin and a yang . . . [It's] both all the time, at the same time." To focus only on the recession was to miss America's blessing. To pity the jobless person during the economic downturn was to miss how much harder such a difficulty would be during a time of prosperity. "It's interesting, it's not as big a blow to a man to lose his job in a recession as when in a boom time," Warren said. "In a boom time, it's 'what's wrong with me?' In a recession, it's 'okay, I'm one of the guys that got laid off.' So, it actually doesn't hurt as bad emotionally if 600,000 are getting laid off. It doesn't feel like a personal attack."[6]

To further illustrate this point, Warren situated his laid-off worker as still better off than most. He said the United States was still more blessed, and so still more exceptional, than other nations. To find true suffering, both the laid-off worker and Warren's listener would have to go elsewhere. The proper mindset was not anger at the system, or worry for one's future, but a commitment to thanksgiving and service. "Let me take you to Darfur, or Chad, or a hundred other places where most of the world would love to have your upside-down mortgage, would love to have your debt, would love to have your car that can't be repaired," Warren said. "Our problems are the rest of the world's riches. So, we just need a clearer perspective." He concluded by inviting Hewitt to drive an hour south of where they sat in the radio studio, to cross the Mexican border, and to "go over to the Tijuana dump, and . . . see how people are living just like Slumdog."[7]

For Warren, and for many evangelical megachurch pastors during the recession years of 2008 to 2012, there was the United States and its "so-called" suffering, and there was the rest of the world. There is little doubt that conservative, white evangelicals as a constituency never embraced the promise or politics of the Obama presidency—when he left office in 2016, his approval among this group remained the lowest for any individual group that was polled.[8] But from the beginning, these believers pushed back on any narrative framing that positioned the United States as globally faltering or that imagined America as having lost its place as the most enviable nation in the world. Instead, inside their churches, these Bible-believers listened to sermons about economic and values issues that urged restoration and remembering traditional American mores like individual initiative, hard work, and saving. They were reminded of the nation's presumed prominence and providence. And, like the audience listening to Warren's radio interview, they heard stories that insisted that actual anguish always existed outside of the United States. While the current crisis was bad, things beyond the nation's borders were always worse.

In this chapter, I examine the stories the pastors of the nation's largest churches told about the Great Recession and what it meant for the American future, as I heard it during my digital rhetorical ethnography in the years from 2009 to 2012. The narratives I describe shed light on two things. The first is clear and straightforward. It makes plain how some of the leaders of the most highly religious constituency in the United States framed the worst economic crisis to face the country in generations. Pastors told stories of business and capitalist triumph, and so maintained rhetorical support for the financial orthodoxy of the Republican Party, in general, and, to a lesser degree, the then-emergent Tea Party and its platform, which emphasized individual responsibility for getting through the recession, rather than government spending. Ministers also crafted sermons that emphasized traditional values and the American founding. They did not tend to mention structural inequality, let alone macro-economic structural collapse. The second issue is less forthright but still significant. The stories of the recession years hinted already at how these same traditionalist believers could come to embrace the candidacy of Donald J. Trump in 2016, only ten years after the recession, and while still adhering to the moniker "values-voter."

The sermons I heard were based on narratives that affirmed American exceptionalism and the American Dream. Many depended on a framework that mirrored Kenneth Burke's guilt-redemption cycle. This theory uses religious language (guilt, redemption, and purification) and concepts (Jesus died to save sinners) to understand the secular world. Burke applied his guilt-redemption theory to explain the persuasive appeal of Adolf Hitler's tome *Mein Kampf*. He showed how Hitler had idealized the meaning of German citizenship by scapegoating the Jewish people, and had promised that the nation would regain its former glory through vanquishing this common foe.[9] While the pastors whose sermons I heard in my study never deployed language or ideas as abhorrent as Hitler's, the certainty in the providential goodness of the United States that pervades conservative evangelical discourse is somewhat similar to the confidence that the notorious dictator had in Germany. During the recession era, pastors of the nation's largest churches urged their congregants to sustain belief in the natural bounty and privilege that was theirs by birthright. To live in the United States, they said, was to occupy a land that afforded them every blessing and opportunity. Even during a period of national economic turmoil, the light at the top of the "city on the hill" shone bright. The task before born-again Christians was to dig in and live out the same habits that had brought the country through hard times before, and so could be counted on to bring it through again. While many investigations into traditional, nonapocalyptic, culture wars rhetoric take as their point of departure the white, conservative Protestant disillusionment with social values questions, recession-era discourse revealed storylines that urged the faithful to live out the American Dream and protect themselves from further loss, or else to do whatever they could as individuals to join the ranks of the prosperous. Key words such as "discipline," "responsible," "faithful," "choice," and "decide," filled the sermons I watched and heard. Conservative evangelicals did not have to become statistics to the recession, pastors said. Neither did believers have to join those who had given up on the country and saw it as losing God's favor—or, even worse, no longer needing His presence at all.

Throughout the more than one hundred sermons to which I listened during the years of financial crisis and recovery, I heard pastors repeatedly situate American born-again Christians as having the ability to both survive and overcome financial hardship. Despite the recession, the United States still had abundant resources and wealth, proof that God remained on America's side. These pastors promoted the country's purported foundational values of self-reliance, divine providence, and Christian faith, and so created a rhetorical context that strengthened the already existing coalition between these believers and the rest of the GOP. Just as economic conservatives disavowed funding the social safety net in favor of low taxes, deregulation, and individual initiative, these sermons promoted similar themes. This was true even when such messages seemed to force the pastors to ignore their broader Christian call to challenge endemic poverty, hunger, or injustice in the United States, and to pay little attention to the country's most vulnerable populations.

Preaching the Culture Wars: Values and America

According to the underlying logic of the culture-war debate, as James Davidson Hunter first described it in his book *Culture Wars*, there are two sides at battle for the hearts and minds of American citizens. On one side are those with an "impulse toward orthodoxy," and on the other are those with an "impulse toward progressivism." Progressives tend to be both secular and at least somewhat relativist. Truth shifts with perspective. Orthodox[10] believers find such diffidence unappealing, even immoral. They prefer traditional culture and, more to the point, believe in "external, definable, and transcendent authority." For white, conservative Protestants, who fit into the orthodoxy camp, this is God as revealed in the Bible, which they understand to be inerrant in its original writing.[11] Truth is fixed, eternal, and beyond question. It demands submission and obedience. Such truth applies to all parts of human life, including the political, social, cultural, and economic realms.[12] Because truth is omnipresent, believers always have a means for divining (and defining) right from wrong, and attributing causation for everything that happens in life, even if this means simply saying, "It must have been God's will."[13]

Even so, for white, conservative Protestants, defining God's will often sounds like something that is passed out in personal doses. While these believers see America as uniformly blessed and called as a collective unit to stand as a shining beacon for the world, there is always an unmistakable tone of individualism in their rhetoric. Personal salvation comes first. Each person must choose either for or against Jesus. To refuse to make a decision is to choose against being saved. This first, essential judgment about heaven creates a fertile soil for other kinds of rhetorical appeals that stress individual agency and accountability. For white evangelicals, choice is always operative when it comes to whether individuals have sex outside of marriage, get pregnant, act on queer impulses, live within their means, have jobs, pay their debts, and more. Good choices make for good Christians. Unstated but often implied is the idea that good Christians make for good Americans, as well.

During the Great Recession, this formative ideal of choice appeared as a construct in three essential parts. First were arguments that began by asserting that the United States was exalted and exceptional, chosen from the beginning by God to be blessed. These appeals then moved to situate the contemporary culture as saturated with overconsumerism, individual ineptitude and laziness, and conservative Protestant apathy. Finally, there were calls to personal action. Here, no matter how collective the country's problems might have seemed, pastors urged their congregants to consider individual changes of behavior. Doing so would bring national restoration. Ministers relied on the theme of the nation, and wondered whether God's purpose in allowing the recession to have even happened was to get the attention of citizens and, more pointedly, of Bible-believers. Clergy reminded their listeners that the nation had an abundance of wealth and resources and so, from a practical point of view, any kind of economic hardship was always, and for anyone, almost absurd. It went against the grain of divine providence. The most reasonable explanation for the recession was disciplinary, pastors said. God wanted His people to demonstrate better character and better stewardship of their wealth. When this happened, He would restore the nation to its place as an exemplar of freedom and hope.

In 2011 Andy (Charles Andrew) Stanley, senior pastor of one of the five largest megachurches in the nation, North Point Community Church in Alpharetta, Georgia, just outside Atlanta, built a six-part sermon series on the obvious wealth of the United States.[14] Tall and lanky, casually dressed in lace-up leather shoes, jeans, and a colorful button-down shirt, the pastor argued that the nation teemed with overabundance. Indeed, he continued, the recession derived from the problem of having too much, rather than too little: "Ultimately our problems don't stem from a lack of prosperity. Come on. We are the United States of America. We're sea to shining sea. We're not way north where you freeze to death. We're not way south where you burn up. We have the ultimate piece of real estate. You realize that. You look all over the world and . . . if you started all over and God said that there aren't any countries, you get to pick one, and here's all the pieces in the world you can look at, you might find some more beautiful ones, but in terms of strategic locations, you'd say, I'll take that one, sea to shining sea, right in the middle, full of resources, that's the way to go."[15] Stanley's belief in American hegemony and exceptionalism was as robust as any that I heard. He ignored American exceptionalism's more traditional meaning, which includes global obligation—the United States as a nation whose good works and moral values engender providential blessing.[16] Instead, exceptionalism appeared in his sermon sui generis, an unquestionable fact, meant to benefit citizens as their birthright and gift.[17] Chaïm Perelman and Lucie Olbrechts-Tyteca describe such reasoning as based in the notion of "unlimited development."[18] This framing allows speakers to "insist on the possibility of always going further in a certain direction, without being able to foresee a limit to this direction."[19] These kinds of appeals "present at the end an ideal which is unrealizable, but whose realizable terms will constitute incarnations that are ever more perfect, ever purer, and ever closer to the ultimate term."[20] Stanley's sermon evoked this kind of emphasis on the "ultimate" nature of American exceptionalism. The United States—as an idea, a concept, and a geographical landscape—represented the definitive historical model, from sea to shining sea, not too far north, and not too far south. Such a privileged positioning meant that, for those who lived in the United States, there would always be more than enough: enough work, enough access to resources, enough freedom.

Along these same lines, Skip Heitzig, the founder and senior pastor of Calvary Chapel in Albuquerque, New Mexico (whose rhetoric I also highlight in chapter 4), worried that an abundance of American freedom led some citizens to take it for granted. They had failed to honor and protect their birthright, he said, thinking it would always be there. When this happened, freedom, like a cloud on the horizon, had begun to slip away. During a 2012 Independence Day sermon, Heitzig said:

> We live in the most unique country in the world . . . The United States of America, you live here. It's a . . . unique place. There are a lot of great places in the world, and a lot of places on earth have their own border issues. Typically, though, it's people wanting to leave their borders and get out of town . . . We have a border problem in our country, but it's the kind where everybody else wants to come over into this country because it is such a great country—and you live here.
>
> My fear is we're becoming less great everyday because we don't care about those same values and standards and goodness and righteousness that have been passed down to us.[21]

Here, Heitzig relied on what I term "founders' rhetoric" to develop his sermonic narrative. Such homilies depend on stories and logics that urge audiences to remember what has been "passed down" to them, in the service of appreciating how the United States is an exceptional nation, with providential roots. Many pastors leveraged these stories that claimed a blessed original status to get congregants to take sincerely their obligations as citizens. Megachurch pastors sought legitimacy and persuasive power for their claims about America's continued, contemporary status as an exceptional nation through entrenching the founders' and the country's constitutional framing in nostalgic terms, infused with Christian meaning. Sometimes, this even included using dubious history, as was the case with Don Wilson's sermon "This Is Freedom," given on July 4, 2010.[22] Wilson is the founder and former senior pastor (he is now retired) of Christ's Church of the Valley, Peoria, Arizona. On Independence Day, 2010, he said: "America is a nation that has been blessed by God. Our nation was founded on godly principles by godly men. Do you realize that fifty-three of the fifty-six men who crafted our Constitution indicated their belief in the word of God and its values . . . All of our country's original documents were based on the Bible. Did you know the separation of governmental powers was taken from Isaiah 33, verse 22, which says, 'The Lord is our judge, the Lord is our lawgiver, the Lord is our king.' From that verse, our forefathers established the judicial, legislative, and executive branches of government."[23] Of course, this is wrong. Political theorists generally hold that the framers were inspired by the writings of Aristotle and by Montesquieu's tripartite system.[24] Nonetheless, for many evangelicals who believe insistently in the Christian founding, such claims may be "true enough." Pastors often highlight individual words of Bible texts in their sermons, then define them in the original Greek (or sometimes Hebrew), to get closer to a phrase's pure meaning. Likewise, in sermons about the United States, pastors often point back to the founding as a time when the nation was most right and most free. Many situate the founders as inherently wise and faithfully—evangelically—Christian, even if they must choose non-mainstream accounts of history to do so.

Dave Stone, then pastor (now retired) of Southeast Christian Church in Louisville, Kentucky, also gave a sermon on July 4, 2010, that deployed this kind of reasoning. Stone's sermon, "Cliffhanger: The Family, the Foundation of a Nation, the Story of Us," is especially fruitful for study, because while he described the American past as an example of unlimited greatness and providence, he also urged that the contemporary nation was at risk of losing God's favor. "At the beginning, America had a solid foundation," Stone said. "It wasn't perfect, but the foundation was solid." The active and open faith of men like George Washington, John Adams, Abraham Lincoln, and Theodore Roosevelt made obvious the nation's Christian underpinnings. Stone emphasized how the Continental Congress had declared May 17, 1776, as a day for national "fasting and prayer." He reminded his listeners that George Washington had spontaneously added the words "so help me God" to the end of his inaugural oath, and then kissed the Bible he used for his swearing-in. John Adams, too, had said the "Constitution was made for a moral and religious people . . . [and was] wholly inadequate to the government of any other." Early American intellectual life privileged sacred over secular knowledge. "In fact, 106 of the first 108 schools in America were founded on the Christian faith," he said. "Did you know that Harvard and Yale began as ministry training schools?" During the Civil War, Abraham Lincoln declared that without the Bible, "we would not know right from wrong." And Teddy Roosevelt delighted in leaving behind the "perplexing problems" of the presidency to attend a weekly worship service.

Stone related each of these examples in a straightforward manner, adding little context or meaning. That so many American founders spoke using such obviously religious language proved that the status of the United States as an exceptional nation stemmed from its conservative Protestant underpinnings. But Stone's message meant to do more than simply celebrate the nation's religious heritage. Instead, like other pastors, Stone situated his homily as part of a larger conversation that worried about how the nation's central narrative no longer included God as its main character. He highlighted a story he had seen on the news about a teenager in Massachusetts who had asked his school for a daily recitation of the Pledge of Allegiance over the loudspeaker, only to be refused. For Stone, that such a simple request could not be granted, "because we might offend someone," made obvious the problems of political correctness, along with those of public education itself. Stone then described some research published by the controversial historian David Barton of WallBuilders[25]—revealing again the tendency of these pastors to develop appeals based on accounts and records from outside of the mainstream—to develop his argument that taking God out of the public schools, and so out of the public square, had caused national decline. According to Barton, the 1962 Supreme Court decision that restricted prayer in public schools, *Engel v. Vitale*, correlated to increases in premarital sex, teen suicide, violent crime, and more. The only category in which the numbers declined was in average SAT scores. "So how do you explain all these statistics, in a dozen different areas?" Stone concluded, his voice rising. "Coincidence? Or maybe, just maybe, there really is power in prayer."

And yet, rather than urge his audience to begin praying more, Stone drew attention to the complicity of conservative evangelicals in having contributed to the cultural decline portrayed in his narrative. As was true of many of the pastors I listened to, Stone included himself in his indictment, along with the congregants to whom he was preaching. This is a sometimes-overlooked factor in analysis of culture-war rhetoric, which often asserts a bifurcated discourse, with those defending and upholding traditional values on one side, and those seeking progressive values on the other. This partly explains why some people outside the conservative evangelical subculture decry hypocrisy at work. However, the stories I heard in my research were more complicated, and there were hints of this complication in Stone's homily. With a touch of grace, Stone asked his audience to listen to his words not solely from a political vantage point and to weigh his words against God's word. "This is a message that many of us need to hear," he said. "This is a message that I need to hear." He had failed in the same ways he suggested his audience had. He then listed a series of specific indictments, emphasizing himself as part of the problems he identified through carefully invoking the word "we": "Christians seem . . . to be oblivious . . . [that] moral standards . . . American values . . . biblical principles and common sense are quickly fading . . . In our efforts to cover our mistakes, we have allowed 51 million abortions to take place. In our quest for more and more possessions, we've racked up huge debts, which rob us of our joy. In our attempt to be tolerant, we have discounted the sanctity of marriage. In our search for the fountain of youth, we have stopped listening to the wisdom of the elderly. In our desire for wealth, we have communicated, 'In gold we trust.' In our efforts for political correctness, we have neutered the power of our Christian witness."[26] One easy interpretation of Stone's message is that his words imagined a more fundamentalist, more traditionalist, less tolerant American society. He argued that if white, conservative Protestants had never ceded their claim to the moral high ground, progressive gains would never have been made. This may well be true. But leaving that analysis to the side for a moment, the other sobering message of Stone's sermon was that these deleterious consequences were the inescapable outcome of having left behind the founders' true intentions for the United States. The only way forward would be to go back. He had used the words of men like Washington, Lincoln, and Teddy Roosevelt to assert the centrality of Christianity to strong leadership, and to the American project itself. So, while Stone never overtly linked the presumed faith of the American forefathers with widespread evangelical belief among the general citizenry, the overall structure of his argument depended on this being true.

If the American people, in general, had never been as religiously motivated as Stone imagined the founders to have been, then there would be no real contrast between the historical era of the American founding and the contemporary moment marked by decay.

Grandma Told You Where to Go When You're Broke: To Work

Stone's rhetorical strategy of nostalgia for earlier times was shared by other pastors during recession-era sermons, although not all were as explicit in their rendering. In sermons that I listened to during my research that had explicitly financial themes, or that took the recession itself as a point of departure, I heard many pastors urge their congregants to notice how they had contributed to the nation's decline by placing their hope in material things, causing them to overspend and become overleveraged. These same messages also tended to romanticize hard work, delayed gratification, and looking to God for fulfillment. Like Stone's conception of a nostalgic founding, these arguments were deeply sentimental. Many drew on the mores of the Protestant work ethic, although this ethos was never mentioned by name. Nonetheless, these sermons almost always defined work and frugality as markers of American character. Pastors encouraged their audiences to demonstrate their Christian faith by respecting their bosses and being faithful to their employers. They depicted human structures of authority as matters of providence. Sometimes clergy encouraged audience members to think of their place on an organizational chart as their workplace ministry, or to consider difficult working conditions as challenges for learning how to overcome, rather than as injustices that might require resistance or rejection. Above all, pastors stressed personal responsibility and the need for self-reflection.

Andy Stanley proved especially pithy in delivering this rhetoric. "I feel like I'm one of the most materialistic people I know," he said in a guest sermon at Willow Creek Community Church on February 14, 2010. "I love stuff. I want every Apple computer product . . . I don't know if this is true of you, but it's true of me, but I never know what I want until I see it, then I know I want it, and then I eventually convince myself that I need it."[27] Stanley used this illustration as a means for drawing his listeners in to the dilemma of consumerism, as he made a case for linking personal character with his individual spending priorities. Like Stone, Stanley included himself in the problem he presumed troubled his listeners, too. The rhetoric was not one of speaker versus audience, but of speaker and audience, together, causing the recession that had financially ruined America.

"People say, 'I don't know where all my money goes,'" Rick Warren told attendees at a special weekend seminar at Saddleback Church. "Money doesn't talk, it just walks away quietly . . . Ignorance of your financial condition plus easy credit equals disaster, because you're spending money you don't have."[28]

Megachurch pastors often told stories about spending and overspending. They said that living beyond a budget evidenced lack of discipline. Ministers avoided conversations about rising costs of insurance or childcare, for example, and instead stressed the problem of the American consumer culture, which led to overindulgence.[29] "We think that we not only need to be clothed, but to wear the latest fashion and have five of everything," Joshua Harris said to his Gaithersburg, Maryland, congregation in a sermon about the recession in January 2009. "We think we need more than just a roof over our heads. We want a bigger house, with a big yard."[30] Similarly, radio host and frequent guest pastor Dave Ramsey did an extended take in his guest sermon at Willow Creek Community Church about the "illegal word . . . that has been surgically removed from all the dictionaries . . . [which is] the ancient word no," and included for the audience instructions in pronunciation.[31] Rather than bingeing and charging, Ramsey encouraged his audience to remember better, old-fashioned mores. "My grandmother used to say there's a great place to go when you're broke," he said. "To work."[32]

Don't spend. Don't covet. Work harder. Respect your forefathers. Remember the nation's founding. Each of these phrases, in its own way, animated and reinforced the recession rhetoric that was at work during the years of the financial crisis for white, conservative Protestants. Pastors at megachurches across the nation told stories about a country imperiled by a citizenry that had grown soft, and so required God's discipline in the form of hardship. At heart, the narrative stressed choice, including chosen suffering. Americans had been slack for too long in their decision making and so were reaping the consequences of bad behavior through lost jobs, upside-down mortgages, high credit card balances, depleted college funds, and more. The answer would not come through looking to government for help, but rather through returning to God's ways and restoring Him to the center of American life. Doing so would lead to better finances, a healthier economy, a restored country, the good Christian life, and the possibility of living out the American Dream. This discourse was bigger than the recession, however. Instead, the larger narrative was about the American project itself. Because of this, pastors were not only interested in advancing appeals about how their congregants might think about the economic downturn and go about recovering from it. Many ministers also sought to define God's bigger purpose in having allowed the financial collapse to even occur. To do this, clergy again highlighted American exceptionalism, and then folded the recession story back into the original, founding narrative. While the recession was probably temporary, pastors said, Bible-believers who developed better work habits and learned to better steward the nation's resources could pull the country through its financial torpor and restore the status of the United States as the most exalted of all lands.

The key to understanding these appeals was accepting that even those who were experiencing hardship were still wealthy by sheer virtue of living in the United States. No matter how hard the recession had hit any individual American, beyond the nation's border, life was always worse. The pastors of the country's largest churches made meaning of the recession's dire nature and still negotiated their belief in unparalleled American exceptionalism by situating true poverty as external. Ministers surmised that God was using the recession to "wake up" sleeping believers and reassert His place as the nation's raison d'être, much' as Rick Warren had suggested was the case in his radio interview with Hugh Hewitt in April 2009.

Sermons based on this "true hardship is elsewhere" storyline depended on claims of universal affluence in American life. John Piper of Bethlehem Baptist Church told his congregation on February 1, 2009, that the financial collapse came like a shout from heaven to "remember!"[33] Don Wilson, in his 2010 "This Is Freedom" sermon, said the root of the problem was boredom. Too many people tried to find fulfillment in things, he explained. "The end result is . . . valu[ing] personal comfort and convenience ahead of everything else," he said. "When that happens, we soon become soft. When we get soft, we take life easy, and then it's so easy to leave God out . . . I think our country needs a little persecution to get us back on purpose. We need to face some persecution so we . . . know what we really stand for. Christianity tends to be the strongest when life is hard."[34] Kevin Myers posed a similar idea as a rhetorical question, asking his listeners whether they had "created a nation with the notion that . . . you can go ahead and cheat the economic process? That it doesn't matter? You don't have to [do the hard work] and sow, plow, plant . . . You can just harvest. And if you find that the harvest doesn't come that you want, well then, somebody owes you a harvest."[35]

This rhetoric of softness versus toughness was an important discursive marker for many pastors. They used it to demarcate the difference between a contemporary conception of the American Dream that relates to acquisition and having the nicest house, car, and boat, along with the prettiest wife, as opposed to one that was about hard work and honoring God, as is evident in Myers's homily.[36] To this end, Mark Driscoll of Mars Hill Church in Seattle claimed that many people facing financial hardship avoided taking responsibility for their situation and engaged instead in blame-shifting. "Nobody calls in and says, 'It's my fault. I apologize. I was not a shrewd steward. I bought stuff I couldn't afford,'" Driscoll said. "[They don't say,] 'I didn't work hard at my job. I didn't give to the poor. I didn't give to God. I didn't save for a rainy day. It's my fault. I ask you all to forgive me.' Nobody says that."[37] As a result, the country was losing its Christian identity in favor of a "purely secular system" that would stop at nothing short of the "de-Christianization of America." If it took a recession—or worse—to get conservative evangelicals to defend the nation against these "lying prophets," then God would continue to allow such events to take place.[38] This was the argument of Lon Solomon of McLean Bible Church in McLean, Virginia (near Washington, DC), in July 2012. As remedy, he urged his audience to stand together in repentance, and do all they could to elect political candidates who promised to support biblical truth and who would commit to doing their utmost to return God to the center of the public sphere.

How Do I Know America is Great? Because It Is Not America the Poor

Not all pastors were as explicitly political as Lon Solomon. In fact, overt politicization is falling out of favor in America's churches, especially megachurches, which are often based in a consumer model of Christianity. This missional style seeks to draw in new converts through outreach techniques that avoid being controversial and divisive, and rather seek to be warm and welcoming.[39] Nonetheless, one of the most powerful ways pastors telegraphed their belief in continued American exceptionalism and made plain their conviction that their fellow believers should be grateful for the blessing of their citizenship, rather than focus on temporary hardship, was through telling stories that distinguished between true and false kinds of suffering. This discourse of "true suffering" had a dual purpose during the time of the recession—two rhetorical strands that were woven together to create a unified narrative about the United States and its status as the world's most essential nation. The first strand emphasized American wealth and bounty. That this wealth was hidden or harder to access during the recession years did not mean it had disappeared. Instead, individuals would have to dig deep and toil patiently to recover. Such recovery, however, was inevitable.

The second strand had to do with poverty, what suffering meant, and who really suffered. Pastors argued that God might well be using the recession to bring global penury to the forefront of public discourse. To truly see need, pastors asked conservative evangelicals to look to the developing world—places like São Paulo, Brazil; sub-Saharan Africa; or Kolkata, India. There they would find people who truly lacked riches and the blessings US citizens took for granted. Taking on this worldview would open the hearts of conservative evangelicals. It would also reinforce the perception of how lucky they were to be American. This line of reasoning, in turn, reinscribed American exceptionalism, because it made plain the benefits of US citizenship and the bounty of the US homeland. The rhetoric of true suffering thus posited that all American suffering was necessarily temporary and relatively easy to bear, because all Americans are blessed by virtue of their status as citizens of the United States. True suffering always existed outside of the nation's borders, because it was both endemic and required external (read: American missionary) intervention to ameliorate.

To this end, John Piper told his Minneapolis congregation that God's main purpose in the recession was to make plain "the constant and desperate condition of the developing world where there is always and only recession of the worst kind."[40] Piper built this claim on the idea that prosperity had made Americans "blind . . . to the miseries of the world."[41] If a temporary recession "bothers us," Piper said, then what of the "one billion people who do not have safe water to drink [or the] . . . sixteen thousand children [who] die every day from hunger related illnesses[?]"[42]

Jay Wolf, a pastor in Montgomery, Alabama, also pointed to the general affluence of American life as compared to the rest of the world, even in the middle of a recession. "If you are an American, and if you have plenty of food to eat, you have a clean source of water to drink, you have indoor plumbing, and you have transportation, you are more wealthy than 80 percent of the people in this world," the pastor said. "That puts you ahead of about four and a half billion people. My dear friend, you are wealthy."[43] Similarly, Andy Stanley insisted that nearly all Americans have more resources than they need, unlike citizens of the developing world: "I never walk through the mall and think to myself, 'Wow, I certainly have a lot of extra, don't I?' When I walk through the mall, I feel poor. I feel like I'm poorly dressed, I feel like I'm behind. And most of culture focuses us on what we don't have, focuses on what we think we need, and so consequently we don't feel like we have any extra. But every once in a while you go on a mission trip . . . and you realize there are people in the world that have so much less than you, and then you have that weird American guilt feeling like, 'Why do I have more?' And then we just kind of move on. But in that moment, when you were . . . focused on the fact that you have more than other people, it was recognition of this fact: You and I have extra."[44]

For Stanley, recognizing this "extra" and being generous with it represented the key to "breaking the power of greed" in American life.[45] He encouraged his audience to acknowledge the ubiquitous prosperity of the United States. Doing so would make plain how wealth among citizens was equal and universal ("you and I have extra"). In Stanley's telling, there was no need to wonder whether any individual might be poor or struggling, or even whether there were important distinctions or income inequalities among Americans that might require redress. If someone in the United States faced economic peril, the likely cause was personal failing, and the proper remedy was gratitude and hard work. American struggle could not be related to citizenship status, race, gender, or geography. The obvious bounty and blessing of the United States—rhetorically animated through the consumer wonderland of the shopping mall—obliterated such a possibility. The real danger for citizens in the United States was wealth, Stanley argued. It caused selfishness, stagnation, and blindness to true need.

"One of the most amazing parts about our culture is how much we are ruled by the messages, the power, around money," Tod Bolsinger of San Clemente Presbyterian Church said. "Around the fact that we are the richest nation of all time, and [around the idea] that we should continue to be the richest nation of all time. That we have gone through difficult times . . . [and the ways in which difficult times] can shape entire people and cultures for a lifetime."[46] Like Bolsinger, other pastors suggested that too much focus on wealth could create a kind of blindness to true need in the world, and so reveal an absence of character on the part of the American citizen. "You need to know that historically and globally, we're the rich. And what tends to happen is we always look at someone who's one rung above us on the class ladder and say, 'When Jesus thinks about the rich, he's thinking about those guys,'" Mark Driscoll said. "No, he's thinking about us, those of us with vehicles and places to sleep and electricity . . . I've had the pleasure of traveling [to developing countries] and it gives you a little perspective."[47]

Driscoll's statement demonstrated how pastors universalized American affluence, without paying attention to the economic situation, circumstance, or class of any individual in particular. This theme of economic flattening erased the real suffering that was happening in the United States during the recession years. It also delegitimized structural economic inequality in America as a problem worth worrying about. Instead, pastors at the nation's largest churches told narratives that depended on themes of presumed prosperity to develop arguments about personal responsibility. Ministers pressed their congregants to recognize that the indisputable bounty of the United States meant that everyone could access whatever resources were necessary to secure financial stability. Thus, individual economic struggle stemmed from hapless management of one's resources, rather than from a lack of access to them. Pastors pointed to the ways in which the problem in the United States was a problem of abundance, rather than a problem of paucity. "The biggest medical problem in our country is obesity. That's really never been a huge issue [before this period in history], right?" Driscoll said in another sermon on May 29, 2011. "We have so much food and so little space for it that we're dying of malted Milk Duds and Chiclets. We are a people who are going to eat until we blow up . . . Go to a third world country. We're the rich."[48]

Being rich, however, did not make Americans happy, said some pastors. The rhetoric of suffering included an ironic twist, as pastors argued that people who lived outside the United States did have something that Americans lacked: perspective. And this perspective was something that conservative evangelicals could learn from, and so restore themselves and the nation. In a sermon titled, "Reverse Engineering: This is What It Looks Like," pastor Jim Burgen of Flatirons Community Church in Lafayette, Colorado, told his audience that because Jesus was "wise," and knew what people were "really like," he talked about money more than he talked about anything else. It was the focus of "one out of every six words he said."[49] "[Jesus] knew the same thing that you, sitting right here today, know," Burgen said, in response to his own question about why Jesus would have paid so much attention to money. "He knew there were very few things on earth that have the power to devastate and destroy [more than money] . . . It's the number one thing people think they need more of to be happy."[50] Nonetheless, Burgen claimed, rich people were world leaders in divorce, suicide, and addiction, proving that money was not the key to happiness.

Similarly, Don Wilson encouraged his Arizona congregation to take every chance they could to travel outside of the United States. He especially stressed the value of short-term mission trips: "It always amazes me, when I go to Mexico, when I go to Africa, you see little kids that have nothing, and they tend to have one thing in common—you know what it is? Huge smiles on their faces. And then you come home to the United States, to your kids and grandkids, and the first thing they say, after you spend the farm to get them what they want, is what? 'I am bored.'"[51] Such boredom, Wilson continued, stemmed from overindulgence and apathy. Too many Americans underappreciate the values of hard work and family, and fail to find pleasure in simple things. Rather, "young people today" demand constant stimuli, comfort, and convenience. Andy Stanley said the problem was that Americans were simply "spoiled." This spoiling would become immediately obvious to anyone who had the chance to visit "a third world country." The citizens of the underdeveloped world "have so little, and they're so happy," he said. "Those people have so much less and they have so much joy."[52] Americans, however, feel entitled, and so have forgotten how much they have and how blessed they really are.

Despite their (perhaps unintentional) condescending tone, there is little doubt that these appeals about global poverty were effective and stinging for audience members to hear. The issue is, in fact, real and significant. Pastors had good reasons to point out the deprivations and poor conditions of life that many citizens in the developing world must daily face. Nevertheless, these remarks often related only tangentially to raising awareness about global poverty or persuading white, conservative Protestants to support global missions. Instead, they more usually worked to create feelings of guilt in the audience for having neglected their responsibility in maintaining the status of the United States as the most essential nation, or else to generate a means for hearers to count themselves as rich and blessed, even if they were actually struggling with real financial hardship. Indeed, the value of American exceptionalism and the goodness of the American Dream ran so deep as assumptions in the stories I heard that these ideals only rarely required explicit articulation. Their fundamental nature as underlying values of the evangelical worldview meant that pastors could talk about the United States as rich and offer very little context or evidence for the claim, or they could assert the nation was exceptionally free without having to qualify the nature of the freedom by race or gender, and could proclaim the country was just and righteous in its causes, without worrying about widespread disagreement. Each of these warrants, in its own way, harkened back to the broader political discourse taking place during the years of the financial crash, and so may well have helped fortify the evangelical place in the GOP base, despite the fact that so-called values issues were said to be losing salience in public debate. More important, each made clear how the debate over America's status as a Christian nation was picking up speed, not slowing down.

Chapter 3

Conclusion

I began this chapter surveying two similar, yet strangely distinct, messages from two evangelical heavyweights in the United States in the early twenty-first century. On the one hand, Albert Mohler described a nation at risk of losing its essential identity as it made an about-face from its Christian roots. On the other, Rick Warren said the future was bright for born-again believers, both at home and overseas. He also minimized the economic uncertainty surrounding the nation at the time. How could two pastors who share the same faith have simultaneously been so positive and so pessimistic? The recession-era sermons I have presented in this chapter offer some insight. During the economic downturn, pastors in the nation's largest churches gave their congregants plenty of advice about how they should work hard, save money, and better handle their debts. Even more common, however, were sermons in which ministers grounded their advice in narratives about how the United States remained a land of providential greatness despite the recession and blamed individual bad behavior for threatening the nation's rightful place of divine privilege.

Kenneth Burke's guilt-redemption-purification cycle is especially useful for understanding such sermonic logic. For evangelicals, the natural order of things is that the United States is *the* exceptional nation. White, conservative Protestants are not Tocquevillian exceptionalists. Theirs is not a framing that situates the United States as simply the first or the oldest democracy, and so exceptional because it is qualitatively different from anything that had come before.[53] Rather, these believers tell a narrative of the United States as the best, most blessed democracy ever to exist. Moreover, much of their discourse tends to suggest that it is always, already, and still God's will for this to be so. However, ineptitude and inattention on the part of contemporary American citizens have put the natural order at risk. This, in Burke's terms, means the order has been polluted. Pastors thus sought to tell stories in their sermons that would create guilt in their audience for having allowed this pollution to happen. Because there was pollution and guilt, purification was needed. Purification in these sermons typically came in the form of suggested discipline. Better behavior meant working harder, saving more, paying down debt, and—even if a person was already doing their best with all of these things—taking responsibility to encourage others while continuing to set a good example. Such actions would lead to redemption and so bring an end to the recession. Better still would be the restoration of the nation's status as the "city on the hill," with God at the center of the public sphere, and the nation again able to reap His promises as the world's most exalted land.

Eight years passed between the onset of the Great Recession (and with it the coinciding election of Barack Obama) and the election of Donald Trump. Over that time, and especially near the end of his second term, Obama's supporters would sometimes insist that he was given too little credit for the job he did stewarding the nation through the financial crisis, and then presiding over national economic growth for most of his two terms. But the recession-era sermons in this chapter suggest that those who attended the nation's largest churches heard a different narrative about the United States during the crisis and the years after than one in which things had gone badly but could have been much worse. Instead, these believers heard sermons in which pastors framed the recession as both optional and chosen by these very believers and by their fellow citizens. Moreover, the recession was actually a necessary consequence, a kind of refining fire, meant to restore the United States to better days.

Seen in this light, the pastors of the nation's megachurches were, in the years from 2009 to 2013, and maybe even inadvertently, already beginning to refortify a campaign message that Donald Trump himself had perhaps not yet discerned. As such, recession-era sermons make plain how "evangelical Republicanism" may not be born only out of obsession with aversion to abortion, marriage equality, feminism, or any other easily named values hot-button issue. Instead, this Republicanism is about the very meaning of America, and the part true Christians must play in tending to this meaning, protecting it from further erosion, while also doing everything possible to restore the nation to its previous place of prominence.

By the time of the 2016 race, white, evangelical Protestants were thought to have lost the culture wars and the battle over who would determine the meaning of America. Demographically, these believers were supposed to be in decline.[54] The economy had long since recovered from recession. Destiny favored the Democrats. But the underlying narrative for these believers hadn't changed. They still wanted to Make America Great Again.

4

Don't Worry, Be Happy—But God Wants You to Vote

On June 26, 2015, the US Supreme Court decided *Obergefell v. Hodges* and affirmed marriage equality in a 5–4 decision. In the immediate aftermath of this pronouncement, which affirmed the right to same-sex marriage, conservative evangelicals around the United States took notice. Some pastors vowed to ceaselessly defend American culture from further perceived decline. For example, National Public Radio (NPR) reported that California ministers in both San Diego and Chino told their congregations that the Supreme Court had erred in its rendering of the case. They claimed the ruling threatened the moral underpinnings of the nation and said they would politically organize to fight back.[1]

Others took a different tack. While few conservative Protestants—and especially conservative Protestant leaders—could be said to have dropped their opposition to same-sex marriage, younger evangelicals in particular are more open than their forebears about the morality of queer love. In the aftermath of *Obergefell*, Laurie Goodstein of the *New York Times* reported that "a wide variety of evangelical churches, colleges and ministries are having the kinds of frank discussions about homosexuality that many of them say they had never had before." This included looking for ways to talk about "how to respond to students struggling with their sexual identities . . . [about] policies on allowing openly gay people in Bible studies . . . [and] pastors . . . preaching and writing about . . . recent books arguing that the Bible can be read to support same-sex marriage."[2] These conversations were evidence, said some observers, of the continuing decline of the culture wars in the United States. The Left had won; the Right should get used to it; life would go on.

As far as the presidential election was concerned, GOP contender and

Texas Senator Ted Cruz immediately came out in opposition to the court's ruling. He said he would make opposition to marriage equality "front and center" in his campaign. He also told Jessica Taylor of NPR that it was time to amend the Constitution to "make members of the Supreme Court subject to periodic judicial retention elections."[3] Comments like these were among the reasons some pundits at the time thought Cruz would prove to be the preferred candidate for conservative evangelicals in the race to become the 2016 Republican nominee for president. At the time, Donald Trump was mostly considered a circus sideshow whose candidacy few observers believed would amount to very much. If he got any attention, it was for making incendiary comments about Mexican and other immigrants.[4]

While Trump did ultimately take home the lion's share of evangelical votes in the 2016 general election, many of these believers expressed discomfort with him from the beginning. Barely a month into his candidacy, he said during an interview on CNN that he had never asked for God to forgive his sins. "I think if I do something wrong, I think, I just try and make it right," he said. "I don't bring God into that picture. I don't."[5] Then there was the time he went to Liberty University in Lynchburg, Virginia, to speak, and said his favorite book in the Bible was "Two Corinthians." Even the most casual readers of the New Testament know that book is usually called "Second Corinthians."[6] And there were clear problems with his character: Trump has been married three times and is publicly unrepentant about having committed adultery. Yet even with these shortcomings, Trump earned endorsements from important evangelical figures. Jerry Falwell Jr., then the president of Liberty University, supported the New York businessman.[7] Conservative activist Phyllis Schlafly also rallied behind him, despite ensuing unrest from the membership of the group she had founded, the Eagle Forum.[8] In June 2016, when Donald Trump's nomination was inevitable, James Dobson of Focus on the Family announced that Trump was a "baby Christian" who had recently been "born again."[9]

This, though, was the national discourse during 2016. Inside American megachurches, the conversation about the election was decidedly less robust and decidedly less passionate. While there were notable exceptions, for the most part those churches that took up the nation's political race did so carefully and tried to seem evenhanded in their analysis. When pastors spoke about the campaign, they almost always began by asking their audience if they would be happy to see it end. Ministers typically agreed that they, too, were keen for the election to be over. Nearly all the sermons I heard during the campaign season that featured political topics professed sentiments that poked fun at the presidential contenders. Pierre du Plessis of The Father's House in Rochester, New York, provided a representative example. Seated on a stool on an elevated stage, wearing dark jeans, a black T-shirt, and a black blazer, du Plessis started his sermon on October 30, 2016, by flashing photos behind him of signs and tweets making fun of the candidates, while reading one of them aloud. "I feel like Trump and Hillary are two divorced parents fighting for custody of us but we, kids, just want to go live with Grandma," he said. "What if nobody was president and we all promised real hard just to be cool . . . Come on, if you feel like that shout 'Yes!' Right?"[10] As this example shows, pastors could develop rapport with their audience by drawing on an assumption of shared antipathy for both Hillary Clinton and Donald Trump. Likewise, Tim Harlow of Parkview Christian Church, in Orland Park, Illinois, just outside Chicago, began his sermon on the Sunday preceding the election by talking about how among the best parts of the recent World Series win by the hometown Cubs was not only that the team had finally broken a more-than-century-long drought between championships, but also the victory had given him something to think about besides how terrible the presidential candidates were.

Then, to audience laughter, Harlow read aloud from a satirical piece written by Andy Borowitz in the *New Yorker* suggesting that Queen Elizabeth had offered to resume rule over the United States given the dire choices facing the 2016 electorate. "The Queen urged Americans to write in her name on Election Day, after which the transition to British rule could begin 'with a minimum of bother . . . Parliament would play no role in this deal. This would be an old-school monarchy. Just me, and then, assuming you'd rather not have Charles, we could go straight to William and those children of his who have mesmerized you so.'"[11]

As these examples show, even in the days immediately preceding the November 8 election, megachurch pastors in the United States were still expressing dissatisfaction with the nation's presidential finalists, Democratic and Republican alike. This simple finding throws into some doubt the idea that conservative evangelicals deeply idealized Trump, his candidacy, or his campaign, at least as far as their church rhetoric goes. Those white, conservative Protestant pastors who led the nation's megachurches and spoke "from the stage," as it were, about the election continued to articulate wariness about the possibility that the New York businessman might become president, and this wariness seems to have matched what they felt about Hillary Clinton. This is somewhat unsurprising given the historic unpopularity of both candidates.[12] Even so, we know from exit polling and postelection analyses that most conservative, white evangelicals ultimately pulled their ballot levers for Trump. Their discomfort for both candidates did not lead them to split their votes, or even to simply stay home. As I argued in chapter 1, literatures in political science anticipate this result. The twin forces of negative partisanship and political identity mean that voters now more than ever tend to stick with the team they have chosen in the past.[13] And Bible-believing Protestants have been a reliable Republican voting bloc since 1980.[14] That these votes were likely to happen, however, tells us little about the stories and reasonings that informed them, or that otherwise allowed these believers to support a nonnormative candidate like Donald Trump, in spite of his character flaws. We could have guessed before the election ever happened that born-again Christians who voted were probably going to support the real estate mogul, simply because he was the GOP's standard bearer. But how did they talk about it with one another? How did they justify it to themselves? Was their thinking overt or subtle? Most significant, how does their political worldview continue to refortify itself, and how did this refortification persist during the campaign of 2016?

The sermons I discovered through intensive immersion in the digital church in the months leading up to November 8, 2016—and especially those given on October 23, October 30, and November 6, the three Sundays just before the election—mostly did not follow a narrative arc about transactional politics or even morality-based politics. For the most part, ministers did not urge their congregations on with phrases like "vote your values." While some pastors did mention issues like opposition to abortion or to marriage equality, such matters were not typically presented as foreground concerns. Instead, ministers often conceded that many of those attending did not want to hear about politics and might even think church was the wrong place for talking about hot-button, divisive issues about which people might fairly disagree. Pastors said churchgoers had not congregated in their pews, in stadium seating, or at their digital screens to get virtual voting guides. These were not messages for a modern moral majority. Instead, what I watched and heard was a discourse that I suggest amounted to a call to "active-passivism." "Active," because pastors typically insisted that as American citizens everyone—and maybe especially believers—had a responsibility to vote. They owed it to those who had died for their freedom. "Passive," because these same pastors were quick to remind listeners that no matter who was elected, God was always in control. I argue that this appeal toward passivity—conservative evangelicals would say toward divine trust—had two targets, one obvious and intended, and the other unintended. The first was overcoming concern about the inadequacy of the candidates. "Would I pick the lesser of evils?" asked Kevin Myers of 12Stone Church in Lawrenceville, Georgia, on October 23, 2016, two Sundays before Election Day. "Of course I would. Jesus isn't running for president, or I'd vote for him. It's just people."[15]

The second target of the pastor's passive call, however, was to subtly discharge conservative Protestants from considering the consequences of their vote, even if unintentionally. In chapter 3, I described how the evangelical narrative of continued American exceptionalism depends on situating true suffering as always existing outside of the United States. Conservative believers see their homeland as a place of plenty. Because of this, anyone who is willing to work hard and make responsible choices will prosper. The nation's beneficent resources make it so. Thus, in an election between two undesirable candidates, where believers could be assured that God was in charge, the already present discourse in conservative evangelicalism that privileged external suffering may have refortified also already present tendencies to vote for the GOP. The discourse of active-passivism allowed believers to vote for Donald Trump without worrying about American constituencies that might face harm through his election—to say nothing of the false equivalency that happened as pastors continuously represented Clinton and Trump as equally bad candidates—because these constituencies had at their disposal whatever they might need to overcome adversity, by virtue of being in the United States. This tendency was strengthened further through an election rhetoric that framed contemporary culture as sick and beyond repair. Votes for moral traditionalism would help and were necessary but—circling back to the fact that God was in charge—believers should also remember that their real citizenship was in heaven and so their first responsibility was always to Jesus. Active-passivism creates rhetorical marginalization, where vulnerable constituencies become elided and obscured through an evangelical discourse that privileges only those issues and consequences that fit a preconceived political worldview. It allows born-again Christians to avoid looking at the things they may not want to see.

To be clear: I do not argue that the majority of American megachurch pastors actively preached messages that elevated Donald Trump over Hillary Clinton or instructed listeners to vote for the GOP nominee. To the contrary, this kind of direct messaging seems never to have happened, although some did come close. Campaign-season sermons typically had one of three themes. First were homilies that sought to reassure believers that the election was but a temporary moment. The call on believers was to participate as grateful citizens of an exceptional nation, but also to trust that God was in control. These sermons, I argue, were the most explicit in their call to active-passivism. Second were sermons that pastors framed as nonpolitical, but that still had electoral connotations. Third were messages that most closely fit the popular stereotype of pastors exhorting believers to vote according to a traditionalist platform and a moral agenda, especially regarding issues like abortion, marriage equality, religious (Christian) freedom, and so on. I offer a detailed example of each of these kinds of sermons in chapter 5. But whichever of these three types of sermons was at play, they were linked via shared premises. Megachurch pastors across the United States constructed election narratives that urged both *surrender* and *reassurance*, as well as *resolve*. In the sermons I studied about the contest between Trump and Clinton, pastors reframed the benefits of citizenship away from exceptionalism and toward the celestial kingdom. A common refrain was that American citizenship is nice but "heavenly" citizenship is better. The key was to *surrender* hope in an earthly leader or an earthly government, in favor of God's government in heaven. This opened the door to the second, corresponding appeal, which had to do with *reassurance*. While most ministers did not mention the candidates by name when they made these arguments, their effect—at least in part—was to diminish Trump's perceived defects. God was already the perfect moral leader, they said. All presidents fail in comparison to Him. And so came *resolve*. No matter who won the election, the national culture would remain a site of temptation, a place of sin, full of souls in need of saving. The real answer would never come through politics, but through God and His grace, and through individual choices to live with character. According to the pastors I observed, politics would never be the answer. Individual conversions were the only real source of hope. These narrative appeals, then, represented an abandonment of the culture wars, because they deemphasized politics as possible avenues for creating change. However, absent the possibility that conservative Protestants stop voting, I argue the natural beneficiary of these types of homiletic stories and appeals is the Republican Party. This is because there is nothing in them that suggests a progressive politics. While many pastors I heard claimed to be speaking as nonpartisan, fellow Christians, and said that believers should vote according to their own consciences rather than according to a preconceived political agenda, the sermonic themes and stories that preachers presented did nothing to disrupt the longstanding discourse that has caused white evangelicals to adhere to GOP candidates, including Trump, and despite his nonnormative rhetoric and issue positions. Indeed, this adherence was made even more likely because Republicans still control the narrative about individualism, individual responsibility, and the nostalgic rendering of the American Dream—as exemplified in Trump's motto "Make America Great Again."

Members of a Supernatural Kingdom

Megachurches have a reputation for lacking the holy mystique of smaller churches. They typically spurn ornate architechture and so don't look particularly "churchy" from the outside. Very few have the trappings of large cathedrals, such as stained glass windows or large towers with crosses that are visible for miles. Many megachures, in fact, appear more like superstores or warehouses, and some are repurposed basketball arenas.[16] But that does not mean these spaces are bereft of deep spirituality. For example, when Greg Holder of The Crossing Church near St. Louis, Missouri, appeared before his congregation on November 6, 2016 to speak about the election, he did so with the Beatles song "Revolution" playing over the loudspeakers. The transition was somewhat jarring to watch. Immediately preceding it, the auditorium/sanctuary had been lit dimly for communion and prayer. An enormous wooden cross filled the left side of the stage—and so my digital screen—as a man played piano and sang the nineteenth-century hymn "I Hear the Savior Say." As the music swelled near the end, a band that included drums and an electric guitar joined to lead the congregation in singing, "O praise the One who paid my debt / And raised this life up from the dead / O praise the One who paid my debt," in a repeated chorus.[17] In the many sermons that made up my digital rhetorical ethnography, this time of worship was among the most extraordinary for its power and use of visual symbolism. There was nothing inauthentic or saccharine in the presentation.

Yet, the sermon Holder gave was ultimately familiar, both in message and in tone. As did many pastors that weekend, he began by mentioning the Chicago Cubs' recent World Series win: the longtime underdogs had delighted the nation by coming from behind in Game 7 to defeat Cleveland and claiming the trophy while ending a more than 100-year drought between championships. Holder next despaired over the the ineptitude of both Clinton and Trump. He wondered if listeners thought his words were a "disaster" in the making, as politics was something good preachers didn't talk about. "I'm not going to tell you who to vote for," he said. "But I believe God has something for us today." Holder promised to avoid mentioning specific issues—from Wikileaks, to *Access Hollywood*, to email servers, to the FBI—and said he would focus instead on a time when Jesus dealt with politics. In so doing, he would make clear that "it is about so much more than a candidate, an election, or whatever it is that you and I are wrestling with over the next few days" (before the time came to vote). This "so much more" was that too many people tried to distinguish between the "real world" and the "spiritual world." True Christians should know, Holder said, that "the Kingdom of God is about real life, right now . . . Politics matters, it just doesn't matter as much as [people] think it does."[18]

As was true for other pastors with similar messages, Holder's argument relied on a claim of basic identity. Because I only included in my study those churches that affirmed the authority of scripture, pastors usually grounded their homiletic claims in particular Bible texts. Holder began by reading from Matthew a passage in which Jesus affirmed paying taxes to the state—that individuals should "give back to Caesar what is Caesar's, and to God what is God's."[19] As Nancy Murphy explains, most pastors use scripture in their sermons "to shape Christian identity" while also "transforming the lives of Christian communities [in the] here and now." Evangelical ministers often emphasize "particular texts" and then develop narratives based on these texts that offer reassurance, challenge beliefs, summon faith or hope, encourage action, and so on.[20] The question is one of primacy. To whom is the Bible-believing Christian foremost responsible? During the election season, pastors like Holder were keen to make clear to their audiences that their primary identity—their primary citizenship—was in heaven, and so their first responsibility was not to a political party, candidate, or agenda, but to God. This, in turn, meant that the authentic believer's ultimate obligation was not to vulnerable constituencies—or even to country—but to their faith, which always privileged converting more souls to Christ. Other types of possible suffering or deleterious consequences were subordinate to the consequence of hell.

"Even though you live here, remember you don't belong here. Remember you march to the beat of a different drummer," said Todd Mullins of Christ Fellowship in Palm Beach Gardens, Florida. "Even though you live here physically . . . you are you are part of a supernatural, otherworldly kingdom, so live that way. Focus. Set your mind on things above, not on things below."[21] For Mullins, this notion of a supernatural kingdom to which believers truly belonged meant that the election was of serious, but still fleeting concern. Mullins urged his listeners to vote (be active), but also to remember that no matter the election's outcome, born-again believers could rest easy in their true identity (that is, wait passively on God).

"We have the luxury of living in a democratic society where we can say what we believe in a ballot box," Skip Heitzig said, making an argument similar to the one Mullins had put forward. "So we should. We should vote. We should voice our concern in the public discourse. That's first. Be responsible in your culture. Second is to be prayerful. Be prayerful for your country." These were Heitzig's calls to action, his words and acknowledgment of American citizenship. But where worry could enter, Heitzig encouraged peace of mind—an embrace of divine tranquility. "Listen, it doesn't matter who's in the White House," he said. "God rules the universe with his feet up. Isn't that good? He's not stressed. He just goes, 'Next. This is easy stuff. I got this. I got this covered.' And you . . . should never come to a place where you are hopeless, where you despair. God causes things to happen. God overrules what men rule."[22]

Imagining God sitting in heaven in an easy chair, watching over the most urgent affairs of humankind with both control and disinterest, only makes sense from an eternal vantage point, where politics and political outcomes have necessarily unimportant effects. God's people—the citizens who count—could rest easy, safe somehow from having to worry about a miscast vote. "We really don't belong here," explained Dary Northrop of Timberline Church in Fort Collins, Colorado. "Our image comes from another place. That means our identity, our hope, our faith, our loyalties, lie within a different kingdom than the kingdom called earth." Emphasizing divine protection in the form of an otherworldly image left Northrop feeling peaceful, he said, even though he felt disheartened in the election and was "learning to lower his expectations, especially when it comes to politics, character, [and] the truth." Despite the temptation to become "apolitical," as some Christians had historically done, Northrop averred that "we are very fortunate to be in a country [where] we have a vote . . . We have our problems, but at least we have a say and we can go to the poll and we can vote and I hope that you will do that. But we need to remember that the system we live in is broken."[23]

The question of a broken system, united with a call to action (vote) and rest (dual citizenship), allowed pastors to frame the election as both urgent and nothing to really worry about. Clinton and Trump were thus presented as equally bad choices who might do harm, but whose harm paled in comparison to the good of the God of the universe. Together, these were homiletic calls to surrender that almost certainly worked in Trump's favor. Any potential deleterious effects of a Hillary Clinton presidency—or those of progressive politics in general—were discursively exacerbated through sermon warrants that situated Democrats as pressing for programs that would ultimately harm culture and families, even when pastors did not specifically identify liberals as more dangerous than their conservative counterparts.

Steven Furtick, pastor of Elevation Church, near Charlotte, North Carolina, told his congregation that Christians should stop fretting over the election. Their worry was evidence of inadequate faith. It meant their attention was fixed on the wrong things. The fever-pitch levels of stress about the election demonstrated declining interest in eternity, in favor of overwhelming anxiety about what was happening on earth. As he took his place in his auditorium-style chapel, more like a basketball arena than a sanctuary, wearing black jeans, a black T-shirt, a black leather jacket, and scuffed brown boots, Furtick read from the first chapter of Second Corinthians. Here, the Apostle Paul wrote that his afflictions were meant for the comfort of others, that his hope was renewed when he shared his suffering, and that he was confident that God would finally deliver those who trusted Him to safety and health.[24] As this verse hung in the air, Furtick asked his already standing congregation to share with one another the title of his sermon: "I Know, But I'm Not Nervous." However, the pastor did not merely want those in attendance to exchange the words of the title, but the title within a "context." He asked them to recite to one another the following words: "Neighbor, it's kind of crazy in the world these days. There's a lot going on. The stakes are high . . . I know, but I'm not nervous [*applause*] . . . I know, I watch the news, I saw what your cousin Jimmy said on Facebook about a conspiracy theory . . . but I'm not nervous . . . I refuse to be. Not gonna be. Not about to be. God is too great and He's been too good for me to be nervous."[25] By beginning with Paul's words, and then transitioning to emphasize a theme of anti-anxiety over the election, Furtick developed a narrative structure in which worrying about politics or who would become president necessarily led to fear and foreboding. Trusting in God's outcome, in contrast, would bring relief. Politics might mean suffering, but reassurance was available by looking past the public sphere to Christ. One could follow the election, and even see its possible repercussions, without distress that those consequences might have any personal effect. And absent such personal effect, and bathed in God's comfort, one could vote with American pride, attention to issues, and relative disinterest—all at the same time. "You notice everybody is so nervous right now, just incredibly nervous. They're either ignorant or nervous. They're either in Canada, or they're nervous," Furtick said. "What if she, and what if he? You know, I'm gonna go press that button, but I might press it with a blindfold on, just to press it, I don't even know. Nervous, they might take my guns. Nervous, they might not take my guns. Nervous, he might really build that [wall]. Nervous, she might take away our civil liberties . . . People get frustrated because you won't get nervous."

Likewise, in a message given much earlier in the election season, on April 4, 2016, David Hughes of Church by the Glades, Coral Springs, Florida, near Fort Lauderdale, told those among his audience who were "all worked up" over the idea that the wrong person might get elected and bring about "Armageddon" that he had "good news."

"The essence of our message as a church is not primarily political," he said. "It is something called the gospel . . . No matter who ends up in the White House, our great God is in control. And God will have the final word. And God is not sweating this election."[26] Other pastors created similar images of God in heaven, stoically watching over the campaign with foreordained knowledge of its outcome and a serene sense of its eternal importance. Todd Mullins of Christ Fellowship Church in Florida was similarly convinced. "God is not freaking out about the election. He's not up in heaven going, 'Oh, dear Lord. Oh, dear me.' He's not freaking out. And so I'm not freaking out. I know exactly what November 9th holds. It holds another day in God's perfect sovereignty over the universe. God is still in control . . . We don't need to fret or worry. God's power, His authority, has never been dependent upon a ruler, a king, or a president . . . So, we can rest in that."[27]

The Election Matters, It's Just Not the Long Play

Rhetorical calls to rest, surrender, and reassurance, while trusting in God's perfect will for the nation, refortified the evangelical discourse that embraces American exceptionalism—better understood in the election context as Christian nationalism—and also held that such exceptionalism was tangential to God's true interest in creating and ruling over the universe. As such, these calls functioned to sanction voting for an imperfect candidate in 2016, while affirming that nothing truly terrible—or insurmountable—was likely to happen no matter the result of the campaign. Thus, even in cases where pastors admitted that God had never promised to favor the United States in world affairs, the rhetorical effect of the sermons I studied downplayed the ultimate significance of politics. This is somewhat surprising, given the reputation conservative Protestants have for being active in the public sphere and for agitating in culture-war questions. However, it also sheds light on how some conservative evangelicals may have negotiated perceived dissonance between voting for Trump, in spite of his character shortcomings, without presuming that these voters "sold out their faith" in a kind of transactional, tit-for-tat "values politics."[28] Rather, worldview, as revealed through sermonic, narrative storytelling, informed their votes about those issues. Recognizing this worldview and the expectations it engenders about evangelical priorities and faith logics makes clear how Bible-believing Christians may have renegotiated what were once clear political alignments with the GOP into more diluted storylines that still favored Republicans in the end. There was nothing in the homilies I studied to suggest the Democrats had become more appealing. If anything, both Clinton and Trump were presented as equally bad, while pastors stipulated that their own role was to lay out Christian principles for voting, no matter which of the two major party candidates—or even a third-party option—a person might prefer.

"The future of our nation, whether it be for your kids or your grandkids or you, really, is more dependent upon how you and I live our lives, than it is on who is elected to the office of the presidency. And it always has been that way," said Troy Gramling of Potential Church, near Miami, on October 30, 2016. "It's the people, and the way in which we choose to live our lives, what we value, what we say is important . . . I mean, there are a lot of politicians and pundits telling you and me what we should do, who we should vote for, how we should respond, all the things that we ought to do. But what does God say we ought to do? I mean, how are we supposed to live every day?"[29] Here, Gramling proposed for his listeners yet another form of individual responsibility, while eliding the importance and influence of either politicians or the public sphere.

An easy dismissal of this rhetoric would be a mistake, because it undermines the nature of how community comes together in the United States, and how government functions as an essential tool for providing for the nation's most marginalized and vulnerable constituencies. That is, while it is undoubtedly true that individual action and character are worthy of attention and consideration for religious and secular citizens alike, and maybe also true that conservative evangelical discourse always privileges personal calls to service and witness, America as a democratic nation depends on a social contract. The particulars of this contract are, in fact, contestable to a large degree, as the rhetoric of terms like "culture wars" makes clear.

However, the policies under debate in every election have real consequences at stake for the lives of real people. These consequences are evident not only in those homiletic discourses that I will take up in the next section, which describes some of the more pointed sermons I heard that did discuss culture and issues—even at a distance. But in considering only those sermons that tried to be more passive—whose position was that citizens should vote while remembering God's ultimate providence—there was often an undercutting admission that something deep and incalculable was at stake, at least for some people. For example, in Greg Holder's sermon that I described earlier in this chapter, he did not stop by simply averring that "politics . . . doesn't matter as much as [people] think it does." Rather, he went on to say that the reason politics matters at all, is "because the things beneath politics matter. Human dignity. Freedom. How we do what we do. All of this stuff matters. But it's not the long play. It's not the ultimate answer."[30]

But it's not the long play: This, I argue, represents the fundamental tension in the sermonic rhetoric of conservative evangelical pastors in the lead-up to the election of Donald Trump. Through appeals such as this, ministers were able to maintain the narrative that democracy matters and that Christians should vote as a moral imperative, thereby sustaining the rhetorical commitment to American exceptionalism, while at the same time diverting attention away from the problematic choice facing the electorate, and especially the character problems of Donald Trump, including the possibility that his candidacy might cause harm to vulnerable populations or even to the United States as a whole. After all, given that these voters may have been unlikely to hold worldviews favorable to Clinton, her candidacy as a viable choice likely did not resonate deeply in the *esprit de finesse* (the sense of things) as described in chapter 1. For Pascal, such an *esprit* is a kind of "intuitive knowing" that a person recognizes when a conversation reverberates with others they are involved in, or a worldview they cherish. It is not the kind of knowledge that is necessarily empirical or exact (an *esprit de géométrie*).[31] Apprehending this distinction and insight is essential for critics of my approach who might say that the discourse I describe is simply that which is always common to evangelicals—likely the same as would have happened in any election, and in the absence of such controversial candidates. But this is precisely the point. Like a river whose water wouldn't stop, couldn't stop, the discourse of conservative Protestants continued unabated, almost certainly because it had to.[32] This is the power of the narrative, its resonant strand. Much of the power of the gospel story rests in its eternal promise and the injunction that believers must "set [their] minds on things above, not on earthly things."[33]

In 2016, however, the failure to notice earthly things or change the conversation meant that even when ministers claimed to be speaking without partisan intent, they were nonetheless often seen as supporting a president who was unwilling to detach himself from the country's extreme Right wing, who had been notoriously disrespectful of women (and who showed little remorse for having done so), and who made little pretense of having a true interest in matters of faith.[34] Pastors returned relentlessly to the notion that because the election and its consequences were necessarily temporary, while

God and heaven are eternal, Bible-believing Christians should vote and thoughtfully consider political issues, but should only *worry* about matters of everlasting concern. "No matter who's elected, God's love never stops. No matter who's elected, God's love will never let you down," said Ray Johnston of Bayside Church, near Sacramento, California. "He did not create you and go . . . 'I am going to put them in . . . the most strategic area of the world at this point in time' . . . and go, 'I've given them one life, one shot, one time to make a difference, and I hope they live it stressed, anxious, and miserable.' God wants better for you than that. Which means this: [You have hope.] And when you have hope, anything is possible."[35] No matter the outcome of the election, anything that happened in the here and now would be okay and sustainable. Indeed, the United States remained exceptional ("the most strategic area in the world"), and nothing that happened in the race between Clinton and Trump had the potential for changing that. So, where others have suggested that the reason so many conservative evangelicals cast ballots for Trump had to do with the Supreme Court vacancy, abortion politics, opposition to same-sex marriage, or other such hot-button issues—what we might call transactional politics—I suggest that the sermonic discourse in American megachurches reveals an alternative "how" of justification. This narrative "how" depended on trusting God and his great provision for the United States. Bible-believing Protestants remained linked to the GOP, even the GOP of Donald Trump, through a discourse that favored voting, not worrying, and remaining committed to America as a whole. Then, for those voters who were vexed over values and cultural decline, there were appeals about defending tradition and further decay. These appeals were sometimes overt and sometimes hidden. In almost every case, though, they worked to the favor of the New York businessman.

Tocqueville, Hollywood, and the Signs of the Times

Many megachurches use video montages to transition from worship and singing to Bible teaching and preaching. In election-themed sermons, these montages were often set to music along with campaign-related images, including shots of Trump and Clinton on the campaign trail or during a debate, as well as photos of citizens in need, whether hungry, engaged in cleaning up after a storm, or being helped in some way by a soldier or a police officer. Sometimes the montages closed with pictures of church members doing some form of service—viewers could usually distinguish them as belonging to the church because they were wearing T-shirts with church logos—like building houses, passing out water at a local fun run, or some other kind of social activity for good. For example, before Dale Hummel's sermon on October 22, 2016, at Wooddale Church in Eden Prairie, Minnesota, southwest of Minneapolis, a video played that included scenes of Syrian refugees, streets on fire, Vladimir Putin, Hillary Clinton, Donald Trump, and more. The final shot was of the White House. When the video closed, Hummel appeared, standing at a lectern. He began his remarks by (mis-)quoting the French philosopher Alexis de Tocqueville, who came to the United States in the early nineteenth century to study American democracy: "I sought for the key to the greatness and genius of America in her harbors . . . in her fertile fields and boundless forests; in her rich mines and vast world commerce; in her public-school system and institutions of learning. I sought for it in her democratic Congress and in her matchless Constitution. Not until I went into the churches of America and heard pulpits aflame with righteousness did I understand the secret of her genius and power. America is great because America is good, and if America ever ceases to be good, America will cease to be great."[36] Hummel's use of this spurious Toqueville excerpt is not entirely blameworthy; Bill Clinton, Pat Buchanan, Ronald Reagan, Phil Gramm, Sean Spicer, and many others have all misattributed it to Toqueville, too. The Christian Defense Fund included it in a compendium of quotations from the founders and other eminent figures in its book *One Nation under God*.[37] The quote is compelling because it makes plain the link conservative evangelicals see between church life, traditional culture, and what it means for the country to be good. "There are a lot of people right now who feel that America is declining in its greatness and in its goodness," Hummel said. "I can understand why, perhaps you can, as well. There are things happening, there are things being said and done that are very discouraging and are very disheartening and one does tend to think—yeah—we are going downhill." By leaving his signifiers open, "things happening" and "things being said," the pastor allowed his hearers to fill in their own worries, while also foreclosing the possibility that the country remained on solid ground (was "still good"). Moreover, his words followed the video imagery of destruction, creating a rhetorical situation for seeing the glass as half-empty and thinking about all that was wrong in the world.

Moving around to the front of his lectern, the gentle-voiced Hummel began speaking directly about the election. Like so many other pastors, he mentioned how citizens across the political spectrum fretted over both Clinton and Trump. He said his concern was different, even though he also believed whoever was elected to the presidency or to Congress would have a "significant relationship to the course of the nation." But the heart of the country, its ability to be "great" and "good," depended not on the result of the campaign, but on "the people who follow God through a relationship with Jesus Christ." Like those ministers who encouraged their hearers to vote and rest in the knowledge that God was in charge, Hummel called on his audience to see beyond the election and what it might do to American life, and to consider instead what those who were listening to him could certainly do, no matter which candidate prevailed. "The hope of this nation is not a politician," he said. "The hope of this nation are God's people, who get serious about God and believe that God, through His people, can make a difference." Born-again believers, Hummel said, could do more than vote. They could pray.

Following these words, Hummel crossed the stage. As he did this, lights flooded a new lectern—this one standing between two US flags and adorned with a mock "Seal of the President of the United States." He said he wanted to speak from this set to allow his congregation to imagine, as he spoke, "the greatest leader in the land, perhaps the greatest leader in the whole world." As his sermon unfolded, it became clear that Hummel hoped his congregation would pray fervently for the nation, and according to traditional values, in the hope of influencing their friends and neighbors for Christ. This is hardly noteworthy. Indeed, it is standard evangelical messaging, from the standard evangelical playbook. However, near the middle of his sermon, Hummel began to argue that the best political leaders would be those who governed by recognizing that neither they nor the party they supported were the "ultimate authority." Instead, the American democracy was subordinate to God and His will. "It is in His name that this nation was founded," Hummel said. "We're the ones that invoked His name, 'In God we trust.' 'Liberty and Justice for All.' Our [founding] documents [are] based on so much of what is taught in the Ten Commandments and throughout the scriptures."[38]

In chapter 3, I noted how pastors sometimes use dubious history to substantiate their claims in sermons. This is true of Hummel's account of the American founding. Even more resonant is his reliance on Christian nationalism. As John Fea explains, Christian nationalism is the mostly erroneous belief among conservative evangelicals "that the United States was founded as, and continues to be, a Christian nation." It is the discourse of American exceptionalism made into American history as a kind of nostalgic American truth. Fea further argues that evangelicals are prone to engaging in nostalgic renderings of the American past because doing so allows them to imagine a time that was safer, less compromised by sin, and so easier to understand.[39]

Such nostalgia can easily function as a defense mechanism against facing social change or demographic upheaval. It acts as a buffer against a lot of things including, perhaps, making room for worldviews and experiences that are different from one's own, or accommodating conceptions of truth that may challenge one's particular set of beliefs.[40]

Ray Johnston, in his "Separation of Church and Hate" sermon, took nostalgia as his explicit theme. Beginning in the 1950s, he went decade by decade and offered one value that had slipped from American life for good, to the detriment of all citizens. First, he said, went innocence. "[We] came back from fighting a World War . . . and all of a sudden the economy explodes, Hollywood explodes, and the number one shaper of values in America stops being parents and is replaced by Hollywood, California," Johnston said. "And Hollywood and movies and media have been the number one shaper of values ever since." Next, in the 1960s, was authority. "It was the decade of protest . . . We lost respect for government authority, for political authority . . . the authority of God and the authority of rules. And what happened is this . . . every single media everything makes the teenager look cool and the dad look like a complete idiot." In the 1970s, Johnston said, Americans lost love. "Starving for love, [we] settled for sex, and that's never changed." In the 1980s, somewhat confusingly, Americans lost values, in general. "The number one movie in the 1980s was the movie *Wall Street.* It starred a character named Gordon Gekko . . . And in that movie, they said this, 'Greed is good.' And it flipped. People's generosity went down ever since. Having a heart of compassion went down."[41] In the 1990s, people lost faith in the future. "For all of American history, if you asked a sixteen-year-old . . . is your future going to be better than your parents'? . . . They always said what? ['Yes!'] . . . Since the 1990s, when they ask teenagers, is your future going to be better than your parents', the vast majority of millennials say, 'No.'" Finally, in the first decade of the 2000s, Americans lost security. "Am I safe or not in my own country? Am I safe if I go into a movie theater? Am I safe if I get onto an airplane? Americans feel more insecure than they ever have."[42]

In Johnston's telling, because the United States was emptied of these foundational, traditional values, citizens have little reason to find hope going forward. The *esprit* of this argument reaches out for other narratives that also situate the American founding and earlier decades of American life as being better examples of fruitful, godly living. From a political perspective, the point of these stories is not whether they are absolutely and authentically accurate. Instead, they find power, explains William F. Lewis, by simply ringing "true to life," which is to say, by being true enough.[43] In addition, Fea has pointed out that Donald Trump never articulated during the campaign when he thinks America actually was great. However, it is clear in sermons like Johnston's that for many white, conservative evangelicals in the United States, that time was sometime before 1950, when, among other things, the country was less diverse and more patriarchal. Such simple clarity as exists in sermons like his makes it possible to link traditional values to the American good and—reaching back to join with the *esprit* of Hummel's sermon—to position liberal progress (like the civil rights movement, the feminist movement, and increasing immigration of non–Western Europeans after the Immigration and Naturalization Act of 1965 that included non-Christian populations) as suspect, because it goes against the nature of the country as it has always been, and so should always be.

The kinds of sermonic appeals that both Hummel and Johnston deployed are essential to notice as they related to the 2016 election. Many evangelicals right up until the end of the campaign expressed discomfort with Donald Trump as a candidate. More worrisome than Trump, it seems, was the state of American culture and the conservative evangelical place inside it. The quick and always threatening pace of this changing culture—by which I mean, in Raymond Williams's terms, a "particular way of life"—was at the root of the claims that reminded conservative Protestants to cling to their dual citizenship in the United States and in heaven.[44] But because conservative Protestants also had to live in this world, and because many ministers also wanted to provide advice and insight about what role these believers might play in turning the tide for good as part of their vote and participation in the election, some sermons did acknowledge both the (perceived) ruin all around, and the potential for moral intervention, whether through prayer or more direct political action. In rare cases, the call was of the fire-and-brimstone type many outsiders imagine as being typical of conservative evangelicalism. For example, Ed Young of Fellowship Church in Grapevine, Texas, stated on November 6, 2016, that "if God does not rain judgment on the United States of America he's going to have to apologize to Sodom and Gomorrah."[45] (I unpack Young's sermon at length in chapter 5.) Much more common were messages like "None of the Above," presented by Rob Ketterling, founder and pastor of River Valley Church, Apple Valley, Minnesota.

Ketterling's sermon "None of the Above" was based on the story of Daniel in the lion's den. In this Bible narrative, Daniel was a faithful follower of God, and a faithful servant to the king of Babylon. In the beginning, Daniel and his fellow Jews arrived in Babylon as captives, and so had to persuade the king to allow them to live out their faith and to keep kosher. It was hard to do, but eventually they succeeded. Daniel, in fact, became the king's most favored servant. The king's other attendants were very jealous of Daniel's status and schemed against him. They convinced the king to sign a decree making it a crime to pray to anyone besides his royal highness. When Daniel was found praying to God in the same way he always had, and despite the royal pronouncement, he was thrown into the lion's den as punishment. But God protected Daniel from harm, a saving grace that delighted the king, because he thought he had been tricked into signing the law forbidding prayer in the first place. In the end, the king threw the scheming servants in with the lions and told Daniel to continue serving him and praying to his God. In short, it is a story about serving well and loving God. It is one that many conservative Protestants hold out as an example of how God ultimately protects the faithful, even though trials may come in the meantime. Referring to this text, Ketterling said:

> I recognize the signs of the times . . . I really feel like, honestly, as a country, as people of faith, we are moving from a Daniel 1 era to a Daniel 3–6 era. This is what I believe. Now, if you don't know your Bible, in [the book of] Daniel, chapter 1, Daniel and a bunch of Jewish people have been brought into captivity in Babylon and they're asked to eat the wrong food, they're asked to violate their conscience. And Daniel goes to his leader and says that [things would go better if they stuck with] God's ways . . . And in Daniel, chapter 1, the leader says, "well, I'll give you a few days, but I don't want to lose my life and so I'll see . . . Let's reason together, let's dialogue about this." And so you see in Daniel, chapter 1, they do it, and all of a sudden they're like, "Wow, you're better! You're like ten times better, we're going to make everybody eat what God says they should eat." Okay? That's Daniel, chapter 1. And I believe we've been living in that type of world.
>
> If you fast-forward to Daniel, chapter[s] 3–6, all of a sudden you see it's changed now, it's against the law to stand up for what they want to stand up [for]. It's against the law for them to do what they've always done and to hold on to the matters of conscience and of their faith . . . You see, with Daniel in the lion's den . . . You see the king is almost like, "Is it true? Is it true that you actually believe this? Is it true that you defy what we say? Is it true? You will pay for this." And it's an amazing thing . . . They have to face the furnace. They have to face the lions. It's no longer "let's negotiate." It's "you must assimilate and you must say that everything we say is right or else." And I think we're on the verge of that . . . And we had better be ready to stand up for that."[46]

What is the logic of this argument? The elements are both straightforward and complex, because they conceive of the United States as both monotheistic and pluralist, at once.

In chapter 3, I described how the pastors of America's megachurches insisted that during the economic downturn the United States remained a land of prosperous plenty, an exceptional nation whose main threat existed from a people who had grown slack and were forgetting the nature of their blessing. "The [2008] recession," said John Piper, had come "like a shout from heaven to remember."[47] Ketterling's sermon fit this mold. But he also suggested that such remembering had not worked or, more to the point, had not been welcomed among those outside the conservative Protestant subculture. As a result, those who, like him and, ostensibly, his listeners, still adhered to the previous conception of what the country is—or is supposed to be—no longer felt welcome or allowed to express their essential identity. For this reason, Ketterling's use of the prophetic phrase "signs of the times" was particularly revealing, made even more poignant because he did not stipulate what those signs might be, except to suggest they went against an open, conservative Protestant faith. The allowance for polysemy of meaning was not complete, however, because the pastor's Bible context—the Daniel story—and the nature of the election timeframe made it almost certain that his audience would join him in seeing the same troublesome signs. It seems unlikely that very many listeners would have imagined concerns over looming bad weather or unpropitious fortunes for the local sports team, for example. Rather, to be able to follow Ketterling's logic, they needed to share—which is to say, needed to have an intuitive sense of—both the pastor's sense of national peril and his sense of loss. For while Ketterling quickly explained the Daniel story, it only resonated insofar as one also worried that dysfunction similar to what had happened during the time of the prophet was present today in the United States. His portrait of life in America was one in which Christians were once able to demonstrate how their ways were better, and so were able to dominate both the private and public spheres ("Wow, you're better! You're like ten times better, we're going to make everybody eat what God says they should eat.") to one where the elites (the king) have made culture increasingly inhospitable to Christians ("It's no longer 'let's negotiate.' It's 'you must assimilate and you must say that everything we say is right or else'"). The result is that born-again believers must stand ready to defend the faith, even to the point of suffering persecution.

But what is confusing about this portrait of Christian nationalism is that it affirms the United States as belonging to God, and so as being best when the majority of citizens acknowledge Him, but also as a place where Christians have always been marginalized and under threat. Such a notion of dissenting Protestantism, as Robert Bellah has described it, is steeped in American evangelical identity. In this view, religion and faith are given their fair place in the post-Enlightenment public sphere. Reason and science are not privileged at the expense of all spiritual things; rather, the nation's religious identity stands as central to how the country understands its culture.[48] The necessary lesson of the first part of the Daniel story—when Daniel convinces the king that life would be better if everyone would follow the culinary restrictions of the Jewish people rather than breaking God's culinary law—is that everyone, and not only the original believers, is better off living according to the dictates of faith. For this to translate forward to Ketterling's "signs of the times" requires a public imaginary in which Christian values were previously dominant and life was "like ten times better!" But as happened with Daniel, such accommodation is no longer the case. The monotheism of Christian nationalism couldn't hold, or was eventually subordinated to a dangerous pluralism. This pluralism disdains and mocks the religious freedom of conservative evangelicalism: "Is it true you actually believe this? . . . You must assimilate (to sin) or else."

Such assimilation, however, seems to strike Ketterling as not only noxious, but impossible. On the one hand, this is his country. America is his culture. From a Christian nationalist perspective, why should he have to assimilate? On the other hand, just as Daniel and his fellows were never really welcome in Babylon, so conservative Protestants really are not welcome in the contemporary United States. This is the heart of the tension in almost all of the election-era sermons I listened to, and it was especially stark in Ketterling's. This tension, I suggest, is why so many pastors fell back on the notion of dual citizenship, not as a theological construct, but as a practical one. However, as ministers moved past dual citizenship into engagement—particularly engagement with issues—this pressure between belonging and being alien grew ever starker, a rhetorical warrant structure that found resonance not only across churches, but in the campaign speeches of Donald Trump.

The Campaign Crosses Over

Among the chief concerns articulated by conservative evangelical pastors in their election-related homilies was a perception of waning religious (Christian) freedom in the United States. As Ketterling did in his "None of the

Above" sermon, megachurch ministers made this worry concomitant to a belief that those who took the Bible seriously were becoming unwelcome in America—they were undesirable aliens whose commitment to a traditional way of life would require a willingness to go against the grain. Against this worry, the words of Donald Trump resounded. In a campaign speech at the Values Voter Summit in Washington, DC, on September 9, 2016, the Republican candidate told a group of conservative Protestants gathered there that if he became president, the nation's "Christian heritage [would] be cherished, protected, defended, like you've never seen before . . . and that includes religious liberty." Later in the same speech, he added, "Our nation today is divided. Nobody likes to say it, but we're living in a very, very divided nation. It will be our faith in God and his teachings . . . that will lead us back to unity." Trump's words framed the United States as previously having had a united Christian heritage that was now under threat and so needed reverence and defense. For the nation to prosper, its citizens should abandon pluralism in favor of returning to the founding intent. As he stated near the end of his speech: "Imagine what our country could accomplish if we started working together as one people under one God, saluting one flag." Such rhetoric works to exclude any who might believe in more than one God (like Hindus or Native Americans) or those who do not believe in any God at all (like Buddhists or atheists).[49]

In his sermon about election issues, "Rehoboam," delivered on November 6, 2016, Don Wilson of Christ's Church of the Valley, Peoria, Arizona (see chapter 3), shared Trump's *esprit de finesse*. "Over 50 percent of Americans believe the church is of no value in the community. Over half of our culture says, 'We don't need churches, they don't add anything,'" Wilson said. "We're the visiting team. Basically, people do not like Christians today."[50] Like Ketterling, Wilson emphasized how Bible-believing evangelicals were out of step with majority culture in the United States and maintained a lifestyle that most other citizens found irrelevant. This sense of irrelevancy led Wilson to make two claims in his sermon that likely worked to Trump's advantage. The first was to affirm that God could use a person of imperfect character for His own ends. "When people say, who are you going to vote for, it's crucial, yes it is," Wilson said. "But you know what? All throughout history God has used corrupt and ungodly leaders to accomplish his purpose. And whether . . . Hillary Clinton or Donald Trump is the next president, whether you like one or the other, really it's not going to make that much difference. God can use either one of them to accomplish His purpose because He is in control." While this remark seems at first glance to be politically neutral—he lumps the Democratic and Republican nominees together and says a vote for one is essentially the same as a vote for the other—recall that literatures surveying both American political identity and the effects of negative partisanship strongly suggest that conservative evangelicals were already predisposed to voting for Trump, in spite of his defects, simply because he was a Republican. Wilson's words, then, likely offered rhetorical "cover" for those in the audience who wished to vote for the real estate mogul. Although he might be "corrupt and ungodly," God could still use him. Any harm he might cause was discursively muted because God is in control. Such logic depends on the passive part of active-passive discourse, allowing hearers to think about the election and listen to Wilson with limited worry about their own votes or the campaign's possible lasting effects.

There is another, starker, reason I suggest Wilson's sermon was ultimately in support of Trump. Soon after Wilson finished his appeal about ungodly and corrupt candidates, he wondered aloud to his audience how they could "make the right decision," without feeling overburdened. To help them, he said, he would share his own voting priorities and how he had gone about deciding how to vote, because he had participated in early voting. Wilson began this part of the sermon with the caveat that listeners could "disagree" with his priorities and "still go to heaven." This claim added levity to his remarks, while making it possible for the pastor to hold to his earlier promise that the sermon would not take sides. It also allowed him to speak in a way that nudged listeners toward his own ostensibly conservative worldview. He began by citing a LifeWay Research poll that showed differing priorities among evangelicals about what mattered most in the election, and so disrupted the idea that born-again Christians have monolithic political opinions. In the poll, which did not differentiate by race or ethnicity, 45 percent of respondents favored Trump, 31 percent Clinton, 15 percent were undecided, and 8 percent went for a third-party candidate. On the issues, 26 percent said the economy was the most important issue, 22 percent picked national security, and 10 percent said the Supreme Court. Only 4 percent of respondents said they were voting based on the abortion issue.[51] Having laid out the framework of this poll, Wilson continued by bifurcating between what he called "short-term issues and long-term issues." Choosing the president, he said, was "very important, . . . [but] it's a short-term issue. For me, the number one, long-term issue, for me, and I'm surprised only 10 percent of evangelicals think that way, is who is going to select the next Supreme Court judges [*audience clapping*]. Here's why. . . . Who the next president is will give us problems for four years. Who the next Supreme Court judge is, that they (the president) nominate, will give us decisions that will impact all of us and our kids and grandkids from twenty to forty years. And so, for me, the most important thing . . . I tried to vote for the person that I thought would put in the Supreme Court judges that I believe will impact . . . on most of those short-term decisions." While Wilson did not enumerate exactly what those "short-term decisions" were, it is hard to imagine his words would have moved listeners toward Clinton, or would have created a worldview imaginary among the audience of a Supreme Court full of justices selected by her.[52] He followed this entreaty with an appeal about how different the nation would be if more Christians would register to vote and then go to the polls to elect those candidates who shared similar values to those he proffered in his sermon. In making this appeal, Wilson seemed to assume that his hearers shared his way of thinking about issues.

"Fifty percent of Christians are not even registered to vote, and of the 50 percent that are registered to vote, only 50 percent vote," Wilson said. "That means only 25 percent of Christians vote. God forgive us. We complain and talk a good game, but we don't back it up with our actions. If all Christians voted their values and their beliefs, every candidate who had the same beliefs would win by a landslide."[53] Other ministers, too, envisaged a unified conservative Protestant electorate who could shore up the Christian nation against a secular onslaught if more Bible-believers would register and then vote. "Think about it this way," said Waylon Sears of Victory Worship Center, Tucson, Arizona. "Four million evangelical believers didn't vote in the last election. Do you know that the president was elected with 17 million votes? You hear what I'm saying? That's how many people elected him."[54] In making this (erroneous) claim, Sears meant to emphasize the power of born-again voters, while also proposing a "biblical approach to voting . . . There's far too many believers being quiet. Being intimidated."[55] Instead, they should speak out to defend themselves in the public sphere. Such an approach, in turn, would allow traditional values to prevail once again in the United States, and would resituate at the center of American life such Christian principles as the patriarchal family, personal success through self-reliance and self-control, the restoration of the American Dream, conservative sexual ethics, and more.

Although Todd Mullins of Christ Fellowship Church in Florida began his "Decision 2016" sermon with clear advice to his listeners that they could trust in God's perfect will for the election, he still reminded them that there were tangible issues at stake that his audience should take seriously: "There's a choice that we as a nation are going to make this week . . .[and] that choice has consequences. There's going to be religious freedom consequences. There's going to be consequences that speak to life and the unborn, there's consequences that speak to social issues and morality issues, there's consequences that speak to racial issues, and immigration issues, all of these are going to be dealt with this week. Make sure you understand the consequences of the choices that you are making and that I am making."[56] While Mullins did not go so far as to suggest which candidate or party would be better on these issues, only one of them—racial issues—was front and center in Clinton's campaign. Each of the others related more closely to the GOP and, as I suggested earlier, Trump was especially keen near the end of the campaign to tie religious freedom into his public rhetoric.

Like Don Wilson—and relating to my broader point about how a perhaps unintentional but long and historical discursive *esprit* existed among megachurch pastors in how they spoke about elections, in general, and politics, in particular, during 2016—Mullins tried to find a way to help his audience think about voting even if they found the candidates unbecoming or distasteful. Mullins encouraged his listeners to think about each party's platform instead of focusing on individual candidates, and he used unsubstantiated "facts" to make his point. "Sometimes I think we get so caught up in the personalities that we forget the platform," he said. "You just gotta understand the platform for Republican, Democrat, Independent . . . Because they say that about 80 percent of a platform of a party that gets into the presidency—about 80 percent of it just automatically gets put into play." He did not stipulate which platform was better, or which one was worse. However, he did remind his audience that should the United States choose leaders who operated in "opposition to the word of God, there [would be] consequences, a lack of blessing that [would] come."[57] Likewise, Wilson—after explaining the difference between short-term and long-term issues—said that, given the chance, he'd remind any American president that "we are not the exception. God's judgment will come on any nation that turns their back on God."[58]

Appeals such as these furthered the narrative of Christian nationalism within a conservative Protestant imaginary. For the nation to prosper, its citizens would have to re-embrace traditional values, which included evangelical religious freedom, a pro-life agenda, the appointment of conservative judges, and so on. Those pastors who reached beyond active-passivism created a narrative frame that favored Trump in 2016. This happened even when they began by situating their sermons as nonpartisan. The homilies I studied were mostly grouped around the idea that (contrary to assertions that God was in control and so not ultimately worried about the voting outcome) God did, indeed, have a stake in the election, and would remove His hand of protection from the country if the wrong person were to take office, or if the nation should fail to remain faithful to His way of structuring life. This, in turn, required that born-again believers recognize the peril facing them. It was essential for the faithful to engage in prayer and politics to help the United States retain its status as the exceptional land it had always been. Such an exceptional nation was traditional, not progressive. It was founded and finished, not still being made. To this end, Calvary Chapel's Skip Heitzig said: "I think most of us believe our country is in trouble. I don't think I need to sell that. I think most of us would say our country needs God's help. I think we all agree on that. So we understand we need God to forgive us our sin, to heal our land. And prayer is our declaration—not of independence, but of dependence upon God . . . I'm asking God for a revival in this country. Another chance . . . It's happened before. Christians came at times in our national history when it looked like things were falling apart to them, and they got on their knees and they prayed for revival. And there were Great Awakenings in this country . . . I want God to bless America. But first America needs to bless God. We need to praise Him and be one nation under God like it says so on our money."[59] In this passage, Heitzig offered both a critique of the country and an invitation to his audience to identify with his assessment of this critique. Indeed, he assumed his hearers did identify with his perspective. The country was "in trouble," he said. "I think we all agree on that." However, the trouble is ill defined. In what way, exactly, does the country require God's help? What are the sins? What healing is required? Heitzig left his narrative open to some interpretation, but this interpretation was bounded by the ideas of a "revival" and a "Great Awakening." Whatever problem the nation faced could be cured—not by policy or politicians—but through a public resurgence and revitalization of faith. This was Heitzig's essential call, and, quite frankly, it was the call of many other pastors I heard. Such a call makes sense inside the church. As a believer of the Bible, you think every person on earth would be better off with Jesus, or you don't. You think culture is healthier when it is full of Christians, or you don't. You think God is in charge, or you don't. And if you don't, it makes little sense for you to identify as a conservative evangelical Christian.

Heitzig didn't stop with this call, however. Like so many other pastors to whom I listened, he acknowledged the tension of the 2016 presidential race and said, "This election is not like any other election. And I am not going to tell you who to vote for. I'm going to tell you to vote." Heitzig encouraged participation and electoral activism. He also conceded that that neither Clinton nor Trump was particularly appealing, and said maybe the best that could be done was to choose the one who "wouldn't be against us," who would support Christian religious freedom. But in the most surprising turn of all, Heitizg referred to the 2016 election as a "Bonhoeffer moment," referring to Dietrich Bonhoeffer, the German pastor and anti-Nazi dissident who was eventually hanged in a concentration camp:

> Bonhoeffer noted that so many people in his day couldn't be bothered with politics . . . "That's not my thing" . . . Just not informed, not engaged, not involved. And so he came along, and he was calling people to stand up against injustice, asking the church to do it, sounded the alarm. But if you know what happened, very few heeded his call. The rest is history. The policies of Adolf Hitler took over Germany, threatened Europe, threatened the free world.
>
> So, I don't think we have the option to sort of sit in the corner and whine and despair. I don't think we have that option. Edmund Burke said . . . "The only thing needed for evil to triumph is for good men to do nothing" . . . So you want it to get worse? Do nothing at all. Don't get engaged. Don't get involved.[60]

Heitzig's narrative palpitates with a call to social justice. One can hardly hear of Hitler without imagining gas chambers and emaciated victims behind barbed wire. Accounts like this usually lead listeners to ask themselves what they would do in such a situation, and to identify with the behavior of the hero—the Bonhoeffers of the world—rather than as one of Burke's "good men" who "do nothing." Accounts like this, if they are anything, are calls to action on behalf of the oppressed.

These words from Heitzig were among the most urgent and moving of the sermons I heard during the 2016 race. They brought to mind victims of an earlier era who were helped too late, and made it seem as if such a situation might be at hand again. Moreover, in invoking the phrase "Bonhoeffer moment," Heitzig seemed to be saying there was something new or especially appalling in the race between Clinton and Trump, rather than a continuation of the same culture-war issues that have been with Americans for generations. So, it was jarring when he did not go on to mention the threat the election posed to immigrants and refugees, to women, or to other members of minority culture, as a narrative about Nazi Germany would suggest, but rather returned to the familiar. His advice, given the urgency of the moment he had just described, was to "think about the issues": "issues like the sanctity of human life in the womb. Issues like marriage and family.

Issues like human rights. Issues like federal judges in the Supreme Court. Issues like national defense. Issues like terrorism. Issues like the stability of Israel in the very volatile Middle East. All of these are issues that you have a voice in." The *esprit de finesse* was clear. Despite rhetoric that suggested the presidential contest between Clinton and Trump posed Hitler-like peril to at least some American constituencies, Heitzig still emphasized the same politics that has united conservative evangelicals to the GOP for decades. Even if Heitzig imagined Clinton as representative of the "Bonhoeffer moment" requiring response, it remains unclear how this voting issue-set reflects that. In short, the Bonhoeffer lead-up suggested some awareness of how, as Greg Holder said, politics matters because of what it references underneath: dignity, freedom, the ways in which we live our lives. The "how" of Heitzig's narrative, though, was not about this. Rather, like the narrative "how" of so many other pastors who spoke about 2016, Heitzig's "how" was about recognizing the need to protect religious liberty and to continue the fight for the same values conservative Protestants in the US have fighting for decades. Nothing else rose to the surface, despite the pastor's own words that claimed so much more was at stake. Even so, these were not words of transactional politics, but an ongoing story that has long existed. During the 2016 campaign this story was not disrupted, even though many megachurch pastors, across many pulpits, expressed concern over Trump and said—flatly, yet with conviction—that his candidacy failed their expectations and hopes.

Conclusion

The public rhetoric I have presented in this chapter is both predictable and surprising, mundane and worrisome. Particularly, the active-passive discourse that I describe makes sense given the longstanding tendency in white, conservative Protestantism in the United States for embracing American exceptionalism and American democracy, while at the same time acknowledging that all religion is a means for orienting and understanding life. Additionally, evangelicalism refers to itself as a saving religion. Its whole point is a life hereafter. Its whole point is heaven. As Saint Augustine explained, with words very much like those of the pastors I heard who described themselves as having obtained "dual citizenship": "From here each of us has the end of going home. We end in the place we are going to. So now then, here we all are, engaged in life's pilgrimage, and we have an end we are moving toward. So where are we moving to? To our home country. What is our home county? Jerusalem, mother of the faithful, mother of the living."[61] Christians use this language of "going home" to describe going to heaven. It is a language of hope, of thinking beyond the here and now, and seeing into the future. Absent this hope, the appeal of faith seems slight.

There is also evidence that many conservative Protestant churches, especially megachurches and other seeker-friendly institutions, are trying to distance themselves from the idea that they do spend, or even should spend, enormous amounts of time on politics. Indeed, while this study highlights precisely such messages, the churches and pastors I have introduced here spend far more time on other things. For example, during 2016, the churches that I have foregrounded as having taken up the election did so only as one part of an entire year of sermons that necessarily addressed other facets of the Christian life, things far removed from the race between Clinton and Trump, including messages about faith, spiritual growth, doubt, family issues, how to become a Christian in the first place, and more. Moreover, I heard many pastors express wariness about addressing the election. They talked about feeling anxious, and admitted that they understood how dangerous the territory was. "I'm wondering who's more nervous me, you, our elders, my family," said Rob Ketterling of River Valley Church. "On the way to church today our youngest son Logan said, 'Dad, be careful, they're listening.' I was like, 'Don't they listen every week?' He was like, 'No, *they're listening.*' It's almost like anything you say can be used against you in a court of law, that type of thing [*audience laughter*]."[62]

But the acknowledged reticence on the part of these pastors may have advantaged Trump. To be clear again: I do not argue that these sermons were determinative in forming a worldview among those who heard them that favored the GOP nominee. That worldview has long been in place, as research in political science affirms. Rather, I suggest that these sermons did nothing to interrupt this already extant conversation that has kept white, conservative Protestants adhering to the GOP since the election of Ronald Reagan. And so, even when the pastors I heard admitted that this election was somehow different, or that it featured unattractive candidates, the message that seemed to come through was that because voting (being active) remained essential to one's democratic duty, voting for Trump would be okay because God was ultimately in charge, and He would work things together for good.

From a critical perspective, such a passive stance from pastors seems inadequate. I argue that those ministers—a large majority of those I studied—who engaged the rhetoric of active-passivism, or the rhetoric of active-passivism combined with diluted calls to traditional values, were giving de facto endorsements to Donald Trump. Moreover, as these pastors discursively exempted themselves and other Bible-believers from the worst effects of politics through appeals that claimed God was in control, they also obscured the potential harms a Trump presidency posed, especially to refugees, immigrants, women, people of color, and more. Votes for Trump were quite obviously valid and permissible choices for any American citizen to make, including conservative Protestants. However, through active-passivism, pastors elided the reasons why Trump was different from previous Republican nominees or why he might merit closer scrutiny as a candidate.

5

Do Unto Others?

Taking part in a church service online begins as a completely personalized experience. Most megachurches have websites preloaded with worship videos and sermons from which to choose. Unless a person attends the same online church every week, a megachurch website affords a menu of choices that lets users choose the topics they want to hear about and avoid the ones they do not. There is no reason a person should ever have to be challenged by, or even encounter, topics or sermon types they do not like. Quitting a service is as easy as closing a tab or web browser. There is no real cost, besides some time invested, to watching a recorded sermon online.

In fact, access to this kind of choice was precisely how I managed to complete the research for this book. Because I was only interested in sermons with political and economic themes, I was able to visit the websites of megachurches that were spread geographically throughout the United States, looking for homilies that fit my subject. To be clear, I paid no attention to whether the individual pastors said something I found agreeable. Neither did I have a preconceived sense of what any minister should be saying. After codifying my selection criteria and starting my formal research period, I actively guarded against cherry-picking by listening to almost every message I found.[1] However, most megachurches neatly catalogue their sermons into series with themes, and include clear titles and descriptors. For website users, there is almost a Netflix-like feel to the experience: what do I feel like watching today? Some churches even have menus for easy searching, along with sermons with catchy titles, descriptions, and click-friendly icons. While I did not watch many sermons outside of my research genre, there were times something would catch my eye, and I would view a message or series that seemed interesting. For example, during my research I visited the website of Watermark Community Church in Dallas, where I live and teach. I was especially curious about Watermark because several of my students had told me they like to go to church there. So, after I listened to a few sermons from the series "One Nation under God" that Watermark pastors gave about the election, I decided to listen to a different sermon to see and hear what it was like.[2] To do this, I began to click through the many options available, quickly perusing and deciding between what looked interesting and what did not. I found a sermon about self-esteem and the problem of comparing oneself to other people, rather than to God's perfect standard.[3] I found another sermon about anxiety and learning to overcome it.[4] I found yet another about distinguishing between fake and real Christianity.[5] And these are just three examples among many possibilities. I eventually decided to watch several sermons from a series called "Relationship Goals," a special group of messages from 2016 aimed at single Christians. I was curious about what kinds of advice my students were getting from church about love, sex, marriage, and gender equality. In the two messages I watched, I heard pastors define sexual purity as remaining a virgin until marriage, and only dating for the purpose of finding a lifelong mate. To make these arguments, Garrett Raburn, then director of Watermark's ministry for young adults, argued that because sex is dangerous—having sex means risking exposure to sexually transmitted infections, pregnancy, and heartbreak—the only way to stay truly safe is to stay pure until one's wedding night. To illustrate these dangers and the need for self-protection, Raburn told the story of his own courtship and recent wedding, and showed a picture of himself with his bride at an altar on a beach. He said that he and his wife had not even kissed each other before taking their vows. "Some things are just too powerful to play with," he said. "Too powerful to take a chance on." The idea was that sex outside of marriage was not merely sinful, but self-harming.[6]

I begin this chapter with this brief sketch of my tour of Watermark's online archive of sermons for several reasons. First, the collection of messages allows anyone to have their own experience of the church. I described in chapter 2 how attending church online does, in fact, have a feeling of community. Whenever I participated in an online service, I felt pulled in to the imagined community of believers, both digital and physical, who attended the churches I studied. Even so, whenever I first entered an online worship space, my choices were up to me. This deep personalization is both unique to the digital church, and part of the contemporary culture of American evangelicalism, especially as it is practiced in megachurches.[7] This personalization means that many of the pastors I listened to during my research framed their messages as individual missives. The stories ministers told were usually about personal sin, possibilities for personal growth, or forms of personal enrichment. This framing rang true in Raburn's sermon about sex, something that generally happens between at least two people. The reason he encouraged his audience to wait for marriage had to do with fear about individual risk of disease, pregnancy, heartbreak, or spiritual damage. He said little about how sex—or sex without consent—sometimes hurts other people. Raburn's argument structure was typical for evangelical purity culture, a topic I will take up, in part, in chapter 6. For now, what I want to emphasize is that, just as the digital church allows users to get what they want out of "going to church," at least to a certain extent, the words of many pastors also often take shape mostly as spiritual advice for meeting individual needs.[8]

This personalized focus resonates with how conservative discourse has changed over the years in the United States.[9] For the most part, contemporary American conservative discourse now resonates less strongly with the theory and philosophy of Edmund Burke than with that of Friedrich von Hayek and Milton Friedman, among others. When evangelical outsiders criticize Bible-believers for failing to support public policies that would prop up the poor or otherwise mitigate harms to vulnerable constituencies, part of what they mean is that these Christians should be better Burkean conservatives. For the most part, until Ronald Reagan's election to the presidency in 1980, this was the kind of conservative thinking that prevailed in America. Like most conservatives, Burke valued liberty, honored hierarchy, and defended tradition. However, Burke also believed that proper human behavior should not only take into account what one owes to the present generation, but also pay proper deference to those who came before, along with those who will come after.[10] His philosophy was, in this way, reminiscent of Jesus's admonition that individuals should "do unto others as they would have done unto themselves," but extended out to embrace all humans, across all time periods.[11] For Burke, meeting this obligation required cherishing established customs and acquiescing to existing systems of authority.[12]

However, as I outlined in chapter 1, conservative evangelicals in the United States since the election of Reagan have been loyal members of the Republican base. Reagan's campaign and administration emphasized a new kind of economic theory and discourse that promoted strict laissez-faire economic policy, while also refusing the very idea of individual obligation. This philosophy, most closely associated with the writings of Hayek and Friedman, insists that human liberty requires vigilant defending. To argue that people are obligated to one another is really to champion coercion.[13] Very few megachurch pastors in my study were as stark in their discourse as this. In fact, many talked about serving others as a good thing to do, but as a good thing that people could choose, not necessarily as a good thing that God requires. One of the subtexts of the rhetoric of active-passivism that I detailed in chapter 4 was an emptied sense of responsibility for the consequences of the votes evangelicals were casting in the 2016 election. The pastors I studied tended to tell their audiences that participating in the election was an essential, democratic duty. Many also reminded their hearers about their importance as a constituency of voters. Bible-believers, they said, should take seriously their potential to come together and vote, as a bloc, in favor of traditional values and government responsibility. At the same time, pastors also said they shared the sense of antipathy many citizens were feeling with regard to both the campaign and the candidates. Megachurch ministers fretted that the public sphere had become depraved beyond recognition. In response, they reminded their hearers that God was in control and so, whoever became president of the United States, nothing truly terrible could happen. The election was important, but also not worth worrying about. However, when pastors told their audiences to vote without anxiety because God was in control, they were necessarily ignoring those vulnerable populations—including immigrants, refugees, and people with disabilities, among others—whose welfare was threatened by Trump's candidacy. Pastors were transposing a theological belief—God's transcendent sovereignty—onto the material conditions of real human lives.

In this chapter, I consider four sermons up close. I unpack how three different pastors used the rhetorics of active-passivism and traditional values to craft politically themed messages during the campaign of 2016. I also assess how the logic and positions of the Republican platform were present in these homilies, even when ministers did not necessarily mean to take sides in the election. The four sermons I present reveal how megachurch pastors often began their remarks by advancing appeals that seemed to embrace political open-mindedness—all three pastors I include here said their audiences should decide for themselves how to vote, based on their own values and principles—but ended by at least tacitly favoring Trump with their words. Pastors did not have to formally endorse the real estate mogul for his candidacy to seem like the better option. Instead, Republican values drifted to the top, making Trump the beneficiary of the homilies. Whether pastors were asking their hearers to vote and trust in God's perfect will for the country, or to do everything they could to return the nation to its traditionalist roots, the stories they told resonated much more closely with the GOP than with the

Democratic Party. These sermons make plain how the pastors of America's largest churches developed a narrative structure—a storytelling "how"—that invited not only rhetorical identification with themselves (which is almost always true of speakers and audiences), but ultimately continued identification with the Republican Party as a whole and so with its presidential nominee. This continued and ongoing sense of identification gives insight into why so many of these believers cast votes for Trump, despite his non-normative candidacy.

The Republican theology—to use Benjamin Lynerd's term—of the American megachurch pastors I present is sometimes subtle, and sometimes apparent. With this term, Lynerd described how American conservative evangelicals embrace the claim that human freedom is the product of limited government and God's perfect law. It also stipulates that people best experience freedom through Christian virtue. They experience suppression and exploitation through regulation and the rules of the state.[14] But what may be most useful for readers is to situate each homily I analyze as it pertains to the theme of obligation and, more particularly, how obligation in Burkean terms gives way as the messages shift from least to most political in tone. In the first message I present, Jud Wilhite, senior pastor of Central Church, near Las Vegas, offered an exemplary presentation of active-passivism. He also talked about obligation as something people owe to each other, as a means of advancing the gospel and making politics less important in daily life. The second two messages were a set of homilies given by Kevin Myers of 12Stone Church just outside Atlanta. Myers repeatedly stipulated in his sermons that he was not taking sides and was not trying to be political. Even so, his homilies were replete with partisan themes and GOP talking points. Myers emphasized unity as a form of obligation, for citizens and believers alike. He argued that concordance as a people was the value that informed all others, even if this meant sometimes tolerating racial injustice. The final message was the least common sermon type I encountered. Nevertheless, it may represent for outsiders the most stereotypical illustration of an election homily. Readers should be careful not to overdetermine its influence. However, excluding it would underestimate its sway, because its emphasis on traditionalism and economic conservatism made it resonant with elite evangelical discourse, including that articulated by political religious groups, such as Focus on the Family and the Family Research Council. The sermon, given by Ed Young of Fellowship Church in Grapevine, Texas, took values issues and the state of American culture as its point of departure. Without saying so directly, Young left little doubt that Hillary Clinton's progressive approach to politics was the less desirable choice. For Young, the problem was one of failed obligation, particularly as this failure pertained to secular Americans who misunderstood the nation's Christian founding, and Bible-believers who too meekly defended traditional mores and absolute truth.

I chose to closely analyze these sermons and these churches because they were ordinary—I heard many sermons like them during the course of my research. They are representative samples of the messages in my archive. I also chose to analyze them because they were extraordinary—the pastors I present here are very vivid storytellers, and I found myself captivated when I watched and heard them speak. As well, although these messages exist in virtual locations (cyberspace) on the respective megachurch websites, they come from a variety of geographical sites: Henderson, near Las Vegas (Central Church); Lawrenceville, near Atlanta (12Stone Church); and Grapevine, near Dallas, (Fellowship Church). This geographic diversity is further increased by the vastness of megachurches. Most, including those I present here, have multiple locations beyond their "home" church, sometimes in several states or countries. Nevertheless, this "multi-site-ness" imbues these churches with a necessary, and built-in, ambiguity.

Who's That Kid with the Oreo Cookie?

A primary way that conservative evangelical pastors talked about the election was through the rhetoric of active-passivism. Ministers often framed and supported this discourse through stories that were both nostalgic and supportive of Christian nationalism. Jud Wilhite did too, in his election-themed sermon given on November 6, 2016. Wilhite is currently senior pastor of Central Church, which has its home site in Henderson, Nevada, just outside Las Vegas. Central is a nondenominational Protestant church with a young vibe and ten brick-and-mortar locations, in several places, including Nevada, Arizona, Florida, and Morelia, Mexico. In 2018, researchers who maintain the database at the Hartford Institute for Religious Research estimated that more than 21,000 people attend Central weekly, making it the thirteenth-largest church in the nation—clearly a "megachurch," indeed.

Wilhite's sermon, "Hope beyond Politics," was the fourth in a six-part series about keeping "hope alive" when everything in life "looks bleak." The series aimed to encourage Christians to remain filled with "great expectation" even when they feel worn out and worn through. As far as politics go, Wilhite thus acknowledged that while the election mattered, it was less significant than even the most mundane matters of faith. To create this narrative structure of more important and less important things, the pastor affirmed voting as part of the evangelical duty for maintaining the American democracy; reminded believers that although this duty mattered to the nation, true believers were actually dual citizens of the United States and heaven, with heavenly citizenship as always primary; and argued finally that God has little concern with earthly politics, anyway. Wilhite further buttressed these appeals through a reasoning style that depended on examples and narratives that resisted change—progress was worse than tradition—and encouraged feelings of sentimentality in heartfelt human relationships. These stories were very powerful and hard to resist. However—and even if the pastor did not intend for them to have this effect—they likely worked against any notion of progressive or collective politics. In a sermon that was ostensibly about the election and its issues, Wilhite talked about cookies and about a little girl who made friends with an elderly widower at a grocery store and so made him a little less lonely. Almost no one is "against" gestures and friendships like this. However, in filling his election-themed homily with such stories, Wilhite subtly suggested that politics is—or can be—the fruit of personal acts of service and mutual obligation.

Wilhite appeared on stage after a time of worship, wearing a jean jacket over a black T-shirt, and sporting horn-rimmed retro-style glasses. He gave off a cool, relaxed, yet nerdy vibe throughout his half-hour-long talk. His connection with his audience was obvious. The pastor oozed friendliness, as he derived his speaker's authority via deep empathy and knowledge of scripture. He kept his leather-bound copy of the Bible close to him throughout his talk. Such authority based on sacred texts is common for megachurch pastors, who often lack the clout that comes from ordination or formal church structures. Additionally, Wilhite's expository preaching style added weightiness to his words, as it did for almost all the preachers I listened to, including those whose sermons I describe in this chapter. Teaching straight from a text enhances a speaker's credibility, something that is especially useful in instances where "the question involved is in danger of being debated," which is to say, where more than one point of view is possible, or differences of opinion might occur.[15] Political discussions almost always fall into this category. Wilhite defended against such deliberation in two ways. First, he translated a values-based claim—a faith-based claim—into a reason-based claim. Second, he demonstrated the lived truth of this translation through narrative.

In sermons during the 2016 campaign, pastors like Wilhite often developed a shared political identity with their audiences by emphasizing feelings of antipathy toward the two candidates and talking about how depressed the campaign had made them, personally, feel. Beginning this way built a bridge from the material world of politics to the immaterial world of the Bible. Creating this political community of minds generated momentum for pastors to talk about questions of values and faith as though they were also matters of political reason. Ministers implicitly encouraged their audiences to endorse their interpretation of the Bible as a viable guideline for thinking about how to vote, even as they also often said that everyone was free to cast a ballot for whomever they wished. When it came to Bible texts and God's thoughts about political matters, pastoral words were presented as truth.

In his sermon, Wilhite wanted to shift his audience's attention from the temporary to the eternal. Like other pastors across the nation on November 6, Wilhite spoke first about the Chicago Cubs's recent World Series triumph, and teased several of his fellow pastors for crying tears of joy at seeing their long-suffering team finally take home the trophy. The long-suffering Chicago team's come-from-behind Game 7 win over Cleveland had broken a more than one-hundred-year drought between championships, and had been very exciting to watch. Wilhite then remarked how quickly joy and triumph can fade, whether humans realize such victories in athletic feats or politics. Further narrowing his focus, he said he would like to emphasize one "core idea." This simple, two-word locution allowed Wilhite to quickly shift his audience's attention and establish his own speaker's authority. With his introduction about sports and the problem of contemporary politics, the pastor had made plain how easy it is to accidentally put one's hope in an appealing but insecure place. The only spot of true stability, he would soon suggest, is heaven. It was the only thing that is truly eternal—his "core idea." Joining the *esprit de finesse* of looking beyond life on earth to eternity, whereby pastors claimed that evangelical believers did not need to overstress themselves about the election, Wilhite encouraged his audience to remember that "when your hope comes from beyond this world, you can rise above this world . . . In other words, when it's not just in your circumstances, when it's not just in your team, when it's not just in . . . your political person; when your hope comes from beyond this world—what's the result of that? Then you can rise above this world."[16] Wilhite's point was that while the nation and its citizens, including his audience, were in the process of choosing leaders to be in charge, the only One who really mattered and so deserved attention was in heaven. Because of this, no one who really believed in the Bible needed to worry about what was happening or lose hope in their (earthly) circumstances. Further, by framing the election in terms of hope, rather than concern or peril, Wilhite freed his audience from any responsibility to consider the significance of their vote, or to think about their obligation to any constituency beyond themselves and their own political priorities. Their only real duty was to participate in the democratic process itself.

"Jesus Christ is the hope beyond politics," Wilhite said. With this statement, the pastor emptied politics of meaning, and proposed that what people really need from life is to be saved. He then bridged into the main part of his sermon, which was largely based on the same rhetoric of active-passivism that I described in chapter 4. His order was different than that used by other pastors, but the result was the same. Wilhite began with the passive: rest, trust, and remember you are a citizen of heaven first. He then encouraged his audience to vote and to engage in individual acts of service. "As a follower of Jesus today, you have a dual citizenship," Wilhite said. "You have a citizenship to your country, but you have a citizenship that's even greater in heaven. That's where you're truly a citizen." Wilhite's use of the word "truly" privileged his notion that there existed something akin to an invisible but still real kingdom where believers already lived. Residence in this kingdom took precedence over their domicile in the United States.

In chapter 4 I explained how pastors during the 2016 campaign used the logic of "dual citizenship" to dilute the urgency of the contemporary election context. It was like saying, "Your American citizenship matters, but take a deep breath. Everything will be all right." This reasoning stood in stark contrast to the kinds of claims I heard in the recession-era sermons I described in chapter 3, in which pastors like Andy Stanley of North Point Community Church, Alpharetta, Georgia, said that the nation occupied "the best piece of real estate in the world." It stretched from "sea to shining sea."[17] Contrary to this type of conception, Wilhite's foremost intention in drawing his audience's eyes toward their "dual citizenship" was to emphasize Christian over civic obligation. This ostensibly was the "beyond" in his sermon's title, "Hope beyond Politics." Indeed, there was very little political matter to be had in the sermon. He did not mention any hot-button issues, whether on the Left or on the Right. The words "abortion," "climate change," "gay marriage," and "taxes" were not uttered. His focus was starkly personal and aimed at individual lives, even when it came to the campaign and God's purposes in it. "What does God care about this election? What does He care about this season? What does He care about that's going on in the world?" Wilhite asked. "God cares about people more than politics," he replied. "And God's heart is that people would come to know Him and believe in Him and follow Him and be changed by Him. And He is available to people for that purpose."[18] This is a deeply evangelical call in an avowedly seeker-friendly evangelical church.

There is nothing overtly political about Wilhite's rendering of his faith or his belief in God's ultimate priority. However, the narrative necessarily works against progressive politics because it asks hearers—particularly those who share his faith—to situate the civic sphere as unimportant to God. Some might suggest it also pushes back against the impulse to wage culture wars or argue values questions or worry about trying to legislate moral rectitude. While this may be true, in part, the next move in Wilhite's sermon left intact the impulse toward moral traditionalism, as he created a metaphor that anchored the sense of true citizenship with the sense of an authentic American past.

"Things are always changing in our culture," Wilhite said. "How many of you have recently just sort of felt like . . . things are changing. You woke up one day and it just feels different." He then described a series of disorienting technological changes, including the continuous advance of cellphone technology, the ubiquitous presence of Twitter as a conversation starter, and how Facebook had become a main source of news when "ten years ago it didn't exist."

"Even Oreos are changing, and I'm very disturbed by this," he said. Walking toward a table staged at the middle back of the platform where he was speaking, Wilhite reached out for one of several packages of the Nabisco snack cookie he had left there, with flavors that included Candy Corn Oreos, Reese's Peanut Butter Cup Oreos, and Swedish Fish Oreos. "I don't know about you, but I'm in the grocery store and I'm like, look, man, this is stressing me out. What happened to just plain Oreos? Do you know? They were always good enough for me. I love Oreos! Why are you changing Oreos? Pretty soon they are going to phase these out or something. That won't be right."[19]

Talking about Oreos did several kinds of rhetorical work for Wilhite. It situated anything unfamiliar or new as necessarily suspect—as a disheartening disruption of time-honored cultural codes. Oreo cookies are the ultimate American confection. Their two chocolate cookies stuffed with creamy filling are the flavor of childhood, of safety, and of tradition. In the context of a sermon about politics, and the Christian's role in a divisive election, using Oreos as an example produced nostalgia for a former way of life, soon writ larger than a simple cookie. As Wilhite began tossing packages of cookies to the audience, he assured everyone that he was only sharing "classic Oreos, real Oreos." The snacks people could really count on.

Now standing firmly in a narrative logic that affirmed rootedness over chaos, and control over instability, the pastor began to show how his small cookie example could be generalized to the United States as a whole.[20] "Things are changing," Wilhite said. "And I wonder, in the political season, how many people have just had this thought, like, I feel like my country is changing. No matter where you're at on the political spectrum, just you read the news, you see things that are said . . . And you think, I don't know, my country is changing." The minister then pointed to (uncited) research that 53 percent of "people" agreed the country was changing. The fact that Oreos had changed, and that a majority of respondents to a survey agreed the country had changed, proved the rule that distortion was afoot. The meaning and order that individuals relied upon for sense-making in both politics and life had been disrupted. To remediate this tension, the pastor reengaged the theme of passivism, and argued that the early church, too, had faced political trouble and disorder, but God had always been faithful. To illustrate this point, Wilhite spoke of the Roman emperor Nero, whom most historians—secular and Christian alike—regard as having been hugely corrupt and incompetent in his imperial role. Returning to the Bible, and pointing to the text in 1 Peter where he had begun his sermon, the pastor highlighted 1 Peter 2:3, which tells believers that they should, "for the Lord's sake, submit to all human authority." With this remark, Wilhite began to deliver an argument that slowly discharged the steam from the negative aspects of both the campaign and the candidates. Instead, he suggested, the audience should forgive the presidential frontrunners their faults and imperfections.

Over several minutes, Wilhite focused intently on the call to Christian submission, emphasizing and repeating its essential nature, while also acknowledging that obeying such an injunction is hard, particularly in the face of corruption. "Let's just sit here for a minute," he said. "I didn't write it, don't get mad at me. It says, 'For the Lord's sake,' right? For nobody's sake but the Lord's. For nobody other's sake but the Lord's. For the Lord's sake. [The Apostle Peter] says, 'Submit to the king.' Now, what's fascinating to me is, what king is he talking about? Well, Peter is writing when Nero is the emperor of the Roman world."[21]

Wilhite next described Nero's sins and schemes in some detail: he poisoned his fourteen-year-old stepbrother. He was publicly unfaithful to his wife. He had his mother killed. He partied, raced chariots, and made his subjects sit for his terrible theater performances. The great philosopher Seneca tried to tutor him, only to give up in frustration. Nero ran Rome into bankruptcy, all the while showering gifts on his friends. He then refused to pay his soldiers. And when the nation had finally had enough and was set to dethrone him, Nero slit his own throat. He was dead by age thirty.

But before he died, Rome caught on fire. No one knows for sure who started the blaze, but some scholars suggest it may have been Nero himself, so that he could rebuild the city according to his liking.[22] "Nero found Christians to be this handy little scapegoat, and so he blamed Christians for starting the fire," Wilhite said. "It started this persecution that went out across the empire. So, Christians were being killed . . . some of them were being tortured, some of them were finding themselves drug out of their house[s], it was all this sort of religious hate and intolerance that turned toward the Christian community—when? Exactly around the time that Peter is writing this letter that we're reading right now."[23] Joining the *esprit* of arguments that placed conservative evangelicals as always already outside of the cultural mainstream, Wilhite's message positioned Bible-believers as continuous cultural misfits. Going back to at least 64 CE, Christians had been out of step with the political climate and were persecuted for refusing to conform.

At this point in the sermon, Wilhite left little doubt that he perceived evangelicals as members of a long-persecuted minority who occupied a liminal space in culture that required defense and protection from perceived threat. As such, he finally, but briefly and subtly, moved from the language of electoral "passivism" to take up the rhetoric of political "activism" to further develop his argument. Wilhite had left little doubt that Nero was as "immoral" and "ruthless" as a ruler could be. But he reminded his audience that Peter's primary teaching was one of submission to all authorities, whether godly or corrupt. He reaffirmed this teaching by quoting Paul's writing in 1 Timothy 2:1–2 that individuals should pray for their leaders, whether good or bad, so "people would be saved and come to a knowledge of the truth." This was God's priority, for everyone, at all times, the pastor claimed, even when it came to politics.

"So, where does that leave us today [two days before the election]?" Wilhite asked. In line with evangelical values and affirming American exceptionalism and the superiority of the US democratic system, he encouraged everyone to vote, according to the dictates of their "conscience" and who they believed God to be. The pastor pressed his listeners to do all they could "to ensure the freedom that we are so thankful we have." But these broad, transcendent appeals lacked specificity, even as they also constituted the whole of Wilhite's call for active participation in the election. Returning instead to the discursive *esprit* of God's already existing reign and the hope to be found in waiting—in choosing electoral passivity—he said, to applause, "But don't ever confuse this fact: No matter . . . who gets elected president next week, Jesus is still the king. Right? He's the king." As I explained in chapter 4, this logic was essential to the sermonic storytelling of megachurch pastors who preached messages about the election of 2016. It situated true believers as exempt from the worst consequences of a bad president—even a bad president they might have had a hand in helping to elect. Should the leader turn into a Nero— or should a candidate show signs of becoming a Nero—there was no need to truly worry, because things would be all right in the end. And if things were not yet all right, then it was not yet the end.

To emphasize how God's rule in His kingdom superseded any possible human position—elected or otherwise—Wilhite spoke for several minutes about the many names God has throughout the Bible, including "king of kings," "ruler of all the kings," and more. Then, in language deeply resonant with the recession-era sermons I wrote about in chapter 3, Wilhite absented elected leaders and, indeed, politics more generally, as having deep relevance to the life of the true believer. He began to read from an email he said he had received from a friend years before, with words that both encouraged him and explained his faith. The logic of this email, however, claimed that God could, and would, provide His subject with every necessary thing, simply because His subject existed.[24] To be fed, clothed, housed, schooled, or loved required nothing more than faith: "He is my lord, and He rules my life. I serve Him because His bond is love, His burden is light, and His goal for me is eternal life. He will never leave me, never forsake me, never mislead me, never forget me. When I fall, He lifts me up. When I am weak, He is strong. When I am lost, He is the way. When I stumble, He steadies me. When I hurt, He heals me. When I'm broken, He mends me. When I'm blind, He leads me. When I'm hungry, He feeds me. When I face trials, He is with me. When I face problems, He comforts me. When I face death, He carries me home. He is everything, for everybody, everywhere, every time, in every way. He is God. He is faithful. He always was. He always is. He always will be. He is unmoved, unchanged, undefeated, and never undone [*applause*]." These kinds of words are typical of conservative evangelical rhetoric. They are also typical for Bible-believers to say and hold dear. But in this context, within the time period of the campaign season and in a sermon about the election, they cannot be extracted from the broader moment. Wilhite was speaking about his faith and his belief that God was bigger than politics—a valid belief for all Christian believers all the time, but an explicitly theological one. At the same time, however, the pastor was suggesting that God's greatness could ameliorate or even annul the potential harm of a corrupt leader.

"So, whoever you vote for, remind yourself that Jesus is our king," he said. "Maybe you're here today and you look at your mortgage, and it's a mess—well, look to Jesus, because He's the ruler of the kings of the world. Maybe you look at your kid's situation right now, and it's a mess. Look to Jesus, He's the ruler of the kids—of the kings of the world . . . Maybe depression is creeping in your heart . . . Maybe you feel discouraged and frustrated and you aren't sure what the future holds, and maybe it feels like everything is changing around you. Look to Jesus, He is the ruler of the kings of the world . . . So, listen, remember, your true citizenship is in heaven."[25]

By making tangible problems that politics does address—societal problems such as affordable housing or children's issues or mental health—into spiritual questions best laid at the feet of Christ, Wilhite elided the possibility that the election had consequences or that the candidates on the ballot had different positions worth thinking about. He created a worldview about individuals in need, but in a sermon about the election, he repeatedly declared that this same election was not important at all. For a constituency of voters who may well already have supported Trump, such a pastoral rhetoric likely had the effect of holding them in place. Wilhite then concluded his sermon with a heartwarming story of a young girl who befriended an elderly widower in a grocery store.

In the story, four-year-old Nora went birthday-cake shopping with her mother. While there, she walked up to a "grumpy old man," and said, "Hi, old person, it's my birthday today." Feeling embarrassed, the girl's mom wished her daughter would stop. Precocious Nora, however, would not stop, but insisted on having a picture taken. Soon, Nora and "Mr. Dan" became fast friends, and the little girl began to sleep clutching a framed picture of her new companion. She filled a space in his heart that had started to close after the death of his wife. "She gave Dan a reason to get up and shave in the morning," Wilhite said. "She gave him a reason to wash his hair, clean himself up and get out and be among people . . . And the mom said this: 'Sometimes talking to strangers turns into the most beautiful thing in the world.' People need hope."[26] Where some might look to elections as sites of collective action, or moments when citizens join their voices for change, the pastor instead drew the audience's attention to a personal act of kindness between a child, her mother, and an elderly man. The unspoken assumption was that if everyone behaved like Nora, with simple awareness of and attention to the outcast, the need for politics would cease. Our obligations to one another—as Edmund Burke first described—could be fulfilled through simply noticing the needs of the elderly stranger, rather than through political action.

It might be easy to dismiss the logic of Wilhite's sermon as an example of the kind of individualistic message, focused on personal salvation, that is typical of the storytelling arc megachurch pastors use for their messages to their congregations. In large part, it was precisely that. However, it also rejected politics as a site of possible change. It was a homily that likely reaffirmed longtime support among conservative evangelicals for the GOP, and so at least implicitly advantaged Trump over Clinton. Even a moderate message that asked hearers to cast ballots according to their "conscience" tacitly, perhaps even unwittingly, encouraged votes for the New York businessman. This nonpartisan message still had a partisan effect.

How Much Do Black Lives Matter?

Although Jud Wilhite mentioned the word "politics" in his sermon, as well as the names of both presidential candidates, he never talked about any actual issues. Instead, he stuck mostly to the rhetoric of passivism and encouraged his listeners to remember that whoever won the election, God still reigned in heaven. In the next sermons I consider, given by Kevin Myers of 12Stone Church in Lawrenceville, Georgia—just outside Atlanta—the theme of politics was more resonant, even as the pastor also tried to eschew any association with direct partisanship. Although Myers sometimes admitted that he was talking about controversial topics, or advancing opinions rather than an absolute truth, he also couched these claims with disclaimers and rhetorical add-ons that disavowed discussing politics in church. This sermonic construction allowed Myers to stake out the middle ground between Wilhite and the final sermon I will consider in this chapter. Myers was not stridently political or overt in support of the GOP. But he did not avoid all mention of the most urgent issues facing the American electorate. In particular, Myers forcefully discussed the question of race. In so doing, he spoke about Christian obligation and the idea that love means taking inequality seriously, including the experiences and pain of fellow citizens. However, he framed this duty as secondary. First, Myers said, evangelicals needed to unify in faith and citizenship, even if doing so required marginalized individuals to change their political priorities to forgive past discrimination along with ongoing injustice.

Myers founded 12Stone Church in 1987, along with his wife, Marcia, and another couple. Like many other megachurches, the church began small. It originally met in a borrowed movie theater, then in a "Jazzercise" space, before opening its first permanent site in 1993. Its main campus now covers 82 acres, including a 2,500-seat worship center. There are also eight satellite campuses, each with its own "host" pastor. In 2010, *Outreach* magazine named 12Stone "the fastest growing church in America."[27]

Myers gave two sermons related to the presidential campaign. The first was on September 11, 2016, and the second was on October 23, 2016. I will also briefly interpret a third sermon from 12Stone from the summer of 2020, after the death of George Floyd. This message was similar to the October 23, 2016, sermon. Myers's preaching style is blunt and friendly, authoritative and inviting. His rhetorical point of departure for each of the two politically themed sermons I consider here was the concrete value of identity—both God's identity and that of the authentic believer—along with citizen unity. In chapter 4 I explained how many pastors use their sermons to talk about what it means to be a believer. When it came to political sermons, these arguments about Christian identity may have proved particularly salient because of the power that political identity now has in America. Recent research suggests that our political affiliations are as important to our understanding of ourselves as are other kinds of demographic markers. More bluntly, our demographics define our political affiliations.[28] We are evangelicals, and we are Republicans. We are secular Jews, and we are Democrats. This sorting via identity has real consequences. In a polarized and sorted world and public sphere, we do not just want our side to win, we also want the other side to lose.[29]

As well as this foregrounding of identity, Myers stressed in both sermons that because God could be known and understood through the Bible, and because His chief concern was always for eternity, all other human worries—and particularly political worries—paled in comparison. Because the nation belonged first to God, His wish was always that its people would be united in Christ. This value of unity, and the Christian's obligation to seek it with others, always structured his storytelling logic. Myers's focus on eternity mirrored Wilhite's logic in some ways. Both pastors sought to draw attention away from the mere "moment" of the election toward the more important "fact" of eternal salvation.

The first sermon was a retrospective on Christianity and the United States in the fifteen years that had then passed since the terrorist attacks of September 11, 2001. The second was an explanation of why clergy at 12Stone purportedly avoid presenting political sermons and political topics "from the stage." However, even as Myers repeatedly disclaimed partisan intent, each message was replete with partisan overtones, especially about what it means to belong as white or Black in the United States.

Myers began his September 11 sermon by talking about God's identity. In so doing, he tapped into both a theological concept and a politically charged idea. He also denied the intention of doing so. "Right off the top, I want to make sure we know something about who God is and His heart because we're talking about events that led to thousands of Americans dying, even as a result of war, as well as some of our enemies," Myers said. "And there is something about God we should all know." Myers then quoted Ezekiel 18:32, which says that God takes "no pleasure in death." Rather, Myers said, God wants everyone to be forgiven and to go to heaven. Myers thus began the main argumentative work of his sermon, which was to advance a logic that the United States is best when it stands as one nation unified under (the conservative Protestant version of) God.

To rhetorically generate a sense of unity among his hearers, Myers began playing a series of familiar video clips while asking people to remember where they were and what they were doing when they learned about the September 11 attacks. As Myers's voice played through my computer's speakers, the screen filled with images of New York City: the Twin Towers smoldering, fire trucks rushing to the wreckage and a fireman running up the stairs as scared office workers filed down. "We discovered that we have an enemy," Myers said. "American lives [were lost] . . . The old normal has gone. A new normal has come upon us, and . . . reshape[d] some things in our nation."

Myers's invocation of "we" and "our" appeared both natural and purposeful, as he slipped from asking his listeners to individually remember their own placement during and memories of the terrorist attacks, to presuming the common realization of a "new enemy and a new normal." This, too, reached back and contextualized his earlier comments about God and his character-identity in favor of universal belief and salvation. Muslims, for instance, might be enemies, but they could become friends through Christ. For Myers, while September 11 was a tragedy, its hidden benefit was that it showed the best of what America could be. Afterward, people came together, trusted and sought God, promised to serve and protect, and renewed their commitment to good. Each of these benefits made the country great, but each was lost over the years that had passed since the towers fell. The flag no longer flies in front of most homes. Race relations have fractured. People protest public prayer. Most struggle to find the good.

Here, like Wilhite, Myers reflected that he didn't mean to be political and take sides. He said he would address "Why PK (Pastor Kevin) doesn't talk about politics" in the forthcoming October 23 sermon. Even so, Myers soon turned to an ongoing and urgent public conversation—one that was getting almost as much attention at the time as the presidential election: the decision of San Francisco 49er quarterback Colin Kaepernick to sit (later kneel) during the playing of the national anthem in protest of police brutality against Black citizens. For Myers, Kaepernick's protest and the public controversy it sparked made manifest how divided Americans were. Over the course of five minutes, Myers offered his own opinion about the quarterback's necessarily political protest. It was a sermonic moment that would go viral. After the church posted this part of the pastor's sermon on its Facebook page, more than 3,000 people shared it, and it garnered more than 200,000 page views.[30]

Myers first talked about how the Kaepernick controversy was one in which everyone had "an opinion." The ferocity of this public discourse meant that parents had to talk to their kids about what was going on.[31] He said he had told his own son, Jaden, who was thirteen years old, that the United States is a "free country" where everyone should be allowed to make their own decision about whether to stand or sit for the flag. As the audience began to applaud, he said, "If fans want to turn off the NFL when [players sit], and they just don't want to watch because they think that's the wrong place and the wrong time, [that's okay, too]." As those listening approved of this notion—that to refuse to watch was better than to support dissent—Myers asked them to stop clapping. "I'm not looking for this," he said. He reiterated that he was not trying to take sides. But to speak about Kaepernick was, by necessity, to engage with the nation's race politics. Myers next quoted the quarterback, who told reporters that he had decided to sit during the anthem because he refused to "show pride in a flag for a country that oppresses Black people and people of color." Myers said he had told his son that Kaepernick was right that the United States was rife with racial injustice, and that if the flag were only about race, he would "stand" with Kaepernick on "that issue," but he couldn't "sit with him when the flag was flown . . . That seems disrespectful to me, the flag, and the country." Further, to engage in such a way alongside Kaepernick would elevate racial discrimination as a cause over other kinds of inequities:

> If standing for the flag is only done when the country is free of all injustice, then no one will ever be able to stand again. Ever. Because there are injustices happening across our nation. I can give lists, and so can you. I jotted a few down. Injustice for young women being trafficked for sex. Huge injustice, and they are innocent, enslaved, and sold like cattle. That's an injustice. Domestic violence prevails with great injustice to women and children in the country . . . Racism on many fronts is crippling this country . . . The unconstitutional and unaccountable corruption in Washington is a national travesty. Growing injustice toward some Christians is heinous. Injustice for some among the poor is tragic. I grew up, and I was called

> white trash. The prejudice was palpable. The unjust shooting of police is horrifying and intolerable. Injustice by the IRS—well those are alarming and destructive, and I could go on. I could give hundreds, so could you—hundreds of educational, economic, social, ethnic, moral, constitutional, religious injustices on all sides. . . . If the existence of some injustice is the reason not to stand for the flag, then nobody will ever be able to stand for the flag again, because I'm not sure we've ever been to the place where there's never been an injustice somewhere, in some pocket of this nation. And so what I told my son is, "Jaden, the reason I stand for the flag is the same reason Kaepernick sits . . . Because I pledge allegiance to the flag of the United States of America; and to the Republic for which it stands; one nation—one nation—under God [*applause*]; indivisible with liberty and justice for all. Justice for all." . . . If we can't stand together on the pledge of "justice for all," then when can we stand together?[32]

This moment in Myers's sermon was noteworthy for several reasons. Myers moderated his authority through emphasizing the supposedly non-political intention of his remarks. This was just his opinion, a kind of aside in the sermon. Nonetheless, he spoke "from the stage," as pastor, a positioning that necessarily endowed his remarks with extra influence. As Myers spoke, he gained momentum and added examples of national injustice that both supplemented the political gravity of the situation, and simultaneously subtracted substance from Colin Kaepernick's protest. Myers created coincident fallacies, including several non sequiturs (an argument about malfeasance at the IRS, for example, is not an appropriate response to an argument about police brutality against people of color) and a kind of reverse slippery slope (because we cannot simultaneously protest all injustice, it is illegitimate to protest any), among other tactics, to discredit the quarterback's dissent. Most noteworthy, however, was how Myers's words spoke to ongoing evangelical discomfort about what the United States is, to whom the nation belongs, and to which citizens the US government has a foremost obligation. Myers's comment about Kaepernick's protest resonated as both nostalgic and defensive. Although his first, explicit argument was about the quarterback's actions, his actual concern regarded the country and the flag. Following the logic of this appeal was somewhat difficult—or, at least, complex—because the pastor deployed a heterogeneous hierarchy of values. By listing so many kinds of injustices, Myers clouded the importance of the original one, while subordinating each equally to his original claim. To refuse to stand for all these injustices—or for any of them—was to disrespect the ultimate value of the flag. This reasoning, in turn, depended on Myers's invocation of "for all" at the end of these remarks. Here, the pastor subtly turned responsibility back to the quarterback, as he argued that Kaepernick was failing in his obligation to support American unity. Myers suggested that sitting during the national anthem and refusing to salute the flag were not protests, but rather illegitimate dissents based on a refusal to participate in the nation's collective call. This affirmation of the American pledge to justice, finally, insisted that the promise of it eventually being true was what really counted. Kaepernick's argument-by-bodily-dissent that such justice only mattered as it was being practically lived by people of color on the streets and in their confrontations with police was secondary to the promise as articulated in the pledge. For Myers, the idea of America ranked higher than the experience of actual injustice in the lives of his Black fellow Americans.

On October 23, 2016, Myers returned, as promised, to the topic of politics. This time, he said, he wanted to explain why the church's pastors usually avoided talking about partisan issues, even when they seemed like the topic of everyone else's conversation. "There is only one, ultimate, throne," Myers said. "And God is on it—permanently." This hierarchical positioning of God as always at the top ran through Myers's sermon and informed his logic throughout. First, he said, came God. Second, was the country. And third, was politics. By creating this hierarchical ranking, Myers affirmed again—as he had during his September 11 sermon—that unity is the preeminent Christian value. He said unity in God comes through the Bible. Unity as a nation comes through the Constitution. "Politics," he continued, has no value, but is "filled with disunity." In order to hold together both faith in Christ and the nation as a whole, Myers encouraged his audience to take a pessimistic approach to the public sphere. "I'm not trying to figure out how to unite us in politics," he said. "My agenda is to unite us in Christ." Myers wanted the church to talk about Jesus, His character, and how to get to heaven. "In fact, if I had my way, I'd rather not talk with you about politics," Myers said. "At least not until we agree on the teachings of Christ and that the Bible is God's word." Discussing the tenets of citizenship and public engagement required a strictly Christian worldview.

This requirement ran so deep in his assumptions, in fact, that he soon used it to conflate biblical and political issues. Any issue the Bible mentioned belonged to the church, even if politicians talked about it, too. "The biblical supersedes the political," he explained. Any hot-button, out-of-bounds, that's-not-fit-for-church topic could become fair game if it was also a focus of scripture:

> Now I am aware that some people would say [we] talk plenty about politics. When you talk about racism, you're talking about politics. And when you talk about economics and this $20 trillion irresponsible debt in our nation you're talking politics. When you talk about God's design in marriage and family and the role of husband and wife, you're talking politics. When you talk about a gay lifestyle and gay marriage stuff, you're talking politics. When you talk evolution and creationism kind of things, that is political. When you, . . . talk about injustice in this country, it's political. When you go to the state capitol and you pray, that's political. You go to Washington, DC, and you pray at the Capitol, that's political. So, let me give you my, our perspective . . . If a matter is a biblical issue, addressed in the Bible, then to me it's a biblical issue first. So, when I teach on biblical issues that happen to be made into political issues by our country—oh, well—it's political for the nation, but it's first and foremost biblical for me.[33]

This joining of political and theological issues likely resonated for many in Myers's audience. Evangelicals in the United States cherish scripture, believing it to be true and trustworthy. More important, "Americans by the millions have found that the Bible speaks to the heart."[34] Situating the authority of the Bible as coming both before and above politicians and political issues—even when they were speaking about the same things—allowed the pastor to move quickly through this question set while also claiming authority to speak about each one. He told his audience that God "established pastors for the purpose of teaching" and helping individuals to become "mature in Christ" so that they would not become confused by the "heresy of the world." This language privileged Myers's own interpretation of the meaning of biblical-cum-political issues, and allowed him the freedom to do exactly that which he had said he would not do earlier: speak about the nation's politics, in general, and the 2016 election, in particular.

Returning to the presumed value of unity, Myers said that the United States could only hold together as a country so long as there was "truth and justice" in the land. "Truth and justice" were also God's priority for His people, the pastor continued. Under a perfect system, the government that pleased the citizens would also please God, because such a government would be based on truth and justice—however haphazardly or ill defined. Unfortunately, Myers continued, Washington, DC, was filled with "corruption . . . half-truths, and injustice." To illustrate, like so many other pastors during the 2016 campaign, the pastor flashed photos of Trump and Clinton on a large screen that was positioned behind him while he sat on a stool. He said that the photos—and the audience's presumed reaction to them—made plain how divided the nation was. "You see hope in whichever candidate you choose, but otherwise you're looking at the other and it's offensive, and [sparks] indignation and polarization, and division." Myers then joined the *esprit* of the discourse I described in chapter 4, which characterized the two candidates as equally bad, among the worst choices for president the nation had ever faced. "In this election we are dealing with candidates who disrespect the law, who disrespect people, and for whom there might be way too much evidence of corruption," he said. "Which candidate am I talking about? Don't answer. I'll answer it for you: Both."

Myers's appeal to corruption simultaneously indicted the candidates and the audience. The reason the nation had to choose between Clinton and Trump, rather than between other, superior choices, was because citizens had also become corrupt and unclean. Like those pastors I described in chapter 4, who spoke about how the nation had turned its back on traditional values and so had become unmoored, or who said that the United States was losing its exceptional status through disregarding biblical values, Myers claimed that Clinton and Trump were quintessential examples of widespread ungodliness. The candidates represented the rule, not the exception. "What if they are a mirror to who we are becoming as a people?" he asked. "What if we are simply getting the candidates we deserve?" To wit, he said, while the "media [were] indignant over indecent comments," most people had long since given up believing in traditional, heteronormative sexual ethics. Lying and cheating were commonplace. And culture had become so poisoned that women not only were objectified but had participated in their own objectification. The result was a country lost to itself, its better days behind it. "I pray for our nation, I really do," Myers said. "And sometimes I quietly weep. Because I know we are far from God and drifting all the more, and we don't really care about truth and justice."

Myers's notion of moral decline that left the United States at risk of losing God's favor, coupled with nostalgia for better days, resonated with the recession-era sermons I described in chapter 3, which called on believers to remember the nation's exceptional nature and do their own part to restore the country to a position of prominence, as well as with those sermons I highlighted in chapter 4, which emphasized Christian nationalism and the nation's presumed Christian founding. Because so many people had turned away from moral traditionalism, Myers could find little reason to hope things would turn around. Yet, there was an election at hand. Embracing the rhetorical logic of activism—the same logic so many other pastors also espoused—Myers prodded his audience to vote despite the poor choices they faced. To figure out how to choose between such objectionable candidates, Myers suggested reading "scripture alongside the platforms." He said taking this step would put God in control, and eliminate the anxiety anyone might be feeling over the candidate slate. This appeal also re-elevated the authority of the Bible and allowed Myers to escape the claim that he was advocating for either Clinton or Trump. As pastor, he was not saying how anyone should vote. Rather, hearers would be able to decide for themselves as they placed the issues—the party platforms—next to scripture. To illustrate how this worked, Myers talked about how this process had unfolded for him:

> You get to make some issues more important than others . . . Things like VP is influential in the voting factor. Things like that $20 million [*sic*] in debt and growing, that has to change. Things like taking the life of unborn children when the mother's life is not at risk ought to weigh heavy on us . . . [Things like who] would [pick] the [next] Supreme Court justices . . .
>
> So, what are you going to put as more important than others? . . . And by the way, I've always voted the lesser of evils in every presidential election because it's always been fragile and imperfect human beings . . . I'm not voting on a pastor. . . . I'm voting on a president and I have limited options. And . . . let me say one more thing. . . . Saying that because I vote for someone means that I endorse their lifestyle is like saying I endorse Apple's corporate values because I have an iPhone, or that I endorse atheism because my surgeon doesn't believe in God, or that I endorse Hollywood because I watch movies.[35]

Although Myers began by encouraging his audience to start with reading the Bible, and then to think about both political platforms, when he talked about his own decision-making process, he spoke only about his voting priorities ("you get to make some issues more important than other issues"). He did not say, for example, the Democratic platform emphasizes these issues, the Republican one these, and scripture says this. Instead, Myers described a longstanding set of values associated with the GOP and so with Donald Trump. He mentioned the deficit (financial conservatism), abortion, and who would serve on the US Supreme Court. Having done this, he finished with a move toward rhetorical dissociation.

Myers spent much of his sermon outlining the degraded nature of politics and the American public sphere. He also made clear his belief that Bible-believers should concentrate foremost on eternal and spiritual matters, not temporary and earthly ones. God was perfect. Humans were not—especially the two humans running for president. Even so, the pastor wanted to endorse the American democratic system and to encourage his audience to vote. He legitimized this participation immediately after affirming the importance of a mostly conservative agenda. To reunite a flawed candidate with this preferred agenda, Myers delinked that candidate from the requirements of godliness or high character ("Saying that because I vote for someone means I endorse their lifestyle . . ."). As Perelman and Olbrechts-Tyteca explain, such a rhetorical strategy allows speakers to stress an "act . . . [independent of] the opinion held of the person."[36] Or, in this case, Myers stressed the politics of a presidential contender, despite nonnormative behavior and discourse. Without saying Trump's name, Myers indemnified the candidate's positions and potential acts as president from criticism, thus granting his own agreement and approval to any hearer who might have been thinking of voting for the New York businessman.

In the final part of Myers's sermon, he drew the audience's attention back to his message from September 11. He said that among the most important issues facing the nation were the problems of racism and injustice against people of color. He also acknowledged that there are few things more confusing, or harder to talk about, than the division between races in the United States, which events like the killing of Michael Brown in Ferguson, Missouri, or the killing of Freddie Gray in Baltimore exposed. For a moment, Myers seemed poised to articulate progressive talking points about the structural disadvantages that come from being born into America's inner cities, or how people of color find themselves incarcerated at rates much higher than whites, for similar crimes, and for longer periods of time. But he did not. Instead, Myers returned to the theme of unification, and said that God never plays favorites. Everyone counts the same in heaven. "And we know that in the church," Myers said. "But this racism thing is political, as well."

Recall that in his September 11 sermon, Myers privileged the flag, and, by implication, the country, over questions of racial harm. To make this happen, the pastor listed a series of injustices, and said that each of these inequalities also merited citizen pushback and protest. But this kind of continuous protest would be impossible. It would cancel out the promise of the Pledge of Allegiance, in favor of attention to the practices of sin. This appeal, in turn, suggested that the point of dissent should be to foster unity—to call others to join, in kneeling or standing—rather than other possible goals, such as noticing hidden pain as a means for demanding change. To this end, in his second sermon, Myers said that because racism was not just a spiritual issue, but a political one, too, people needed to have a "conversation" about race.

To illustrate the kind of conversation he meant, the pastor played a video of a recent (staged) conversation he had had with three Black men who attend 12Stone Church: Cameron Glasper, a businessman and part-time worship leader; Ron Gary, also a businessman and a church usher; and Derreck Kayongo, CEO of Atlanta's Center for Human and Civil Rights. Myers told the congregation that the four men had talked for nearly 90 minutes, of which he showed a 13-minute clip. (The quotations from the four men in the following paragraphs are all drawn from this video clip.) The conversation meandered, and it is difficult in a short space to fully explicate all its discursive contours. Most important to this analysis is how Myers leveraged his prestige as pastor to lend authority to his interlocutors to speak on behalf of all African Americans in the United States, including those who founded and are involved in the Black Lives Matter (BLM) movement. This loaned authority, in turn, allowed a conversation to develop that superficially affirmed the struggles facing people of color in the United States, but situated them mostly in a historical lens. Critically, the conversation disavowed Black pushback as manifest through BLM, specifically because it creates disunity. When this happened, many in the white audience may have felt exonerated if they were having negative reactions toward African American protest, or even supported in their feelings against it.

Myers began the conversation by calling out his own white privilege and asking whether this meant "the system works for me and against you." With this question, Myers sought to create a sense of joint rhetorical identity, both with his immediate interlocutors and those who would become the video's audience. He needed to generate good feelings with those who were in the room with him, while also not alienating those who would watch later. To do this, Myers emphasized intent. "Systemically, even if I don't intend it, the system works for me, that's my privilege, whether I see it or not, and it works against you," Myers said. "How do you respond to that? Do you think that's true? Whether it's intended or not?"

By emphasizing intention, but also situating this intention as a rhetorical question, Myers invited an answer that could acknowledge the existence of white privilege, while also discharging any feelings of guilt and responsibility the existence of this privilege might produce in the audience. If any of the three men had wanted to sharply challenge the pastor's privilege, they would also have had to challenge his authority and goodwill. After all, he was a white man offering to stand in and have a conversation about race. The alternative was to accept the pastor's questions at face value, answer them, and so borrow some of his credibility to speak. Doing this, however, left Glasper, Gary, and Kayongo to have a conversation about Black life on white discursive turf. This meant that while they could admit they did face racism, they also had to downplay its significance or otherwise sanitize the Black struggle.

To illustrate, Glasper responded to Myers's question about white privilege by talking about slavery in the simplest of terms. He described how his ancestors were brought from Africa to the United States and were unable to "read . . . write or speak the language." In short, he identified illiteracy as the chief problem of slavery. That enslaved people could not read or write and, importantly, were forbidden from learning to do so meant that when the Civil War ended, they were mostly unemployable. This claim softly affirmed the historicity of systemic oppression, but also joined the much louder and longstanding evangelical *esprit* of personal responsibility for success or failure, as described in chapter 3. If Black people could not succeed like white people, it was because they lacked the same opportunities to acquire the necessary skills to take part in traditional (white Protestant) culture. That reading and writing were unnecessary skills for many occupations during the era of Reconstruction—which is to say that Glasper appeared to transmute the necessary skill-set for an information economy onto an agrarian and industrial one—did not figure into the logic of the conversation. Instead, Glasper emphasized how white institutions of higher education were first closed to Black students, even as degrees from historically Black colleges were seen as less prestigious. So, even in the contemporary United States, he said, where education is open to everyone, it can still feel like "it doesn't matter."

The tone of Glasper's remarks embraced white ideals of success in 2016. He framed the cause of Black struggle as their exclusion from learning and education stretching back to the time of slavery. There is no doubt that his analysis is true. African Americans in the United States have never had the same access to the best schools (or to schools at all) as white citizens. One need only look at the Supreme Court's decision in *Brown v. Board of Education* (1954) to see that this is true. The country's desegregation process has been long, slow, and incomplete. However, when scholars who study race speak about white privilege, access to education is but one part of their critique. Nothing in Glasper's response was about poverty, crime, incarceration, police brutality, or other, more controversial claims that many Black Americans (including Colin Kaepernick) make about systemic oppression.[37] Rather, he spoke in terms most palatable to a white audience. He closed his remarks by saying that when it came to Black and white people, privilege versus exclusion could now be understood through what happens in a job interview. "When you [pointing to Myers] walk into an interview room, you're given the benefit of a doubt. You're given the, 'Hey, this guy could work here,'" Glasper said. "I'm given the 'Why should we?' You're given the 'Why not?'"

"Is that what's fueling Black Lives Matter?" Myers asked. Gary responded first. He said that "all this"—leaving open what "this" referred to—was nothing new, but instead had passed down through generations. He related the problem again to a lack of education about history, though he stopped short of interrogating who was uninformed. Instead, he spoke in collective terms, blaming both Black and white Americans for a bad situation. Because he posited shared—and equal—culpability for the nation's racial injustice, while also omitting from the conversation the problem of police violence against people of color, those in the audience who harbored doubts about the goals of BLM may have felt affirmed for their position. If these Black men were unconvinced by the group's motives and methods, how could white people be expected to offer their wholehearted endorsement? Glasper, too, soon distanced himself from BLM, and offered a history of the movement that ran counter to the one it gives for itself.[38] "Black Lives Matter was never intended to be a hate group," he said. Engaging this false frame allowed the conversation to skip over any history of racism and racial violence in the United States, from the true horrors of slavery, to the era of lynching, to Jim Crow, and so on. Instead, Glasper developed a narrative based on self-esteem for African Americans that—again—depended on already existing evangelical good reasons, which affirm individual responsibility and personal worth through self-control and moral acts. Still missing, too, was any mention of structural racism or white sanctioning of state-sponsored (police) violence. "I believe that its [BLM's] basis was on . . . it was to say to fellow Black people, 'Hey, man, your life matters,'" Glasper said, while Gary and Kayongo nodded along affirmatively. "It was trying to raise empowerment in the Black community . . . No matter what you see on the news, if that guy gets killed on the street and nothing happens to him . . . your life still matters. What are you going to do with it? It was trying to build hope, to say to that kid who feels like he has no future that your life matters."

Such a narrative has many possible effects, but from an election standpoint, one of the most important was how it held in place a logic of limited blame. The conversation likely affirmed those listeners who wanted to limit their share of complicity for a system of unequal justice, or who did not want to believe that people of color were facing police prejudice, or who simply didn't like Black Lives Matter. Speaking about the protest movement as a "hate group" positioned its supporters as problems, and potentially dangerous ones at that. Such "radicals" had an agenda that went too far and was too aggressive. Even African Americans like Gary, Glasper, and Kayongo could see why so many people in the white community rejected their message. They did, too. Moreover, the conversation may have fortified the pro-police, anti-crime language that Trump was forwarding at the time—rhetoric that also ran counter to empirical truth.[39]

The conversation closed with two questions from Myers. He asked the three men to imagine what they would like to say to white people to help them better understand BLM, and what they would like to say to the leadership of BLM to help them get back on track. Kayongo framed his answer to the first question around 12Stone's approach to diversity. He said that the church had done a good job of ministering to "God's diversity" near Atlanta. He also said that the city's diversity was evident in the individuals who filled the auditoriums every weekend. "What you did is you loved," he said. "If you love people, you don't have to worry about diversity and inclusion. [People] will immediately come to you. That's what God does. All He does is love . . . And people who really understand this love come and seek Him out." Myers pointed out that Gwinnett County, north of Atlanta and where 12Stone is located, was among the most ethnically diverse counties in the nation. "We are uniquely positioned to demonstrate a unity across . . . ethnic lines, probably unlike any other place in the Southeast."

This rhetoric is the church and the gospel at its best. Indeed, I suggest it is what outsiders hope to hear, and feel disheartened in its absence. But it was a strange response to a question about what people could or should take from the messaging of Black Lives Matter. Instead, Kayongo joined Myers's theme of unification and gave the white pastor credit for creating a space of racial reconciliation at 12Stone Church. While 12Stone may, indeed, be such a space, focusing on it as a response to what white people might take away from the BLM movement rhetorically worked to let the audience off the hook for their participation in any system of hegemonic racial privilege, through being members of a church in one of the most ethnically diverse counties "in the nation." Moreover, still missing from the conversation was any mention of the problem of violence against minorities or police brutality against bodies of color.

As for how the men might speak to the Black Lives Matter movement, by this point the response was predictable. Myers wondered aloud whether a movement that had been "hijacked" (note here the use of violent language rife with terrorist overtones) from its original meaning to encourage African American youth and remind them they matter as much as anyone else could even be saved. As Glasper and Kayongo again looked on in support, Gary replied that he would tell the organization that it needed to "get back to the original basis" of its mission or else start a new movement altogether. To do otherwise would be engaging in "evil . . . the same as the KKK." Kayongo next described how the civil rights movement was one based across races, where white men and women came together with Black people to fight for equality. Once more the theme—the solution—of unity foregrounded the problem of racial injustice. This rhetorical construction allowed audience members to be participants and even potential heroes in a still unfolding narrative of ethnic and social justice. The BLM activists who were criticizing police and demanding to be heard were "radicals," and "the same as the KKK." It is hard to imagine a more damning critique. White people like Myers and the members of 12Stone who were willing to receive all with "love" could be like Freedom Riders during the 1960s. The act of simple openness—but not protest—would transform them into brave crusaders with moral courage who were willing to risk their own comfort for national unity and the good of the gospel.

Curiously missing from the discussion among the four men was the presidential election. This is curious because the sermon during which the video was shown was still about politics and, ostensibly, about the 2016 campaign. However, its tone and message resonated with the longstanding discourse of the GOP, as well as the words of Donald Trump. Republicans, since at least Barry Goldwater's 1964 presidential campaign, and with marked prominence beginning with Richard Nixon's campaign in 1968, have linked themselves to a rhetoric of "law and order." This rhetoric includes language that frames Black Americans, especially those in the inner cities, as lacking in values and virtue.[40] While the conversation between Myers and three of his congregants affirmed the existence of Black struggle, the narrative thread relied on the notion that what constituents of color needed most was love—to be welcomed—education, and economic access. They did not talk about how the very experience of being American often differs depending on the color of one's skin. In some ways, this fits how church happens in the United States. One of the most frequently quoted lines from Martin Luther King Jr. after "I have a dream" is his remark that "at 11:00 on Sunday morning when we stand and sing . . . [the hymn] 'Christ Has no East or West,' we stand at the most segregated hour in this nation."[41] As of 2012, about eight in ten churchgoers in the United States attended "mono-racial" congregations, meaning a place of worship where at least 80 percent of the members belong to the same racial group.[42] Protestants of different races, whether they belong to mainline or evangelical congregations, simply do not worship together. This separation contributes to a discourse that frames racial politics in different ways. Conservative evangelicals, as was evident in Myers's repeated calls for unity, have responded to racial strife and grievance in the United States by urging Black citizens to join them in respecting police and honoring service as ways to bring about change and reduce state-sanctioned violence. And, as was clear in Myers's sermons, when Black and white people do come together in conversations about race and racial politics, there can be pressure for congregants of color to deemphasize past pain or contemporary injustice. The reasons they do this may be myriad, but likely include a wish to avoid conflict.

Indeed, in the summer of 2020, the United States erupted in protests again after George Floyd was killed during an arrest in Minneapolis.[43] Videos from security cameras and bystanders' cellphones showed how a white officer, Derek Chauvin, had asphyxiated Floyd by kneeling on his neck and pinning him to the ground for more than eight minutes.[44] Demonstrators soon filled all of America's major cities, including Minneapolis, New York, Chicago, Los Angeles, Houston, Seattle, and more. A similar racial reckoning happened online, as users across Twitter, Facebook, and Instagram shared pictures and opinions about what the United States should do about police violence against people of color, especially Black Americans.[45] Some megachurches preached special messages about the protests, and tried to offer insight about how the church could respond to racial injustice. Among those that took this approach was 12Stone Church.

The sermon at 12Stone happened on June 7, thirteen days after George Floyd's death. Two pastors delivered the message: Myers and Associate Executive Pastor Jason Berry. As with the 2016 sermons, the two ministers focused on unity, and how the church was called to be "one family," one body. Speaking first, Berry said that while "the world" might be "divided" about race, Christians should recognize the bigger truth that "we are one. . . . Look at the news. How can anyone say, 'We are one?' . . .See, what Jesus said is, 'You are one . . .as a kingdom fact, you are one.'" Berry's words joined the *esprit* of active-passivism from the 2016 campaign, making plain that this rhetoric persists for conservative evangelicals beyond sermons and conversations explicitly related to elections or presidential politics. While the nation was ablaze with protests over longstanding racial injustice, God's invisible kingdom had already achieved perfect equity and total righteousness. "This [overcoming racism] is not a political agenda, this is a kingdom agenda," Berry said.[46]

About twenty minutes into Berry's remarks, Myers joined him onstage, accompanied by another Black member of 12Stone, Gary (last name not given). Myers and Gary sat down on stools behind a high-top table to have another conversation about race in the United States. Myers soon explained that he had invited Gary to assist in the sermon after he had listened to him during a roundtable discussion he had attended earlier in the week. "You said, 'Relationship solves racism,' and I was immediately captivated." This statement did two things. First, Myers, a white man, spoke for Gary, a Black man. Although Gary did participate in the conversation, before that happened, Myers told the audience what Gary had said—the reason he had been invited into the privileged white preaching space—and emphasized that he had been invited because the pastor was impressed and "captivated." Second, Myers made plain that the solution to racism was small and interpersonal—it would come through relationships rather than through systemic and structural change, as those in the streets protesting against police violence were insisting. As was the case in 2016 with Myers's words against Colin Kaepernick and in his earlier videotaped conversation, the audience was thus invited to ignore the nation's longstanding history of racial discrimination and legalized segregation, and to listen instead to Gary, who would tell them a story about a policeman he had known when he was a child in Buffalo, New York. This officer, named Herman, had been kind, treated Gary and his brother to candy, and often played basketball with the boys in the front yard. "This was going on in 1965," Gary said, "there was a lot going on racially, but he was our friend. [When] I found out he was a policeman, I had to make a decision, how I [felt about him]. Well, we loved Herman. We didn't care about any of the other stuff that he was."[47] Gary's story thus personalized police, refortified cops as both friendly and good, and armed the conversation with a necessary safety and nostalgia. Gary was not talking about a murder that happened in Minneapolis on May 25, 2020. He was talking about being a child and playing basketball with his neighbor, who happened to also be a policeman, in the mid-1960s.

Collectively, Myers's sermons from 2016, along with the more recent 12Stone message from 2020, embraced both active-passivism and the longstanding discourse of the Republican Party in favor of law and order. Although Myers made sure to stipulate that he was not talking about politics and forswore any partisan intent, his sermons still formed a narrative arc that affirmed traditional values and, especially, a longstanding white conservative evangelical story about how Christians are obligated to move past the problem of race in favor of reconciliation and unity.[48] Moreover, Myers argued for this unity through a discourse of values hierarchy. He said American solidarity should matter more to believers than the problem of racial injustice or, quite frankly, any kind of injustice, because such solidarity mattered more to God. Indeed, in the October 23 sermon, he even engaged African Americans in a conversation about race to legitimize this worldview. I have little doubt that Myers—like many of the other clergy I studied in my digital rhetorical ethnography—cares deeply about the loss of life that has occurred due to police shootings in the United States. However, the *esprit* of this conversation remains consonant with that of the GOP, which insists that most police are good, and for this reason, officers are properly due respect. Suspects and other individuals in contact with law enforcement should act with deference to reduce the possibility of bad outcomes.

This logic, in turn, relies on individual initiative and personal responsibility. Structural disadvantage is absent in this story. Good behavior and good decision making are the fruit of a good life, and they are adequate defenses against injustice. Myers nodded to this kind of thinking when he said that, as a voter, he got to "make some things more important than other things." He then suggested that he preferred a candidate who would reduce the deficit, fight abortion, and appoint conservative justices to the Supreme Court. Such a candidate easily fits the Republican mold, taken generically. So, although he never said (perhaps for both legal and practical purposes) which candidate he cast his ballot for, he also didn't have to do so. Instead, he set out a rhetoric of "prescribed" political thinking, when it comes to voting. This rhetoric went as follows: Put your faith first. Remember the country belongs to God. Politics and parties don't matter. Issues do. Read your Bible to figure out which issues matter most. Then, vote accordingly.

Such prescription was common during my study. This is particularly true in the last sermon I will analyze in this chapter, which was both the least common thematically and the most stereotypical. This sermon worked from the premise that the election was of both immediate and eternal importance. While the pastor who gave it stopped short of saying for whom the audience should vote, he left little doubt about which issues mattered, or what he thought of progressive politics writ large.

Like a Drunk Fan at a Football Game

White, conservative Protestants in the United States take seriously American exceptionalism, small government, traditional values, and personal responsibility for success. Most of the narratives I described in chapter 3 about the evangelical response to the Great Recession emphasized these themes. American evangelicals likewise stress the role of individual human action for understanding how life turns out, over that of systems or structures. Each person must receive redemption, pursue success, be a good citizen, and more. Many pastors in my study told sermonic narratives that acknowledged human depravity (sinfulness), but also insisted that blessing—meaning the ability to self-sustain, free from government intervention—is always available to those who are industrious and live according to "God's rules."

These rules, of course, may elicit images of fire-and-brimstone stereotypes in outsiders. There is some truth to these stereotypes, as will become clear in the sermon I analyze next. To live according to the conservative evangelical rules is to disapprove of abortion, and to support a traditional "one man, one woman" definition of marriage, while also opposing other possible formulations of family as ungodly (gay marriage, living together without marriage, single parenthood, and so on). The rules further require seeking employment and being employed, while disparaging all forms of government entitlement programs—even, increasingly, Social Security and Medicare. The rules are anti-Hollywood and pro–family game night. The rules prefer business over government. And so on.

Some observers—like Thomas Frank in his book *What's the Matter with Kansas?*—have suggested that while some of these rules find obvious *esprit* with the Christian faith (perhaps opposition to abortion or insistence on hard work), others are less obvious (business over government, no social welfare for the poor). And yet, since at least the late 1970s, this has been the political-economic rhetoric that has resonated with American evangelicals. It is a discourse of individual obligation and traditional values.[49] When I began my rhetorical ethnography during the Great Recession, these were the kinds of messages I mostly expected to hear.

However, most of the pastors I heard in my study did not frontload their sermons with language about hot-button issues. Instead, when topics like abortion, marriage equality, government debt, entitlement programs, school prayer, and more were mentioned, they usually came up as parenthetical asides, as was the case in Kevin Myers's sermons. Most pastors during the 2016 campaign deployed the logic of active-passivism. Vote and don't worry, they said. The result was a de facto endorsement of Trump. By telling their congregations to vote, then reminding them God was in control and He was not worried, yet still situating issues of values as primary in politics, even with an attenuated tone, pastors maintained alignment with the GOP and its nominee, although less obviously so.

Some pastors, however, continued to be direct in their admonitions about the perils of progressive politics. For example, Ed Young, of Fellowship Church in Grapevine, Texas, preached such a message on November 6, 2016, called "How to Pick a President."[50] Fellowship is a multisite church with campuses in Texas, Oklahoma, and Florida. As of 2018, the Hartford Institute for Religious Research estimated that Fellowship was the sixth-largest megachurch in the United States, with more than 24,000 people in weekly attendance. Young has gained national attention for his willingness to speak openly about sex, including one stunt that involved staying in bed with his wife for twenty-four hours—on the roof of the church. The marathon "bed-in" was streamed live over the internet. Young is also a best-selling author, especially popular for his writings about family, parenting, marriage, and sex.

Like many of the sermons I watched, Young's sermon began with a montage of pictures and voice-overs from previous presidents, including Franklin D. Roosevelt, Ronald Reagan, John F. Kennedy, Barack Obama, and more. The short film ended with an image of Hillary Clinton and Donald Trump facing each other against a blue screen. As my computer screen cleared, Young appeared. He was wearing a gray fitted suit, a white shirt unbuttoned at the neck, and no tie. Behind him, the image of Clinton and Trump facing off was projected onto a giant screen, where it remained for the rest of his sermon. Young began with a short welcome and then said that he would be talking about the election, which he described as "one of the most important and consequential in our history." This argument stood in contrast to those of other pastors in my study, who had engaged the active-passive rhetoric of trying to downplay the campaign's significance. Like so many of those preachers, however, Young agreed that the two candidates in the election were less than ideal. "Let's just be honest," he said. "They're the best? They're the best out there?" To escape the conundrum of bad nominees, while maintaining his argument that the election was essential, he said that their personalities mattered little as compared to their positions and policies. Then, as Kevin Myers had done, Young encouraged his audience to read the party platforms alongside scripture and so discover how to vote from a "biblical perspective, a Christo-centric perspective, from a Christ follower's worldview." But first, Young said, believers needed to see American culture for the mess it had become.

To make plain this mess, Young crafted his sermon around the metaphor of a drunk sports fan at a football game. He said that years before he had attended a "big game" at a packed stadium. For most of the first quarter, however, the four seats immediately in front of him remained empty. As the quarter ended, drunk fans filled the seats. One of the four began to hector the pastor, excited to see him there. American culture, the pastor continued, was drunk, too: "There's a game going on and we're so drunk with deception, so inebriated with our own thing, our own independence that we don't even realize there's a contest out there. There's a game going on, a conflict for the very heart and soul of our nation . . . Could it be that we don't really understand the trajectory of where our nation is going?"

Continuing with the metaphor of the football game, Young explained that many play-by-play announcers emphasize individual matchups between teams. Likewise, he said, the United States was facing a matchup between those who favor a secular approach to life, and those who favor the Bible. He structured his sermon around this idea of matchups, with a secular side pitted against a Christian side in a struggle over the essential meaning of the keywords "truth," "tolerance," "responsibility," and "wisdom." These words represented both good citizenship and the good life. Because Young began with truth and ended with wisdom, he created a self-contained value-set that endowed conservative evangelicals with better, fuller knowledge than other people. Christians were the ones who knew best what kind of country the United States had always been and so was always supposed to be. It was up to true believers—true Americans—to sober up and do the necessary voting work to restore the nation's traditional culture and work ethic.

Before taking up these keywords, however, Young engaged the rhetoric of activism with urgent, patriotic overtones. This urgency overwrote the rest of his sermon. God called Bible-believing Christians to the nation's service: "Need I mention the responsibility each one of us has to vote? Jesus said we're under the authority of our rulers. We have an opportunity in this great nation to cast a vote. And I would implore you to vote for one or the other. I wouldn't suggest . . . to go third party . . . You're wasting your vote. Also some people that I've talked to, even well-meaning Christians, [say], 'I'm just sitting this one out . . .' Well, don't do that. Twenty-five million Christians sat the bench in 2012. We're the most influential voting bloc in America. Step up and vote." Like many other pastors, Young affirmed political authority in this appeal. Even in a democratic society, evangelical political rhetoric situates citizens as under rulers—be they presidents, governors, mayors, or heads of school boards—rather than rulers as responsible to citizens. This rhetorical positioning as "under" is complicated and blurred, however, by the fact of modern democracy. Unlike in Bible times, now most citizens can vote. Caesar does not exist as an unquestioned fact that requires contention, whether or not he is just. Rather, citizens have a say in their government, and in who will represent them. This fact was obvious in Young's use of words like "opportunity" and "great nation" to describe the franchise endowed to each citizen. It became even clearer as he developed his appeal and urged his audience not to "waste" their votes on third-party protests and not to opt out of the election based on a belief that both Clinton and Trump were distasteful choices for president.

The idea that neither of the two major party candidates was suitable for the presidency ran through Young's sermon. His message was not about Clinton or Trump, in particular. Rather, his sermon was issues-based, as he defined and explained each of his keywords, and then tied these words back to his notion of a proper Christian political worldview. He encouraged his audience to think about how this Christian worldview lined up with each party platform, and then to vote with each platform in mind. Over the course of the sermon, Young decried moral relativism, marriage equality, reproductive freedom, big government, advanced education, and more. So, while the minister never overtly endorsed Trump, he created an election narrative that resembled the traditionalist, anti-elite message of the GOP and its nominee.

"The first word is 'truth,'" Young said. "Just truth." With this simple statement, the pastor moved into the main section of his sermon, which was based on word pairs and dissociations—a worldview based on "this" and "not that." He described truth as something that exists outside of individuals, while falsity embraces postmodernity and lived experience. For thousands of years, he said, humans have believed that a "transcendent God has set forth universal truths, objective truths, that are true everywhere, all the time, for yours and mine." This truth is knowable and discoverable through the Bible. Such truth is not based on feelings or individual identity. Moral relativism, in contrast, represents the opposite of truth. It is "the belief that there are no absolute or objective standards, . . . to determine right and wrong." Returning to the metaphor of a football game—and drawing a false equivalency—Young said that moral relativism would be like a quarterback who told the referee he needed seven chances to make a first down. "You know what, I'm sick and tired of four downs, I really think we should have seven downs, that's true to me," Young said, taking on the quarterback's voice and vantage point. Such a scenario would be impossible, Young continued, because it would ruin the game. "Well, in our culture, the referee [should agree], because both truth sources are equal," the pastor said. "That's insane." Offering another example, Young said that relativism is like dropping an anchor without knowing whether the chain could reach the bottom of the sea. It would not work if it was too short. The boat would bob about, adrift. He then told a story about how as a boy he had tried to make an anchor with sand and an empty bleach bottle but had failed to measure the string. When he went out to play with his invention on the local pond, he was disappointed by failure.

This easy dismissal of extra-Christian interpretations of truth provided Young with a launching pad for continuing his sermon. It made sense for him to begin with this appeal, because he was speaking as a pastor to a special (theological) audience, who were predisposed to believe in absolute, discernible and discoverable truth, as given in the Bible. This truth, however, did not merely rely on theology, although theology was present (Young cited both John 8:32 and Judges 21:25). Rather, because the pastor was also telling stories, he depended on the "good reasons" that make up evangelical political narratives. He illustrated the truth of his "good reasons" through jokes and asides to make his case about what it meant to vote as a proper Christian. He thus created a shared political identity and a social reality with his audience through theology, narrative, and laughter that reaffirmed truth as having a singular, static, and easy-to-understand meaning.[51] "As you go to the polls, think about truth," he said. "Which platform believes in . . . absolute truth? Which platform has anchors and which one is just floating on the seas of relativism?" He then encouraged everyone to think about "transcendent" truths, including love, honesty, unity, and respect for life, and said that one side—the truth side—esteemed these values, while the other did not.

The second keyword was "tolerance." As Young had done with truth, he defined tolerance in two ways, one authentic and Christian, the other inauthentic and ungodly. True tolerance, he said, was the "willingness to accept feelings, habits or beliefs" that differ from one's own. "Faux tolerance," contrarily, was "forced acceptance, approval, and applause of beliefs" that differ from one's own. Young argued that Christians should be the most tolerant of all people. However, he did not detail what that tolerance meant, beyond mere "acceptance." Instead, he situated Bible-believers as targets of intolerance: "Not only do you have to accept gay marriage, transgender bathrooms; not only do you accept people who feel that they are homosexual, or maybe they feel that they are the opposite sex, at the moment. We should accept them, that's tolerance. The faux tolerance is we should approve and applaud their behavior [*here he began clapping for emphasis*]. We need to say that they are as right as we are. Believers. Now, you've got to be kidding me. You mean the homosexual community is going to tell me that their deviant behavior is the same thing as being a minority? You've got to be [*here he inhales while pretending to hold a joint*] smoking some crazy stuff." This argument depended on two things. First was Young's earlier definition of truth. When he compared the lives of the LGBTQ community to the lives of born-again Christians, and particularly the idea that lifestyles and ways of being in the world were equal, he dismissed the possibility of equivalency with one word: "believers." Believers could be tolerant, the pastor argued, but believers also lived according to (his definition of the) truth. This truth denied the validity of LGBTQ claims to love, marriage, honesty, and unity. "Faux tolerance" was the province of the unbeliever. Second, like other pastors in my study, including Kevin Myers of 12Stone Church, Young then fortified his claim by saying, "Homosexuality is not a political issue . . . it's a Bible issue . . . Abortion is not a political issue, [either]." While tolerance might allow conservative Protestants to, well, tolerate someone who experienced gay feelings or who had exercised their rights to reproductive freedom, a true Christian could never vote for anyone who refused to renounce these practices.

One of the clearest lines of *esprit de finesse* to emerge from the recession-era sermons that I studied was the theme of personal responsibility. Conservative evangelicals in the United States routinely emphasized a narrative that prized individual obligation for success. This discourse also included vibrant language favoring free enterprise, entrepreneurialism, hard work, and private charity (as opposed to state-sponsored welfare programs). Escaping from poverty and the recession's worst effects required working, saving, tithing, and trusting God instead of the government. Young spoke about the election in a similar way.

"Do you realize the gospel—the death, burial, and resurrection [of Jesus]—is about responsibility?" the pastor asked. "I have to take responsibility for my sinfulness, for my behavior. I turn from that, turn to Jesus . . . I know the truth, and the truth sets me free." Like tolerance, responsibility as a keyword required embracing Young's definition of truth, along with the conservative evangelicals' exclusive claim to it. Truth began with confessing sin and believing in Jesus, full stop. Without this faith, there was no truth. And without this truth, there could be no taking of responsibility. Everything that followed from this claim necessarily situated Bible-believers on one side—the right side—and everyone else on the other. The responsibility to be saved, in turn, presented true Christians with other, necessary obligations: to be good citizens, to work, and to be self-sustaining.

"God gave us the desire to work before sin entered the human equation," Young said. This is a common claim in evangelicalism. Pastors sometimes explain that God Himself worked when He created the world. Others muse that God gave Adam and Eve the garden to tend as a kind of holy toil.[52] But Young skipped such appeals. Instead, he moved to make a moral argument about welfare, and suggested an epidemic of avoiding work. He quoted 2 Thessalonians 3:10 where the Apostle Paul wrote: "We gave you this rule: The one who is unwilling to work shall not eat." The audience responded with light applause. Stepping away from the podium, Young said, "We have to help . . . the downtrodden and destitute. We have to help those who can't help themselves. The physically challenged, the mentally challenged, we have to help people who cannot work." However, he continued, most people who depend on government do so because of fraud. They are lazy and have figured out how to cheat the system.

In chapters 3 and 4, I showed how pastors sometimes use dubious statistics to support their stories and claims. In crafting his narrative around responsibility, Young did this several times. He also created an imaginary monster for his audience to think of as their political enemy: Fedzilla. Fedzilla was a Godzilla-like government creature that sucked up the motivation, money, and morale of good people so that it could be redistributed to the lazy and indolent: "I read several years ago that 31 percent of Medicare is fraud. Now, those of you who have businesses, what if 31 percent of your business was fraud? . . . I mean, name one thing that the government runs that is run well—one thing.[53] Fedzilla's role is to protect. Not to rob us. We live in a free country. Yet Fedzilla has taken so much. And now when anyone achieves anything, the taxes on businesses are at the top of the world . . . Forty percent! Fedzilla! . . . [He] takes it, shifts it through the government, and then redistributes it. That's what Fedzilla does." Young's argument rested on an unarticulated but resonant story about takers in the United States who were robbing the nation of both its bounty and its spirit. The pastor did not have to explicitly tell this story for its *esprit* to ring true. He suggested that most people were takers who lacked the moral character to work and be personally responsible.[54] Young referred to this as an "assault on achievement" that came with a side of a "victim mentality." To counter this trend, and again drawing from an unspoken but still present narrative about the softness of those who rejected absolute truth and engaged in faux tolerance, Young said, "Our nation was built on taking responsibility. Our nation was not built on 'everybody gets a trophy' . . . Let's have a smaller government."

The final keyword was "wisdom." This term looped back to "truth" and so closed the circle. According to the pastor's logic, only those who acknowledged biblical truth could ever be wise because "wisdom begins with God." A fancy degree could suggest intelligence, he said, "but there are so many intellectual idiots out there . . . so many dummies with doctorates; so many loony lawyers; so many morons with master's degrees. Isn't that the truth?"

It was as though Young were quoting directly from Richard Hofstadter, the mid-twentieth-century historian who identified a "paranoid style" in politics. This paranoid style mistrusts elites of all kinds, in favor of traditional values and common sense.[55]

"Common sense is uncommon. It comes to us from our God," Young explained, once again narrowing his audience to only those ("us" and "our") who agreed with his conceptions of truth and wisdom. "It's wisdom. It's the ability to discern. The ability to negotiate the maze of life. So, you can have all the intelligence in the world and that doesn't mean a thing. We have to have wisdom." Biblical intellect, Young suggested, would lead true believers to vote according to a platform that rejected abortion, marriage equality, government spending, and gun control. It would also recognize the value of votes casts in favor of religious freedom and greater government accountability.

As Young prepared to close his sermon, he recalled the drunk fan at the football game. He said that like that spectator, American evangelicals needed to sober up and return to the truth of the Bible. Born-again believers would have to choose between misinformation—lies promulgated by a permissive culture—and wisdom and truth. "All we have to do is have the platform in one hand and the Bible in the other," he said. However, he never actually stated what it meant to vote biblically. The signifier was open. The key to understanding the message was to agree with Young's definition of each of the four keywords. It was also to affirm the longstanding *esprit* of the narrative he had presented. Young framed obligation as something individuals performed as citizens by working hard and adhering to traditional values. His sermon was, therefore, resonant with contemporary conservative political rhetoric that emphasizes individual behavior as a primary measure of good character, with limited attention to mutual obligation. While Young did briefly talk about the Christian duty to offer care to "the downtrodden and destitute," he tempered this call by overstating government malfeasance and claiming most people have what it takes to be self-sufficient. In building his homily around the four keywords of truth, tolerance, responsibility, and wisdom, Young crafted a narrative of failed obligation on the part of secular Americans. They were the ones who posed a danger to the American way of life and refused to do their part to defend the nation from cultural decay.

As the sermon concluded, Young spoke one last time about the drunk fan at the football game. However, now that fan had become a "friend" who embraced those values the pastor held dear. He "traded in his beer for ice cream and nachos and coffee . . . I watched him sober up," Young said. As the congregation clapped their approval, he said the time had come for those who agreed with him to do the same and so "turn the tide" for America.

Conclusion

Ed Young's sermon was among the most politically pointed I heard in my study. Only about 10 percent of the messages I studied during my digital rhetorical ethnography fit into this category. His was the most open in rejecting American secular culture. When he denigrated individuals who are poor or of queer identity, I found the homily hard to watch. His open assault on other hot-button topics, such as abortion, gun control, and government spending, was also unusual. For many who reside outside of the evangelical subculture, this sermon may well be what they would have expected to hear. Indeed, Young's message may represent what outsiders fear is true of conservative evangelical discourse, even while its tone gives them their own good reasons for dismissing these believers as judgmental and hardly worth getting to know. But as my research shows, many other kinds of sermons exist that use rhetorical effects similar to Young's, without being nearly so strident. For this reason, readers should be careful not to overemphasize this example, but read it in context with the others.

Indeed, Young's sermon shared *esprit* with other campaign season messages for its affirmation of Christian nationalism and waning American exceptionalism, coupled with his call to voter activism. Conservative Protestants must vote, Young said. The nation depends on their voice. All the other sermons I have analyzed in this chapter also relied on this rhetoric. However, the sermons by both Jud Wilhite and Kevin Myers were much more entrenched in the discourse of "active-passivism." This rhetoric has two essential features. First, it is grounded in conservative evangelical affinity for American exceptionalism and democracy, which insists believers should always vote as a way to show respect for the nation's founders and those who have died in defense of freedom. Voting was the hallmark of activism, of participation. Second was the acknowledgment that both Trump and Clinton were unlikable candidates, and so the 2016 presidential election presented an especially noxious choice. To overcome this, both Wilhite and Myers—along with most other ministers in my study—exhorted that God was always already on His throne, and that He would continue to be, no matter who won the election. Pastoral calls to trust, to passivism, likely gave those listeners who already identified as Republicans, and who were already predisposed to vote for Trump, even with pinched noses, final permission to do so. This reasoning provides much of the "how" of the discourse for understanding the good reasons behind the majority support of conservative evangelicals for the New York businessman, despite his many flaws as a candidate.

Yet, each of the sermons I highlight in this chapter engaged the discourse of active-passivism in a slightly different way. Wilhite depended almost entirely on a traditionalist discourse that was based on nostalgia. His Oreo cookie metaphor encouraged his audience to treat change and progress as suspect and framed the past as better than the present or even the uncertain future. He also argued that Bible-believing Christians have always been unwelcome in majority culture, going back to the earliest days. No politician is as trustworthy as God. Because of this, social and political solutions pale in comparison to individual acts of service, like the little girl in the grocery store reaching out to create community with a grieving elderly widower. For Wilhite, both citizen and Christian obligation is the product of personal service. Such narratives, while powerful, work against progressive politics that tend toward collective solutions that include safety nets and the taxes that pay for them.

Myers's sermons, in contrast, were more overtly conservative even as they sometimes suggested liberal tendencies. He developed his messages largely on the theme of race and racial tensions in the United States and, in some moments, sustained the complaint that Black Americans face more police violence and structural racism than the majority population. However, his sermons ultimately emphasized a hierarchy of arguments that situated unity as the foremost value. This privileging of unity meant Myers always chose passivism over activism, from refusing to support Colin Kaepernick's protest during NFL games, to reappropriating the Black Lives Matter movement into a positive message for youth, rather than a remonstration against police violence. In the latter case, Myers recruited men of color in his congregation to help forward this idea. I do not argue that the pastor was insincere or sinister in his intent. Rather, I suggest his rhetorical wish to defend the nation from perceived threat—too much racial strife meant lost unity—coupled with a desire to talk about the election without seeming to take sides ("we don't talk about politics") put the pastor in the position of telling a story about race that was incomplete, and that left marginalized constituents with the obligation to accept the status quo.[56]

To be clear, no pastor, no matter how influential, and no sermon, no matter how noxious, can be blamed for any particular ill effect of the election of 2016, or any other political or public event, past or future. But this is precisely the point. A conservative discourse based on personal responsibility, with inattention to vulnerable constituencies, is not the sole responsibility of any single speaker. The *esprit de finesse* of contemporary American conservatism has been created over decades by religious and nonreligious speakers alike. As the nation's largest churches have become less overtly engaged in partisan battles (while Young's sermon was pointed in tone, he is not usually so caustic), and have tried to become more "seeker friendly" in the last decades, many among their leadership have tried to exempt themselves from responsibility for the nation's divisive political discourse. I suggest it is not so easy. Whether the pastors I studied like it or not, they are already associated with the American conservative political movement and the discourse it has engendered. In 2016, Donald Trump was the presidential nominee affiliated with that movement. So, when pastors encouraged their hearers to vote but not worry, the necessary rhetorical effect was to absolve their hearers from responsibility for the votes they were getting ready to cast. While this might seem obvious, what I want to draw out is how these pastors were also muting for believers any sense of obligation to others, despite Trump's campaign language against women, refugees, immigrants, people with disabilities, people of color, and more. But votes add up, and they have consequences. Pastors had awareness of this, as is evident when they would encourage their audiences to realize their potential to form a powerful voting bloc in favor of traditional (Christian) values. Perhaps, for the pastors I studied, such values mattered most.

However, another interpretation exists. In the 2016 campaign discourse that I have presented in chapters 4 and 5, when pastors told their congregations to vote and not worry because they were citizens of heaven first and God was in control, pastors rhetorically transposed a valid theological belief in God's transcendence from a metaphysical perspective onto the individual, material votes that people were planning to cast. They recast something spiritual into something tangible. Pastors talked about American values, culture, and economics in moral and immoral terms that believers could do something about. But they talked about voting as though its outcome were out of both the individual's and the nation's control. Participation in the election was a duty; its outcome, no matter the possible harm, belonged to God. This was a lost opportunity to think through obligation and duty, whether the pastoral speakers realized it or not.

6

#MeToo Goes to Church

Eleven days after the *Washington Post* released the *Access Hollywood* tape of Donald Trump bragging about his penchant for mistreating and even assaulting women, Troy Gramling, pastor of Potential Church in Cooper City, Florida, began a three-week-long sermon series about the election. The video had seemed to change the dynamic of the campaign. In early October, Clinton led most national and swing state polls,[1] and it seemed plausible that the so-called pussy tape would solidify and widen her lead. Even Republicans had begun to distance themselves from Trump. House Speaker Paul Ryan said the remarks "sickened him" and cancelled a joint campaign appearance with the New York businessman. Senate majority leader Mitch McConnell called Trump's words "repugnant, and unacceptable in any circumstance." Trump's running mate, Indiana governor Mike Pence, said he was "offended by the words and actions described by Donald Trump . . . and [could not] defend them."[2] It did not seem like a stretch to think that the campaign was all but over, and that Clinton would win.

The tape put Gramling in a bit of a rhetorical quandary. He wanted to talk about the election and why it was of significance to both the nation and to God but, like so many other pastors in my research, he did not want to take sides or seem overly political. However, like Republican leaders and—it seems reasonable—because he identifies as a Christian, Gramling did not want to condone Trump's lewd comments. He began his sermon by calling the election "crazy." He said it left a lot of people confused about how to vote. This craziness, he said, even created a "temptation to not vote." Giving in to such temptation would be foolhardy, Gramling continued. "It's one of the ways to honor those who have given their life, for you and I to experience the freedom that we have. And so it's almost dishonoring to not participate." He next reassured those members of his audience who were unsure about how to vote. "God is in control no matter who wins this election," he said. "He's on His throne. You could even say it stronger: He is Lord." Within the first five minutes of the first in his three-week sermon series about the election, Gramling had already laid out the rhetoric of "active-passivism" that dominated so much of the discourse in evangelical megachurches in 2016. All citizens, and especially Bible-believing Christians, should vote as a matter of civic duty. But no matter who won the presidency, God was ultimately in charge of both the universe and the United States.[3]

Although the beginning of Gramling's message matched the narrative about the 2016 presidential campaign writ large that was being presented in megachurches across America, his next rhetorical move was unique. He spoke directly about the *Access Hollywood* tape and suggested that the conservative tendency to immediately defend Trump was misplaced:

> Mr. Trump says that . . . happened ten years ago, he is not that person any longer, and he says that he has apologized. You'll have to weigh [for] yourself whether or not you believe that he's changed, or if he has apologized . . . I want to talk about those who are defending him, especially Christ followers. Because we know that the words that he said were unchristian and evil . . . Now, if you want to defend him, that he is a changed man, that was ten years ago, great. If you want to say that he's apologized and we need to accept that, fine. But what I hear a lot of it is, "That is locker room talk." I hear a lot of, you know, "Bill Clinton has done far worse," and I hear a lot of, "We've all heard those kinds of words before." And I want you and I, as Christ followers, to be able to go to the water cooler . . . Or to the family reunion when it comes to our family, and not lose our credibility. See, when you use any of those excuses as a Christ follower, you lose credibility . . . It doesn't matter if you've heard those words before. As a Christ follower, we are to speak in a certain way . . . If you're going to defend him in this case, it needs to be on [the basis of] his apology and on the fact that he says he's changed.[4]

Gramling's condemnation of Trump's comments was rare among those pastors I listened to during my research. Most ministers avoided mentioning the tape. Some talked about Trump's words in comparison to perceived equal shortcomings on Clinton's part. "God is not freaking out about the election. He's not up in heaven going . . . 'More Wikileaks!'" said Todd Mullins of Christ Fellowship Church, Palm Beach Gardens, Florida. "[God's not saying,] 'Oh, I didn't know he was gonna say that!'"[5] Others, like Allan Lockerman of First Baptist Cleveland, avoided direct mention of the remarks by describing Trump's character faults, and then comparing them to personal flaws in Clinton. "We've been given two choices," he said. "The choice is between two very, very human beings . . . one who sometimes acts like a schoolyard bully and the other, people [are] saying they just can't trust."[6]

But for Gramling, Trump's words were not schoolyard bullying or something that happens in locker rooms. While he stopped short of reproving a vote for the real estate mogul, he disavowed the temptation to accept Trump's excuses for having bragged about his sexual impulses with vulgarity and the suggestion of violence. Gramling said he himself had played basketball in college and knew that "you don't have to use that language in the locker room." He rejected the moves toward false equivalency ("Bill Clinton has done far worse") that other pastors relied on to relieve tension about Donald Trump's character problems.

National evangelical figures, however, mostly deployed the discourse that Gramling disavowed. Their public conversation about Trump and his candidacy for president, even when it came to the *Access Hollywood* tape, resonated with those ministers who tried to frame Trump's comments as bad, but still tolerable, given that his opponent was also imperfect. Ralph Reed, who in 1989, together with Pat Robertson, had founded the Christian Coalition, and had said in 1998 during the Clinton-Lewinsky scandal that he would "not rest until we have leaders of good moral character," conceded Trump's remarks were "inappropriate." However, the comments were no match for Clinton's "corrupt use of her office to raise funds from foreign governments and corporations and her reckless and irresponsible handling of classified material on her home-brewed email server, endangering US national security." Franklin Graham, son of Billy Graham and an evangelist in his own right, engaged the rhetoric of equivalence exactly when he said, "The crude comments made by Donald J. Trump more than 11 years ago cannot be defended. But the godless progressive agenda of Barack Obama and Hillary Clinton likewise cannot be defended." And Robert Jeffress, a member of Trump's evangelical advisory board and senior pastor of First Baptist Church in Dallas (a megachurch), said, "While the comments are lewd, offensive, and indefensible, . . . they are not enough to make me vote for Hillary Clinton." After all, Jeffress continued, he was choosing a president, not a "Sunday School teacher." The comments were not evidence that "Hillary Clinton is more moral than Donald Trump."[7]

I begin this chapter by recalling how some conservative evangelical men responded to Trump's worst remarks about women because their overall reluctance to condemn the GOP nominee—and, indeed, their continued rhetorical embrace and justification of him—led some Christian women to speak out. The *Access Hollywood* tape marked the beginning of a discursive split between the movement's most prominent men and some of its most admired women. Popular (if also controversial) writer and blogger Rachel Held Evans took to Facebook on October 9 to urge her fellow believers against voting for Trump. "Do you really think a man who mocks people with disabilities will speak out against aborting babies with Down Syndrome? Do you really think a man who believes women are either a 'nice pieces of ass' for him to grope or 'fat, ugly pigs' for him to demean will help the pro-life movement become both pro-life and pro-woman?" she wrote. "Donald Trump is not a champion for the voiceless. He is an exploiter of the voiceless, a mocker of the voiceless. He uses people to get what he wants and he is using pro-life evangelicals to try and get the presidency."[8] Evans, who died suddenly in 2019, grew up in a conservative evangelical home and attended a conservative Bible college in Tennessee. She was a "cheerful" critic of the tendency in conservative evangelicalism to refuse women leadership positions, along with the subculture's general resistance to LGBTQ inclusion.[9] Evans joined an Episcopal church in 2014, but retained a loyal and enthusiastic following of conservative evangelical readers, some of whom found comfort in her words, while others enjoyed debating her positions.[10]

Evangelical author and speaker Jen Hatmaker was even more direct in her criticism of ongoing elite support for the GOP nominee. To those evangelical men who were defending Trump, she tweeted, "We will not forget. Nor will we forget the Christian leaders that betrayed their sisters in Christ for power."[11] She followed this with an Instagram and Facebook post on October 11 refuting Trump's words and excuses. The post included a square photo of a person with their back to the camera, wearing a tan corduroy coat and a knit cap. Across the coat the words "Don't Believe It" were written in all caps. Alongside the photo, Hatmaker wrote that it was a "national disgrace" that the GOP contender for the presidency had been caught on tape "degrading women and normalizing sexual assault." She wrote that Trump's words were "disqualifying" and that she was "sorry" for "every woman" who had ever experienced the kinds of sexual trauma the real estate mogul described. She finished her post by countering Trump's claim that his words were "locker room talk." "The hell it is," she wrote. "This wasn't 'guy banter'—this was a description of terrifying, habitual, sexually abusive behavior toward women." She urged everyone in her audience—women and men, alike—not to listen.[12]

Most prominently, Beth Moore, a prolific Bible study writer, joined the conversation. Conservative Protestant congregations across the United States, whether small or large, have long relied on scripture studies by Moore to bring women together to talk about God's word as it applies to their life. In 2020, Moore had nearly one million followers on Twitter and 485,000 on Instagram. "She's a singularly influential figure among evangelicals as a woman leader," Ed Stetzer, the executive director of the Billy Graham Center at Wheaton College, told the *Atlantic*'s Emma Green in October 2018 in a profile about Moore. "Beth just is a category by herself."[13]

Moore built this following by tying conservative theology to a conservative worldview. Though she traveled frequently and fed her own family takeout meals on a regular basis, she affirmed complementarian gender roles that included wifely submission.[14] Her Bible studies and books were both written for and marketed exclusively to women. She almost never spoke about politics before 2016. All this changed after the *Access Hollywood* tape. She had been attending a weekend ministry event when the news of Trump's comments first broke, and so she was only vaguely aware of what had happened. On her flight home, she read the story in full and saw how national evangelical leaders had justified the GOP nominee's words or said they would support him anyway. She felt betrayed and worried for the women who had shared their own stories of assault and abuse with her over the years.[15]

In response to the *Access Hollywood* tape, and apparent evangelical apathy or acquiescence to Trump's behavior, Moore tweeted out a seemingly political response—a missive of protest. "Wake up, Sleepers, to what women have dealt with all along in environments of gross entitlement & power," she wrote. "Are we sickened? Yes. Surprised? NO."[16] The tweet was not meant as an endorsement of Clinton. Instead, it was an affirmation for her female followers and, especially, a shot across the bows to let male evangelical leaders know that women were watching. Moore, one of conservative Protestantism's best storytellers, was asking the movement's men to incorporate into their narratives an accounting of some of evangelicalism's own wrongs. These included a culture that allowed women to be demeaned in the name of submission and abused in the name of obedience. She—more than Hatmaker or Evans, who had both transgressed conservative Protestant theology at other times and in other ways[17]—had a solid standing and so the most rhetorical agency inside the subculture to speak back to male power. She had always been a "good girl" who agreed to the rules. This positioned her to make plain how the rules had to change.[18]

In the aftermath of speaking out, Evans, Hatmaker, and Moore all lost followers on social media.[19] Trump won the election. The large majority of conservative Protestants found their way to voting for Trump. But the cracks in the movement were real. In the remainder of this chapter, I briefly examine how Trump's debasement of women offers a lens of rhetorical ambiguity worthy of examination. Although much of the narrative I found in my research was consistent across congregations and years, the story that began to emerge from women in conservative American evangelicalism in the aftermath of the *Access Hollywood* tape acknowledged new plotlines. Like their male counterparts, the women who engaged in public dissent affirmed American exceptionalism and celebrated the promise of American democracy. They acknowledged God's grace and love as omnipresent in the life of the believer. However, women also spoke about systems of abuse and their own personal encounters with sexual harassment and sexual violence. They said they had faced harms that shaped their daily lives, including the ways they experienced the church and public sphere. Words like "patriarchy," "regret," "pain," "shame," and "silencing" emerged into the evangelical discourse. Jen Hatmaker, who followed up her rejection of Trump by revealing that she believed there was a spot in heaven for those who identify as LGBTQ, wrote on Good Friday 2017 that "things died during the election season . . . The Christian Machine malfunctioned, and we are all still staring at each other, trying our damnedest to figure out how we understand the gospel so differently, unsure if we will ever find our way back to each other."[20]

Disrupting the Narrative

In chapter 3, I discussed Kenneth Burke's rhetorical theory of guilt, redemption, and purification. I noted that recession-era sermons made use of this type of argumentative logic. America had been ordained by God to be exceptional and great. Citizens had failed to live up to this calling, and so the recession had happened. Redemption would come when God's people turned back to Him and lived according to His rules. This prescriptive narrative included traditional values like heteronormative marriage, conventional gender roles, the Protestant work ethic, and an affirmation of free market capitalism. Similar themes dominated the stories of pastors throughout my research. Whether pastors mentioned them specifically as a way out of the recession or suggested that the way to "make America great again" was to remember the country's "true" founding, ministers relied on tales that framed old-fashioned virtues as godlier—and so more authentically American—than progressive values like equality, diversity, or enhanced opportunity.

However, there is another part of Burke's theory that has entered the evangelical discourse in the aftermath of Trump's win: ambiguity. Ambiguity in discourse allows for disruption in seemingly set narratives. With ambiguity, a story with clear and predictable patterns is open for reassessment. Previously hidden nuances come to the fore.[21] In the case of the 2016 election and the women's and #MeToo movement that followed Trump's ascension to the presidency, conservative Protestant women in the United States began a new and ambiguous public conversation.

There were pro-life evangelical women who fought to be part of the Women's March on Washington on January 21, 2017, the day after Trump's inauguration—not as protesters, but as participants. Born-again women started professional mentoring organizations with credos similar to Sheryl Sandberg's popular advice in her book *Lean In*. Others advocated publicly for paid maternity leave.[22] Then came October 2017 and the Harvey Weinstein sexual abuse scandal. Weinstein's fall from his powerful position in the world of Hollywood prompted women across the world to flood Twitter with stories of their own experiences of sexual assault and abuse alongside the #MeToo hashtag. Soon a number of men across media and popular culture were exposed as predators and expelled from their industries. They included Kevin Spacey, Matt Lauer, Charlie Rose, Garrison Keillor, Steve Wynn, and more. As this happened, women who had been hurt inside the church took notice. Two in particular, Hannah Paasch and Emily Joy, launched a hashtag of their own, #ChurchToo.[23] They encouraged survivors of abuse inside conservative evangelicalism, and those who had left because of mistreatment, to speak out and tell their stories. Women (and some men) responded with accounts of rape and assault at the hands of pastors and church elders. They likewise tweeted about how mores of "purity culture" (saving sex for after marriage and only having sex within the confines of heteronormative marriage) made the shame stronger and the impulse toward silence about forced sexual contact more acute.

The #ChurchToo conversation typifies Burkean ambiguity. Nonetheless, not all of the conservative Protestant women whose names I have mentioned responded in the same way, or at the same time. While Rachel Held Evans tweeted support,[24] Beth Moore did not wholly add her voice. She never tweeted with the #ChurchToo hashtag, although she does identify as a victim of sexual abuse. (Moore was abused as a child.) She co-signed a statement affirming that "#SilenceIsNotSpiritual."[25] Then came April 2018. That was when things appear to have reached a boiling point for Moore.

That month, the "Baptist Blogger" (a blog created by Benjamin Cole) released audiotapes of comments made by the then-president of the Southwestern Baptist Seminary, Paige Patterson. Patterson was regarded as a lion in the Southern Baptist Convention (SBC) because he had helped lead the effort during the 1970s to get Southern Baptists to return to the doctrine of biblical inerrancy and so reengage theological conservatism over the liberalism of their northern counterparts.[26] In the tapes that were released, Patterson advises women who were abused by their husbands that they should focus on prayer and being "submissive in every way" possible, rather than pursuing divorce. Soon thereafter, evidence emerged that he had encouraged a rape victim to forgive her assailant rather than report the crime to the police. He was fired from his seminary position for these actions, but not immediately.[27] Moore spoke out on Twitter against the conservative Protestant conversation that privileges forgiveness over the experience and pain of victims. "I'm pro marriage. Nearly 40 years of ups and downs to back that up," she tweeted. "But when we as a church culture demonize divorce as the worst possible outcome—the sin of all sins—we truly have no clue on this ever loving earth what some people are enduring. We do not submit to abuse. NO."[28]

Both Patterson and Moore had published with LifeWay, the publishing house for the Southern Baptist Convention. LifeWay was among the first to formally condemn Patterson for his remarks. Thom Rainer, founder and president of LifeWay, issued a statement that said "there is no type or level of abuse of women that is acceptable."[29] Moore followed on May 3 with a blog post to her own site at Living Proof Ministries—a Christian nonprofit she founded for sponsoring her speaking events and publicizing her Bible studies. She titled her post "A Letter to My Brothers."[30] It quickly went viral.

To outsiders, Moore's post may seem saccharine, even hard to swallow. It lacks a plaintive cry on behalf of those who have been abused, and there is no disavowal of the evangelical purity culture that some—including Paasch and Joy—claim cultivates systemic abuse because it makes women vulnerable and often frames them as responsible for male lust.[31] Instead, Moore began by affirming her lifelong commitment to the tenets of her conservative Baptist faith, including the doctrine of complementarian gender roles. This theology stems from Paul's writing in 1 Timothy 2:11–12, which holds that men lead and women serve, men dictate and women submit.[32] "Being a woman called to leadership within and simultaneously beyond those walls was complicated to say the least but I worked within the system," she wrote. "After all, I had no personal aspirations to preach nor was it my aim to teach men. . . . My unwavering passion was to teach and to serve women." It was within this context that she began writing Bible studies, work that had made her famous enough that she became a sought-after speaker and visible leader. Most men graciously allowed her to lead, so long as she stayed in her place, she explained. She had planned to wait to talk about how hard it was to be a woman in ministry "in the conservative Evangelical world" until she was on her deathbed. Delaying would have saved her the pain of being "fried like a chicken." But "recent events" (especially the revelations about Patterson) and the "harrowing" eighteen months that followed the release of the *Access Hollywood* tape convinced Moore to speak out.

Most conservative Protestant men had treated her well, Moore began. For her part, she had

> learned early to show constant pronounced deference—not just proper respect which I was glad to show—to male leaders and, when placed in situations to serve alongside them, to do so apologetically. I issued disclaimers ad nauseam. I wore flats instead of heels when I knew I'd be serving alongside a man of shorter stature so I wouldn't be taller than he. I've ridden elevators in hotels packed with fellow leaders who were serving at the same event and not been spoken to and, even more awkwardly, in the same vehicles where I was never acknowledged. I've been in team meetings where I was either ignored or made fun of, the latter of which I was expected to understand was all in good fun. I am a laugher. I can take jokes and make jokes. I know good fun when I'm having it and I also know when I'm being dismissed and ridiculed. I was the elephant in the room with a skirt on. I've been talked down to by male seminary students and held my tongue when I wanted to say, "Brother, I was getting up before dawn to pray and to pore over the Scriptures when you were still in your pull ups."[33]

With this paragraph, Moore painted a picture of submission. She began by acknowledging the difficulty of the subject—the tenuous relationship between men and women in the theologically conservative church. She also acknowledged the truth of the tension. She even allowed for it to be God's will that men are above women.

However, Moore also used this paragraph to begin a slow process of showing how men had used their authority to disrespect and abuse her. Recall the title of the post: "A Letter to My Brothers." Although Moore's typical audience is evangelical women, Moore meant to speak as a representative of these women, to men, particularly men in power. This is easy to forget, but the revolutionary nature of the post only holds so long as this audience remains present. For other audiences, particularly external, nonevangelical audiences, Moore's writing is likely to register as barely revolutionary, even weak.[34] For those inside the evangelical community, however, Moore is among the best known and most visible women alive. If she can be rendered invisible, silenced, or condescended to by men decades younger with less well-known names and credentials, any—and so every—woman in the community is vulnerable. The power of her story is in its mundanity. As a woman among men, she is an elephant (easily noticed as different), but also delicate (wearing a skirt). This is how they have always seen her.

As the post continued, Moore wrote that she tolerated the misogyny and reproach she faced because "anyone out in the public eye gets pelted with criticism." She loves what she gets to do and "would not trade lives with a soul on earth." She "accepted the peculiarities accompanying female leadership in the conservative Christian world," even when she did not wholly share the beliefs these peculiarities were rooted in, because she thought they stemmed from deep convictions with which she happened to disagree. Sometimes the battle was not worth risking the chance to keep fighting in the war.

But then came Donald Trump and #MeToo, Moore wrote. As the election and its aftermath unfolded, she realized that more than conviction drove conservative Protestant misogyny. Instead, the abuse was the fruit of bad behavior—of "sin." This was among "the most demoralizing realizations of [her] adult life." Here, Moore made an argument based in degree. She accused her male readers of allowing, at best, or engaging in, at worst, a "colossal disregard and disrespect of women." Moore used the superlative ("the most demoralizing")—something she usually reserved for God in her writing—to describe a feeling she had about treatment by men, toward women, and for being a woman. For male readers, this had to be shocking. She then leveraged her role as a female leader to specifically address these male offenders. Again, in a complementarian system that depends on the words "submit" for women and "lead" for men, Moore's language was bold and telling.

"I cry foul and not for my own sake," she wrote. "I do so for the sake of my gender, for the sake of our sisters in Christ and for the sake of other female leaders who will be faced with similar challenges." Moore then relayed a personal anecdote that exemplified the treatment she was writing about, and so created a shared reality with her readers, this time likely those who were female. Her words operated as an empathic call to community, even as they also produced shame in those men who may have behaved similarly or failed to speak out when witnessing such behavior: "About a year ago I had an opportunity to meet a theologian I'd long respected. I'd read virtually every book he'd written. I'd looked so forward to getting to share a meal with him and talk theology. The instant I met him, he looked me up and down, smiled approvingly and said, 'You are better looking than ______.' He didn't leave it blank. He filled it in with the name of another woman Bible teacher." This anecdote articulated into both the #MeToo and the #ChurchToo movements. Moore's experience resonated as current (it had happened only a year before), believable (it was neither out of the ordinary nor over the top), and painful (her disappointment in finding out someone she had respected was a cad comes through). By telling this story, she positioned herself among the many women whose lives had been touched by men's bad behavior, though she wrote from a place of privilege as one of the few female voices that was more likely than not to be heard in the culture of conservative Protestantism. The anecdote could not function on behalf of all women, precisely because it belonged to Moore and was not especially graphic.

Rather than detail the horrors of rape and abuse that others had described with the #MeToo and #ChurchToo hashtags, Moore conceded that her story might "seem fairly benign in light of recent scandals of sexual abuse and assault." This move drew victims of worse crimes into her circle and endowed their accounts with gravity and power, while forcing her male readers to see that every act of misogyny—whether in thought, word, or act—grew "from the same dangerously malignant root." She closed by granting that those men most apt to take her seriously likely "do not possess a whit of the misogyny" she condemned. She asked them to become more aware of how "churches quick to teach submission are often slow to point out that women were among the first followers of Christ." In drawing on the life narrative of Jesus, Moore placed women at His forefront and asked her readers to do the same. This worked to rhetorically affirm their place in the gospel, as well as to legitimize their stories of shame and pain. Tying her call immediately back to Christ's work and relationship with women made plain how urgent and real was the need to take seriously women and their stories of misuse, exploitation, and violence, perhaps especially because she was writing for those men she believed were less guilty of obviously abusive behavior. For too long, she wrote, those with power and a voice had failed to speak up for those in harm's way. In this failing, she included herself. This move once again created a new audience of the powerful with the ability to effect change, should they choose to act, as opposed to those who must wait for such action. "My acquiescence and silence made me complicit in perpetuating an atmosphere in which a damaging relational dynamic has flourished," she wrote. "I am grateful for the privilege to be heard . . . I long for the day . . . when we can sit in roundtable discussions to consider ways we might best serve and glorify Christ as the family of God."

By closing with a symbol of a roundtable, Moore ended with an image of equality in which, as Paul writes in Galatians 3:28, "There is neither Jew nor Gentile, neither slave nor free, nor is there male and female, for . . . [all are] one in Christ Jesus." Again, for those outside of the evangelical subculture, this may seem mundane and straightforward. However, a roundtable works to undo complementarian theology. Without a head at the table, women are equal to men. No one is first, no one is last. For this to happen, male leaders of the movement must recognize sexual assault and acknowledge the legitimacy of female shame and pain. Women must matter as whole members of the community. In a culture steeped in traditional gender roles, these are radical words. Her post elucidated a problem long hidden and set it into the evangelical system and structure. It augmented longstanding sexual violence with legitimacy. As such, Moore framed wounds that were at least partly justified through scripture—abuse disguised as submission—into what they actually were—harms of violence and exploitation. In so doing, she claimed authority for herself and her own experiences, and she also elevated the experiences of sexual abuse and harassment that other women had experienced. She made it safe for others to speak out, as well.

Moore tweeted a link to her post that was liked more than 13,000 times and retweeted nearly 4,000 times.[35] Russell Moore (no relation), president of the Southern Baptist Convention's Ethics and Religious Liberty Commission, retweeted Moore's blog and thanked her for encouraging him during a difficult time during his own ministry. Andrew Walker, who also works for the Ethics and Liberty Commission as policy director, noted that Moore wasn't even asking for anything "extraordinary. It's simple decency, kindness, and respect." Pastor Thabiti Anyabwile, who is African American, was most extensive in his public apology. Anyabwile, who is on the board of the Gospel Coalition, said he regretted his silence, his complicity, and his complacency. "I've been in rooms where your name was mentioned with disparaging tone. And rather than ask a few basic questions . . . I said and did nothing," he wrote in a public letter asking for forgiveness. "I wasn't any different from Saul standing by holding clothes while Stephen was stoned."[36]

The viral nature of Moore's blog and coincident tweet, along with the responses it engendered, made clear she had touched a nerve. Its *esprit de finesse* reached out to the community of minds that exists among those evangelical and "exvangelical" women who had been tweeting and Facebooking under the #ChurchToo hashtag. Moore invited those women to join her narrative with their own stories. Jen Hatmaker tweeted to Moore an account of a time when she had been invited to preach at a church. The pastor had told the men in attendance she was there to share with the "ladies" and had said the men could "peek over their shoulders" until Hatmaker was finished. She said the minister's words were "condescending, shocking even since he invited me to preach." Kaitlin Curtice, a Native American Christian writer, tweeted that the culture of conservative Protestantism had "embedded [the notion that women] don't matter." She added that when she spoke at a recent retreat and her male colleagues greeted her with respect, "it actually surprised [her]" and made her cry. Less famous voices tweeted their endorsements of Moore's post, passed along their condolences for how she had been treated, and told of their own sadness for the sexism present in the church.[37]

Moore's post was only one example of how the narrative inside evangelicalism was becoming less prescribed and more ambiguous. Other women also revealed their own experiences of abuse and were heard. In February 2018, Andy Savage of Highpoint Church in Memphis resigned after admitting to having sexually assaulted a seventeen-year-old girl when he was a youth pastor two decades earlier.[38] The biggest news came in August 2018, when Bill Hybels, one of the pioneers of the megachurch and seeker-friendly missions movement, was forced from Willow Creek Community Church, near Chicago, after being accused by multiple women of sexual misconduct.[39] Nonetheless, white, conservative evangelicals remained one of Donald Trump's and so the GOP's biggest sources of support—at least so far as the polls went. But the ambiguity sparked among women was real, and ongoing.

#ChurchToo Goes to Wheaton

In summer 2018, Justice Anthony Kennedy retired from the Supreme Court. To replace him, Donald Trump nominated Brett Michael Kavanaugh, a federal judge for the District of Columbia Circuit of the US Court of Appeals. During Kavanaugh's confirmation process, Christine Blasey Ford, a professor and research psychologist, came forward with an account accusing Kavanaugh of attempted rape in high school. She was criticized by some on the Right for waiting so long to speak out. In response, the #WhyIDidntReport hashtag went viral on Twitter. Survivors of assault erupted with their own stories of sexual violence and the subsequent shame, fear of being disbelieved, vulnerability, and humiliation that kept them from reporting their stories. Once again, Beth Moore contributed her own account to the discussion.

"He lived in my house," she tweeted. "#whyididntreport."[40]

Her message was retweeted 1,800 times and liked more than 11,000 times. Moore's five-word missive revealed a shared pain that exposed, yet again, a different conservative evangelical public conversation from the one happening at front stage in the public sphere. That one framed conservative Protestant believers as mostly in support of Kavanaugh's nomination, despite the allegations against him. His conservative bona fides against abortion and in favor of the traditional family and limited government meant his alleged past actions could be forgiven.[41] But the truth was more complicated. As the *Washington Post* reported, some born-again women talked about Kavanaugh using language similar to the active-passive rhetoric I have described. Speaking in reference to his confirmation hearings and, specifically, to a tension-filled day when Ford and Kavanaugh had both testified before the Senate Judiciary Committee, one woman told *Washington Post* reporters Samantha Schmidt and Michelle Boorstein, "No hearing will thwart the will of God for the court . . . What God intends is far more just—and God knows what happened or didn't with Dr. Ford and Judge Kavanaugh."[42] Another took to the *Huffington Post* to explain how purity culture had created an atmosphere in conservative evangelicalism that made women ready to see sexual assault as their fault. Under this logic, even if Kavanaugh had assaulted Ford, she must have been asking for it. "In our world, we were taught that our bodies [don't] belong to ourselves. God owned them [but that really] meant that men owned them. Our fathers. Our pastors. Our husbands. Our politicians. Never ourselves," wrote Carly Gelsinger. She then described being "violently assaulted" when she was fifteen. Rather than go after her attacker, Gelsinger's youth leaders wondered what she had been wearing. She knew the message was to keep quiet and fix herself. "I shut up about that assault for a good decade after that."[43]

In the aftermath of Kavanaugh's confirmation and, especially, the growing #ChurchToo movement, the Billy Graham Center at Wheaton College announced in October 2018 that its final conference of the year would be a summit on sexual violence and the conservative Protestant church. More than 700 attendees gathered on December 13, 2018, at Edman Chapel on the Wheaton campus for "Reflections: A GC2 Summit on Responding to Sexual Violence." I was among those who attended. Thousands more watched online. Those who spoke in front of Christmas trees and holiday wreaths included Max Lucado, a Texas pastor and best-selling evangelical author—who revealed during his talk that he had been abused as a child—and Eugene Cho, former pastor of Quest Church in Seattle, a rapidly growing congregation that occupies the building of Mars Hills Church, which has dissolved in the aftermath of Mark Driscoll's resignation amid controversy surrounding his leadership style, including abusive treatment of women.[44] But most of the speakers were women (eleven out of fourteen), many of whom were also survivors of sexual assault. Beth Moore spoke second.

The day was not without criticism. Neither Paasch nor Joy was included among the speakers, for example. Many of those who did take the stage focused on forgiveness and the problem of individual sin.[45] None spoke out against patriarchy, or suggested that the discourse emphasizing sexual purity in the church might have to change. Moore spoke with force. She insisted that believers could no longer look away or feign ignorance. "I believe we will be held responsible for knowing," she said. "All that is left for us to hide behind in the midst of all this exposure is a blindfold we wrapped around our own heads." A call to conservative Protestants to recognize and see hurting women was the primary warrant of Moore's twenty-five-minute address. Sexual violence is hard to look at, she said. But ignorance is evil. To illustrate this truth, she talked about the 2015 Oscar-winning film *Spotlight*. The movie made plain how priests had been able to abuse hundreds of children because so many of Boston's Catholic citizens had stood idly by. "Light that spares itself awareness of the darkness has moved from the doors and windows to airless inner offices where it becomes nothing more than a fluorescent bulb, turned on and off by a switch, possessing not a whit of holy fire," she said.

By allowing for the presence of darkness inside the church, Moore was again differentiating her audience in her speech, and calling out to different kinds of Christian listeners. One audience was victims of abuse. Another was those who protected abusers, whether they meant to or not. To distinguish between the two, Moore brought to mind the metaphor of darkness and light, a frequent theme in the Bible.[46] Christians are called to be light to the world. Victims of sexual crimes, however, typically suffer from shame, humiliation, and self-silencing. They remain in darkness, both by choice, and by systems that keep them there. This darkness undoes the virtue—the very possibility—of light. Having begun with this narrative based in metaphor, Moore answered the unasked but often present questions: Why do victims stay silent? Why don't they report what has happened? What do they have to lose? She answered: "Victims fear incurring the wrath of God . . . They fear losing the only community they have. They fear being the downfall of the church. They fear not being believed. They fear being blamed and shamed and named. Their fears have too often proved founded." Moore situated victims as being afraid of losing everything, for nothing. The seriousness of this threat seems clearer if we return to her first metaphor and recall the scene of a light flicking on and off in an interior office, and then imagine a scared victim of assault hunched inside, scared but seen only in flashes. This victim may also rely on another—the one who opens the door—for the presence of light. The abused has little control over the light, when or if it is turned on, or whether the office door remains shut, locked, and so darkened for good.

Moore concluded her remarks by challenging her audience to stop confusing sexual immorality with sexual criminality. Here, again, for those outside of the conservative evangelical subculture, her words may ring hollow or half-hearted. Critics insist change is impossible until leaders like Moore disavow purity culture along with the born-again commitment to heteronormative sexual politics. When shame becomes intensified because sexual abuse is happening outside of marriage, and because sex itself is hard to talk about inside a community that can only imagine its act occurring in one legitimate way, these critics have a point. However, setting these reproaches to the side for now, Moore was still able to speak to the problem of the system, and how it had to change. She talked about her own experience of abuse, and how the church was a place of respite for her. "I have often wondered what a difference it might have made if that safe harbor had not only been a place to hide but a place to heal," she said. "What if I'd heard my pastor or my teachers or any of my leaders address what I was going through, call it what it was, say that I wasn't to blame and not to be ashamed?"

Moore closed by telling a story of meeting a ten-year-old girl and her mother at one of her events. The mother told Moore that the child had been sexually abused. Moore described her sadness at knowing the girl would have to carry a burden like the one she had carried, but "as much as I wanted to weep, this was no time for that. It was not what she needed from me." Moore told her young friend she would learn to hold the abuse as a gift because it would teach her "how precious" she is to Jesus. "Somebody very wrong made us feel really small, but now we get to learn how to stand really, really tall." By retelling this anecdote, Moore created a community with children and with her audience, and rhetorically generated a sense of having to choose between despair and hope. How many more children would find themselves in interior offices without light, waiting for someone to open the door? How many would have to find a strength they did not know they had? By beginning the close of her talk wondering how her life would have been different had her own church been more than a refuge, but rather a place for healing, and ending with the image of a child now facing a similar journey, Moore revealed conservative evangelical Protestantism as in need of systemic change, with a long and ongoing problem of sexual violence toward children and women. Nobody was safe. Ever faithful, Moore had hope in the gospel. Others worry that nothing will change, that the movement will give out to hypocrisy and crumble under its own weight.[47]

Conclusion

For many women who have objected to the hegemonic narrative happening inside conservative evangelicalism, particularly since the election of Donald Trump, a conversation around safety and valuing female voices and contributions has been gaining strength. Whether this ambiguity in the narrative will show up at the ballot box has yet to be seen. In the 2018 midterm election, three-quarters of white conservative Protestants voted for Republican candidates, according to Pew, and about the same number had at least a somewhat favorable view of the president, according to NBC News.[48] But there is a new narrative at hand, being composed by female writers. These women share the same stories of faith that come from the pastors I highlighted in chapters 3–5. For this reason, their objections are worth noticing. Will their rhetoric of ambiguity create lasting fissures or engender lasting change?

One thing seems sure: the early conversation that was mostly about sexual assault in the church and disgust over conservative evangelical willingness to look past Donald Trump's most objectionable behavior has motivated born-again women to agitate about other issues. In the leadup to 2018, even politicians who tried to align themselves as evangelical stalwarts found themselves facing opposition from women of faith. In Republican Texas, the *New York Times* featured a story about white conservative Protestant women who backed El Paso Congressman Beto O'Rourke in his race for the Senate over Ted Cruz. Cruz made headlines in 2016 as Trump's longest standing challenger for the GOP presidential nomination. He ran as a social values conservative. He made his opposition to the Supreme Court's decision in favor of marriage equality central to his campaign.

Among those who supported O'Rourke was Tess Clarke. Clarke, who lives in Dallas, told *Times* reporter Elizabeth Dias that before 2016 she had always voted for Republicans, and she had done so mostly because of the abortion issue. But the presidency of Trump and, especially, the policy of separating migrant and refugee children from their parents, which came to light during the summer of 2018, led her to rethink this support.[49] She described as mortifying her previous, automatic backing of the GOP based solely on the abortion issue. "I care as much about babies at the border as I do about babies in the womb," she was quoted as having said in the *Times* article. "We've been asleep. Now, we've woke up."[50]

This "waking up" meant expanding the universe of issues about which evangelicals cared and about which they wanted to tell stories, including immigration. Clarke had long been an advocate for refugees. She and her husband, Jason, lived for a while in low-income housing in Dallas to be available to give hands-on help to people who had only recently arrived in the United States. After having children themselves, they moved to a house nearby, but still made time to give advice and assistance to anyone who asked.[51] She went to the border during the separation crisis in the summer of 2018 and felt outraged. Her indignation deepened when a male member of her church told her it was not possible to be a believer and vote for a Democrat.

Clarke and several of her friends were interviewed for the *New York Times* article. They talked about how they had become open to the possibility of voting for Democrats because of Trump's behavior on the campaign and during his presidency, and not entirely out of opposition to Ted Cruz. Some, though not Clarke, were forced by their husbands to keep their Leftish conversions under wraps. Clarke hoped that women speaking out would allow the narrative to open. "My hope would be that women in similar places as us would feel liberated from the expectation that you're just doing the same thing you've always done, because it's safe, because it's what your pastor is telling you to do, or your husband," she told reporter Dias. "We have to own it."[52]

We have to own it. This sentence signifies the essential truth about the new ambiguity in the conservative evangelical narrative and that is being driven primarily by women. These individuals, who are both insiders and outsiders of the subculture, at once, have the necessary agency to force open the stories to include new plotlines and actors. In the 2018 midterm election, the votes went mostly the same, although, as I noted previously, only 75 percent of conservative evangelicals voted for the GOP, as opposed to 81 percent who went for Trump in 2016. This six-point decline in support is potentially significant. More important is whether this one subordinated group—women—will speak up loudly enough, and with enough conviction, on behalf of other subordinated groups to make a difference, whether those groups are composed of people who identify as abused, abandoned, poor, young, immigrant, disabled, gay, or some intersectional component of all of these. To make this happen, they will have to own it.

Conclusion

When I began to ask the questions that finally led to this book, there was nothing in my imaginary that foresaw Donald Trump as president. It was 2010, and Barack Obama was still in his first term. But this is the nature of research. As Valerie Hartouni once wrote, "Rare is the case that the end we imagined at the beginning of a project is the end that we find or that finds us once all is at least provisionally said and done."[1] I can still see myself, in my mind's eye, on some of those runs I took during the early phases of my research, listening to the very first sermons I found, even though I long ago erased the contents of those messages from my iPod, and then stopped using that device altogether. I had no idea then how valuable those homilies would eventually become. The trail I was embarking on was still dark. Indeed, I had no intention of following it through to where it has now led. I was thinking about leadership discourses, conservative social movements, the Tea Party, and whether the fight over marriage equality—I had worked hard on the campaign against Proposition 8 in California—would push young, conservative Protestants to the Left. Emergent research suggested that queer issues, along with environmentalism, might have that effect.[2]

But then, this is not really a book about Donald Trump or the Tea Party. This is a book about conservative evangelical rhetoric, and the people who bring this rhetoric to life. No matter who wins the White House in the next or future elections, this constituency of voters will remain important to the American public sphere. While others who study politics may think issues like abortion, marriage equality, tax policy, and so on best explain the political inclinations of conservative Protestant voters, students of rhetoric know that stories prevail over facts, and narratives triumph over data. Stories are what make us human. They join us to our communities. They help us make sense of our beliefs. They order our lives. And the more a story gets repeated, the more a story rings true. The more a story rings true, the more it gets repeated. This is the nature of Pascal's *esprit de finesse*.

Among the most important narratives to emerge during the time of my digital rhetorical ethnography was the rhetoric of active-passivism. This rhetoric emphasized citizen participation and duty as necessary, but also privileged God's providence as sufficient for true Christian believers. The recession-era sermons I described in chapter 3 were replete with activism and reminders about God's will and authority. Pastors foregrounded the believer's obligation to work hard, delay gratification, and uphold the nation's founding values, all the while remembering that suffering is something that happens elsewhere—outside of the United States. By advancing these virtues, Bible-believers could restore America to its rightful place as the most blessed nation on earth. But by the time of the presidential campaign between Clinton and Trump, the emphasis had slipped to passivism. In chapters 4 and 5, I showed how pastors developed narratives that limited the believer's duty to voting, which was patriotic and necessary. Megachurch ministers urged evangelicals to cast ballots to show their gratitude to the founders for having gifted Americans with the Constitution, as well as to veterans for having died to preserve democratic freedom. But this call to participation was narrowly tailored. Once the voting was over, pastors encouraged their hearers not to worry about the result. Whatever happened, God was on the throne and tending to the polity that truly counted: heaven.

Under the rhetoric of active-passivism, megachurch pastors were able to rank priorities for evangelical hearers and so to hide, even unwittingly, some constituencies from consideration, even if such constituencies were vulnerable and needed defense or protection. In chapter 5, for example, I wrote about Trump's attacks on refugees and people of color and suggested that pastors privileged narratives of Christian unity as being more important to God, and so more important to voters, than protests and other acts of dissent. To be clear, I do not argue that the pastors of the nation's largest churches do not care about vulnerable constituencies, marginalized people, or real harms like racism in the United States. On the contrary, I believe that they do. Rather, I argue that ministers often subordinate these concerns to other anxieties. When megachurch pastors talk about the American public sphere and American political issues, the constituent of foremost concern is always the nation itself. Defending the country and maintaining its presumed exceptional status always comes before any person or group, no matter how at-risk they may be. Indeed, the warrant of exceptionalism does double duty for conservative Protestants. First, it fuses together their faith and their patriotism. Second, it allows them to create a story about the country such that no one should be at risk or in need in the first place, because there is always already enough for everyone. This notion of "always already enough" works to relieve Bible-believers of responsibility for helping individuals in need and frees them from seeing large institutions or structures that might be causing harm. The very fact of national abundance means that any person in a condition of vulnerability must necessarily be in that condition from having engaged in bad actions or from having made bad choices. The responsibility is not on the evangelical believer to find ways to change systems or to support (or even see the need for) structural change. The responsibility is on the individual in harm's way to do better and choose better—ideally with God's help.

This, then, is the key tension and disconnect between those inside conservative evangelicalism and those outside it. In chapter 1, I wrote that among the key questions of those seeking to understand the political priorities of Bible-believers who vote for Republicans is this: why is a party that seems to be against poor people supported by those whose faith includes a specific call to care for poor people? To answer this question, I have forwarded in these pages their narratives—what I have called their storytelling "how." This discourse frames the United States as both exceptional and at risk, the best of all lands and in constant need of defense. The country itself is the constituency evangelicals prioritize and for which they vote. But for those outside the subculture, the point is almost always the people—they are the ones in need. For those inside, the point is the nation. The individuals at risk, if they are spoken of at all, are framed in the story as characters contributing to decline, who need to do better, to set the nation back on its providential trajectory toward exceptionalism.

A Question of Agency

The rhetoric of active-passivism is itself a narrative. In the introduction, I briefly mentioned Paul Ricoeur's theory of emplotment. Emplotment, for Ricoeur, was the process by which individuals make meaning of their lives. Moments that may actually have little to do with one another become connected when people look back over them and create plausible stories and narratives.[3] Sometimes this is easy to do. For example, I might say that today I had breakfast, drove to work, and then had a meeting with my boss. These are all things that happened, and none may be especially noteworthy.

However, in a phone call with my friend I might explain that I spilled egg on my blouse and almost ran a red light, all because I was nervous about asking for a raise. Now I have engaged in emplotment. My nervousness about asking for a pay raise has become the meaning behind three events that, at first, were typical, but not necessarily related. According to Ricoeur, the creation of these narratives is the ongoing experience of being human, and is also how we create communities and social worlds. The things that happen to us are also stories waiting to be told—moments we share with our neighbors, partners, students, and friends.

However, for born-again Christians, God's hand is in everything. Events are always related, can be explained, and have cosmically significant meaning. This is the ultimate message of the rhetoric of active-passivism. Through it, pastors were able to argue that regardless of what happens—whether in one's own life, in an election, or in the future—God is already, and will always be, in control. Whether we are thinking about a national recession, the race between Donald Trump and Hillary Clinton, or some other event down the road, no option exists but for God to have a plan that He will see through to completion. As evangelical megachurch pastors set about telling a story about American politics during the first decades of the twenty-first century, they were forced, in the words of William Dowling, to create a narrative that would drive the "story toward an anticipated conclusion."[4] Such a conclusion had to be based in providence and exceptionalism in order to maintain a shared sense of the American past, while privileging traditional values and American hegemony to defend against seeming irrelevant, wishy-washy, or hypocritical. Under active-passivism, the anticipated conclusion was twofold. On the one-hand, it allowed believers to claim they were the ones on the side of providence in the election. On the other hand, it allowed them to divest interest in the outcome of politics, in favor of heaven and eternity.

This divestiture of interest was, rhetorically, a divestiture of agency. As a critic, this was both the most surprising and the most difficult finding to sort out during the years of my digital rhetorical ethnography. Agency is at the heart of both political and democratic theory. It is the reason why voting is an essential human right in a democracy. Among the foundational assumptions at work in both the humanities and the social sciences is that people want ultimate control over their own lives.[5] Moreover, being free and having agency are good. These ideals make self-determination possible, and self-determination is among democracy's highest goals. Political rights to speech, religion, association, representation, and so on are the reinforcement of political and human agency. These endowments assure us that we are equal in the eyes of the state, and that state authority responds to the will of the people, rather than the other way around. When the megachurch pastors to whom I listened told stories based on founders' rhetoric, and talked about how the nation was originally made as Christian and free, they were drawing on idealized frames of political theory that include political agency as a moral good.[6]

In using the term "agency," I have in mind Karlyn Kohrs Campbell's definition that it is the "capacity to act, that is, to have the competence to speak and write in a way that will be recognized or heeded by others in one's community."[7] This definition is useful for its emphasis on action (capacity), ability (competence), and community. Such competence is not merely skill or proficiency. Rather, Campbell urges that agency requires the coming together of possibility and capacity so that—and this is key—one's community will be willing to recognize and heed one's words. Joining Campbell's notion of rhetorical capacity and competence with the political ideal of self-determination I highlighted previously suggests that being a wholly realized person means being able to speak and then register one's civic priorities to others who are, at a minimum, willing to listen.

The rhetoric of active-passivism, however, obfuscates this sense of civic wholeness. When pastors encouraged their audiences to vote (speak) but not to worry because God was in control, they were encouraging their hearers to cede not only responsibility, but also agency. This is profoundly confusing, even if it also makes sense.[8] As I suggested earlier, and as Campbell also writes, agency is the sine qua non of life.[9] Agency is an essential condition. There is no freedom without it. We expect people to want agency, and to rebel against not having it. This is a crucial tension in the rhetoric of active-passivism. It allows for action, but denies agency. Its logic permits speakers to forsake calls to obligation or even to relinquish deep interest in the consequences of their words.

In chapter 5, I wrote that when conservative evangelicals embraced a rhetoric of passivism, they were embracing a valid theological belief. It makes perfect sense for born-again believers, who base their lives in the authority of scripture, to look for God's will on earth. But this is a question of trust, not of democratic participation. To this critique, conservative evangelical pastors may well reply that, for them and, they hope, their fellow believers, asserting their voices and votes is not a primary value. Their gift to their community, as well as their gift to God, is to deny their agency out of submission to the One who holds the universe in His hands. "Have we begged God? Have we taken off from work and spent an entire day on our face, 'Lord, please, please,

please,'" exhorted Jonathan Pokluda of Watermark Community Church in Dallas on October 25, 2016. "Save our country. God help us. We need your help."[10] Pokluda's words are an example of how such rhetoric might sound. While the pastor was speaking about the election, his true appeal was for his audience to beg God to change their hearts, along with the hearts of their fellow citizens, so that sin, especially sexual sin, would be eradicated from the land, and the nation would be restored. When this happened, the easy result would be a return to godly leaders who would preside over a godly people. Unlikable or unfit candidates for president, like Hillary Clinton and Donald Trump, would never again be a problem.

The easy conclusion is the cynical one: Pokluda's prayer will never be answered. The conditions of postmodernity that include religious plurality, liberalized sexual mores, women's equality, and shifting notions of truth are unlikely to give way. But this is not really the point. Rather, the conservative evangelical abdication of agency is actually double, and this doubling is what makes it problematic. Active-passivism wants to have it both ways. It is a rhetoric that says, "vote but don't worry" *and* "vote because doing so could make a difference in restoring the country." In admitting that votes had the potential to influence the election, pastors conceded that the conservative evangelical vote had sway. It was significant. So, what the rhetoric of active-passivism actually does is allow Bible-believers to only pay attention to the consequences they wish.

As difficult as this assessment might sound, and even if it was unintentional on the part of many pastors, the truth is that there were constituencies at risk during the recession and during the presidential campaign of 2016, just as there will be in any future election. These at-risk constituencies are the reason outsiders to evangelicalism have sometimes found confusing the tendency of born-again Christians to support the GOP. Writers like Thomas Frank have argued that Republican policies hurt the poor, for example, while Arlie Hochschild has suggested that environmental deregulation has cost jobs and made people sicker. Yet, the conservative evangelicals they met in their research still vote and identify as conservatives.[11] In 2016, because Donald Trump's language against women, people of color, refugees, immigrants, people with disabilities, and more was so far outside the political norm, the failure of conservative evangelical pastors to at least regularly include these constituencies in their homiletic rhetoric seemed all the more striking. I suggest that because white evangelicals do have agency and power as a voting bloc, these rhetorical omissions were, indeed, problematic, if also predictable. Through their silence, pastors framed vulnerable groups as mattering less than did traditional values or than simply trusting God that things would be okay. The failure to speak out meant that groups with already limited power to act were delegitimized rhetorically for a second time.

To be clear, I do not argue that evangelical believers had an obligation in 2016, or in any election, to vote for any Democrat over any Republican. I am also not suggesting that evangelicals are responsible for any bad outcome of the 2016 election. Nor do I mean to deny agency to any group that opposed Trump, even if they operated from a space of vulnerability. Rather, I suggest that the pastors of the nation's largest churches have been telling an incomplete story about economics and politics in the United States, and this incomplete story has consequences. Especially in 2016, pastors stopped short of asking hard questions about what was really going on, or what it would mean for those in their audience to continue voting in much the same way they had always done. By using a mostly nostalgic frame about traditional values, while also promising that nothing truly terrible could happen because God was in control, megachurch preachers engaged in an emplotment about the past and the future that failed to properly account for the perilous present. The values discourse about returning to better times, which was evident in Pokluda's pleas that true believers should pray that God would heal the nation, created a story that framed the United States as having been better before. The rhetoric of active-passivism that asked believers to vote and not worry affirmed this values discourse, while also telling a story that said the future would be okay, even if nothing got better. However, besides limited conversation about the dangers of marriage equality, abortion, and creeping secular humanism, ministers tended to avoid speaking about how politics affects any community beyond the one that populated their pews and auditoriums, along with those who watched online.

For those outside of the evangelical subculture, the question is whether to try to interrupt these stories or to suggest variant plotlines. Many of the pastors in my study did express wariness about being overly partisan, along with weariness at the division in the public sphere. This could suggest a readiness to listen. The women I described in chapter 6 who are pushing back against being silenced and trying to open new dialogues about equality, feminism, and immigrant rights offer a model for how new conversations might begin. For researchers and activists, the technique I have forwarded in this book also provides a useful means for discovering pathways of conversation. What I thought I knew about conservative evangelical stories—and evangelicals themselves—at the beginning of this project, and what I think I might know now, are very different. The humility of knowledge that comes from diving deeply into a community to learn its language, its community, and its structure creates space for hearing in new ways. Active-passivism as a storyline has likely existed for a long time. However, it is also continuously being re-created anew.

In 2010, when I decided to study the narratives of conservative evangelicalism, I did so because I was an outsider. I mostly thought of evangelicals as voters—probably because this is how they tend to be framed in the media—and as having outsized power in the American public sphere. As I wrote in the introduction, I was also intrigued about why my personal experiences with Bible-believers tended not to match the way these individuals were talked about in the news and in popular culture. I wanted to understand the difference. Even so, a part of me wondered if I should be trying to join a less hegemonic movement, or be working to draw out the voices of those who had not already received so much attention.

Refining and practicing digital rhetorical ethnography has taught me that sometimes the best way to see how silencing and marginalization work is through experiencing and troubling spaces of power. It was only because I could attend church all across the country, over the course of years, and also at once, that I was able to discover the rhetoric of active-passivism, and then to find how insidious it was. Active-passivism as a narrative is uniform yet also dispersed—I heard it many times over the course of many sermons, but typically only once per megachurch that I visited. Traditional in situ ethnography or rhetorical criticism almost certainly would not have allowed for this finding. It only came from digital immersion and deep listening. Through carefully creating my own archive, and then attending to sermons empathically and methodically, I came away with an understanding of the political and economic rhetoric of American megachurch pastors—who do influence American evangelicalism writ large—that reaches beyond media sound bites and already well-known texts by already well-known speakers.

Many other such digital communities exist online for discovery, though they may not be immediately obvious. Those who wish to follow my approach might also find that what we think we know about hegemonic discourses is actually more complicated and nuanced upon closer study. While not every experience can be replicated via digitization, the fact of digital space makes it possible to move into the quiet of one's own home or office and then to go around the loudest voices in the public sphere, to enter some of the most important sites of public engagement. This act, in turn, opens possibilities for creating new conversations or suggesting new stories across constituencies.

Doing the work to discover these narratives is long and painstaking, but it reaches beyond easy understanding—and misunderstanding, as well.

Finally, during the years I was working on this book, many people asked me if there was one sermon that had stayed with me more than any other. I often demurred in answering, but the truth is, there was one. It was delivered by Nate Ross of Northside Christian Church in New Albany, Indiana, on October 28, 2016. The sermon, "Who Are You Voting For," was not exceptional because it was atypical in its message.[12] Quite the contrary: near the end of the homily, Ross referred to his audience as "ambassadors" who lived in the United States but had a true "homeland in heaven." He also said that God "was bigger than the election" and so believers should "trust Him with the results." Active-passivism. Instead, the reason the sermon stayed with me had to do with a video Ross used to set up the sermon, along with his call to humility and authentic—even rhetorical—listening.[13]

The video was nearly five minutes long and played immediately after a time of worship and prayer. Many churches in my study used similar visual aids to transition from singing and announcements to teaching. This video was different, however. It did not begin with pictures of past presidents, the Washington Monument, the US flag, or Clinton and Trump. Its purpose was not to engender feelings of pride or to reinforce American exceptionalism or a sense of duty to participate in the democratic system. Instead, as the song "Wasteland" by the Christian rock band Needtobreathe played in the background, a black screen faded onto an image of disaster outside of the United States: Hurricane Matthew raining down over the Caribbean. Images followed of Black Lives Matter protesters; a boy in Aleppo, Syria, wounded, alone, and surrounded by rubble; a grieving soldier's wife receiving a flag; a ruined mobile home park after a tornado; pro-choice activists; pro-life activists; Black bodies being held down by police; white bodies left lonely in nursing homes; and more. Through my speakers the song's lyrics played:

> All of these people I meet
> It seems like they're fine
> Yeah in some ways I hope that they're not
> And their hearts are like mine
> It's wrong when it seems like work
> To belong all I feel is hurt
> Oh, if God is on my side . . .
> Then who can be against me?[14]

The video closed with an image of a young boy, perhaps six years old, being baptized in the ocean by his parents. Before they walked into the water, the boy kissed his mom. The show of gender equality was touching and unusual to see over the course of my study. Fairly or not, almost all the sermons I discovered were given by men. When the video ended, Ross appeared onstage wearing jeans and a dark gray Under Armour polo shirt, his dark brown hair swept up into a fauxhawk. "It's been hard to watch that video all week in preparation for this sermon because we want to hang on to those words, 'If God is for me, who can be against me?'" he began. "But if we're honest . . . sometimes it doesn't [feel that way] . . . Especially as I look at that little boy [from Aleppo], I can't help but think of my little four-year-old girl, and I sit there in that moment, and . . . I'm overwhelmed by the darkness in this world."

By beginning with disconsolate images and then admitting he felt overcome by the magnitude of despair he saw—a level of brokenness that he dared not suggest he had an easy answer for, just because he was a Christian—Ross created rhetorical identification through shared experience. As a viewer, I had also watched the video and wondered how a world—and country—so filled with pain and grief could find justice or community in the public sphere. I had also thought about young people I know, my friends who have weathered storms literal and figurative, and individuals in my life on both sides of the political spectrum. Although I did not share Ross's faith, I shared his sense that the narrative, as it was being told, was wrong. By talking about and showing pictures from different perspectives—pro-life and pro-choice, a soldier's wife and the wife of a Black man who had been shot, Ross had brought into stark relief the possibility of conversation, along with the difficulty that ensues when we are asked to see and hear things outside of our own worldview.

As his sermon unfolded, Ross spoke about political conversations, and the problem of hiding rather than choosing to engage. Unlike so many pastors who used active-passivism as a way to give their audiences an easy exit from worrying about the election, Ross said that because born-again Christians had dual citizenship, their call was to be rooted in their community. "Ambassadors," he said, live in a foreign country and "speak the language." While an ethnographer is not an ambassador, this is exactly what I, too, was trying to do with the research I have presented in these pages. I have tried to bring the language and stories of conservative evangelicals to those outside of the subculture, in the hope of starting a new and more nuanced conversation. The digital church was, in some ways, a foreign country that I had to learn to navigate.

In the middle of his sermon, Ross talked about how he had initially misunderstood Black Lives Matter, but had been lucky when one of his African American congregants, an ex–football player and West Point cadet, took time to talk to him, email him, have breakfast with him, and so open his world to Black experience. Ross, a white pastor, realized he had a lot to learn about race in America. His worldview expanded when he took seriously the words of his friend. "There's beauty when we can sit down and listen," Ross said. "I'll never know [another's] story unless I'm willing to stop and [hear]."

Ross's honest evaluation of American politics, along with his willingness to take responsibility for the evangelical role in a broken system, was unusual, no doubt. He modeled candid conversation and an awareness that citizens outside of the church—and outside of the United States—might have opinions and worldviews that were different and worth hearing. He reminded me that no election is ever final, just as every story has a sequel. The *esprit de finesse* goes on.

Appendix A

RHETORICAL SAMPLE OF SERMONS FROM THE GREAT RECESSION AND RECOVERY

LOCATION	CHURCH	PASTOR	SERMON TITLE	DATE DELIVERED	GENERAL TOPIC
Alabama	Church of the Highlands	Chris Hodges	Financial Peace on Earth—Part One	December 4, 2011	Working hard
Alabama	Church of the Highlands	Chris Hodges	Financial Peace on Earth—Part Two	December 11, 2011	Spending and saving
Alabama	Church of the Highlands	Chris Hodges	Financial Peace on Earth—Part Three	December 18, 2011	Tithing
Alabama	First Baptist Church	Jay Wolf	Be Wise with Wealth	February 6, 2011	Wealth, money, the shrewd manager
Arizona	Central Christian Church	Cal Jernigan	What If: God Were Your Financial Advisor	September 16, 2012	Being faithful to God with your money; tithing
Arizona	Central Christian Church	Cal Jernigan	What If: You were Able to Live Debt Free	September 23, 2012	Debt
Arizona	Central Christian Church	Cal Jernigan	What If: Money Were No Object	September 30, 2012	Generosity

LOCATION	CHURCH	PASTOR	SERMON TITLE	DATE DELIVERED	GENERAL TOPIC
Arizona	Central Christian Church	Cal Jernigan	What If Giving Came Easily	October 7, 2012	Generosity
Arizona	Grace Community Church	Darryl DelHousaye	Kingdom Economics	November 21, 2010	Mostly tithing
Arizona	Christ's Church of the Valley	Don Wilson	Freedom	July 4, 2010	
Arkansas	Fellowship Bible Church	Mark Henry	Profile of a Sluggard	July 26, 2011	Laziness
California	Menlo Church	Scott Scruggs	Believing and Choosing	March 20, 2011	Financial priority setting
California	Menlo Church	John Ortberg	Make It All about Money	January 17, 2010	Greed
California	Menlo Church	John Ortberg	Financial Freedom	March 22, 2009	Generosity; priority setting
California	Menlo Church	John Ortberg	God's Heart for the Poor	March 6, 2010	Lazarus and the rich man; noticing those who have less
California	Menlo Church	Kevin Kim	Because Justice Matters	February 27, 2010	International issues of injustice and what a good Christian response should be
California	Menlo Church	Kevin Kim	The Power of Greed	August 19, 2012	Greed
California	Saddleback Church	Rick Warren	The Five Foundations of Financial Freedom	June 4, 2010	Getting one's finances in order, taking personal responsibility for that; five steps to getting it done
California	Saddleback Church	Rick Warren	Set Free from Me	July 10, 2011	Financial crisis; problems of self-discipline

LOCATION	CHURCH	PASTOR	SERMON TITLE	DATE DELIVERED	GENERAL TOPIC
California	San Clemente Presbyterian Church	Charlie Campbell	Make It All about Success	January 23, 2010	Problem of self; worry; selfishness
California	San Clemente Presbyterian Church	Tod Bolsinger	Raised Down to Earth	January 24, 2010	Suffering and idols
California	San Clemente Presbyterian Church	Tod Bolsinger	When What's in Your Hand Gets in Your Way	November 21, 2010	Obsession with success; feeling "owed"
California	San Clemente Presbyterian Church	Tod Bolsinger	The Most Personal Matters	February 12, 2012	Sex, money, identity
California	San Clemente Presbyterian Church	Tod Bolsinger	God Is the Boss of You	March 4, 2012	Work
Colorado	The Next Level Church	Brian Gray	Money	April 11, 2011	Money, generosity, giving
Colorado	Flatirons Community Church	Jim Burgen	Reverse Engineering: This Is What It Looks Like	January 22, 2012	Wealth, generosity, and tithing
Georgia	North Point Community Church	Andy Stanley	Momentum: Our Financial Peace Declaration	December 12, 2010	Being a slave to financial stress distracts from a fulfilling life within the community and with God
Georgia	North Point Community Church	Andy Stanley	On Location Part 1: Head Count	January 28, 2007	A little bit of righteousness goes a long way
Georgia	North Point Community Church	Andy Stanley	On Location Part 2: Being There	February 4, 2007	Righteous people are the stewards, the "salt" and the preservative of the earth

LOCATION	CHURCH	PASTOR	SERMON TITLE	DATE DELIVERED	GENERAL TOPIC
Georgia	North Point Community Church	Andy Stanley	On Location Part 3: Shine	February 11, 2007	Finding purpose in life when the "momentum years" run out
Georgia	North Point Community Church	Andy Stanley	On Location Part 4: Road Trip	February 18, 2007	A "how-to" on converting and being a light in the workplace as a means of understanding your purpose in life
Georgia	North Point Community Church	Andy Stanley	Recovery Road Part 1: We the People	August 21, 2011	How can a nation with so much wealth have a financial crisis?
Georgia	North Point Community Church	Andy Stanley	Recovery Road Part 2: Taking Inventory	August 28, 2011	Should our nation's recovery take its cue from twelve-step recovery programs? Personal recovery requires personal reflection
Georgia	North Point Community Church	Andy Stanley	Recovery Road Part 3: The Credibility Factor	September 3, 2011	Moral integrity and credibility of leaders as a remedy for national crisis
Georgia	North Point Community Church	Andy Stanley	Recovery Road Part 4: Declaration of Dependence	September 9, 2011	A call to the nation to depend on God in our time of crisis. How accurate is our national motto "In God We Trust"?

LOCATION	CHURCH	PASTOR	SERMON TITLE	DATE DELIVERED	GENERAL TOPIC
Georgia	North Point Community Church	Andy Stanley	Recovery Road Part 5: The Spending Crisis	September 18, 2011	Spending
Georgia	North Point Community Church	Andy Stanley	Recovery Road Part 6: Entitled	September 25, 2011	What will you do with what you're "entitled" to? The church can lead the way to recession recovery
Georgia	North Point Community Church	Joel Thomas	The Immeasurable Life Part 1: Immeasurably More	November 6, 2011	There is an inherent desire within all of us to desire more (materially and spiritually)
Georgia	North Point Community Church	Mike Minter	The Almighty Dollar and the Almighty God	November 21, 2010	Greed
Georgia	12Stone Church	Kevin Myers	How We Work	November 27, 2011	Budgeting, spending, wisdom
Idaho	Cole Community Church	Jackson Cramer	A Believer's View of Work	May 1, 2011	Work, employment, labor conditions
Illinois	Evangelical Free Church	Rick Wagner	Lie #4: Money Equals Happiness	November 1, 2009	Greed
Illinois	Willow Creek Community Church	Bill Hybels	Recession Lessons	February 20, 2011	Recession
Illinois	Willow Creek Community Church	Dave Ramsey	Enough	March 1, 2009	Greed, spending
Illinois	Willow Creek Community Church	Andy Stanley	In God We Trust	March 1, 2010	Debt, spending, generosity
Indiana	The Chapel	Rick Hawks	God's Wisdom on Money, Part 6	February 12, 2012	God's money management plan

LOCATION	CHURCH	PASTOR	SERMON TITLE	DATE DELIVERED	GENERAL TOPIC
Indiana	The Chapel	Rick Hawks	God's Wisdom on Money, Part 9	March 4, 2012	Five steps to handling money wisely
Iowa	Third Church	Jason Nelson	Creation—The Story of God, The Story of Us	August 28, 2011	Creation, identity, work
Kansas	Olathe Bible Church	Carl & John Blackburn	Invest Generously	May 15, 2011	Generosity, giving
Kentucky/ Indiana	Southeast Christian Church	Dave Stone & Bob Russell	Where Should It Go	March 6, 2011	Personal income, spending, giving wisely
Kentucky/ Indiana	Southeast Christian Church	Kyle Idleman	Ownership Rights	March 13, 2012	Tithing
Kentucky/ Indiana	Southeast Christian Church	Dave Stone	On the Job	May 29, 2011	Work, working for God
Louisiana	Healing Place Church	Brady Boyd	Lessons in Crisis	March 18, 2012	Recession, why was there a Financial Crisis
Maryland	Covenant Life Church	Joshua Harris	The Good Recession, Part One	January 11, 2009	Recession, greed
Massachusetts	Grace Chapel	Bryan Wilkerson	Good Work	June 6, 2010	Labor, employment, work
Michigan	Central Weslyan Church	Lynn Bruce	Can I Be Trusted with Money? The Story of the 10 Apples	February 27, 2011	Greed, spending, generosity
Michigan	Northridge Church	Brad Powell	Rudy . . . Be Diligent	October 2, 2011	Work hard, work for God
Michigan	Northridge Church	Brad Powell	It's a Wonderful Life . . . Be Generous	November 27, 2011	Tithing, generosity

LOCATION	CHURCH	PASTOR	SERMON TITLE	DATE DELIVERED	GENERAL TOPIC
Minnesota	Bethlehem Baptist Church	John Piper	What Is the Recession For	February 1, 2009	Recession; why was there a financial crisis?
Mississippi	Pinelake Church	Gene Henderson	Giving Up Ownership	April 25, 2012	Tithing, generosity
Missouri	Capefirst Church	Gary Brothers	Money Matters Part I	July 26, 2009	Stewardship
Missouri	Capefirst Church	Gary Brothers	Money Matters Part II	August 2, 2009	Debt, saving
Missouri	Capefirst Church	Gary Brothers	Money Matters Part III	August 9, 2009	Tithing
Nebraska	Lifegate	Les Beauchamp	Hit the Road "No More to a Guilty Conscience	October 16, 2011	What is real conscience and what is a false conscience
Nebraska	Lifegate	Les Beauchamp	Hit the Road "Learning to Say No More"	October 2, 2011	Jesus's presence and sin's deception, especially regarding the sin of catering to self
New Hampshire	Manchester Christian Church	Bo Chancey	Giving, Not Getting	November 20, 2011	Generosity, giving
New Hampshire	Manchester Christian Church	Bo Chancey	It's His, Not Mine	November 6, 2011	Tithing
New Jersey	Fellowship Baptist Church	Brennan Coughlin	Kingdom Finances	July 31, 2011	Tithing
New Mexico	Faith Christian Family Church	David Swann	The Principle of First Fruits	January 8, 2012	Tithing
North Carolina	Forest Hill Church	David Chadwick	Live to Give, Give to Live	October 23, 2010	Generosity, giving
North Dakota	Bethel Church	Matthew St. John	Our Financial Peace Declaration	November 12, 2010	Saving, getting out of debt, tithing

LOCATION	CHURCH	PASTOR	SERMON TITLE	DATE DELIVERED	GENERAL TOPIC
Ohio	Cuyahoga Valley Church	Rick Duncan	Fear Not Part I	March 22, 2009	Recession, greed
Ohio	Cuyahoga Valley Church	Rick Duncan	Fear Not Part II	March 29, 2009	Saving, getting out of debt, tithing
Oregon	Morningstar Church	Scott Nelson	Worshipping in the Workplace	Jun 15, 2009	Work
Pennsylvania	Calvary Fellowship Church	Jeff Allem	Submission: Home, Work, World	May 30, 2010	Work, being an employee who honors God
South Carolina	Grace Church	Mark Bailey	Confrontation with Grace	March 17, 2012	Serving God with money
South Carolina	Grace Church	Bill White	An Act of Worship	March 3, 2012	Serving God with money
South Dakota	Celebrate Community Church	Keith Loy	What's in Your Wallet—Week One	Not on website	Debt
South Dakota	Celebrate Community Church	Keith Loy	What's in Your Wallet—Week Two	Not on website	Saving
South Dakota	Celebrate Community Church	Keith Loy	What's in Your Wallet—Week Three	Not on website	Generosity; you can give more than you think you can
South Dakota	Celebrate Community Church	Keith Loy	What's in Your Wallet—Week Four	Not on website	Fearless finances
Tennessee	Grace Chapel	Steve Berger	Courage—To Be a Faithful Steward	May 6, 2012	The generous servant
Texas	Beltway Park Baptist Church	David McQueen	Grace of Giving	February 19, 2012	Tithing
Texas	Beltway Park Baptist Church	David McQueen	Money, Money	February 5, 2012	God's plan for your money

LOCATION	CHURCH	PASTOR	SERMON TITLE	DATE DELIVERED	GENERAL TOPIC
Texas	Community Bible Church	Rober Emmitt	God's Miraculous Plan of Economy	September 5, 2011	Work, be faithful, be generous
Virginia	Cornerstone Chapel	Gary Hamrick	Malachai—on Matters of Marriage and Money	July 6, 2008	Money and marriage
Virginia	Fairfax Community Church	Rod Stafford	Recovery Begins with Me	January 9, 2012	Personal responsibility and the recession
Virginia	Fairfax Community Church	Rod Stafford	Addicted to Spending	January 15, 2012	Greed and spending
Virginia	Fairfax Community Church	Rod Stafford	Financial Integrity	January 22, 2012	Debt and spending, personal responsibility
Virginia	Fairfax Community Church	Rod Stafford	Dealing with Entitlements	January 29, 2012	Personal responsibility problem of greed—personal and national
Washington	First Christian Church	Eric Atcheson	Spending Less	November 27, 2011	Spending
Washington	Mars Hill Church	Mark Driscoll	Parable of the Rich Fool	November 7, 2012	Greed—the problem of wanting too much
Washington	Mars Hill Church	Mark Driscoll	The Parable of the Dishonest Manager	March 13, 2011	Handling money well vs. handling money foolishly
Washington	Mars Hill Church	Mark Driscoll	Jesus on Money, Idolatry, and Comedy	May 29, 2011	The difference between being rich and poor; idolatry and money

LOCATION	CHURCH	PASTOR	SERMON TITLE	DATE DELIVERED	GENERAL TOPIC
Washington	University Presbyterian Church	George Hinman	Work Is a Gift	October 3, 2010	God gives us work and we should honor Him with it
Washington	University Presbyterian Church	Ryan Church	Work Is Hard	October 10, 2010	Work is difficult—prepare yourself
Washington	University Presbyterian Church	George Hinman	Work Is Eternal	October 17, 2010	We will always work, even in heaven
Washington	University Presbyterian Church	George Hinman	Work Is Common	October 24, 2010	Everyone works—and everyone should
Washington	University Presbyterian Church	George Hinman	Work Is Ministry	October 31, 2010	We work to heal the world. And each other.
Washington	University Presbyterian Church	Bruce Baker	Work Is Inspired	November 7, 2010	No matter your work, work at it with your whole heart
Washington	University Presbyterian Church	George Hinman	Work Is Purposeful	November 14, 2010	Your work has meaning
Washington	University Presbyterian Church	George Hinman	Work Is Transforming	November 21, 2010	Your work will change you
Washington, DC	Capitol Hill Baptist Church	Henry Forums	The Financial Breakdown: A Spiritual Diagnosis	April 22, 2009	Recession: an explanation
Wisconsin	Christ the Rock Community Church	Mitch Lautenslager	Who's the Boss	September 2, 2012	You work for God; and for your boss—submit to both
Wisconsin	Christ the Rock Community Church	Bill Lenz	Helps & Hinderances to Growth, Part One	September 23, 2012	The economy—why it is broken and not growing; it's a spiritual problem, too

LOCATION	CHURCH	PASTOR	SERMON TITLE	DATE DELIVERED	GENERAL TOPIC
Wisconsin	Door Creek Church	Marc Maillefer	How to Find Comfort When Bankrupt	April 26, 2009	Moving through tough times
Wyoming	Highland Park Community Church	Milo Miller	ThanksLiving	November 27, 2011	Generosity

Appendix B

RHETORICAL SAMPLE OF SERMONS FROM THE PRESIDENTIAL CAMPAIGN OF 2016

LOCATION	CHURCH	PASTOR	SERMON TITLE*	DATE DELIVERED (IN 2016)
Arizona	Palmcroft Church	Jim Bull	Don'tcha Know?	November 6
Arizona	Christ's Church of the Valley	Don Wilson	Letters to the Next President	November 6
Arizona	Victory Worship Center	Waylon Sears	Who Do I Vote For?	October 9
Arkansas	Church at Rock Creek	Greg Kirksey	True North Part 1	July 17
Arkansas	Church at Rock Creek	Greg Kirksey	True North Part 2	July 17
California	Mariners Church	Christian Mungai	Celebrate Differently	November 6
California	Bayside Church	Ray Johnston	Separation of Church and Hate	November 6
California	Grace Church	Hohn Cho	Christians and Politics	July 3
California	People's Church	Dale Oquist	#45: Who Will It Be?/Does It Matter?	October 16
California	Menlo Church	John Ortberg	How Not to Be Anxious During an Election	October 30
California	Menlo Church	John Ortberg	Greatest Political Decision Ever Made	November 6

LOCATION	CHURCH	PASTOR	SERMON TITLE*	DATE DELIVERED (IN 2016)
California	Menlo Church	John Ortberg	How Not to Fall Apart	November 13
California	Menlo Church	John Ortberg	Why the Best Is Yet to Come	November 20
Colorado	Timberline Church	Dary Northrop	Pressure Points: Politics	October 16
Florida	Potential Church	Troy Gramling	Big Decisions	October 23
Florida	Potential Church	Troy Gramling	Battleship for the Heart	October 30
Florida	Church by the Glades	David Hughes	Who Would Jesus Vote For	April 3
Florida	Church by the Glades	David Hughes	Looking for a Leader	April 10
Florida	Christ Fellowship Church	Todd Mullins	Decision 2016	November 6
Georgia	12Stone Church	Kevin Myers	Faith. Freedom. Church.	September 11
Georgia	12Stone Church	Kevin Myers	Faith. Politics. Church.	October 23
Illinois	Parkview Christian Church	Tim Harlow	How to Love Those People	November 6
Illinois	Community Christian Church	Dave Ferguson	Choose Your President	July 3
Indiana	Northside Christian Church	Nate Ross	Who Are You Voting For?	October 28
Indiana	Warsaw Community Church	Denny Wilson	The Myth of the American Dream	May 1
Louisiana	Simple Church	Justin Haigler	We Believe in Heroes	September 11
Massachusetts	Grace Chapel	Bryan Wilkerson	Thinking Biblically about Politics	October 30
Michigan	Grace Community Church	Jerry Weinzierl	Lord, Heal Our Land	July 10
Michigan	Grace Community Church	Jerry Weinzierl	Celebrate Freedom	July 3
Michigan	ResLife Church	Eric Everhart	Veterans Day	November 6
Michigan	Mount Hope Church	Kevin Berry	The America of Yesterday	July 10

LOCATION	CHURCH	PASTOR	SERMON TITLE*	DATE DELIVERED (IN 2016)
Michigan	Mount Hope Church	Kevin Berry	Recalculating to the Right Path	July 17
Michigan	Calvary Church	Jim Samra	God and Government	November 6
Minnesota	Wooddale Church	Dale Hummel	Dear Mr. or Mrs. Next President	October 22
Minnesota	River Valley Church	Rob Ketterling	None of the Above—Part 1	November 6
Mississippi	Crossgates Church	David Jett	We the People of God Must Fight	November 6
Missouri	The Crossing	Greg Holder	Common Ground	November 6
Montana	Harvest Church	Vern Streeter	Jesus for President	November 6
Nebraska	Lifegate Church	Les Beauchamp	How to Pick a President	July 3
Nevada	Central Church	Jud Wilhite	Hope beyond Politics	November 6
New Jersey	The Chapel	Dave Gustaven	Land of the Free: Free to Challenge Our Culture	October 30
New York	The Father's House	Pierre du Plessis	Questions, Part 1: Politics	October 30
North Carolina	Elevation Church	Steven Furtick	I Know, But I'm Not Nervous	November 6
Ohio	Vineyard Cincinnati	Rob King	One Nation	November 6
Oregon	Rolling Hills Community Church	Bill Towne	Stand Strong Together	September 11
Pennsylvania	Parker Hill Church	Mark Stuenzi	I Am a Foreigner	November 6
South Carolina	Seacoast Church	Greg Surratt	Building a Platform of Leadership	October 16
South Carolina	Seacoast Church	Greg Surratt	Too Many People, Not Enough Leaders	October 30
South Carolina	Taylors First Baptist Church	Paul Jiminez	Culture, Politics, Church	November 6
Tennessee	Hope Church	Eli Morris	Casting Your Vote for God's Word	November 6

LOCATION	CHURCH	PASTOR	SERMON TITLE*	DATE DELIVERED (IN 2016)
Texas	Church Unlimited	Bil Cornelius	Election 2016: The Mess We're In	November 6
Texas	Fellowship Church	Ed Young	How to Pick a President	November 6
Texas	Watermark Church	Garrett Raburn	How to Choose a Leader	November 1
Texas	Watermark Church	Jonathan Pokluda	Sex and Government	October 16
Virginia	Cornerstone Chapel	Gary Hamrick	Election Day Sermon	October 16
Washington	Gold Creek Community Church	Dan Kellogg	How Would Jesus Vote	September 11

*Unlike Appendix A, this table lacks a column specifying a sermon topic. All sermons for this part of the study were about American politics. Most were specifically about the campaign between Hillary Clinton and Donald Trump.

Notes

Introduction

1. In July 2020, Ortberg came under fire for failing to be forthcoming after one of his sons, John "Johnny" Ortberg III, revealed to him pedophilic impulses. Johnny had confessed these feelings to his father in July 2018, after he lost his computer. He was then a youth volunteer at the church and for a Bay Area ultimate Frisbee team. For more than a year, the pastor kept his son's revelation secret and also didn't stop him from continuing to volunteer with children. In November 2019, Ortberg's other son, Danny, alerted Menlo Church's elder board to the situation. John Ortberg, the pastor, was placed on leave while an investigation took place. Ortberg was eventually cleared of wrongdoing, although church members were never told that it was the pastor's own son who had made the original confession. This was the information that became known in July 2020, sending the church membership reeling. Ortberg finally resigned from Menlo Church, effective August 2, 2020. Menlo Church is not the only megachurch that has faced similar clergy misconduct or accusations of sexual impropriety during the years I was writing this book. For more about the church's response to these issues, see chapter 6. Carol Kuruvilla, "A Megachurch Reels after Learning Pastor Let His Professed Pedophile Son Work with Kids," Huffington Post, July 14, 2020, https://www.huffpost.com/entry/john-ortberg-menlo-church_n_5f04e820c5b67a80bbffcdc4. Carol Kuruvilla, "Pastor Steps Down after Megachurch Learns He Let Pedophile Son Work with Kids," Huffington Post, July 30, 2020, https://www.huffpost.com/entry/john-ortberg-resignation_n_5f22d01ec5b68fbfc87fc983.

2. Gregory A. Smith and Jessica Martinez, "How the Faithful Voted: A Preliminary 2016 Analysis," Pew Research, November 9, 2016, http://www.pewresearch.org/fact-tank/2016/11/09/how-the-faithful-voted-a-preliminary-2016-analysis/.

3. "Election 2016: California Results," *New York Times,* August 1, 2017.

4. John Ortberg, "How Not to Be Anxious during an Election," sermon, October 30, 2016, Menlo Church. See also Ortberg, "Greatest Political Decision Ever Made," sermon, November 6, 2016, Menlo Church.

5. See, for example, William Wan, Tanya Sichynsky, and Sandhya Somashekhar, "After Trump's Election: 'There Are Two Americas Now,'" *Washington Post,* November 21, 2016; Sabrina Tavernise and Katherine Q. Seelye, "Political Divide Splits Relationships—and Thanksgiving, Too," *New York Times,* November 15, 2016.

6. John Ortberg, "How Not to Fall Apart," sermon, November 13, 2016, Menlo Church.

7. Thomas Frank, *What's the Matter with Kansas? How Conservatives Won the Heart of America* (New York: Henry Holt, 2004); Kirk Noden, "Why Do White Working-Class People Vote against Their Interests? They Don't." *The Nation,* November 17, 2016, https://www.thenation.com/article/why-do-white-working-class-people-vote-against-their-interests-they-dont/.

8. Robert Reich, "Fear Is Why Workers in Red States Vote against Their Economic Self-Interest," Berkeley Blog (blog), January 16, 2014, https://blogs.berkeley.edu/2014/01/16/fear-is-why-workers-in-red-states-vote-against-their-economic-self-interest/; Bruce Y. Lee, "Why People Vote against Their Own Interests," Forbes.com, November 8, 2016, https://www.forbes.com/sites/brucelee/2016/11/08/heres-why-you-may-vote-against-yourself/#3ca55bab25fa; Michael Wear, "Why Democrats Must Regain the Trust of Religious Voters," *Atlantic,* November 21, 2018, https://www.theatlantic.com/politics/archive/2017/11/why-democrats-must-regain-faith-among-religious-voters/546434/.

9. Frank, *What's the Matter with Kansas?*

10. Federal tax law prohibits churches from "engaging in any political activity." Known as the "Johnson Amendment," as part of the IRS tax code, the rule requires churches to maintain postures of political neutrality as part of their tax-exempt status. Clergy may still be politically active in their private lives (they do not forfeit their first amendment rights to political speech or association). However, they cannot speak for the church. The Johnson Amendment does not proscribe politically neutral activities such as voter drives or prohibit sermons on political issues such as abortion or the morality and necessity of aid to the poor, or those other issues I specifically mention here. "Charities, Churches and Politics," Department of the Treasury, Internal Revenue Service, updated June 5, 2020, https://www.irs.gov/newsroom/charities-churches-and-politics; Tom Gjelten, "The Johnson Amendment in 5 Questions and Answers," NPR News, February 3, 2017, https://www.npr.org/2017/02/03/513187940/the-johnson-amendment-in-five-questions-and-answers.

11. In her book *Between Jesus and the Market: The Emotions That Matter in Right-Wing America,* Linda Kintz developed the idea of rhetorical resonance. Resonance, Kintz explains, is the familiarity that comes when values and ideas are repeated, by different speakers, across spheres. Hearers come to recognize a tune that is rhetorical resonance. Kintz argues that the culture wars in the United States are mostly about familiarization built through resonance about, for example, opposition to feminism. Such opposition is found in arguments against women's empowerment given by congressional leaders, church leaders, media personalities, and others. These arguments join in a rhetorical timbre that is resonant. Likewise, in my own research, I chose to

use large churches with especially visible leaders, because I thought that while they were typically less famous than other conservative evangelicals in the public sphere, their reach extended farther than those who led smaller churches. As such, their ability to create rhetorics of cultural resonance was greater. Linda Kintz, *Between Jesus and the Market: The Emotions That Matter in Right-Wing America* (Durham, NC: Duke University Press, 1997), 6–9.

12. Not everyone attends a megachurch, and that is a limit to this study. But a lot of people do. Megachurches themselves, and their attendees, are also wealthier and more media savvy than other churches and church populations. Nonetheless, Scott Thumma and Dave Travis wrote in their 2007 book, *Beyond Megachurch Myths*—which I read when I began my research and which was much newer in 2011 than it is now—that while only 1,250 (just over one-third of one percent) of the 335,000 churches in the United States were megachurches, they attracted the same number of weekly attendees as the 117, 250 smallest churches (35 percent of the whole) in the country. This is a lot of people. More relevant to me as I was designing my study, Thumma and Travis described the importance of the internet presence of these churches, and their confidence that these web pages vastly increase their reach and influence. They wrote: "The pastors of these churches wield tremendous power within their denominational groups, in the larger Christian world, and even in the public and political realms. The ministry activities and worship styles of the megachurches affect tens of thousands of smaller churches in the country and, thanks to the Internet, literally millions of pastors around the world." Thus, and bearing in mind the notion of resonance I describe in note 9, I developed my study using megachurch pastors and megachurch rhetoric, despite the limitations this necessarily entailed. I describe my method of sermon selection more fully in chapter 3.

13. Megachurches tend not to co-affiliate with one another in the ways that denominations do—Baptists, Methodists, Presbyterians, and the like. However, in the architecture of the internet, churches' presence often mirrors one another, and this may have to do with the underlying market and industry of conservative evangelicalism. For example, the company Subsplash, headquartered in Seattle, designed the websites for many megachurches I encountered and studied, including Saddleback Church, 12Stone Church, Highpoint Church, and more. This meant that although I was looking at different churches all together, there was a similar feel to them, and so a similar skill set was necessary for navigating and understanding the pages and online communities I encountered. Subsplash, "Subsplash: The Ultimate Engagement Platform," http://www.subsplash.com/.

14. Conservative evangelicals almost always use capital letters to refer to God and Jesus, including the pronouns "He" and "Him," and the possessive "His." I follow this convention throughout this book, out of respect for the tradition and for reader clarity. Because the pastors I studied were almost exclusively male, using uppercase "He"/"Him" to refer to Jesus, and lowercase "he"/"him" to refer to pastors was one way to create clean distinction between actors in the text. For understanding my rationale for defining evangelicals, see Randall Balmer, *Evangelicalism in America* (Waco, TX:

Baylor University Press, 2016); Christian Smith, *Christian America? What Evangelicals Really Want* (Berkeley: University of California Press, 2000); Frances FitzGerald, *The Evangelicals: The Struggle to Shape America*, (New York: Simon & Schuster, 2017). The "Great Commission" is the resurrected Jesus's injunction to his disciples to spread the word of God to all the world.

15. James Boyd White, "Law as Rhetoric, Rhetoric as Law: The Arts of Cultural and Communal Life," *University of Chicago Law Review* 52 (1985): 690; Benedict Anderson, *Imagined Communities: Reflections on the Origin and Spread of Nationalism* (New York: Verso, 2006).

16. Charles Taylor, *Sources of the Self: The: Making of the Modern Identity* (Cambridge, MA: Harvard University Press, 1989); Taylor, *Modern Social Imaginaries* (Durham, NC: Duke University Press, 2004). For Taylor, humans can be understood only insofar as they participate in community. Humans use language both to talk about themselves *and* to give shape and reality to the world around them. Words perform—they make the world, and they make relationships. That is, language is essential to mutual understanding and intersubjectivity. See Craig Calhoun, "Charles Taylor on Identity and the Social Imaginary," unpublished working paper, 1999, http://eprints.lse.ac.uk/48046/1/Charles%20Taylor(lsero).pdf.

17. Pew Research Center, "Religious Landscape Study," http://www.pewforum.org/religious-landscape-study/.

18. Within the field of ethnography, Susan Harding descibed how important pastors are when it comes to influencing how believers interpret and talk about the world. Concerning her study of Jerry Falwell Sr. and the Thomas Road Baptist Church, Harding wrote, "Preachers 'stand in the gap' between the language of the Christian Bible and the language of everyday life. . . . Preachers convert the ancient recorded speech of the Bible once again into spoken language, translating it into the sequence of Biblical stories. Church people, in their turn, borrow, customize, and reproduce the Bible-based speech of their preachers and other leaders in their daily lives." Research by Glen H. Utter and James L. True found that conservative evangelicals trust their pastors more for leadership than do members of mainline churches. "Thus evangelical pastors can rely more confidently on their claim to have biblical sanction for their social and political pronouncements. . . . Evangelical clergy are also in greater agreement with their congregations on political matters than are mainline clergy." Susan Friend Harding, *The Book of Jerry Falwell* (Princeton, NJ: Princeton University Press, 2000), 12; Glenn H. Utter and James L. True, *Conservative Christians and Political Participation: A Reference Handbook*, ed. Raymond A. Smith (Santa Barbara, CA: ABC-CLIO, Inc., 2004), 31.

19. Aristotle, *On Rhetoric: A Theory of Civic Discourse*, trans. George A. Kennedy, 2d ed. (New York: Oxford University Press, 2006), 4.

20. "Seeing the available means of persuasion" includes, of course, paying attention to rhetorical genre (forensic, epideictic, and deliberative). Sermons are sometimes epideictic and sometimes deliberative. With respect to politics and economics, they are usually deliberative. Pastors rely on *ethos* (their experiences and education); *logos*

(facts, Bible proofs, and history, including sometimes dubious history); and *pathos* (emotional appeals about character, Christian good, and more).

21. Ortberg, "How Not to Be Anxious during an Election." Ortberg is probably referring to an article written in April 2016 by Elizabeth King, a Chicago-based writer for *Time*, about the relationship between the 2016 campaign and stress. See Elizabeth King, "Stressed? Blame the 2016 Election," *Time,* April 26, 2016, https://time.com/4299527/election-mental-health/.

22. Michael C. Leff and Gerald P. Mohrmann, "Lincoln at Cooper Union: A Rhetorical Analysis of the Text," *Quarterly Journal of Speech* 60, no. 3 (1974); Leff, "Dimensions of Temporality in Lincoln's Second Inaugural," *Communication Reports* 1, no. 1 (1988); Ronald C. White, *Lincoln's Greatest Speech: The: Second Inaugural* (New York: Simon & Schuster, 2002); Greg Weiner, "Of Prudence and Principle: Reflections on Lincoln's Second Inaugural at 150," *Society* 52, no. 6 (2015).

23. Ortberg, "How Not to Be Anxious during an Election."

24. In *Civic Hope*, Roderick P. Hart uses letters to the editor to argue that a "culture of complaint" (by which he means argument and disagreements between citizens and aimed at leaders) is essential for keeping democracy going. Hart writes, "The vitality of a democracy, that is, lies not in its strengths but in its weaknesses, and in the willingness of its people to address those weaknesses without surcease. It is the imperfections of democracy that call forth a people." Roderick P. Hart, *Civic Hope: How Ordinary Americans Keep Democracy Alive* (Cambridge, UK: Cambridge University Press, 2018), 10.

25. C. S. Lewis, *Mere Christianity* (New York: Harper Collins, 2015), 137.

26. When born-again Christians discuss "being in the world but not of it," they typically have 1 John 2:15–19 in mind. "(15) Do not love the world or anything in the world. If anyone loves the world, the love of the Father is not in him. (16) For everything in the world—the cravings of sinful man, the lust of his eyes and the boasting of what he has and does—comes not from the Father but from the world. (17) The world and its desires pass away, but the man who does the will of God lives forever." (All scripture quotations are drawn from the *New International Version.*)

27. Christine J. Gardner, *Making Chastity Sexy: The Rhetoric of Evangelical Abstinence Campaigns* (Berkeley: University of California Press, 2011), 18.

28. Colby Itkowitz, Emily Davies, and Hailey Fuchs, "Latest Sexual Assault Allegation against Trump Draws Muted Political Reaction," *Washington Post*, June 25, 2019; Irin Carmon, "The Allegations Women Have Made against Donald Trump," NBCNews.com (2016), " https://www.nbcnews.com/politics/2016-election/allegations-women-have-made-against-donald-trump-n665731.

29. The evangelical magazine *Christianity Today* ran several online editorials, mostly by younger writers, advocating various options for the 2016 election, beyond Clinton or Trump, including not voting at all, or choosing either Stein or Johnson. See O. Alan Noble, "Evangelical Views of the 2016 Election: Not the Lesser of Two Evils, Choose Candidate Evan McMullin Instead," *The Exchange with Ed Stetzer* (blog), *Christianity Today,* October 3, 2016, https://www.christianitytoday.com/edstetzer

/2016/october/evangelical-views-of-2016-election-in-support-of-third-part.html; Stephen Waldron, "Evangelical Views of the 2016 Election: 'Jill Stein Is My Imperfect Candidate,'" *The Exchange with Ed Stetzer* (blog), *Christianity Today,* October 6, 2016, https://www.christianitytoday.com/edstetzer/2016/october/evangelical-views-of-2016-election-jill-stein-is-my-imperfe.html; Ron Sider, James Dobson, and Sho Baraka, "Clinton, Trump, or Neither? 3 Views on the 2016 Presidential Election." *Christianity Today* (Special Section), September 23, 2016. https://www.christianitytoday.com/ct/2016/october/clinton-trump-or-neither-3-views-on-2016-presidential-elect.html.

30. Russell Moore, "Why This Election Makes Me Hate the Word Evangelical," *Washington Post*, February 29, 2016.

31. "Here's Donald Trump's Presidential Announcement Speech," Time.com, June 16, 2015, http://time.com/3923128/donald-trump-announcement-speech/; David Fahrenthold, "Trump's Lewd Chat Captured on Tape," *Washington Post*, October 8, 2016; Farai Chideya, "Evangelicals, Once Skeptical of Trump, Have Rallied to His Side," FiveThirtyEight, September 27, 2016, https://fivethirtyeight.com/features/evangelicals-have-rallied-to-trumps-side/.

32. What about voting *against* Clinton (rather than *for* Trump) as a viable option? Could this not be a possible framing? My answer is yes and no. First, the pastors I studied almost never spoke about the candidates by name. We only know the outcome of the vote as represented by poll data: 81 percent of self-identifying conservative evangelicals voted for Trump. To engage a conversation about whether their votes were repudiations of Clinton is to revert to *why* these believers voted this way. My aim, however, is to understand *how* pastors formulated their arguments. I suggest the formulation worked in Trump's favor, and thus the arguments necessarily rhetorically worked to let believers off the hook for paying attention to the New York businessman's character defects and proposed threats to vulnerable constituencies.

33. In *Superchurch: The Rhetoric and Politics of American Fundamentalism*, Jonathan J. Edwards wrote about the shift away from fundamentalist congregations such as Jerry Falwell's Thomas Road Baptist Church and toward megachurches such as Bill Hybels's Willow Creek. "Megachurches . . . offer a friendly and open kind of evangelicalism that seems to challenge many of the negative connotations associated with Christian Fundamentalists in the popular imagination." Part of this shift—and this was true of many of the sermons I heard—was movement from appeals set in "authoritarian terms" to those set in "individualistic, grassroots" terms. Many of the pastors I listened to, for example, gestured toward ideas that congregants should study the Bible and vote their consciences; they did not so much exhort truths for voting. Of course, sermons are only one form of evangelical rhetoric. But this finding still suggests something about how pastors create and maintain rhetorical identification and claim rhetorical agency within their communities. Many pastors in my study shied away from speaking explicitly about the hot-button issues I have mentioned, including abortion and Supreme Court appointments, which many have assumed drove evangelicals to vote for Trump. The question going forward is whether this

shyness had to do with bad candidates or a truly changing discourse away from overt partisanship. I argue in this book that it is more likely the latter.

34. Andrew Hartman, in his history of the culture wars, writes that they should be understood as refusals by conservatives in the United States to acknowledge fundamental transformations in American life. Those on the Right want to hold the line against what liberals insist is inclusion and progress. This struggle goes on and is resonant in the rhetoric I discovered in the sermons I heard during the 2016 presidential campaign. Although I only engage this argument peripherally, some have argued that Trump's antagonism toward "political correctness" represents rhetorical strength to conservative evangelicals, while liberals supposedly demand a willingness to speak up in favor of queer families, abortion rights, and more. Trump spoke up for supposedly delegitimized opinions (gay is bad, women should be at home with children, spanking is good, the United States was founded by and belongs to Christians first) and insisted they be readmitted to the public sphere and accepted as viable. See Andrew Hartman, *A War for the Soul of America: A History of the Culture Wars* (Chicago: University of Chicago Press, 2015); Alex Altman and Elizabeth Dias, "Why Trump Is Winning over Christian Conservatives," *Time,* January 22, 2016, https://time.com/4189587/donald-trump-christian-conservatives/; George Lakoff, "Understanding Trump," *University of Chicago Press* (blog), August 2016, https://www.press.uchicago.edu/books/excerpt/2016/lakoff_trump.html.

35. Kenneth Burke's theory of comic and tragic frames is useful for understanding the symbolic and rhetorical dance that conservative evangelicals engaged in during Trump's campaign for the presidency (and that they still engage in). Burke argued that there are two kinds of frames humans use for making meaning in the world—frames of acceptance and frames of rejection. A frame of acceptance allows a person to accept a historical situation and adopt to their role within it. A frame of rejection does the opposite. Here, a person rebels against a reigning symbol of authority, shifts allegiance, and seeks a fundamental overhaul in the status quo. Rebellions are born out of frames of rejection. Democracies usually operate under frames of acceptance. However, democratic figures can be framed as either comic figures or tragic figures. Tragic figures are inherently bad and should be punished. Punishment can take the form of rejection. This rejection fulfills the truth that the world is a cold, hard place. Some are irredeemable. For evangelicals, Hillary Clinton fits a tragic frame. Comic figures are fools. Their folly allows us to laugh at them, and learn from them. They can be corrected and taught because they are not inherently evil. For evangelicals, Trump is often presented in a comic frame. This treatment in framing—sometimes made explicit and sometimes implicit—is supported by the political science literatures. Kenneth Burke, *Attitudes toward History*, 3d ed. (Berkeley: University of California Press, 1984), 166–73; William H. Rueckert, *Encounters with Kenneth Burke* (Urbana: University of Illinois Press, 1994), 118.

36. Paul Mason, *Meltdown: The End of the Age of Greed* (Brooklyn: Verso, 2009), x. Political scientist Stephen Skowronek argues that presidents serve during both chronological time (a four-year term) and "political time." Political time has to do

with the prevailing ideology of an era, and how much power a president has to change it. Only some presidents, like Franklin Delano Roosevelt and his New Deal or Ronald Reagan with neoliberalism, serve during a political moment—a political time—that is ready for what Skowronek calls "regime change." Some thought Obama might be such a leader during such a time. The emergence and strength of the Tea Party, along with other factors, proved otherwise. Also see chapter 1, note 6 in this book, *Decoding the Digital Church*; Stephen Skowronek, *The Politics Presidents Make: Leadership from John Adams to Bill Clinton,* rev. ed. (Cambridge, MA: Harvard University Press, 1997). See also Stephanie A. Martin, "Transformational Presidents, New Media Strategies, and the Necessity of a Universal Audience," in *Columns to Characters: The Press and the Presidency Enter the Digital Age*, ed. Martin (College Station: Texas A&M Press, 2017).

37. Theda Skocpol and Vanessa Williamson, *The Tea Party and the Remaking of Republican Conservatism* (New York: Oxford University Press, 2012), 35.

38. Demographic data specific to megachurches are not especially easy to get. The 2014 "Religious Landscape Study" conducted by the Pew Research Center found that of the 26 percent of American citizens who identify as evangelical Protestants, 35 percent of households earn less than $35,000; 22 percent earn between $35,000 and $49,999; 28 percent earn between $50,000 and $99,999; and 14 percent earn $100,000 or more. Pew *did not* break these numbers down to say whether incomes were for a single-family income or dual family earners. In 2009, the Hartford Institute for Religious Research issued a report specific to megachurches. Hartford said that young and single adults were more likely to attend megachurches, meaning that these congregations trended younger and their members were less likely to be married than those of smaller churches. Hartford found that 39 percent of megachurch congregants made less than $50,000; 35 percent made between $50,000 and $99,999; and 26 percent had household incomes above $100,000.

39. Timothy Egan, "How Obama Saved Capitalism and Lost the Midterms," *New York Times*, November 2, 2010.

40. Clifford Geertz, *The Interpretation of Cultures: Selected Essays* (New York: Basic Books, 1973).

41. Walter R. Fisher, "The Narrative Paradigm: An Elaboration," *Communication Monographs* 52 (December 1985).

42. Walter R. Fisher, "Narration as a Human Communication Paradigm: The Case of Public Moral Argument," *Communication Monographs* 51, no. 1 (1984): 8.

43. Barbara Warnick, "The Narrative Paradigm: Another Story," *Quarterly Journal of Speech* 73, no. 2 (1987): 172; Robert Rowland, "The Narrative Perspective," in *Rhetorical Criticism: Perspectives in Action*, ed. Jim A. Kuypers (New York: Rowman & Littlefield: 2016), 125; John Louis Lucaites and Celeste M. Condit, "Re-Constructing Narrative Theory: A Functional Perspective," *Journal of Communication* 35 (1985); Michael Calvin McGee and John S. Nelson, "Narrative Reason in Public Argument," *Journal of Communication* 35, no. 4 (December 1985).

44. William F. Lewis, "Telling America's Story: Narrative Form and the Reagan Presidency," *Quarterly Journal of Speech* 73 (1987): 292.

45. Kenneth Burke wrote about the relationship between anthropology and rhetoric in *A Rhetoric of Motives*. "Gaining courage as we proceed, we might even contend that we are not so much proposing to import anthropology into rhetoric as we are proposing that anthropologists recognize the factor of rhetoric in their own field." Kenneth Burke, *A Rhetoric of Motives* (New York: Prentice Hall, 1950), 43.

46. In his 1992 essay "Ethnography, Rhetoric and Performance," Dwight Conquergood wrote that rhetoric, anthropology, and performance studies are more open to partial truths than are other fields in social science, and more willing to see beyond the usual or expected. Quoting Geertz, Conquergood wrote, "If we wanted home truths, we should have stayed at home." Dwight Conquergood, "Ethnography, Rhetoric, and Performance," *Quarterly Journal of Speech* 78, no. 1 (1992): 82.

47. *Text + Field : Innovations in Rhetorical Method*, ed. Sara L. McKinnon, Robert Asen, Karma R. Chávez, and Robert Glenn Howard, Kindle ed. (University Park: Penn State University Press, 2016), loc. 161.

48. Carole Blair, Marsha S. Jeppeson, and Enrico Pucci, "Public Memorializing in Postmodernity: The Vietnam Veterans Memorial as Prototype," *Quarterly Journal of Speech* 77, no. 3 (1991); Harding, *The Book of Jerry Falwell*; Phaedra C. Pezzullo, "Touring 'Cancer Alley,' Louisiana: Performances of Community and Memory for Environmental Justice," *Text and Performance Quarterly* 23, no. 3 (2003); Gardner, *Making Chastity Sexy*; Robert Asen, *Democracy, Deliberation, and Education* (University Park: Pennsylvania State University Press, 2015); Robert Glenn Howard, *Digital Jesus: The Making of a New Christian Fundamenatlist Community on the Internet* (New York: New York University Press, 2011); Candice Rai, *Democracy's Lot: Rhetoric, Publics, and the Places of Invention* (Tuscaloosa: University of Alabama Press, 2016).

49. I think here of films like the documentary *Jesus Camp* and Bill Maher's *Religulous*, and of books like Chris Hedges's *American Fascists* and Michelle Goldberg's *Kingdom Coming*. Each of these works shows important episodes and characters who have played roles in the evangelical movement in the last twenty-five years, and who do things that many find objectionable. However, while these works—each similar to and different from the others—make important arguments about the danger that religious extremism, including Christian religious extremism, can pose, they can cross over into purveying the view that conservative evangelicalism is necessarily dangerous because it necessarily includes dangerous characters and beliefs. The churches and pastors I studied suggest that the effects are usually not as dramatic as they are typically portrayed in these kinds of works. Heidi E. Ewing and Rachel Grady, directors, *Jesus Camp*, documentary film (Los Angeles: Magnolia Home Entertainment, 2006); Bill Maher, *Religulous*, documentary film, dir. Larry Charles (Santa Monica, CA: Lionsgate, 2009); Chris Hedges, *American Fascists: The Christian Right and the War on America* (New York: Free Press, 2006); Michelle Goldberg, *Kingdom Coming: The Rise of Christian Nationalism* (New York: W. W. Norton, 2006).

50. I have placed these examples into topic "areas" as examples. Obviously, one can—and often does—bleed into another.

51. I am following Krista Ratcliffe's explanation of Barthes in her book *Anglo-American Feminist Challenges to Rhetorical Traditions*. The role of gender—that this is mostly a study of the rhetoric of men, that is, male pastors—is mostly beyond the scope of what I am able to take up within the pages of this book. Yet, evangelicalism is a deeply patriarchal movement, and this fact cannot be entirely overlooked. Its maleness is always already part of its argument. I refer readers to Roxanne Moutford's early rhetorical examination of the role and disruptive power of female preachers within fundamentalism and evangelicalism, for understanding the role of the body and gendered voice as it works in Christian preaching in America. See Roxanne Mountford, *The Gendered Pulpit: Preaching in American Protestant Spaces* (Carbondale: Southern Illinois University Press, 2003); Krista Ratcliffe, *Anglo-American Feminist Challenges to the Rhetorical Traditions: Virginia Woolf, Mary Daly, Adrienne Rich* (Carbondale: Southern Illinois University Press, 1996), 17.

52. Paul Ricoeur, *Time and Narrative*, vol. 1 (Chicago: University of Chicago Press, 1990), chap. 2.

53. See, for example, Jonathan J. Edwards, *Superchurch: The Rhetoric and Politics of American Fundamentalism* (East Lansing: Michigan State University Press, 2015); Sharon Crowley, *Toward a Civil Discourse: Rhetoric and Fundamentalism* (Pittsburgh: University of Pittsburgh Press, 2006); Michael L. Cobb, *God Hates Fags: The Rhetorics of Religious Violence* (New York: New York University Press, 2006); Gavin Flood, *Importance of Religion: Meaning and Action in Our Strange World* (Hoboken, NJ: Wiley, 2011); James Francis Darsey, *The Prophetic Tradition and Radical Rhetoric in America* (New York: New York : University Press, 1997); Molly Castelloe, "The Podium, the Pulpit, and the Republicans: How Presidential Candidates Use Religious Language in American Political Debate," *Journal of Psychohistory* 41, no. 3 (2014); Bethany Albertson, "Dog-Whistle Politics: Multivocal Communication and Religious Appeals," *Political Behavior* 37, no. 1 (2015).

54. Clifford Geertz, "Deep Hanging Out," *New York Review of Books,* October 22, 1998.

55. See Edwards, *Superchurch;* Harding, *The Book of Jerry Falwell*; Kintz, *Between Jesus and the Market*.

56. Betsy Cooper, Daniel Cox, Rachel Lienesch, and Robert P. Jones, "The Divide over America's Future: 1950 or 2050? Findings from the 2016 American Values Survey" (Washington, DC: PRRI, 2016).

57. Alan I. Abramowitz and Steven W. Webster, "Negative Partisanship: Why Americans Dislike Parties But Behave Like Rabid Partisans," *Political Psychology* 39 (2018).

58. Ed Stetzer, "Why Evangelicals Dislike and Distrust Hillary Clinton So Much," *Christianity Today,* October 31, 2016, http://www.christianitytoday.com/edstetzer/2016/october/why-evangelicals-dislike-and-distrust-hillary-clinton-so-mu.html.

59. Alexis de Tocqueville, *Democracy in America* (New York: Alfred A. Knopf, 1948).

Chapter 1

1. Dan Kellogg, "How Would Jesus Vote," September 11, 2016, Gold Creek Community Church, Mill Creek, WA.

2. Thomas Frank, *What's the Matter with Kansas? How Conservatives Won the Heart of America* (New York: Henry Holt, 2004), 2.

3. See, for example, David Ricci, *Politics without Stories: The Liberal Predicament* (New York: Cambridge University Press, 2016); Kirk Noden, "Why Do White Working-Class People Vote against Their Interests? They Don't." *The Nation,* November 17, 2016.

4. Gil Troy, *The Reagan Revolution: A Very Short Introduction* (Oxford: Oxford University Press, 2009), 39.

5. Robert P. Jones, *The End of White Christian America*, Kindle ed. (New York: Simon & Schuster: 2016), loc. 1171 of 5676; Darren Dochuk, *From Bible Belt to Sunbelt: Plain-Folk Religion, Grassroots Politics, and the Rise of Evangelical Conservatism* (New York: W. W. Norton, 2011).

6. Especially useful here is Stephen Skowronek's theory of "political time." Skowronek posits that presidential history follows a pattern. The transformative power of presidents relates more to when a leader serves, and not to their individual characteristics. There are four kinds of plausible presidential regimes: articulation (an era of continuation); preemption (somewhat oppositional to the prevailing politics of the time, but not wholly alternative); disjunction (an era that comes before large change); and reconstruction (new eras). Also see the introduction of this book (*Decoding the Digital Church*), note 36. As well, Judith Stein's economic history of the 1970s offers a rich telling of how the economic politics fundamentally changed during this time. Particularly useful is her chapter 10, "1979–80: 'The Gnomes of Zurich Got Their Way.'" See Stephen Skowronek, *The Politics Presidents Make: Leadership from John Adams to Bill Clinton*, rev. ed. (Cambridge, MA: Harvard University Press, 1997); Judith Stein, *Pivotal Decade: How the United States Traded Factories for Finance in the Seventies* (New Haven, CT: Yale University Press, 2010); Godfrey Hodgson, *America in Our Time: From World War II to Nixon—What Happened and Why* (Princeton, NJ: Princeton University Press, 1976).

7. Randall Balmer, *The Making of Evangelicalism: From Revivalism to Politics and Beyond* (Waco, TX: Baylor University Press, 2010), 55.

8. Balmer, *The Making of Evangelicalism,* 55.

9. Arlie Russell Hochschild, *Strangers in Their Own Land: Anger and Mourning on the American Right* (New York: New Press, 2016), 145.

10. As Benedict Anderson argues, it takes imagination for people to develop the sense of community required for holding a nation together. Similar imagination is necessary for belonging to other kinds of groups, including subcultures like evangelicalism. One important way humans imagine themselves into community is through constitutive rhetoric: making meaning through shared stories and symbols that create worlds through language before these worlds are created materially. Maurice Charland

used Kenneth Burke's theory of identification to explain how people sometimes come together *as a people* and are jointly influenced outside "the realm of rational or even free choice, beyond the realm of persuasion." Using a case study of how citizens of Quebec were motivated through speeches to go from identifying as individuals who lived in a city, to individuals of French-speaking identity who demanded separation from the Canadian government, Charland argued that the "ideological trick" had been performed through constitutive rhetoric. The new identity was created through language. This kind of creating was also present in the "deep story" Hochschild suggested, and also happens when pastors preach every Sunday. Quoting Walter Fisher, Charland wrote that shared narratives, "give order to human experience and . . . induce others to dwell in it to establish ways of living in common, in communion in which there is sanction for the story that constitutes one's life." See Benedict Anderson, *Imagined Communities: Reflections on the Origin and Spread of Nationalism* (New York: Verso, 2006); Maurice Charland, "Constitutive Rhetoric: The Case of the *Peuple Québécois*." *Quarterly Journal of Speech* 73, no. 2 (1987): 133–50, at 142.

11. Walter R. Fisher, "Narration as a Human Communication Paradigm: The Case of Public Moral Argument," *Communication Monographs* 51, no. 1 (1984): 1–22.

12. John Louis Lucaites and Celeste M. Condit, "Re-Constructing Narrative Theory: A Functional Perspective," *Journal of Communication* 35 (1985): 90–108, at 95.

13. Ricci, *Politics without Stories*, 23–24; Jacques Barzun, *The Culture We Deserve* (Middletown, CT: Wesleyan University Press, 1989).

14. Milton Lodge and Charles S. Tabor, *The Rationalizing Voter* (Cambridge: Cambridge University Press, 2013).

15. William F. Lewis, "Telling America's Story: Narrative Form and the Reagan Presidency," *Quarterly Journal of Speech* 73, no. 3 (1987).

16. Fisher, "Narration as a Human Communication Paradigm."

17. Lewis, "Telling America's Story," 292.

18. M. M. Bakhtin, *Speech Genres and Other Late Essays*, trans. Vern W. McGee (Austin: University of Texas Press, 1986). See also Paula S. Tompkins, *Practicing Communication Ethics: Development, Discernment, and Decision Making*, 2d ed. (New York: Routledge, 2019), 12–14.

19. Balmer, *Evangelicalism in America* (Waco, TX: Baylor University Press, 2016), xi–xii. In *Christian America?* Christian Smith affirms Balmer's more recent definition: Christian Smith, *Christian America? What Evangelicals Really Want* (Berkeley: University of California Press, 2000), 16, 84.

20. William G. McLoughlin, *The American Evangelicals, 1800–1900; An Anthology* (Gloucester, MA: Peter Smith, 1976), 1.

21. Frances FitzGerald, *The Evangelicals: The Struggle to Shape America* (New York: Simon & Schuster, 2017), 4.

22. Corwin E. Smidt, *American Evangelicals Today* (Lanham, MD: Rowman & Littlefield, 2013), 15.

23. Christian Smith and Michael Emerson, *American Evangelicalism: Embattled and Thriving* (Chicago: University of Chicago, 1998), 89. See also Christine J. Gardner,

Making Chastity Sexy: The Rhetoric of Evangelical Abstinence Campaigns (Berkeley: University of California Press, 2011), 537–47.

24. George M. Marsden, *Fundamentalism and American Culture*, 2d ed. (New York: Oxford University Press, 2006), parts II and III. See also Jones, *The End of White Christian America*, Kindle ed., loc. 407 of 5676.

25. Conservative Protestants remain proud of their support for abolition. I heard pastors speak about it to remind Christians of their heritage in fighting for marginalized constituencies and standing up for what is right in society. However, the history of born-again support for the abolition of slavery is complicated. Evangelical scholar Mark Noll wrote that the Civil War exposed a theological crisis between North and South. Northern believers thought God was on their side because they were trying to abolish an unjust institution. Southern believers thought God was for them because they mentioned Him in their Constitution. To this, John Fea adds that Confederate citizens believed God had ordained slavery by allowing it to be mentioned in the Bible. Mark A. Noll, *The Civil War as a Theological Crisis* (Chapel Hill: University of North Carolina Press, 2006), 75; John Fea, *Was America Founded as a Christian Nation? A Historical Introduction* (Louisville, KY: Westminster John Knox Press, 2011). See also John D. Wilsey, *American Exceptionalism and Civil Religion: Reassessing the History of an Idea,* Kindle ed. (Downers Grove, IL: IVP Academic, 2015), loc. 1656 of 5108.

26. FitzGerald, *The Evangelicals*, 65–69; Omri Elisha, *Moral Ambition: Mobilization and Social Outreach in Evangelical Megachurches* (Berkeley: University of California Press, 2011), 14; Stephanie Muravchik, *American Protestantism in the Age of Psychology* (Cambridge, UK: Cambridge University Press, 2011).

27. FitzGerald, *The Evangelicals*, 39.

28. Michael Katz, *In the Shadow of the Poorhouse: A Social History of Welfare in America, Tenth Anniversary Edition,* rev. ed. (New York: Basic Books, 1996).

29. George M. Marsden, *Fundamentalism and American Culture*, 57; FitzGerald, *The Evangelicals,* 100–102. Special thanks, too, to Rev. Charlie Campbell, pastor, Northminster Presbyterian Church, Diamond Bar, California, for helping me to understand millennialism and premillennialism and pointing me toward useful texts.

30. Daniel Bell, *The Cultural Contradictions of Capitalism* (New York: Basic Books, 1976), xiii, 22.

31. There is some conventional wisdom suggesting that in the years after the Scopes trial fundamentalists stopped engaging secular society. George Marsden, among others, wrote that the trial changed fundamentalism into a mostly southern and rural movement, instead of having an urban influence. James Davidson Hunter added that fundamentalists largely believed the Depression was God's punishment for American sin. However, while there is some truth to this portrait, it overstates the case. As Robert B. Horwitz explains in *America's Right: Anti-Establishment Conservatism from Goldwater to the Tea Party*, fundamentalists were "hyperpatriots by the end of World War I" and were always present in the agitations against communism during New Deal legislation and after World War II. Of special import was the staunch

fundamentalist Carl McIntire, who criticized Billy Graham but also openly politicked against communism. See Marsden, *Fundamentalism and American Culture*; James Davison Hunter, *American Evangelicalism: Conservative Religion and the Quandary of Modernity* (New Brunswick, NJ: Rutgers University Press, 1983); Robert B. Horwitz, *America's Right: Anti-Establishment Conservatism from Goldwater to the Tea Party* (Cambridge, UK: Polity Press, 2013), 72–78.

32. Quoted in FitzGerald, *The Evangelicals*, 135. FitzGerald describes in detail some of the reporting about the trial. She pays particular attention to how reporters wrote about William Jennings Bryan, three-time Democratic nominee for president, who prosecuted the case. FitzGerald describes a time when Bryan "went up into the hills and preached to two hundred people about a great religious revival. . . . The mountaineers, said the [*New York*] *Times*, listened to him with a 'reverential hush.' To these plain folks, the reporter concluded, 'Bryan is more than a great politician, more than a lawyer on trial, more even than one of our greatest orators, he is a symbol of their simple religious faith.' Mencken naturally took a more jaundiced view. Describing Bryan's admirers as 'gaping primates,' 'yokels,' 'hillbillies,' and 'morons,' he wrote, 'There were many who believed that Bryan was no longer merely human, but had lifted himself up to some level or other of the celestial angels.' As for [Clarence] Darrow (the prominent attorney who defended Scopes), 'All the local sorcerers predict that a bolt from heaven will fetch him in the end'" (FitzGerald, *The Evangelicals,* 134–35).

33. Clyde Wilcox, *Onward Christian Soldiers: The Religious Right in American Politics*, 2d ed. (Boulder, CO: Westview Press, 2000), 28; Susan Friend Harding, *The Book of Jerry Falwell* (Princeton, NJ: Princeton University Press, 2000), 61–82; Joel A. Carpenter, "From Fundamentalism to the New Evangelical Coalition," in *Evangelicalism and Modern America*, ed. George Marsden (W. B. Eerdman: Grand Rapids, MI, 1984), 6. Peter Berger described the separatist impulse, along with the coincident desire to create sacred institutions free from worldly influence, as a "plausibility structure." By this he meant to describe how these believers set out to create a world so complete that it could stand alone and become wholly credible to those who would populate it, even against the attacks of outsiders who might find it ridiculous or otherwise mock its beliefs, routines, or very existence. Peter Berger, "A Sociological View of the Secularization of Theology: Presidential Address, Society for the Scientific Study of Religion, 1966," *Journal for the Scientific Study of Religion* 6, no. 1 (1967).

34. FitzGerald, *The Evangelicals*, 143–44.

35. William C. Martin, *A Prophet with Honor: The Billy Graham Story*, updated ed. (Grand Rapids, MI: Zondervan, 2018), 93–94.

36. Owen Strachan, *Awakening the Evangelical Mind: An Intellectual History of the Neo-Evangelical Movement* (Grand Rapids, MI: Zondervan, 2015), 13.

37. Quoted in William Martin, *With God on Our Side: The Rise of the Religious Right in America* (New York: Broadway Books, 1997), 33; Strachan, *Awakening the Evangelical Mind.*

38. Jones, *The End of White Christian America*, Kindle ed., loc. 476 of 5676; Strachan, *Awakening the Evangelical Mind*, 22–23.

39. For example, see Ron Sider, James Dobson, and Sho Baraka, "No Clear Choice: 3 Perspectives on the 2016 Election"; Sho Baraka, "Why I'm Voting for Neither Candidate"; and Jen Wilkin, "Where Kids Get Their Political Views," all in *Christianity Today* (Special Section), September 23, 2016. Also Tish Harrison Warren, "I Overlooked the Rural Poor—Then Trump Came Along," *Christianity Today* August 22, 2016, https://www.christianitytoday.com/ct/2016/september/i-overlooked-rural-poor-then-trump-came-along.html. Of particular note is Warren's article, which critiques conservatives (like her) and evangelicals (like her) for not "seeing Trump coming" and revealing "a large demographic of Americans who were off [her] radar." Like the so-called liberal elites that members of the GOP and conservative evangelicals were so fond of criticizing, Warren wrote that perhaps in their efforts to evangelize areas of "strategic impact" (cities like New York, Seattle, or San Francisco), the megachurch-planting believers—like those in my study—had neglected to pay attention to Trump voters. Her writing sounds very much like that of so many mainstream reporters when it comes to describing working-class and white rural voters, although tinged with the language of conservative Protestantism. "The rise of Trump brought for me conviction of sin: I did not have ears to hear and take seriously the suffering and frustration of impoverished white Americans in what one reporter has called 'the vast open reaches of the country.' Many small-town and rural communities face unprecedented crisis. Their pain is now driving our national political life." She called for the church to respond to racism, much as many had previously called it to respond to those who identify as queer—to hate the sin and love the sinner. This, she admitted, was hard to do. It seemed all the more peculiar as the article reached its end. She quoted an interview she conducted with a man named Dave, who said it was easier to love college students having premarital sex than elderly rural white people who referred to Mexicans as wetbacks. But the rural white Americans were now, as Trump had shown, the weak, marginalized, and forgotten. "We serve a Savior whose ministry on earth was often 'nonstrategic,' one who reaches the forgotten, despised, and marginalized. Jesus was from a backwater town, a ridiculed, nowhere place. America's Nazareths are longing to hear the Good News."

40. Among the most vociferous critics was Carl McIntire of the ACCC. McIntire was a devout fundamentalist and riveting preacher who urged that while the United States had to defend against the Russian threat of communism—even launch a preemptive nuclear strike if necessary—so, too, did true believers have to remain separate from secular culture to remain pure and free from sin. Martin, *With God on Our Side*, 36–37.

41. Carl F. H. Henry, *The Uneasy Conscience of Modern Fundamentalism* (Grand Rapids, MI: Eerdmans, 1947).

42. Elisha, *Moral Ambition*, 16. The Chicago Declaration was part of the founding effort of the group Evangelicals for Social Action. The Lausanne Covenant came out of the International Congress on World Evangelization.

43. A. James Reichley, "The Evangelical and Fundamentalist Revolt," in *Piety & Politics: Evangelicals and Fundamentalists Confront the World*, ed. Richard John Neuhaus and Michael Cromartie (Lanham, MD: University Press of America, 1987), 76–77.

44. A. James Reichley writes, "During its first year, the Moral Majority concentrated on getting its name well known and on registering voters for the 1980 election. At the first of these objectives it was spectacularly successful. A Gallup poll in December 1980 found that 40 percent of a national sample had heard of the Moral Majority. Surveys taken in the South and Southwest found levels of recognition almost twice the national figure. Part of the Moral Majority's fame stemmed from the use of its name by national media and liberal publicists to designate the entire religious new Right. Many of the people who had heard of the Moral Majority did not like it" (Reichley, "The Evangelical and Fundamentalist Revolt," 83).

45. Evangelical voters almost certainly switched their support from Jimmy Carter in 1976, to Ronald Reagan in 1980. How much is a bit of an open question. In return for their support, Reagan spoke the language of conservative Protestants, even if he was not always open to actively pushing legislation that forwarded their agenda. Randall Balmer, *Thy Kingdom Come: How the Religious Right Distorts the Faith and Threatens America: An Evangelical's Lament* (New York: Basic Books, 2006), xvi; Martin, *With God on Our Side*, chap. 8, "Moral Majority."

46. Elisha, *Moral Ambition*, 16.

47. Groups like the Moral Majority and the Christian Coalition can probably be categorized as primarily political organizations. They talked a lot about Washington, DC and its problems, and the need to change laws and policies to defend the family and society from harm. Others, like Focus on the Family and Concerned Women for America, gained public influence through advancing a conversation with symbolic and affective dimensions. See David Snowball, *Continuity and Change in the Rhetoric of the Moral Majority* (New York: Praeger, 1991); Linda Kintz, *Between Jesus and the Market: The Emotions That Matter in Right-Wing America* (Durham, NC: Duke University Press, 1997).

48. Since Trump was elected, the US Supreme Court majority has swung toward the conservative side, so it is possible that *Roe v. Wade* may finally be overturned. However, this would only return the legality of reproductive freedom and access to abortion to the states. A patchwork system would inevitably result, where women in progressive states like California would likely still be able to get abortions, while women in more conservative states like Texas would not. Christian conservatives who are politically motivated are unsatisfied with abortion restrictions that merely make it hard to access; they want it to be absolutely illegal.

49. Frank, *What's the Matter with Kansas?* 6.

50. Dan T. Carter, "The Rise of Conservatism since World War 2," *OAH Magazine of History* 17, no. 2 (2003): 15.

51. Kim Phillips-Fein, *Invisible Hands: The Making of the Conservative Movement from the New Deal to Reagan* (New York: W. W. Norton, 2009), 258.

52. Phillips-Fein, *Invisible Hands*, 237.

53. J. Brooks Flippen, *Jimmy Carter: The Politics of Family and the Rise of the Religious Right*, ed. Claire Potter and Renee Romano (Athens: University of Georgia Press, 2011), 289.

54. Wilcox, *Onward Christian Soldiers*, 89.

55. Wilsey, *American Exceptionalism and Civil Religion*, Kindle ed., loc. 130 of 5108.

56. Omri Elisha has written extensively about why so few conservative Protestants participate in ministries with goals that aim to reach poor and needy populations, even in spite of loosened government regulations that would provide taxpayer funding to help pay for them. Many give lip service to the need to do better at this, but participation rates are low. This could be for reasons other than a lack of compassion (being busy or otherwise committed, for example). It minimally suggests a tendency to privilege evangelization and "saving souls" over meeting basic needs. See Elisha, *Moral Ambition*.

Chapter 2

1. In *Beyond Megachurch Myths*, Thumma and Travis discuss how megachurches use adaptive methods like the one I describe at Taylors First Baptist as a way to ensure continued growth and attract new people to Christianity. Rather than trying to be one-size-fits-all institutions, or trying to capture a particular vibe that will ensure growth, some churches develop different kinds of services that are meant to attract different kinds of people. The services usually have the same message, however, which is how these congregations maintain shared identity. Scott Thumma and Dave Travis, *Beyond Megachurch Myths: What We Can Learn from America's Largest Churches* (San Francisco: Jossey-Bass, 2007), 172–73.

2. Paul Jiminez, "Culture, Politics and the Church, Week 2," November 6, 2016, Taylors First Baptist Church, Taylors, SC.

3. Omri Elisha, *Moral Ambition: Mobilization and Social Outreach in Evangelical Megachurches* (Berkeley: University of California Press, 2011); Christine J. Gardner, *Making Chastity Sexy: The Rhetoric of Evangelical Abstinence Campaigns* (Berkeley: University of California Press, 2011); James S. Bielo, *Words upon the Word: An Ethnography of Evangelical Group Bible Study* (New York: New York University Press, 2009); Susan Friend Harding, *The Book of Jerry Falwell* (Princeton, NJ: Princeton University Press, 2000).

4. Clifford Geertz, *The Interpretation of Cultures; Selected Essays* (New York: Basic Books, 1973).

5. Megachurches are an admittedly limited and imperfect dataset. In note 12 of this book's introduction, I explain my reasoning for using these bodies, and not smaller churches. Moreover, although megachurches have "home sites" in particular places, they also often have satellite sites and additional campuses that extend into other states and, sometimes, other countries. This, too, extended my reach in various, albeit nebulous, ways. This reach—and imprecision—was extended by the very fact of my presence in cyberspace.

6. Annette N. Markham, *Life Online: Researching Real Experience in Virtual Space* (Walnut Creek, CA: Altamira Press, 1998).

7. From the earliest days of internet expansion, leaders of the megachurch movement—including David Yonggi Cho, one of the founders of Yoido Full Gospel Church, Seoul, South Korea (possibly the world's largest church), and Richard Duane (Rick) Warren of Saddleback Church, Lake Forest, California—thought the internet had great missional potential. The two spoke of how it would allow churches into places where "Christianity was absent or marginalised." Questions have proliferated about how much "church" can really be done online—could a valid baptism or wedding ceremony ever be performed, for example? But the idea persists that the internet presents a way to "draw in people who could not (or would not) get to 'regular church, particularly those who were computer savvy.'" See Tim Hutchings, *Creating Church Online: Ritual, Community, and New Media* (New York: Routledge, 2017), 12, 14.

8. Jud Wilhite, "Hope beyond Politics," November 6, 2016, Central Church, Henderson, NV.

9. Theda Skocpol and Vanessa Williamson, *The Tea Party and the Remaking of Republican Conservatism* (New York: Oxford University Press, 2012).

10. Linda Kintz, *Between Jesus and the Market: The Emotions That Matter in Right-Wing America* (Durham, NC: Duke University Press, 1997), 6.

11. Tod Bolsinger, "What Wikipedia, AA, Al Qaeda, and the Early Church Have in Common," *Tod Bolsinger* (blog), October 3, 2008, https://bolsinger.blogs.com/weblog/2008/10/what-wikipedia-aa-al-qaeda-and-the-early-church-have-in-common.html; San Clemente Presbyterian Church, http://www.scpres.org/#/welcome. Bolsinger was at this time senior pastor and head of staff at San Clemente Presbyterian Church, San Clemente, California. He has since left this position to become vice president for vocation and formation, and an associate professor of practical theology at Fuller Theological Seminary. When Bolsinger led SCPC, as it is known colloquially, the church described itself on its website as both Presbyterian and a church of "evangelical" conviction. Moreover, Bolsinger talks and writes often about how he received both his master's of divinity and his PhD from Fuller Theological Seminary in Pasadena, one of conservative evangelicalism's flagship institutions. That he graduated from Fuller and later returned there as a vice president gives me confidence that he led and identifies as an evangelical, even though many Presbyterian churches in the United States are more mainline than conservative Protestant.

12. An example of the kind of notes I took is as follows: "This week Rev. Bolsinger did talk about leadership in his sermon, but leadership as a function of following. It was a sermon that made fruitful cross-pollination between entrepreneurship, leadership, and theology. To do this, he used the viral TED talk by Derek Sivers. Sivers's key contribution is to link courage with being a follower; the courage required in 'following'; specifically in being a *first follower. He argues that the first to trust a leader or an innovator is on to something.* 'The first follower transforms the lone nut into something more,' Bolsinger said, quoting Sivers. Bolsinger suggested this is key to the Christian life. Following first, following even if no one else does. I wonder: is this another way, a less forceful way, of articulating Christian Smith's theory that evangelicals see themselves as 'embattled but thriving' and 'in the world but not of it'?

Derek Sivers is a business entrepreneur (music). This is an example of narrative resonance across spheres that I have been looking for. Sivers does not identify as any kind of Christian in his publicly available materials, so far as I can find." Author's research notes, September 22, 2011.

13. My decision to exclusively study megachurches necessarily constitutes an important limitation to this work, and a fertile opportunity for further study.

14. Churches based in thirty-seven states are included in this study, from Washington to Massachusetts, and from California to Alabama. See the appendixes.

15. I use "cultural studies" here as an umbrella term to identify myself, across disciplines, with those scholars who privilege questions (as Mountford wrote) of "race, class, and gay, lesbian, and bisexual issues." This list is necessarily incomplete but must be expanded to include gender and economic inequality.

16. Roxanne Mountford, *The Gendered Pulpit: Preaching in American Protestant Spaces* (Carbondale: Southern Illinois University Press, 2003).

17. Aaron Hess, "Critical-Rhetorical Ethnography: Rethinking the Place and Process of Rhetoric," *Communication Studies* 62, no. 2 (2011); Phaedra C. Pezzullo, "Resisting 'National Breast Cancer Awareness Month': The Rhetoric of Counterpublics and Their Cultural Performances," *Quarterly Journal of Speech* 89, no. 4 (2003); Dwight Conquergood, "Ethnography, Rhetoric, and Performance," *Quarterly Journal of Speech* 78, no. 1 (1992).

18. Pezzullo offered the notion of copresence from Michael Warner's work on publics and counterpublics. According to Warner, a public did not necessarily depend on the presence of the researcher. To this, Pezullo wrote, "it is worth considering when and why participant observation of a public might make a difference." Pezzullo, "Resisting 'National Breast Cancer Awareness Month.'"

19. Pezzullo, "Resisting 'National Breast Cancer Awareness Month,'" 350.

20. Louis Althusser, "Ideology and Ideological State Apparatuses," https://www.marxists.org/reference/archive/althusser/1970/ideology.htm.

21. Elisha, *Moral Ambition*; Gardner, *Making Chastity Sexy*; Bielo, *Words upon the Word;* R. Marie Griffith, *God's Daughters: Evangelical Women and the Power of Submission* (Berkeley: University of California Press, 1997); Harding, *The Book of Jerry Falwell.*

22. See also Marsha Houston Stanback and W. Barnett Pearce, "Talking to 'the Man': Some Communication Strategies Used by Members of 'Subordinate' Social Groups," *Quarterly Journal of Speech* 67, no. 1 (1981).

23. Sharon Crowley, *Toward a Civil Discourse: Rhetoric and Fundamentalism* (Pittsburgh: University of Pittsburgh Press, 2006).

24. Heidi Campbell, *Exploring Religious Community Online: We Are One in the Network* (New York: Peter Lang, 2005).

25. David Zarefsky, "Knowledge Claims in Rhetorical Criticism," *Journal of Communication* 58, no. 4 (2008).

26. Ricci argues that one important advantage conservatives have over liberals in American politics is that conservatives tell good stories and liberals do not. By stories,

Ricci means grand narratives that explain big things—markets and morals, patriotism and personal responsibility. Those on the Right, Ricci says, have a touchstone ability to evoke "common sense" and so create "*large* and *lasting* tales" about what it means to be an American. Examples include the power of open markets for individual freedom, the benefits of small government, and how prosperity is not inherited, but is always the product of the American Dream. David Ricci, *Politics without Stories: The Liberal Predicament* (New York: Cambridge University Press, 2016), 16–17.

27. An *esprit de finesse* is similar, but grander, I think, than the idea of "rhetorical resonance" that Linda Kintz described. Kintz, *Between Jesus and the Market*.

28. Ricci, *Politics without Stories*, 23–24; Jacques Barzun, *The Culture We Deserve* (Middletown, CT: Wesleyan University Press, 1989).

29. Lilliana Mason, *Uncivil Agreement: How Politics Became Our Identity* (Chicago: University of Chicago Press, 2018); Alan I. Abramowitz and Steven W. Webster, "Negative Partisanship: Why Americans Dislike Parties But Behave Like Rabid Partisans," *Political Psychology* 39 (2018): 119–35; Julia Azari and Andrew Gelman, "Rejoinder: How Special Was 2016?" *Statistics and Public Policy* 4, no. 1 (2017).

30. Harding, *The Book of Jerry Falwell*, 12; William M. Keith and Christian O. Lundberg, *The Essential Guide to Rhetoric* (New York: St. Martin's Press, 2008), 2; Max Weber, *The Sociology of Religion* (Boston: Beacon Press, 1993).

31. Chaïm Perelman and Lucie Olbrechts-Tyteca, *The New Rhetoric: A Treatise in Argumentation* (Notre Dame, IN: University of Notre Dame Press, 2010), 66, 74–79.

32. Near the beginning of *The New Rhetoric*, the authors define argumentation as "the study of the discursive techniques allowing us to induce or increase the mind's adherence to the theses presented for assent." This definition connects "discursive techniques" (how something is said) with "theses presented" (arguments). In short, evidence does not stand alone; it is framed and presented. A dissertation written in 2008 by Miriam Yvonne Perkins helped me understand how the theory of Perelman and Olbrechts-Tyteca was especially useful for unpacking formal homiletic rhetoric. Perelman and Olbrechts-Tyteca, *The New Rhetoric*, 4; Miriam Yvonne Perkins, "Preaching and Rhetorical Responses to Terror: American Evangelican Sermons Delivered in Reaction to September 11, 2001" (PhD diss., Catholic University of America, 2008), 22–31.

33. Perelman and Olbrechts-Tyteca, *The New Rhetoric*, 14.

34. In the parable of the talents, Jesus tells the story of a master leaving for extended travel. He entrusts three servants with his property while he is away. Each of the first two servants grow the master's wealth, but the third, being afraid of the master, buries his share of the property for safekeeping. Nothing is lost, but nothing is gained. When the master returns, he is angry at this result. He shuns the servant and casts him into the darkness. By contrast, the first two servants are congratulated and given more to manage in the future.

35. Kip Redick and Lori Underwood, "Rationality and Narrative: A Relationship of Priority," *Philosophy & Rhetoric* 40, no. 4 (2007).

36. Wallace Martin, *Recent Theories of Narrative* (Ithaca, NY: Cornell University

Press, 1986), 187. Also, as Fisher wrote, "the narrative paradigm challenges the notion that human communication—if it is to be considered rhetorical—must be argumentative in form." He added that the narrative paradigm also denies "that reason is to be attributed only to discourse marked by clearly identifiable modes of inference an implication." Walter R. Fisher, "Narration as a Human Communication Paradigm: The Case of Public Moral Argument," *Communication Monographs* 51, no. 1 (1984): 1–22.

37. This is the statement of faith at Willow Creek Community Church, South Barrington, Illinois. Willow Creek was established by Bill Hybels, a founder of the seeker-friendly church movement. Hybels stepped down in 2018 after being accused of sexual misconduct. See Willow Creek Community Church, "Statement of Faith," http://www.willowcreek.com/about/statement_faith.asp.

38. Robert D. Putnam and David. E. Campbell, *American Grace: How Religion Divides and Unites Us* (New York: Simon & Schuster, 2010), 111. See also Christian Smith and Michael Emerson, *American Evangelicalism: Embattled and Thriving* (Chicago: University of Chicago Press, 1998); Randall Balmer, *Evangelicalism in America* (Waco, TX: Baylor University Press, 2016).

39. Conquergood, "Ethnography, Rhetoric, and Performance."

40. Candace Rai, *Democracy's Lot: Rhetoric, Publics, and the Places of Invention* (Tuscaloosa: University of Alabama Press, 2016), 16–17.

41. Jiminez, "Culture, Politics and the Church, Week 2."

Chapter 3

1. Jon Meacham, "The End of Christian America," *Newsweek*, April 3, 2009, https://www.newsweek.com/meacham-end-christian-america-77125.

2. Meacham, "The End of Christian America."

3. For some scholarship that explores the role of Obama and his multicultural influence in American politics, see Peter Beinart, "Is Barack Obama American Enough?" *Time*, October 9, 2008, 34–35. See also Michael Haas, ed., *Barack Obama, the Aloha Zen President: How a Son of the 50th State May Revitalize America Based on 12 Multicultural Principles* (Santa Barbara, CA: ABC-CLIO, 2011).

4. Hugh Hewitt, "Rick Warren on the Newsweek 'End of Christian America' Article, Pt. 1," transcript of interview, April 8, 2009, http://www.hughhewitt.com/rick-warren-on-the-newsweek-end-of-christian-america-article-pt-1/.

5. Hugh Hewitt, "Rick Warren Reflects on Why Christianity Is Not Dead in America as Newsweek Proclaims," transcript of interview, April 13, 2009, http://www.hughhewitt.com/rick-warren-reflects-on-why-christianity-is-not-dead-in-america-as-newsweek-proclaims/.

6. Hewitt, "Rick Warren Reflects."

7. Hewitt, "Rick Warren Reflects."

8. Betsy Cooper, Daniel Cox, Rachel Lienesch, and Robert P. Jones, "The Divide over America's Future: 1950 or 2050? Findings from the 2016 American Values Survey" (Washington, DC: PRRI, 2016).

9. Kenneth Burke, *The Philosophy of Literary Form: Studies in Symbolic Action* (Los Angeles: University of California Press, 1974); Burke, *Rhetoric of Religion* (Berkeley: University of California, 1970); Burke, "The Rhetoric of Hitler's Battle," in *Landmark Essays on Rhetorical Criticism*, ed. Thomas Benson (Davis, CA: Hermagoras Press, 1993).

10. It is worth noting that Hunter includes Orthodox Jews and conservative Catholics as also among the American "orthodoxy," although I am only considering white, conservative Protestants in this study. See James Davison Hunter, *Culture Wars: The Struggle to Define America* (New York: Basic Books, 1991).

11. Hunter, *Culture Wars*, 33.

12. Hunter, *Culture Wars*, 44.

13. Hunter, *Culture Wars*, 54.

14. In general, I list both the specific suburban locations of these congregations and the major cities to which they are closest because I am trying to emphasize that these churches have their largest sites—where their "main" pastors preach—near, but not in, major cities. It is more useful for readers to know that these are places near Atlanta, Chicago, Charlotte, Dallas, etc., than to know they are in suburbs they might never have heard of.

15. Andy Stanley, "Recovery Road, Recession Lessons," sermon, August 21, 2011, North Point Community Church, Alpharetta, GA (MP3 audio file).

16. Deborah L. Madsen, *American Exceptionalism* (Edinburgh: Edinburgh University Press, 1998), chap. 1, "Origins: American Exceptionalism and American Cultural Identity," and chap. 2, "Contemporary Interpretations of Exceptionalism." See also Seymour Martin Lipset, *American Exceptionalism: A Double-Edged Sword* (New York: W. W. Norton, 1996).

17. I use the term "sui generis" in the sociological sense following Emile Durkheim. Durkheim used the term to describe "social facts"—those things that exist outside of individuals and are essential to the creation and maintenance of societies. Social worlds and ideas exist "sui generis." They have independent realities and cannot be reduced to composite parts. Rather, such social facts *are* society. No person can escape society or become exempt from society's sturm and drang. Likewise, the point in Stanley's sermon was not whether one approved of the idea of American exceptionalism. American exceptionalism simply exists. It came before. It exists after. It is an American "social fact." Anthony Giddens and Philip W. Sutton, *Essential Concepts in Sociology*, 2nd edition. (Malden, MA: Polity, 2017); Emile Durkheim and Steven Lukes. *The Rules of Sociological Method*, 1st American ed., ed., intro., Steven Lukes ; trans. W. D. Halls. (New York: Free Press, 1982).

18. Chaïm Perelman and Lucie Olbrechts-Tyteca, *The New Rhetoric: A Treatise in Argumentation* (Notre Dame, IN: University of Notre Dame Press, 2010), 307.

19. Perelman and Olbrechts-Tyteca, *The New Rhetoric,* 307.

20. Perelman and Olbrechts-Tyteca, *The New Rhetoric,* 309.

21. Skip Heitzig, "Freedom Celebration 2012," sermon, July 4, 2012, Calvary Chapel, Albuquerque, NM, https://podcasts.google.com/.

22. Don Wilson, "This Is Freedom," sermon, July 4, 2010, Christ's Church of the Valley, Peoria, AZ. For self-evident reasons, the 2010 Independence Day holiday, which fell on a Sunday, proved especially fruitful for research into sermonic discourse about how pastors frame the role of the United States in the world. Many sermons were given across the country on this day about freedom and the meaning of freedom, both for Christians in particular, and for Americans in general.

23. Don Wilson, "This Is Freedom," sermon, July 4, 2010. Isaiah 33:22 is *not* the source from which the framers are believed to have drawn their inspiration. Rather, most political theorists believe the framers drew from Aristotle and Montesquieu.

24. Montesquieu, *Selected Political Writings*, ed. Melvin Richter (Indianapolis: Hackett, 1990).

25. WallBuilders describes itself on its website as "an organization dedicated to presenting America's forgotten history and heroes, with an emphasis on the moral, religious, and constitutional foundation on which America was built—a foundation which, in recent years, has been seriously attacked and undermined. In accord with what was so accurately stated by George Washington, we believe that 'the propitious [favorable] smiles of heaven can never be expected on a nation which disregards the eternal rules of order and right which heaven itself has ordained.'" Wallbuilders, "About Us," https://wallbuilders.com/about-us//. Barton's publisher, Thomas Nelson, once had to pull his book about Thomas Jefferson from shelves and stop publishing it because it was inaccurate. *Time* named Barton one of the twenty-five most influential evangelicals in 2005.

26. Dave Stone, "Cliffhanger: The Family, the Foundation of a Nation, the Story of Us," sermon, July 4, 2010, Southeast Christian Church, Louisville, KY (MP3 audio file).

27. Andy Stanley, "In God We Trust—Part One," sermon, February 14, 2010, Willow Creek Community Church, South Barrington, IL (MP3 audio file).

28. Rick Warren, "The Five Foundations of Financial Freedom," seminar, June 4, 2010, Saddleback Church, Lake Forest, CA (video file).

29. During the years of the recession, costs for housing, transportation, and food were rising faster than wages for families, at all but the very top of the income scale. Bureau of Labor Statistics, "Economic News Release: Consumer Expenditures 2010" (Washington, DC: US Department of Labor, 2011).

30. Joshua Harris, "The Good Recession, Part One," sermon, January 11, 2009, Covenant Life Church, Gaithersburg, MD (MP3 audio file). Harris is no longer a pastor, and indeed has renounced his Christian faith. See "After Kissing Christianity Goodbye, Joshua Harris Joins Vancouver's LGBTQ Pride Parade," *CBN News*, August 6, 2019, https://www1.cbn.com/cbnnews/entertainment/2019/august/ex-pastor-joshua-harris-shows-lgbtq-support-at-vancouvers-pride-parade.

31. Dave Ramsey, "Enough," Willow Creek Community Church, South Barrington, IL, March 9, 2009. Although Dave Ramsey is not an ordained pastor, I include his sermons for the following reasons. Ramsey is one of the very visible figures in evangelical Christianity and has been profiled several times in *Christianity Today*.

He has a radio broadcast that is based in Nashville, Tennessee, and airs on 325 affiliate stations, and he also serves as a frequent guest on programs for the Fox Business Network. But his most significant contribution may be his "Financial Peace University," a program that churches can use as a tool to help people get their finances in order and as a community outreach program. *Christianity Today* estimated that while "military bases, corporations, and other non-religious groups host Financial Peace classes, the majority of the 20,000 held [in 2010] were at churches." The magazine further wrote that about 1.3 million people have attended a Financial Peace seminar since its inception in 1992. Ramsey is also a frequent guest speaker at megachurches like Willow Creek and Saddleback. Rob Moll, "Dave Ramsey Goes Beyond Credit Card Shredding," *Christianity Today*, August 2011, https://www.christianitytoday.com/ct/2011/august/dave-ramsey-money-church.html. See also Stephanie A. Martin, "Money and the Electronic Church: Decoding Dave Ramsey's Debt-Free Gospel," in *The Electronic Church in the Digital Age: Cultural Impacts of Evangelical Mass Media*, ed. Mark Ward (Santa Barbara, CA: Praeger, 2015).

32. Ramsey, "Enough."

33. John Piper, "What's the Recession For," sermon, February 1, 2009, Bethlehem Baptist Church, Minneapolis (MP3 audio file). After thirty-three years as pastor at Bethlehem Baptist, Piper is currently active in his own organization, of which he is founder and teacher, Desiring God.

34. Wilson, "Freedom."

35. Kevin Myers, "How We Work," sermon, February 19, 2012, 12Stone Church, Lawrenceville, GA.

36. Although today's megachurches emit a seeker-friendly vibe that often includes pastors wearing jeans paired with T-shirts or loose-fitting twill sport shirts, there is still an unmistakable misogyny in the sermonic discourse. This is probably because many of these churches still uphold traditional gender roles in marriage and in church structure (see chapter six). Nearly all of them have male senior pastors, and many forbid women from serving in senior pastor roles, or even in regular teaching roles. It is also not uncommon to hear pastors try to moderate their masculine appeals by trying to deliver them as tongue-in-cheek or with asides like, "Right, ladies?"

37. Mark Driscoll, "The Parable of the Dishonest Manager," sermon, March 13, 2011, Mars Hill Church, Seattle (MP3 audio file). Driscoll was forced to resign from Mars Hill in 2014, accused of "creating a culture of fear at the church, of plagiarizing, of inappropriately using church funds and of consolidating power to such a degree that it has become difficult for anyone to challenge or even question him." Michael Paulson, "A Brash Style That Filled Pews, until Followers Had Their Fill: Mark Driscoll Is Being Urged to Leave Mars Hill Church," *New York Times,* August 22, 2014. See also Morgan Lee, "Mark Driscoll Steps Down While Mars Hill Investigates Charges," *Christianity Today,* August 24, 2014, http://www.christianitytoday.com/news/2014/august/mark-driscoll-steps-down-while-mars-hill-investigates-charg.html.

38. Lon Solomon, "The Lying Prophets of America," sermon, July 4, 2012,

McLean Bible Church, Vienna, VA. Solomon served as senior pastor at McLean from 1980 to 2017, during which time the church was based in McLean, Virginia.

39. Monique El-Faizy, *God and Country: How Evangelicals Have Become America's New Mainstream* (New York: Bloomsbury, 2006); Kristopher Norris and Sam Speers, *Kingdom Politics: In Search of a New Political Imagination for Today's Church* (Eugene, OR: Cascade Books, 2015).

40. Piper, "What's the Recession For."

41. Piper, "What's the Recession For."

42. Piper, "What's the Recession For."

43. Jay Wolf, "Be Wise with Wealth," sermon, February 6, 2011, First Baptist Church, Montgomery, AL (MP3 audio file).

44. Stanley, "In God We Trust—Part One."

45. Stanley, "In God We Trust—Part One."

46. Tod Bolsinger, "Talking to the Powers That Be," sermon, November 14, 2010, San Clemente Presbyterian Church, San Clemente, CA (MP3 audio recording).

47. Mark Driscoll, "Parable of the Rich Fool," sermon, November 7, 2010, Mars Hill Church, Seattle (MP3 audio file).

48. Mark Driscoll, "Jesus on Money, Idolatry, and Comedy," sermon, May 29, 2011, Mars Hill Church, Seattle (MP3 audio file).

49. Jim Burgen, "Reverse Engineering: This Is What It Looks Like," sermon, January 22, 2012, Flatirons Community Church, Lafayette, CO.

50. Burgen, "Reverse Engineering."

51. Wilson, "Freedom."

52. Stanley, "Recovery Road, Recession Lessons."

53. Lipset, *American Exceptionalism*, 18.

54. Robert P. Jones, *The End of White Christian America*, Kindle ed. (New York: Simon & Schuster, 2016).

Chapter 4

1. Tom Gjelten, "Conservative Pastors Deliver Sharp Criticism of Same-Sex Marriage," *NPR News: All Things Considered,* November 29, 2015, https://www.npr.org/2015/06/29/418641115/conservative-pastors-deliver-sharp-criticism-of-same-sex-marriage.

2. Laurie Goodstein, "Evangelicals Open Door to Debate on Gay Rights," *New York Times,* June 8, 2015. See also Andrew Hartman, *A War for the Soul of America: A History of the Culture Wars* (Chicago: University of Chicago Press, 2015); Ross Douthat, "The Culture War's Sore Winners," *New York Times,* July 1, 2014.

3. Jessica Taylor, "Cruz: Opposition to Same-Sex Marriage Will Be 'Front and Center' in 2016 Campaign," *NPR News: Morning Edition,* June 29, 2015, https://www.npr.org/sections/itsallpolitics/2015/06/29/418398912/cruz-opposition-to-gay-marriage-will-be-front-and-center-in-2016-campaign.

4. Alexander Burns, "Donald Trump, Pushing Someone Rich, Offers Himself,"

New York Times, June 16, 2015, https://www.nytimes.com/2015/06/17/us/politics/donald-trump-runs-for-president-this-time-for-real-he-says.html; Michelle Ye Hee Lee, "Donald Trump's False Comments Connecting Mexican Immigrants and Crime," *Washington Post*, July 8, 2015, https://www.washingtonpost.com/news/fact-checker/wp/2015/07/08/donald-trumps-false-comments-connecting-mexican-immigrants-and-crime/?utm_term=.967220e8ebe7.

5. Eugene Scott, "Trump Believes in God, But Hasn't Sought Forgiveness," *CNN Politics*, July 18, 2015, https://www.cnn.com/2015/07/18/politics/trump-has-never-sought-forgiveness/index.html.

6. Jessica Taylor, "Citing 'Two Corinthians,' Trump Struggles to Make the Sale to Evangelicals," *NPR News: All Things Considered*, January 18, 2016, https://www.npr.org/2016/01/18/463528847/citing-two-corinthians-trump-struggles-to-make-the-sale-to-evangelicals.

7. Jonathan Easley, "Trump Lands Jerry Falwell Endorsement," The Hill, January 26, 2016, https://thehill.com/blogs/ballot-box/presidential-races/267032-trump-lands-falwell-endorsement. In August 2020, after a series of controversies, Jerry Falwell Jr. was asked to resign from the presidency of Liberty University. Sarah Pulliam Bailey, Susan Svrluga, and Michelle Boorstein, "Jerry Falwell Jr. Resigns as Head of Liberty University, Will Get $10.5 Million in Compensation," *Washington Post*, August 25, 2020, https://www.washingtonpost.com/education/2020/08/25/fallwell-resigns-confirmed/.

8. The Eagle Forum is an all-volunteer conservative organization that chiefly advocates politically for laws and policies that favor the "traditional," patriarchal family. Kevin McDermott, "Conservative Icon Schlafly Faces Revolt over Trump Support; Ed Martin Possibly Removed," *St. Louis Post Dispatch*, April 11, 2016, https://www.stltoday.com/news/local/govt-and-politics/conservative-icon-schlafly-faces-revolt-over-trump-support-ed-martin/article_8268e112–4f2f-560c-9e7d-f445078fc5a8.html.

9. Trip Gabriel and Michael Luo, "A Born-Again Donald Trump? Believe It, Evangelical Leader Says," *New York Times*, June 25, 2016, https://www.nytimes.com/2016/06/26/us/politics/a-born-again-donald-trump-believe-it-evangelical-leader-says.html.

10. Pierre du Plessis, "Political Questions," sermon, October 30, 2016, The Father's House, Rochester, NY.

11. Tim Harlow, "How to Love Those People," sermon, November 6, 2016, Parkview Christian Church, Orland Park, IL. See also Andy Borowitz, "Queen Offers to Restore British Rule over United States," *New Yorker*, October 29, 2016, https://www.newyorker.com/humor/borowitz-report/queen-offers-to-restore-british-rule-over-united-states.

12. Gallup, "Trump and Clinton Finish with Historically Poor Images," November 8, 2016, https://news.gallup.com/poll/197231/trump-clinton-finish-historically-poor-images.aspx.

13. Alan I. Abramowitz and Steven W. Webster, "Negative Partisanship: Why

Americans Dislike Parties But Behave Like Rabid Partisans," *Political Psychology* 39 (2018): 119–35; Bethany Albertson, "Dog-Whistle Politics: Multivocal Communication and Religious Appeals," *Political Behavior* 37, no. 1 (2015): 3–26; Lilliana Mason, *Uncivil Agreement: How Politics Became Our Identity* (Chicago: University of Chicago Press, 2018).

14. Frances FitzGerald, *The Evangelicals: The Struggle to Shape America* (New York: Simon & Schuster, 2017); William Martin, *With God on Our Side: The Rise of the Religious Right in America* (New York: Broadway Books, 1997).

15. Kevin Myers, "Faith. Politics. Church," sermon, October 23, 2016, 12Stone Church, Lawrenceville, GA.

16. Scott Thumma and Dave Travis, *Beyond Megachurch Myths: What We Can Learn from America's Largest Churches* (San Francisco: Jossey-Bass, 2007).

17. Greg Holder, "Common Ground," sermon, November 6, 2016, The Crossing Church, Chesterfield, MO . The final chorus of the hymn, which the worship band led, came from a remix of the song that was released by Kristian Stanfill in 2006. Kristian Stanfill, "Jesus Paid It All," music recording, Sixstepsrecords, Nashville, 2006. The song became a hit and has been used often in contemporary worship services since Stanfill first performed it at a music festival in January 2014.

18. Holder, "Common Ground."

19. Matthew 22:21.

20. Nancy Murphy, *Reasoning and Rhetoric in Religion* (Valley Forge, PA: Trinity Press International, 1994), 93.

21. Todd Mullins, "Decision 2016," November 6, 2016, Christ Fellowship Church, Palm Beach Gardens, FL, http://gochristfellowship.com/messages/.

22. Skip Heitzig, "Christians and Politics," sermon, September 16, 2016, Calvary Chapel, Albuquerque, NM, https://www.youtube.com/watch?v=EPEGtj_AKeU.

23. Dary Northrop, "Politics," sermon, October 16, 2016, Timberline Church, Fort Collins, CO.

24. Steven Furtick, "I Know, But I'm Not Nervous," sermon, November 7, 2016, Elevation Church, Matthews, NC, https://www.youtube.com/watch?v=tsdVmFWL-b_c; 2 Corinthians 1:6–10.

25. Furtick, "I Know, But I'm Not Nervous."

26. David Hughes, "Looking for a Leader," sermon, April 11, 2016, Church by the Glades, Coral Springs, FL, https://www.cbglades.com/archive.

27. Todd Mullins, "Decision 2016," sermon, November 6, 2016, Christ Fellowship Church, Palm Beach Gardens, FL.

28. Neil J. Young, "White Evangelicals Win White House for Trump, But Lose Big," *Religion Dispatches,* November 9, 2016, http://religiondispatches.org/white-evangelicals-win-white-house-for-trump-but-lose-big/.

29. Troy Gramling, "Battleship for the Heart," sermon, October 30, 2016, Potential Church, Cooper City, FL, https://potentialchurch.com/teaching-archives/.

30. Holder, "Common Ground."

31. Jacques Barzun, *The Culture We Deserve* (Middletown, CT: Wesleyan University

Press, 1989), 3–22; David Ricci, *Politics without Stories: The Liberal Predicament* (New York: Cambridge University Press, 2016), 23–24.

32. In creating this river metaphor, I suggest that the discourse of conservative evangelicals, especially the political discourse, might be thought of as a kind of river with competing streams, some fast and some slow, that converge. For those outside of the community, and those who are critics of Trump, we might picture a raft on that river, carrying citizens. During the election, the raft was approaching a steep waterfall or difficult-to-pass, Class V or VI rapids. Seeing a raft in such a situation requires more than passively watching it go by and hoping for the best or promising its inhabitants that even if they're hurt, they'll go to heaven. My argument is that the active-passive discourse of the preachers I studied had this effect. The raft has long been in the river, and so even as many evangelical megachurches have tried to become less overtly political than their Moral Majority forebears, the refusal to engage effectively shot the discursive raft into perilous water.

33. Colossians 3:2.

34. Evan Osnos, "Donald Trump and the Ku Klux Klan: A History," *New Yorker*, February 29, 2016; Michael Barbaro and Megan Twohey, "Crossing the Line: How Donald Trump Behaved with Women in Private," *New York Times*, May 14, 2016.

35. Ray Johnston, "Separation of Church and Hate," sermon, November 6, 2016, Bayside Church, Granite Bay, CA.

36. Dale Hummel, "Dear Mr. or Mrs. Next President," sermon, October 22, 2016, Wooddale Church, Eden Prairie, MN, https://wooddale.org/sermon-series/dear-mr-or-mrs-next-president/.

37. John Pitney, "The Tocqueville Fraud," *Weekly Standard*, November 12, 1995, https://www.weeklystandard.com/john-j-pitney/the-tocqueville-fraud; The Scrapbook, "Fake Tocqueville Lives!" *Weekly Standard*, October 13, 1997, https://www.weeklystandard.com/the-scrapbook/fake-tocqueville-lives. Conservatives do seem to use this made-up quote more than liberals. On July 27, 2018, I did a Google search for it, and the first hundred or so returns (out of 11,200 results) all linked to Right-leaning websites, conservative churches, or Christian bloggers.

38. Hummel, "Dear Mr. or Mrs. Next President."

39. John Fea, *Believe Me: The Evangelical Road to Donald Trump*, Kindle ed. (Grand Rapids, MI: Wm. B. Eerdmans, 2018), loc. 2074–85.

40. Fea, *Believe Me*, loc. 2076–84. See also Svetlana Boym, *The Future of Nostalgia* (New York: Basic Books, 2001).

41. As other pastors did with the historical record and the US founding, Johnston stretched the truth about the popularity and success of *Wall Street*. The film was not the "number one movie in the 1980s" by any normal standard or understanding of "number one." *Wall Street* was not among the top fifty highest grossing movies of the 1980s or even the top twenty-five highest grossing movies of 1987. Although some critics loved it, and Michael Douglas's performance was generally praised, it got mixed receptions or pans from several of the most influential reviewers of the day—including the *New York Times*'s Vincent Canby, Rita Kempley of the *Washington*

Post, the *Chicago Reader*'s Jonathan Rosenbaum, and Julie Salamon of the *Wall Street Journal*. *Wall Street* did not win many awards, either; it was nominated for only one Oscar (Best Actor for Michael Douglas, which he did win). See IMDB, "Feature Film, Released between 1980-01-01 and 1989-12-31 (Sorted by US Box Office Descending)," https://www.imdb.com/search/title/?release_date=1980,1989&title_type=feature&sort=boxoffice_gross_us,desc; Box Office Mojo, "Domestic Box Office for 1987," https://www.boxofficemojo.com/year/1987/; Vincent Canby, "Film: Stone's 'Wall Street,'" New York Times, December 11, 1987, https://www.nytimes.com/1987/12/11/movies/film-stone-s-wall-street.html, Rita Kempley, "Wall Street," Washington Post, December 11, 1987, https://www.washingtonpost.com/wp-srv/style/longterm/movies/videos/wallstreetrkempley_a09f97.htm, Jonathan Rosenbaum, "Wall Street," https://www.chicagoreader.com/chicago/wall-street/Film?oid=1051131.

42. Johnston, "Separation of Church and Hate."

43. William F. Lewis, "Telling America's Story: Narrative Form and the Reagan Presidency," *Quarterly Journal of Speech* 73, no. 3 (1987): 280–302.

44. Raymond Williams, *Keywords: A Vocabulary of Culture and Society* (New York: Oxford University Press, 1976), 12.

45. Ed Young, "How to Pick a President: A Christ Follower's Responsibility in the Election," sermon, November 6, 2016, Fellowship Church, Grapevine, TX.

46. Rob Ketterling, "None of the Above: Part One," sermon, October 23, 2016, River Valley Church, Apple Valley, MN.

47. Piper, "What's the Recession For," sermon, February 1, 2009, Bethlehem Baptist Church, Minneapolis (MP3 audio file).

48. Robert N. Bellah, "American Politics and the Dissenting Protestant Tradition," in *One Electorate under God?: A Dialogue on Religion and American Politics*, ed. E. J. Dionne, Jean Bethke Elshtain, and Kayla Meltzer Drogosz (Washington, DC: Brookings Institution Press, 2004).

49. Donald J. Trump, "Remarks to the 11th Annual Values Voter Summit in Washington, DC, Omni Shoreham Hotel, Washington, DC," September 9, 2016, American Presidency Project, University of California—Santa Barbara, https://www.presidency.ucsb.edu/documents/remarks-the-11th-annual-values-voter-summit-washington-dc-omni-shoreham-hotel-washington. See also Sarah McCammon, "Trump's Vision: Uniting 'under One God' Vs. Religious Freedom," *NPR News: Weekend Edition Saturday,* September 17, 2016, https://www.npr.org/2016/09/17/494360236/trumps-vision-of-uniting-under-one-god-versus-religious-freedom.

50. Don Wilson, "Rehoboam," sermon, November 6, 2016, Christ's Church of the Valley, Peoria, AZ.

51. Bob Smietana, "2016 Election Exposes Evangelical Divides," LifeWay Research, October 14, 2016, https://lifewayresearch.com/2016/10/14/2016-election-exposes-evangelical-divide/.

52. Wilson, "Rehoboam."

53. Wilson, "Rehoboam."

54. Actually, Barack Obama won the 2012 presidential election with more than

65 million votes. Mitt Romney got 60.7 million votes, meaning that Obama won by just more than 4 million votes, not 17 million. This is another example of how white, conservative Protestants often misstate (exaggerate) facts in their sermons for rhetorical effect. Perhaps the pastor meant that had the 4 million missing evangelicals voted, Romney would have won. However, he still would have come up just short, even presuming every single vote had gone to the Massachusetts governor. CNN Politics Election Center, "Election 2012: Results," *CNN,* December 10, 2016.

55. Waylon Sears, "Who Do I Vote For," sermon, October 9, 2016, Victory Worship Center, Tucson, AZ.

56. Mullins, "Decision 2016."

57. Mullins, "Decision 2016."

58. Wilson, "Rehoboam."

59. Skip Heitzig, "Christians and Politics," sermon, September 16, 2016, Calvary Chapel, Albuquerque.

60. Heitzig, "Christians and Politics."

61. Augustine, *The Works of Saint Augustine: A Translation for the 21st Century*, ed. Edmund Hill, John E. Rotelle, and Boniface Ramsey (Brooklyn: New City Press, 1990), s. 16A.9. In this quote, "Jerusalem" can be translated to mean "heaven."

62. Ketterling, "None of the Above: Part One."

Chapter 5

1. Before formally starting to gather my sermon samples, I eliminated a few sermons for being so caustic and over the top in their rhetoric that I determined they were unrepresentative examples. I did not ever eliminate a sermon for not matching the rhetoric or narrative I wanted to hear, unless I determined there was a possibility that using it would frame the evangelical subculture unfairly—which is to say, it would make its members or pastors seem dangerous, scary, or otherwise utterly intolerant. I also omitted a few sermons because they had technical playback issues.

2. Garrett Raburn, "How to Choose a Leader," sermon, November 1, 2016, Watermark Community Church, Dallas.

3. Adam Tarnow, "Everybody Plays But Nobody Wins," sermon, April 26, 2016, Watermark Community Church, Dallas.

4. Jonathan Pokluda, "Anxiety: A Perspective Problem," sermon, December 1, 2015, Watermark Community Church, Dallas.

5. Jonathan Pokluda, "How to Spot Fake Christianity," sermon, July 21, 2015, Watermark Community Church, Dallas.

6. Garrett Raburn, "Sex & Purity," sermon, September 13, 2016, Watermark Community Church, Dallas.

7. I do not argue that the gospel has become personalized, or that conservative evangelical megachurches make everything available wholesale and up for grabs. Rather, individual experience is privileged at the expense of tradition, and this is true online and offline. Stephen Ellingson writes about his field research, and studies that

affirm his findings: "leaders preserve the core teachings while introducing innovations that do not threaten the core . . . Religious groups buffer the core theological teachings but freely borrow and then adapt the ritual practices, recruitment and retention strategies, and technology from other groups in order to increase market share." The things that megachurches borrow include contemporary music led by rock bands, creative use of lighting, and elimination of boring aspects of church, such as reciting creeds or reciting long psalms. These adaptations are aimed at enhancing the individual experience of the church, though they do not translate well to online worship. Stephen Ellingson, *The Megachurch and the Mainline: Remaking Religious Tradition in the Twenty-First Century* (Chicago: University of Chicago Press, 2014), 109.

8. Other research also affirms that megachurch pastors tend to give messages that center on providing audience members with practical, individualized counsel. See Lyman A Kellstedt and John C. Green, "The Politics of the Willow Creek Association Pastors," *Journal for the Scientific Study of Religion* 42, no. 4 (2003); Anne C. Loveland and Otis B. Wheeler, *From Meetinghouse to Megachurch: A Material and Cultural History* (Columbia: University of Missouri Press, 2003); Scott Thumma and Dave Travis, *Beyond Megachurch Myths: What We Can Learn from America's Largest Churches* (San Francisco: Jossey-Bass, 2007).

9. An excellent book for understanding this changed discourse is Michael Lee's *Creating Conservatism: Postwar Words That Created an American Movement* (East Lansing: Michigan State University Press, 2014). Also helpful, particularly for understanding the more contemporary language of the American Right, and its emphasis on economic liberty over traditional and mutual obligation and duty, is Mark A. Smith, *The Right Talk: How Conservatives Transformed the Great Society into the Economic Society* (Princeton, NJ: Princeton University Press, 2007).

10. Robert B. Horwitz, *America's Right: Anti-Establishment Conservatism from Goldwater to the Tea Party* (Cambridge, UK: Polity Press, 2013), 8.

11. Matthew 7:12.

12. John Micklethwait and Adrian Woolridge, *The Right Nation: Conservative Power in America* (New York: Penguin, 2004), 13–14, 319. See also Corey Robin, *The Reactionary Mind: Conservatism from Edmund Burke to Sarah Palin* (New York: Oxford University Press, 2011).

13. F. A. Hayek, *The Collected Works of F. A. Hayek: The Road to Serfdom, Text and Documents, the Definitive Edition*, ed. Bruce Caldwell (Chicago: University of Chicago Press, 2007); Milton Friedman, *Capitalism and Freedom* (Chicago: University of Chicago Press, 1962); Milton Friedman and Rose Friedman, *Free to Choose: A Personal Statement* (New York: Avon, 1979); David F. Prindle, *The Paradox of Democratic Capitalism: Politics and Economics in American Thought* (Baltimore: Johns Hopkins University Press, 2006), 223.

14. Benjamin T. Lynerd, *Republican Theology: The Civil Religion of American Evangelicals* (New York: Oxford University Press, 2014), 40–45.

15. Chaïm Perelman and Lucie Olbrechts-Tyteca, *The New Rhetoric: A Treatise in Argumentation* (Notre Dame, IN: University of Notre Dame Press, 2010), 308.

16. Jud Wilhite, "Hope beyond Politics," sermon, November 6, 2016, Central Church, Henderson, NV.

17. Andy Stanley, "We the People: Recovery Road, Recession Lessons," sermon, August 21, 2011, North Point Community Church, Alpharetta, GA (MP3 audio file).

18. Wilhite, "Hope beyond Politics."

19. Wilhite, "Hope beyond Politics."

20. In *The New Rhetoric*, Perelman and Olbrechts-Tyteca write that argument by example is especially useful in cases where there might be "disagreement over the particular rule the example is invoked to establish." By offering several instances where a rule holds (in Wilhite's case, against change, in the examples of cellphones, Twitter, Facebook, and Oreos), the speaker is able to generalize and so create agreement in favor of a rule. Perelman and Olbrechts-Tyteca, *The New Rhetoric*, 350, 50–57.

21. Wilhite, "Hope beyond Politics."

22. Stephen Dando-Collins, *The Great Fire of Rome: The Fall of the Emperor Nero and His City* (Cambridge, MA: Da Capo Press, 2010).

23. Wilhite, "Hope beyond Politics."

24. This is a ubiquitous Christian poem that appears in books, unsourced, and also across the internet. Wilhite said it came to him in an email, but the email almost certainly was a copy of the poem from somewhere else.

25. Wilhite, "Hope beyond Politics."

26. Wilhite, "Hope beyond Politics."

27. 12Stone Church, "About 12Stone," https://12stone.com/about/.

28. Although there are exceptions, the GOP tends to attract rural voters, older white people, religious conservatives of all stripes, college-educated voters who are married, and, in the aftermath of the Trump election, the white working-class. Democrats attract the young, voters of color, academics, and urban voters.

29. Lilliana Mason, *Uncivil Agreement: How Politics Became Our Identity* (Chicago: University of Chicago Press, 2018), 109–38.

30. Tyler Estep, "Gwinnett Pastor's Response to Colin Kaepernick Protest Goes Viral," *Atlanta Journal Constitution,* September 16, 2016, https://www.ajc.com/news/local/gwinnett-pastor-response-colin-kaepernick-protest-goes-viral/qw5d9JOHftIKYKTxc5HJeP/.

31. More than just protesting, Kaepernick's goal was partly to initiate these kinds of conversations. He said, "Having a conversation with someone can shed a lot of light on what you think is going on versus what's really happening and that's something that . . . as I've talked to people . . . I've seen those things, I've heard those things, and now . . . how do I best maximize my platform and my resources to help these people?" "Kaepernick Explains His Protest," Reuters, September 13, 2016.

32. Kevin Myers, "Faith. Politcs. Freedom," sermon, September 11, 2016, 12Stone Church, Lawrenceville, GA. Note that Myers slipped into quoting the Pledge of Allegiance rather than the National Anthem (the focus of Kaepernick's flag protest).

33. Myers, "Faith. Politcs. Freedom."

34. John D. Woodbridge, Mark A. Noll, and Nathan O. Hatch, "'Holy Bible,

Book Divine': Evangelicals and the Bible," in *The Gospel in America: Themes in the Story of America's Evangelicals*, ed. Mark A. Noll (Grand Rapids, MI: Zondervan, 1979), 133.

35. Myers, "Faith. Politcs. Freedom." Myers said that the country is "$20 million in debt and growing"; in fact, in 2016 the national debt was around $20 *trillion*.

36. Perelman and Olbrechts-Tyteca, *The New Rhetoric*, 312.

37. For example, a very limited, but still useful interdisciplinary sampling of scholarly arguments about Black exclusion finds the following: Lisa Corrigan positing that Black vernacular and specifically discourses of Black power influenced the tendency for white Americans to view constituents of color as criminals needing incarceration; Martin Gilens arguing that media portrayals of Black people emphasize a tendency toward laziness, unemployment, and criminality; Sharon Hays emphasizing how the purported breakdown of the Black family has led to policy outcomes that increase structural inequality and make life harder for marginalized communities; and Michelle Alexander claiming that the nation's drug laws, and, specifically, sentencing disparities between powder and crack cocaine, have led to much higher incarceration rates for Black Americans (especially Black men) than for other American demographic groups (especially white people). See Michelle Alexander, *The New Jim Crow: Mass Incarceration in the Age of Colorblindness* (New York: New Press, 2010); Lisa M. Corrigan, *Prison Power: How Prison Influenced the Movement for Black Liberation* (Jackson: University Press of Mississippi, 2016); Martin Gilens, *Why Americans Hate Welfare: Race, Media, and the Politics of Antipoverty Policy* (Chicago: University of Chicago Press, 1999); Sharon Hays, *Flat Broke with Children: Women in the Age of Welfare Reform* (Oxford: Oxford University Press, 2003).

38. Black Lives Matter was formed in 2013, after a jury in Florida acquitted George Zimmerman on murder charges in the killing of Trayvon Martin, a Black teenager. Though Martin's only "crime" appeared to be walking through a wealthy, white neighborhood while being young, Black, and eating Skittles, Zimmerman—who had been on neighborhood watch—was able to escape responsibility for the shooting. This despite the fact he had been told by a 911 operator to back down and stop following the seventeen-year-old. The Black Lives Matter movement was a response to this event and has since responded and grown as other instances of racial injustice, particularly at the hands of police, have come to light. Its mission is to "build local power to intervene in violence inflicted on Black communities by the state and vigilantes." That is, its mission is protest. Sometimes these demonstrations have turned ugly, as happened in Baltimore in 2015 after the death of Freddie Gray. There, looting and violence broke out. A CVS drugstore was set on fire, along with several police cars. In the summer of 2020, after George Floyd was killed at police hands in Minneapolis, protests and riots broke out across the United States. A poll by Civis Analytics estimated that up to 26 million Americans took part in these demonstrations, making BLM possibly the "largest movement in US history." On June 6, 2020, "a million people turned out in nearly 550 places across the United States," wrote Larry Buchanan, Quoctrung Bui, and Jugal K. Patel of the *New York Times*.

Black Lives Matter, "Herstory," https://blacklivesmatter.com/about/herstory/; Larry Buchanan, Quoctrung Bui, and Jugal K. Patel, "Black Lives Matter May Be the Largest Movement in U.S. History," *New York Times*, July 3, 2020. See also Christopher J. Lebron, *The Making of Black Lives Matter: A Brief History of an Idea* (New York: Oxford University Press, 2017), chap. 1, "American Shame and Real Freedom."

39. For example, as a candidate, Trump sometimes described American cities as hotbeds of crime, even though rates of violent crime had been declining since the 1990s. In his speech accepting the Republican nomination, he said he would "liberate our citizens from the crime and terrorism and lawlessness that threatens their communities." This line had followed claims that framed places like Baltimore and Chicago as rife with murder and police shootings, illegal immigration as out of control, and undocumented immigrants as likely to commit violent acts against hardworking and honorable citizens. Each of these arguments situated people of color as potentially dangerous and untrustworthy. Donald Trump, "Address Accepting the Presidential Nomination at the Republican National Convention in Cleveland, Ohio," July 21, 2016, American Presidency Project, University of California—Santa Barbara, https://www.presidency.ucsb.edu/documents/address-accepting-the-presidential-nomination-the-republican-national-convention-cleveland.

40. This is not to say that Democrats, including Lyndon Johnson and Bill Clinton, have always avoided such law-and-order tacks. But the rhetoric is much more associated with Republicans. See Rick Perlstein, *Before the Storm: Barry Goldwater and the Unmaking of the American Consensus* (New York: Nation Books, 2009); Nathan Angelo, *One America? Presidential Appeals to Racial Resentment from LBJ to Trump* (Albany: State University of New York Press, 2019); Elizabeth Kai Hinton, *From the War on Poverty to the War on Crime: The Making of Mass Incarceration in America* (Cambridge, MA: Harvard University Press, 2016).

41. Robert P. Jones, *The End of White Christian America* (New York: Simon & Schuster, 2016), loc. 66 of 5676. Quoting from Mark Chaves and Shawna Anderson, "Changing American Congregations: Findings from the Third Wave of the National Congregations Study," *Journal for the Scientific Study of Religion* 53 (2014).

42. Jones, *The End of White Christian America*, loc. 66 of 5676. Quoting from Chaves and Anderson, "Changing American Congregations."

43. The death of George Floyd was the proverbial straw that broke the camel's back. The protests came after Americans had endured three-and-a-half months of quarantine during the COVID-19 pandemic, and in response to perceived injustice against other Black citizens, including the death of Ahmaud Arbury near Atlanta; that of Breonna Taylor in Louisville; and more. Matthew Countryman, "2020 Uprisings, Unprecedented in Scope, Join a Long River of Struggle in America," *The Conversation*, June 7, 2020, https://theconversation.com/2020-uprisings-unprecedented-in-scope-join-a-long-river-of-struggle-in-america-139853.

44. Evan Hill, Ainara Tiefenthäler, Christiaan Triebert, Drew Jordan, Haley Willis, and Robin Stein, "How George Floyd Was Killed in Police Custody," *New York Times*, May 31, 2020.

45. Countryman, "2020 Uprisings, Unprecedented in Scope, Join a Long River of Struggle in America."

46. Jason Berry and Kevin Myers, "Communion," sermon, June 7, 2020, 12Stone Church, Lawrenceville, GA.

47. Berry and Myers, "Communion."

48. Jones, *The End of White Christian America*, chap. 5.

49. Michael J. Lee describes how conservatives in the mid- to late twentieth century developed different "dialects" that mutually reinforced one another. One of these was the "traditionalist" dialect that favored words like "tradition" and "hierarchy" and "order." Traditionalists "often treated tradition and religion as indistinct, as if traditions were imbued with divine designs." This, in turn, suggests that human life has evolved into the order and way that it has because it was *supposed to*. It is thus because it always has been, and it always has been because it was thus. Lee, *Creating Conservatism,* 220. See also Stephanie A. Martin, "Recession Resonance: How Evangelical Megachurch Pastors Promoted Fiscal Conservatism in the Aftermath of the 2008 Financial Crash," *Rhetoric & Public Affairs* 18, no. 1 (2015).

50. Ed Young, "How to Pick a President: A Christ Follower's Responsibility in the Election," sermon, November 6, 2016, Fellowship Church, Grapevine, TX. The quotations from Young in the following paragraphs are from this sermon.

51. Walter R. Fisher, "Narration as a Human Communication Paradigm: The Case of Public Moral Argument," *Communication Monographs* 51, no. 1 (1984): 1–22.

52. See, for example, George Hinman, "Work Is a Gift, Take This Job and Love It," sermon, October 3, 2010, University Presbyterian Church, Seattle (MP3 audio file); Bryan Wilkerson, "Good Work, Good People Are Hard to Find," sermon, June 6, 2010, Grace Chapel, Lexington, MA (MP3 audio file).

53. Most experts estimate that the outright fraud rate for Medicare is about 3 percent, while the amount of lost money might be closer to 8–10 percent if billing errors and other wrong charges are included. Exact figures are difficult to come by, but the amount lost is almost surely not 31 percent. Jon Greenberg, "Medicare Fraud Rate Is 8 to 10 Percent, Says Roskam of Illinois," Politifact, June 17, 2013, https://www.politifact.com/factchecks/2013/jun/17/peter-roskam/rep-roskam-says-medicare-fraud-rate-8-10-percent/.

54. Reece Peck has written about how media representations of makers and takers in the United States create a narrative around a "'moral economy' that honors hard work and productivity." Such hard work, however, is allegedly put at risk by government programs that shore up the indolence and bad habits of the undeserving poor. Reece Peck, *Fox Populism: Branding Conservatism as Working Class* (Cambridge, UK: Cambridge University Press, 2019), 157.

55. An important exception to the idea that it has been mostly conservatives who have engaged Hofstadter's "paranoid style" might be Bernie Sanders's campaign for the 2016 Democratic presidential nomination, especially the populist style that agitated against big banks and big business. Richard Hofstadter, *Anti-Intellectualism in American Life* (New York: Alfred A. Knopf, 1963). See also Hofstadter, "The Paranoid Style in

American Politics," *Harper's,* November 1964, https://harpers.org/archive/1964/11/the-paranoid-style-in-american-politics/.

56. Jones, *The End of White Christian America*, chapter 5.

Chapter 6

1. Nate Silver, "Election Update: Are Trump's Polls Getting Worse?" Fivethirtyeight, October 7, 2016, https://fivethirtyeight.com/features/election-update-are-trumps-polls-getting-worse/.

2. Rachel Wellford, "Here's the List of GOP Responses to Trump's Vulgar Comments about Groping Women," *PBS Newhour,* October 7, 2016, https://www.pbs.org/newshour/politics/headline-republicans-react-trump-comments-objectifying-women.

3. Troy Gramling, "Just Words?" sermon, October 16, 2016, Potential Church, Cooper City, FL, https://potentialchurch.com/teaching-archives/.

4. Gramling, "Just Words?"

5. Todd Mullins, "Decision 2016" sermon, November 6, 2016, Christ Fellowship Church, Palm Beach Gardens, FL.

6. Allan Lockerman, "How to Choose a President," sermon, November 6, 2016, First Baptist Cleveland, Cleveland, TN.

7. Sarah Pulliam Bailey, "'Still the Best Candidate': Some Evangelicals Still Back Trump Despite Lewd Video," *Washington Post,* October 8, 2016; Laurie Goodstein, "The Testing of a President: The Conservatives; Christian Coalition Moans Lack of Anger at Clinton," *New York Times,* September 20, 1998.

8. Rachel Held Evans, "Christians, Please Hear Me: Donald Trump Will Not Be a Champion for the Unborn," Facebook post, October 9, 2016, https://www.facebook.com/rachelheldevans.page/posts/christians-please-hear-me-donald-trump-will-not-be-a-champion-for-the-unborn-tha/10154273265129442/.

9. Ruth Graham, "Rachel Held Evans, the Hugely Popular Christian Writer Who Challenged the Evangelical Establishment, Is Dead at 37," Slate, May 4, 2019, https://slate.com/human-interest/2019/05/rachel-held-evans-the-hugely-popular-evangelical-writer-is-dead-at-37.html.

10. Emma Green, "Rachel Held Evans, Hero to Christian Misfits," *Atlantic,* May 6, 2019, https://www.theatlantic.com/politics/archive/2019/05/rachel-held-evans-death-progressive-christianity/588784/.

11. Jen Hatmaker, "We Will Not Forget," Tweet, October 11, 2016, https://twitter.com/jenhatmaker/status/785849362207440899 .

12. Hatmaker, "We Will Not Forget."

13. Emma Green, "The Tiny Blond Bible Teacher Taking on the Evangelical Political Machine," *Atlantic,* October 2018, https://www.theatlantic.com/magazine/archive/2018/10/beth-moore-bible-study/568288/.

14. "Complementarianism" is the theological view that men and women were created by God to have different, complementary, roles in marriage, family life, and the world—essentially, that the two sexes are separate, different, and equal.

15. Green, "The Tiny Blond Bible Teacher."

16. Beth Moore, "Wake up, Sleepers," Tweet, October 9, 2016, https://twitter.com/bethmoorelpm/status/785119502769852418. See also Green, "The Tiny Blond Bible Teacher."

17. Unlike both Rachel Held Evans and Jen Hatmaker, Beth Moore remains mostly in "good standing" within white, conservative Protestantism. Many younger evangelical women, particularly millennials, admire both Evans and Hatmaker. However, both have been criticized for pushing boundaries and taking positions that are supposedly unsound from a theological perspective, especially about evolution, gender hierarchy, and the biblical propriety of queer relationships and queer sex. Moore, meanwhile, has held to conventional teaching and thinking. About Evans, for example, Andrew Walker, director of policy studies for the Southern Baptist Convention's Ethics and Religious Liberty Commission, said, "She [was] a presence because she [was] willing to ask questions and that tap[ped] into a millennial narrative about searching for answers. What she offer[ed] as an answer [was] unbiblical and theologically dangerous." When Jen Hatmaker announced her support for gay people, and said God loved them and they could go to heaven, LifeWay Christian Resources, the publishing arm of the Southern Baptist Convention and owner of LifeWay Christian Stores, stopped selling her books. Sarah Pulliam Bailey, "How Rachel Held Evans Became the Most Polarizing Woman in Evangelicalism," *Washington Post*, April 16, 2015; Kate Shellnut, "LifeWay Stops Selling Jen Hatmaker Books over LGBT Beliefs," *Christianity Today*, October 27, 2016, https://www.christianitytoday.com/news/2016/october/lifeway-stops-selling-jen-hatmaker-books-lgbt-beliefs-chris.html.

18. Karlyn Kohrs Campbell's theory of rhetorical agency is useful for understanding Moore's intervention in the evangelical conversation about gender, sexual assault, and male power. In her article, "Agency: Promiscuous and Protean," Campbell defines agency (the ability to write and speak) as consisting of five things. Most relevant is her assertion that agency is "communal and participatory"; "affected through form"; and "protean . . . and open to reversal." Briefly, what Campbell means is that speakers derive agency *in community*. To act or speak on behalf of oneself is far less important and shows less evidence of agency than to be able to act or speak to—or persuade—a group or community. Moore has this agency abundantly in evangelicalism, based on her years of established authority gleaned through rule-following, Bible study, writing, and speaking. She knows the language and symbols of the movement. This allowed her to speak in the "form," too, that was called for at the moment of the *Access Hollywood* tape and later during #ChurchToo. She used digital media, first, to speak, which allowed her words to reach a wide audience quickly, with a blunt tone that surprised many. She then maintained the audience while also expanding her frame and public through blog entries and public appearances. Finally, her very character as a committed and trustworthy evangelical gave her speech agency and power. Not everyone accepted her words. Nonetheless, her marginal status as a woman actually worked to her credit *because* she had gained earlier agency by knowing the symbols and choosing the proper textual form. Karlyn Kohrs Campbell,

"Agency: Promiscuous and Protean," *Communication and Critical/Cultural Studies* 2, no. 1 (2005).

19. Women lack access to church pulpits in conservative evangelicalism, and so must find ways to speak and hold audiences in other ways. Bethany Mannon explains that because evangelical culture privileges stories, women "develop a personal narrative rhetoric to negotiate contentious currents of religious thought." Social media and blogging are especially effective means for doing this. Bethany Mannon, "Xvangelical: The Rhetorical Work of Personal Narratives in Contemporary Religious Discourse," *Rhetoric Society Quarterly* 49, no. 2 (2019): 142.

20. Jen Hatmaker, "My Saddest Good Friday in Memory: When Treasured Things Are Dead," *Jen Hatmaker* (blog), April 14, 2017, https://jenhatmaker.com/my-saddest-good-friday-in-memory-when-treasured-things-are-dead/.

21. Kenneth Burke, *A Grammar of Motives* (New York: Prentice-Hall, 1945). For an excellent analysis of how ambiguity works, see M. Elizabeth Weiser, "Burke and War: Rhetoricizing the Theory of Dramatism," *Rhetoric Review* 26, no. 3 (2007).

22. Kate Shellnut, "Women's March Sets out to Exclude 40 Percent of American Women:What Pro-Life Feminists Actually Have in Common with Their Pro-Choice Counterparts," *Christianity Today*, January 18, 2017, https://www.christianitytoday.com/women/2017/january/womens-march-sets-out-to-exclude-40-percent-of-american-wom.html.

23. Neither Joy nor Paasch still identifies as evangelical, but rather identifies with the growing "exvangelical" movement. Exvangelicals are ex–conservative Protestants who have lost faith. Many also feel disillusioned over the conservative church's tendency to claim ownership over the American discourse regarding what counts as "moral and patriotic." Bradley Onishi, "The Rise of #Exvangelical," *Religion & Politics,* April 9, 2019, https://religionandpolitics.org/2019/04/09/the-rise-of-exvangelical/; Becca Andrews, "As a Teen, Emily Joy Was Abused by a Church Youth Leader. Now She's Leading a Movement to Change Evangelical America," *Mother Jones,* May 25, 2018, https://www.motherjones.com/crime-justice/2018/05/evangelical-church-me too-movement-abuse/.

24. Rachel Held Evans, "Following #churchtoo with a heavy heart," Tweet, November 21, 2017, https://twitter.com/rachelheldevans/status/933133977484955650.

25. #SilenceisnotSpiritual, statement, https://www.silenceisnotspiritual.org/statement.

26. Ed Stetzer, "Paige Patterson and Doing the Right Thing for the SBC, Again," *Christianity Today,* April 30, 2018. https://www.christianitytoday.com/edstetzer/2018/may/paige-patterson-end-of-era.html.

27. Sarah Pulliam Bailey, "Southern Baptist Leader's Advice to Abused Women Sends Leaders Scrambling to Respond," *Washington Post,* May 2, 2018; Bailey, "Southern Baptist Seminary Drops Bombshell: Why Paige Patterson Was Fired," *Washington Post,* June 1, 2018; Baptist Blogger, "Legitimate Rape vs. Serious Abuse," blog post, April 18, 2018, https://baptist-blogger.com/2018/04/28/legitimate-rape-vs-serious-abuse/.

28. Beth Moore, "I'm pro marriage," Tweet, April 28, 2018, https://twitter.com/BethMooreLPM/status/990417498607468544.

29. Thom Rainer, LifeWay press release, April 30, 2018.

30. Beth Moore, "A Letter to My Brothers," blog post, May 3, 2018, https://blog.lproof.org/2018/05/a-letter-to-my-brothers.html.

31. Christine J. Gardner's book, *Making Chastity Sexy*, explains how this works. In purity culture, young men and women imagine themselves inhabiting fairy tales of romance—virginal lost princesses in need of rescuing from fearless princes. Such princesses must wait for their men, and not dress in ways that will distract or tempt the saviors not yet meant for them. See Christine J. Gardner, *Making Chastity Sexy: The Rhetoric of Evangelical Abstinence Campaigns* (Berkeley: University of California Press, 2011), chap. 3.

32. "A woman should learn in quietness and full submission. I do not permit a woman to teach or to assume authority over a man; she must be quiet." Also important is Ephesians 5, in which Paul writes that wives should submit to their husbands, as to the Lord.

33. Moore, "A Letter to My Brothers" (blog post).

34. Perelman and Olbrechts-Tyteca wrote that rhetoric has everything to do with audience. All argumentation has to be planned and situated with respect to its hearers. Audiences, moreover, must agree to some premises. Perelman and Olbrechts-Tyteca called this the existence of a "community of minds." Without such a community, no rhetoric or conversation could come into existence. Finally, more than one audience may be present at a time, as was evident in Moore's remarks, and audiences may be in flux. Audiences at a speech depend more on a speaker's "mental conception" of them, than on their physical composition. Chaïm Perelman and Lucie Olbrechts-Tyteca, *The New Rhetoric: A Treatise in Argumentation* (Notre Dame, IN: University of Notre Dame Press, 2010).

35. Beth Moore, "A letter to my brothers," Tweet, May 3, 2018, https://twitter.com/BethMooreLPM/status/992035713079267328.

36. Thabiti Anyabwile, "An Apology to Beth Moore and My Sisters," *Gospel Coalition* (blog), May 3, 2018, https://www.thegospelcoalition.org/blogs/thabiti-anyabwile/apology-beth-moore-sisters/.

37. Carol Kuruvilla, "Preacher Speaks Up about the Misogyny She's Faced in Evangelical Circles," *Huffington Post,* May 4, 2018, https://www.huffingtonpost.com/entry/female-preacher-speaks-up-about-misogyny-shes-faced-in-evangelical-circles_us_5aeb7f33e4b0c4f193207bb2.

38. "Opinion: I Was Assaulted. He Was Applauded," *New York Times,* March 9, 2018, https://www.nytimes.com/2018/03/09/opinion/jules-woodson-andy-savage-assault.html.

39. Laurie Goodstein, "Willow Creek Church's Top Leadership Resigns over Allegations against Bill Hybels," *New York Times,* August 18, 2018.

40. Beth Moore, Tweet, September 21, 2018, 9:54 p.m., https://twitter.com/BethMooreLPM/status/1043332804313067520.

41. Jeremy W. Peters and Elizabeth Dias, "Evangelical Leaders Are Frustrated at G.O.P. Caution on Kavanaugh Allegation," *New York Times,* September 20, 2018.

42. Quoted in Samantha Schmidt and Michelle Boorstein, "For Religious Conservative Women, the Kavanaugh-Ford Hearing Was Particularly Disorienting," *Washington Post,* September 28, 2018.

43. Carly Gelsinger, "I Know Why Evangelical Women Support Brett Kavanaugh. I Was Raised to Do the Same," *Huffington Post,* October 3, 2018, https://www.huffingtonpost.com/entry/brett-kavanaugh-evangelical-women_us_5bb3a28de4b0ba8bb211985b.

44. Morgan Lee, "Mark Driscoll Steps Down While Mars Hill Investigates Charges," *Christianity Today,* August 24, 2014, http://www.christianitytoday.com/news/2014/august/mark-driscoll-steps-down-while-mars-hill-investigates-charg.html; Michael Paulson, "A Brash Style That Filled Pews, Until Followers Had Their Fill: Mark Driscoll Is Being Urged to Leave Mars Hill Church," *New York Times,* August 22, 2014.

45. T. J. Geiger wrote about how Moore's blogs and speeches against sexual violence have tried to expand the evangelical (and secular) understanding of forgiveness. Moore urges against a "platitude-based forgiveness" that depends on Christian expectation. Rather, Moore calls her readers and hearers to deliberate over acts of violence to empathize with the experience and pain of victims, without emphasizing the needs or rights of perpetrators to forgiveness. Geiger refers to this as "casuistic tightening" that allows communities to focus on their own role in a process of reconciliation, along with the victim and the perpetrator. T. J. Geiger, "Forgiveness Is More Than Platitudes: Evangelical Women, Sexual Violence, and Casuistic Tightening," *Rhetoric Society Quarterly* 49, no. 2 (2019): 163–84.

46. Light, and light juxtaposed against darkness, is a frequent metaphor in the Bible. Light is mentioned in the Bible at least 250 times. Light comes from God. He created it in the beginning with the phrase, "Let there be light." From this, the Bible suggests repeatedly that what is light is good and what is dark is evil. God is light. Not-God (hell) is dark. For this reason, Christians of all stripes point to the opening lines of the gospel of John to talk about the ministry of Jesus: "The light shines in the darkness and the darkness has not overcome it" (John 1:5). Quite literally, Jesus is the only light that cannot be extinguished. Bible-believers are called to be lights, to shine as lights for Christ, to stay away from darkness. It is this contrast that Moore meant to stress in her talk.

47. Both John Fea and Robert P. Jones argue, though for different reasons, that the religion is in decline. Key to both of their arguments, however, is that those outside of white, conservative Protestantism see the movement as mired in hypocrisy and interested only in power. As well, the new generation is leaving the religion at adulthood, and few are converting to the faith. John Fea, *Believe Me: The Evangelical Road to Donald Trump* (Grand Rapids, MI: Wm. B. Eerdmans, 2018); Robert P. Jones, *The End of White Christian America* (New York: Simon & Schuster, 2016).

48. Elizabeth Podrebarac Sciupac and Gregory A. Smith, "How Religious

Groups Voted in the Midterm Elections," Pew Research Center, November 7, 2018, http://www.pewresearch.org/fact-tank/2018/11/07/how-religious-groups-voted-in-the-midterm-elections/; "NBC News Exit Poll: White Evangelical Women Stand Squarely with the Republicans," *NBC News,* November 6, 2018, https://www.nbcnews.com/card/nbc-news-exit-poll-white-evangelical-women-stand-squarely-republicans-n933236.

49. Miriam Jordan and Ron Nixon, "Trump Administration Threatens Jail and Separating Children from Parents for Those Who Illegally Cross Southwest Border," *New York Times,* May 7, 2018.

50. Elizabeth Dias, "Beto O'Rourke May Benefit from an Unlikely Support Group: White Evangelical Women," *New York Times,* October 9, 2018.

51. Christina Hughes Babb, "Seek the Peace Began with East Dallas Refugees at Vickery Meadow," *Advocate: Lake Highlands,* February 16, 2016, https://lakewood.advocatemag.com/2016/02/19/seek-peace-began-east-dallas-refugees-vickery-meadow/.

52. Dias, "Beto O'Rourke May Benefit from an Unlikely Support Group: White Evangelical Women."

Conclusion

1. Valerie Hartouni, *Visualizing Atrocity: Arendt, Evil, and the Optics of Thoughtlessness* (New York: New York University Press, 2012), 1.

2. Lydia Bean and Brandon C. Martinez, "Evangelical Ambivalence toward Gays and Lesbians," *Sociology of Religion* 75, no. 3 (2014); Justin Farrell, "The Young and the Restless? The Liberalization of Young Evangelicals," *Journal for the Scientific Study of Religion* 50, no. 3 (2011).

3. Paul Ricoeur, *Time and Narrative,* vol. 1 (Chicago: University of Chicago Press, 1990), 31–51.

4. William C. Dowling, *Ricoeur on Time and Narrative: An Introduction to* Temps et Récit (Notre Dame, IN: University of Notre Dame Press, 2011), 6.

5. Political agency, or political liberty, is an enormous concept that is at the heart of this book's argument. Hannah Arendt conceived of agency as "political action." She argued for agency as something distinctly human. She wrote that people, unlike animals, use action to interrupt the course of events and engage the new and unexpected. Humans can change their minds, make new things, and go in new directions. Arendt prized action—agency—because humans used it to speak and thereby to mark their plurality, their difference and distinction, as they conversed and negotiated about the world and the public sphere. The right to speak and decide is agency. Alexis de Tocqueville and John Stuart Mill likewise wrote about the relationship between agency and democracy, though their philosophy related more to problems of declining agency. As such, their work agrees that loss or disinvestment of agency is cause for worry. Hannah Arendt, *The Human Condition,* 2d ed. (Chicago: University of Chicago Press, 1958), 76, 176; Arendt, *Between Past and Future: Eight Exercises in Political Thought*

(New: York: Penguin Books, 2006); Alexis de Tocqueville, *Democracy in America* (New York: Alfred A. Knopf, 1948); John Stuart Mill, *On Liberty* (New York: Compass Circle, 2019).

6. Thomas G. West, *The Political Theory of the American Founding: Natural Rights, Public Policy, and the Moral Conditions of Freedom* (New York: Cambridge University Press, 2017).

7. Campbell, "Agency: Promiscuous and Protean," 3.

8. Here, too, Christine Gardner's findings about purity rhetoric partly match mine. Gardner writes about how evangelicals sometimes situate the problem of AIDS in Africa in agentic terms. She describes how evangelicals resist structural explanations—the prevalence of AIDS as a health epidemic that necessarily touches everyone—in favor of reframing AIDS as a problem of widespread promiscuity. Here nonagency (a problem in the structure) becomes reframed as agency. Those individuals who abstain from sex can be freed from the risk of AIDS. The nonagency rhetoric I point to is different. Pastors encouraged divestment from responsibility. In Gardner's case, evangelicals encouraged taking control of one's health through sexual abstinence. In active-passivism, the call is to forego interest in public matters. Gardner, *Making Chastity Sexy*, 182–83.

9. Campbell, "Agency: Promiscuous and Protean," 3.

10. Jonathan Pokluda, "Sex and Government," sermon, October 25, 2016, Watermark Community Church, Dallas.

11. Thomas Frank, *What's the Matter with Kansas? How Conservatives Won the Heart of America* (New York: Henry Holt, 2004); Arlie Russell Hochschild, *Strangers in Their Own Land: Anger and Mourning on the American Right* (New York: New Press, 2016).

12. Nate Ross, "Who Are You Voting For," sermon, October 28, 2016, Northside Christian Church, New Albany, IN.

13. Krista Ratcliffe, *Rhetorical Listening: Identification, Gender, Whiteness* (Carbondale: Southern Illinois University Press, 2005).

14. Needtobreathe, "Wasteland," from *Rivers in the Wasteland*, music recording, Atlantic Records, 2014.

Bibliography

Abramowitz, Alan I., and Steven W. Webster. "Negative Partisanship: Why Americans Dislike Parties But Behave Like Rabid Partisans." *Political Psychology* 39 (2018): 119–35.

Albertson, Bethany. "Dog-Whistle Politics: Multivocal Communication and Religious Appeals." *Political Behavior* 37, no. 1 (2015): 3–26.

Alexander, Michelle. *The New Jim Crow: Mass Incarceration in the Age of Colorblindness.* New York: New Press, 2010.

Althusser, Louis "Ideology and Ideological State Apparatuses." https://www.marxists.org/reference/archive/althusser/1970/ideology.htm.

Altman, Alex, and Elizabeth Dias. "Why Trump Is Winning Over Christian Conservatives." *Time,* January 22, 2016. https://time.com/4189587/donald-trump-christian-conservatives/.

Anderson, Benedict. *Imagined Communities: Reflections on the Origin and Spread of Nationalism*. New York: Verso, 2006.

Andrews, Becca. "As a Teen, Emily Joy Was Abused by a Church Youth Leader. Now She's Leading a Movement to Change Evangelical America." *Mother Jones,* May 25, 2018. https://www.motherjones.com/crime-justice/2018/05/evangelical-church-metoo-movement-abuse/.

Angelo, Nathan. *One America? Presidential Appeals to Racial Resentment from LBJ to Trump*. Albany: State University of New York Press, 2019.

Anyabwile, Thabiti. "An Apology to Beth Moore and My Sisters." *Gospel Coalition* (blog), May 3, 2018. https://www.thegospelcoalition.org/blogs/thabiti-anyabwile/apology-beth-moore-sisters/.

Arendt, Hannah. *Between Past and Future: Eight Exercises in Political Thought*. New York: Penguin Books, 2006.

———. *The Human Condition.* 2d ed. Chicago: University of Chicago Press, 1958.

Aristotle. *On Rhetoric: A Theory of Civic Discourse.* Trans. George A. Kennedy. 2d ed. New York: Oxford University Press, 2006.

Asen, Robert. *Democracy, Deliberation, and Education*. University Park: Penn State University Press, 2015.

Augustine. *The Works of Saint Augustine: A Translation for the 21st Century*. Ed. Edmund Hill, John E. Rotelle, and Boniface Ramsey. Brooklyn: New City Press, 1990.

Azari, Julia, and Andrew Gelman. "Rejoinder: How Special Was 2016?" *Statistics and Public Policy* 4, no. 1 (2017): 1–3.

Babb, Christina Hughes. "Seek the Peace Began with East Dallas Refugees at Vickery Meadow." *Advocate: Lake Highlands,* February 16, 2016. https://lakewood.advocatemag.com/2016/02/19/seek-peace-began-east-dallas-refugees-vickery-meadow/.

Bailey, Sarah Pulliam. "How Rachel Held Evans Became the Most Polarizing Woman in Evangelicalism." *Washington Post*, April 16, 2015.

———. "Southern Baptist Leader's Advice to Abused Women Sends Leaders Scrambling to Respond." *Washington Post*, May 2, 2018.

———. "Southern Baptist Seminary Drops Bombshell: Why Paige Patterson Was Fired." *Washington Post*, June 1, 2018.

———. "'Still the Best Candidate': Some Evangelicals Still Back Trump Despite Lewd Video." *Washington Post*, October 8, 2016.

Bailey, Sarah Pulliam, Susan Svrluga, and Michelle Boorstein. "Jerry Falwell Jr. Resigns as Head of Liberty University, Will Get $10.5 Million in Compensation." *Washington Post*. August 25, 2020. https://www.washingtonpost.com/education/2020/08/25/fallwell-resigns-confirmed/.

Bakhtin, M. M. *Speech Genres and Other Late Essays*. Translated by Vern W. McGee. 1st ed. Austin: University of Texas Press, 1986.

Balmer, Randall. *Evangelicalism in America*. Waco, TX: Baylor University Press, 2016.

———. *The Making of Evangelicalism: From Revivalism to Politics and Beyond*. Waco, TX: Baylor University Press, 2010.

———. *Thy Kingdom Come: How the Religious Right Distorts the Faith and Threatens America: An Evangelical's Lament*. New York: Basic Books, 2006.

Baptist Blogger. "Legitimate Rape vs. Serious Abuse." Blog post, April 18, 2018. https://baptist-blogger.com/2018/04/28/legitimate-rape-vs-serious-abuse/.

Baraka, Sho. "Why I'm Voting for Neither Candidate." *Christianity Today* (Special Section), September 23, 2016, 63. https://www.christianitytoday.com/ct/2016/october/sho-baraka-why-i-cant-vote-for-either-trump-or-clinton.html.

Barbaro, Michael, and Megan Twohey. "Crossing the Line: How Donald Trump Behaved with Women in Private." *New York Times,* May 14, 2016.

Barzun, Jacques. *The Culture We Deserve.* Middletown, CT: Wesleyan University Press, 1989.

Bean, Lydia, and Brandon C. Martinez. "Evangelical Ambivalence toward Gays and Lesbians." *Sociology of Religion* 75, no. 3 (2014): 395–417.

Beinart, Peter. "Is Barack Obama American Enough?" *Time,* October 9, 2008, 34–35.

Bell, Daniel. *The Cultural Contradictions of Capitalism*. New York: Basic Books, 1976.

Bellah, Robert N. "American Politics and the Dissenting Protestant Tradition." In *One Electorate under God? A Dialogue on Religion and American Politics*, ed. E. J. Dionne, Jean Bethke Elshtain, and Kayla Meltzer Drogosz. Washington, DC: Brookings Institution Press, 2004.

Berger, Peter. "A Sociological View of the Secularization of Theology: Presidential Address, Society for the Scientific Study of Religion, 1966." *Journal for the Scientific Study of Religion* 6, no. 1 (1967): 3.

Berry, Jason, and Kevin Myers. "Communion." Sermon, June 7, 2020. 12Stone Church, Lawrenceville, GA.

Bielo, James S. *Words upon The Word: An Ethnography of Evangelical Group Bible Study*. New York: New York University Press, 2009.

Black Lives Matter. "Herstory." https://blacklivesmatter.com/about/herstory/. Accessed August 31, 2018.

Blair, Carole, Marsha S. Jeppeson, and Enrico Pucci. "Public Memorializing in Postmodernity: The Vietnam Veterans Memorial as Prototype." *Quarterly Journal of Speech* 77, no. 3 (1991): 263–88.

Bolsinger, Tod. Blog. https://bolsinger.blogs.com/weblog/.

———. "Talking to the Powers That Be." Sermon, November 14, 2010. San Clemente Presbyterian Church, San Clemente, CA. MP3 audio recording.

———. "What Wikipedia, AA, Al Qaeda, and the Early Church Have in Common." *Tod Bolsinger* (blog), October 3, 2008, https://bolsinger.blogs.com/weblog/2008/10/what-wikipedia-aa-al-qaeda-and-the-early-church-have-in-common.html.

Borowitz, Andy. "Queen Offers to Restore British Rule over United States." *New Yorker,* October 29, 2016. https://www.newyorker.com/humor/borowitz-report/queen-offers-to-restore-british-rule-over-united-states.

Boym, Svetlana. *The Future of Nostalgia*. New York: Basic Books, 2001.

Buchanan, Larry, Quoctrung Bui, and Jugal K. Patel. "Black Lives Matter May Be the Largest Movement in U.S. History." *New York Times,* July 3, 2020.

Bureau of Labor Statistics. "Economic News Release: Consumer Expenditures 2010." Washington, DC: US Department of Labor, 2011.

Burgen, Jim. "Reverse Engineering: This Is What It Looks Like." Sermon, January 22, 2012. Flatirons Community Church, Lafayette, CO.

Burke, Kenneth. *Attitudes toward History* 3rd ed. ed. Berkeley: University of California Press, 1984.

———. *A Grammar of Motives*. New York: Prentice-Hall, 1945.

———. *The Philosophy of Literary Form: Studies in Symbolic Action*. Los Angeles: University of California Press, 1974.

———. "The Rhetoric of Hitler's Battle." In *Landmark Essays on Rhetorical Criticism*, ed. Thomas Benson. Davis, CA: Hermagoras Press, 1993.

———. *A Rhetoric of Motives*. New York: Prentice Hall, 1950.

———. *Rhetoric of Religion*. Berkeley: University of California Press, 1970.

Burns, Alexander. "Donald Trump, Pushing Someone Rich, Offers Himself." *New*

York Times, June 16, 2015. https://www.nytimes.com/2015/06/17/us/politics/donald-trump-runs-for-president-this-time-for-real-he-says.html.

Calhoun, Craig. "Charles Taylor on Identity and the Social Imaginary." Unpublished working paper, 1999. http://eprints.lse.ac.uk/48046/1/Charles%20Taylor(lsero).pdf.

Campbell, Heidi. *Exploring Religious Community Online: We Are One in the Network*. New York: Peter Lang, 2005.

Campbell, Karlyn Kohrs. "Agency: Promiscuous and Protean." *Communication and Critical/Cultural Studies* 2, no. 1 (2005): 1–19.

Carmon, Irin. "The Allegations Women Have Made against Donald Trump." *NBC News,* October 27, 2016. https://www.nbcnews.com/politics/2016-election/allegations-women-have-made-against-donald-trump-n665731.

Carpenter, Joel A. "From Fundamentalism to the New Evangelical Coalition." In *Evangelicalism and Modern America*, ed. George Marsden. Grand Rapids, MI: W. B. Eerdman, 1984.

Carter, Dan T. "The Rise of Conservatism since World War 2." *OAH Magazine of History* 17, no. 2 (2003): 11–16.

Castelloe, Molly. "The Podium, the Pulpit, and the Republicans: How Presidential Candidates Use Religious Language in American Political Debate." *Journal of Psychohistory* 41, no. 3 (2014): 222–24.

Charland, Maurice. "Constitutive Rhetoric: The Case of the *Peuple Québécois*." *Quarterly Journal of Speech* 73, no. 2 (1987): 133-50.

Chaves, Mark, and Shawna Anderson. "Changing American Congregations: Findings from the Third Wave of the National Congregations Study." *Journal for the Scientific Study of Religion* 53 (2014): 676–86.

Chideya, Farai. "Evangelicals, Once Skeptical of Trump, Have Rallied to His Side." FiveThirtyEight, September 27, 2016. https://fivethirtyeight.com/features/evangelicals-have-rallied-to-trumps-side/.

CNN Politics Election Center. "Election 2012: Results." *CNN,* December 10, 2016.

Cobb, Michael L. *God Hates Fags: The Rhetorics of Religious Violence*. New York: New York University Press, 2006.

Conquergood, Dwight. "Ethnography, Rhetoric, and Performance." *Quarterly Journal of Speech* 78, no. 1 (1992): 80–97.

Cooper, Betsy, Daniel Cox, Rachel Lienesch, and Robert P. Jones. "The Divide over America's Future: 1950 or 2050? Findings from the 2016 American Values Survey." Washington, DC: PRRI, 2016.

Corrigan, Lisa M. *Prison Power: How Prison Influenced the Movement for Black Liberation*. Jackson: University Press of Mississippi, 2016.

Crowley, Sharon. *Toward a Civil Discourse: Rhetoric and Fundamentalism*. Pittsburgh: University of Pittsburgh Press, 2006.

Dando-Collins, Stephen. *The Great Fire of Rome: The Fall of the Emperor Nero and His City*. Cambridge, MA: Da Capo Press, 2010.

Darsey, James Francis. *The Prophetic Tradition and Radical Rhetoric in America*. New York: New York University Press, 1997.

Dochuk, Darren. *From Bible Belt to Sunbelt: Plain-Folk Religion, Grassroots Politics, and the Rise of Evangelical Conservatism*. New York: W. W. Norton, 2011.

Douthat, Ross. "The Culture War's Sore Winners." *New York Times,* July 1, 2014.

Dowling, William C. *Ricoeur on Time and Narrative: An Introduction to* Temps et récit. Notre Dame, IN: University of Notre Dame Press, 2011.

Driscoll, Mark. "Jesus on Money, Idolatry, and Comedy." Sermon, May 29, 2011. Mars Hill Church, Seattle. MP3 audio file.

———. "The Parable of the Dishonest Manager." Sermon, March 13, 2011. Mars Hill Church, Seattle. MP3 audio file.

———. "Parable of the Rich Fool." Sermon, November 7, 2010. Mars Hill Church, Seattle. MP3 audio file.

du Plessis, Pierre. "Political Questions." Sermon, October 30, 2016. Father's House, Rochester, NY.

Emile Durkheim, Emile, and Steven Lukes. *The Rules of Sociological Method*, 1st American ed. ed., intro., Steven Lukes ; trans. W. D. Halls. New York: Free Press, 1982.

Easley, Jonathan. "Trump Lands Jerry Falwell Endorsement." The Hill, January 26, 2016. https://thehill.com/blogs/ballot-box/presidential-races/267032-trump-lands-falwell-endorsement.

Edwards, Jonathan J. *Superchurch: The Rhetoric and Politics of American Fundamentalism*. East Lansing: Michigan State University Press, 2015.

Egan, Timothy. "How Obama Saved Capitalism and Lost the Midterms." *New York Times*, November 2, 2010.

"Election 2016: California Results." *New York Times*, August 1, 2017.

El-Faizy, Monique. *God and Country: How Evangelicals Have Become America's New Mainstream*. New York: Bloomsbury, 2006.

Elisha, Omri. *Moral Ambition: Mobilization and Social Outreach in Evangelical Megachurches*. Berkeley: University of California Press, 2011.

Ellingson, Stephen. *The Megachurch and the Mainline: Remaking Religious Tradition in the Twenty-first Century*. Chicago: University of Chicago Press, 2014.

Estep, Tyler. "Gwinnett Pastor's Response to Colin Kaepernick Protest Goes Viral." *Atlanta Journal Constitution,* September 16, 2016. https://www.ajc.com/news/local/gwinnett-pastor-response-colin-kaepernick-protest-goes-viral/qw5d9JOHftIKYKTxc5HJeP/.

Evans, Rachel Held. "Christians, Please Hear Me: Donald Trump Will Not Be a Champion for the Unborn." Facebook post, October 9, 2016. https://www.facebook.com/rachelheldevans.page/posts/christians-please-hear-me-donald-trump-will-not-be-a-champion-for-the-unborn-tha/10154273265129442/.

———. "Following #churchtoo with a heavy heart." Tweet, November 21, 2017. https://twitter.com/rachelheldevans/status/933133977484955650.

Ewing, Heidi, and Rachel Grady, directors. *Jesus Camp*. Documentary film. Los Angeles: Magnolia Home Entertainment, 2006.

Fahrenthold, David. "Trump's Lewd Chat Captured on Tape." *Washington Post*, October 8, 2016.

Farrell, Justin. "The Young and the Restless? The Liberalization of Young Evangelicals." *Journal for the Scientific Study of Religion* 50, no. 3 (2011): 517–32.

Fea, John. *Believe Me: The Evangelical Road to Donald Trump*. Kindle ed. Grand Rapids, MI: Wm. B. Eerdmans, 2018.

———. *Was America Founded as a Christian Nation? A Historical Introduction*. Louisville, KY: Westminster John Knox Press, 2011.

Fisher, Walter R. "Narration as a Human Communication Paradigm: The Case of Public Moral Argument." *Communication Monographs* 51, no. 1 (1984): 1–22.

———. "The Narrative Paradigm: An Elaboration." *Communication Monographs* 52 (December 1985).

FitzGerald, Frances. *The Evangelicals: The Struggle to Shape America*. New York: Simon & Schuster, 2017.

Flippen, J. Brooks. *Jimmy Carter: The Politics of Family and the Rise of the Religious Right*. Athens: University of Georgia Press, 2011.

Flood, Gavin. *Importance of Religion: Meaning and Action in Our Strange World*. Hoboken, NJ: Wiley, 2011.

Frank, Thomas. *What's the Matter with Kansas? How Conservatives Won the Heart of America*. New York: Henry Holt, 2004.

Friedman, Milton. *Capitalism and Freedom*. Chicago: University of Chicago Press, 1962.

Friedman, Milton, and Rose Friedman. *Free to Choose: A Personal Statement*. New York: Avon, 1979.

Furtick, Steven. "I Know, But I'm Not Nervous." Sermon, November 7, 2016. Elevation Church, Matthews, NC. https://www.youtube.com/watch?v=tsdVmFWLb_c.

Gabriel, Trip, and Michael Luo. "A Born-Again Donald Trump? Believe It, Evangelical Leader Says." *New York Times,* June 25, 2016. https://www.nytimes.com/2016/06/26/us/politics/a-born-again-donald-trump-believe-it-evangelical-leader-says.html.

Gallup. "Trump and Clinton Finish with Historically Poor Images." November 8, 2016. https://news.gallup.com/poll/197231/trump-clinton-finish-historically-poor-images.aspx.

Gardner, Christine J. *Making Chastity Sexy: The Rhetoric of Evangelical Abstinence Campaigns.* Berkeley: University of California Press, 2011.

Geertz, Clifford. "Deep Hanging Out." *New York Review of Books*, October 22, 1998.

———. *The Interpretation of Cultures; Selected Essays*. New York: Basic Books, 1973.

Geiger, T. J. "Forgiveness Is More Than Platitudes: Evangelical Women, Sexual Violence, and Casuistic Tightening." *Rhetoric Society Quarterly* 49, no. 2 (2019): 163–84.

Gelsinger, Carly. "I Know Why Evangelical Women Support Brett Kavanaugh. I Was Raised to Do the Same." Huffington Post, October 3, 2018. https://www.huffingtonpost.com/entry/brett-kavanaugh-evangelical-women_us_5bb3a28de4b0ba8bb211985b.

Giddens, Anthony, and Philip W. Sutton. *Essential Concepts in Sociology*, 2nd edition. Malden, MA: Polity, 2017.

Gilens, Martin. *Why Americans Hate Welfare: Race, Media, and the Politics of Antipoverty Policy*. Chicago: University of Chicago Press, 1999.

Gjelten, Tom. "Conservative Pastors Deliver Sharp Criticism of Same-Sex Marriage." *NPR News: All Things Considered,* November 29, 2015. https://www.npr.org/2015/06/29/418641115/conservative-pastors-deliver-sharp-criticism-of-same-sex-marriage.

———. "The Johnson Amendment in 5 Questions and Answers," NPR News, February 3, 2017, https://www.npr.org/2017/02/03/513187940/the-johnson-amendment-in-five-questions-and-answers.

Goldberg, Michelle. *Kingdom Coming: The Rise of Christian Nationalism*. New York: W. W. Norton, 2006.

Goodstein, Laurie. "Evangelicals Open Door to Debate on Gay Rights." *New York Times*, June 8, 2015.

———. "The Testing of a President: The Conservatives; Christian Coalition Moans Lack of Anger at Clinton." *New York Times*, September 20, 1998.

———. "Willow Creek Church's Top Leadership Resigns over Allegations against Bill Hybels." *New York Times*, August 18, 2018.

Graham, Ruth. "Rachel Held Evans, the Hugely Popular Christian Writer Who Challenged the Evangelical Establishment, Is Dead at 37." Slate, May 4, 2019. https://slate.com/human-interest/2019/05/rachel-held-evans-the-hugely-popular-evangelical-writer-is-dead-at-37.html.

Gramling, Troy. "Battleship for the Heart." Sermon, October 30, 2016. Potential Church, Cooper City, FL. https://potentialchurch.com/teaching-archives/.

———. "Just Words?" Sermon, October 16, 2016. Potential Church, Cooper City, FL. https://potentialchurch.com/teaching-archives/.

Green, Emma. "Rachel Held Evans, Hero to Christian Misfits." *Atlantic,* May 6, 2019. https://www.theatlantic.com/politics/archive/2019/05/rachel-held-evans-death-progressive-christianity/588784/.

———. "The Tiny Blond Bible Teacher Taking on the Evangelical Political Machine." *Atlantic*, October 2018. https://www.theatlantic.com/magazine/archive/2018/10/beth-moore-bible-study/568288/.

Greenberg, Jon. "Medicare Fraud Rate Is 8 to 10 Percent, Says Roskam of Illinois." Politifact, June 17, 2013. https://www.politifact.com/factchecks/2013/jun/17/peter-roskam/rep-roskam-says-medicare-fraud-rate-8-10-percent/.

Griffith, R. Marie. *God's Daughters: Evangelical Women and the Power of Submission*. Berkeley: University of California Press, 1997.

Haas, Michael, ed. *Barack Obama, the Aloha Zen President: How a Son of the 50th State May Revitalize America Based on 12 Multicultural Principles.* Santa Barbara, CA: ABC-CLIO, 2011.

Harding, Susan Friend. *The Book of Jerry Falwell.* Princeton, NJ: Princeton University Press, 2000.

Harlow, Tim. "How to Love Those People." Sermon, November 6, 2016. Parkview Christian Church, Orland Park, IL.

Harris, Joshua. "The Good Recession, Part One." Sermon, January 11, 2009. Covenant Life Church, Gaithersburg, MD. MP3 audio file.

Hart, Roderick P. *Civic Hope: How Ordinary Americans Keep Democracy Alive.* Cambridge, UK: Cambridge University Press, 2018.

Hartman, Andrew. *A War for the Soul of America: A History of the Culture Wars.* Chicago: University of Chicago Press, 2015.

Hartouni, Valerie. *Visualizing Atrocity: Arendt, Evil, and the Optics of Thoughtlessness.* New York: New York University Press, 2012.

Hatmaker, Jen. "My Saddest Good Friday in Memory: When Treasured Things Are Dead." *Jen Hatmaker* (blog), April 14, 2017. https://jenhatmaker.com/my-saddest-good-friday-in-memory-when-treasured-things-are-dead/.

———. "We Will Not Forget." Tweet, October 11, 2016. https://twitter.com/jenhatmaker/status/785849362207440899.

Hayek, F. A. *The Collected Works of F. A. Hayek: The Road to Serfdom, Text and Documents, the Definitive Edition.* Ed. Bruce Caldwell. Chicago: University of Chicago Press, 2007.

Hays, Sharon. *Flat Broke with Children: Women in the Age of Welfare Reform.* New York: Oxford University Press, 2003.

Hedges, Chris. *American Fascists: The Christian Right and the War on America.* New York: Free Press, 2006.

Heitzig, Skip. "Christians and Politics." Sermon, September 16, 2018. Calvary Chapel, Albuquerque, NM. https://www.youtube.com/watch?v=EPEGtj_AKeU.

———. "Freedom Celebration 2012." Podcast, July 4, 2012. Calvary Chapel, Albuquerque, NM. https://podcasts.google.com/.

Henry, Carl F. H. *The Uneasy Conscience of Modern Fundamentalism.* Grand Rapids, MI: Wm. B. Eerdmans, 1947.

"Here's Donald Trump's Presidential Announcement Speech." Time.com, June 16, 2015. http://time.com/3923128/donald-trump-announcement-speech/.

Hess, Aaron. "Critical-Rhetorical Ethnography: Rethinking the Place and Process of Rhetoric." *Communication Studies* 62, no. 2 (2011): 127–52.

Hewitt, Hugh. "Rick Warren on the Newsweek 'End of Christian America' Article, Pt. 1." Transcript of interview, April 8, 2009. http://www.hughhewitt.com/rick-warren-on-the-newsweek-end-of-christian-america-article-pt-1/.

———. "Rick Warren Reflects on Why Christianity Is Not Dead in America as Newsweek Proclaims." Transcript of interview, April 13, 2009. http://

www.hughhewitt.com/rick-warren-reflects-on-why-christianity-is-not-dead-in-america-as-newsweek-proclaims/.

Hinman, George. "Work Is a Gift, Take This Job and Love It." Sermon, October 3, 2010. University Presbyterian Church, Seattle. MP3 audio file.

Hinton, Elizabeth Kai. *From the War on Poverty to the War on Crime: The Making of Mass Incarceration in America*. Cambridge, MA: Harvard University Press, 2016.

Hochschild, Arlie Russell. *Strangers in Their Own Land: Anger and Mourning on the American Right*. New York: New Press, 2016.

Hodgson, Godfrey. *America in Our Time: From World War II to Nixon—What Happened and Why*. Princeton, NJ: Princeton University Press, 1976.

Hofstadter, Richard. *Anti-Intellectualism in American Life*. New York: Alfred A. Knopf, 1963.

———. "The Paranoid Style in American Politics." *Harper's*, November 1964. https://harpers.org/archive/1964/11/the-paranoid-style-in-american-politics/.

Holder, Greg. "Common Ground." Sermon, November 6, 2016. The Crossing Church, Chesterfield, MO.

Horwitz, Robert B. *America's Right: Anti-Establishment Conservatism from Goldwater to the Tea Party*. Cambridge, UK: Polity Press, 2013.

Howard, Robert Glenn. *Digital Jesus: The Making of a New Christian Fundamentalist Community on the Internet*. New York: New York University Press, 2011.

Hughes, David. "Looking for a Leader." Sermon, April 11, 2016. Church by the Glades, Coral Springs, FL. https://www.cbglades.com/archive.

Hummel, Dale. "Dear Mr. or Mrs. Next President." Sermon, October 22, 2016. Wooddale Church, Eden Prairie, MN. https://wooddale.org/sermon-series/dear-mr-or-mrs-next-president/.

Hunter, James Davison. *American Evangelicalism: Conservative Religion and the Quandary of Modernity*. New Brunswick, NJ: Rutgers University Press, 1983.

———. *Culture Wars: The Struggle to Define America*. New York: Basic Books, 1991.

Hutchings, Tim. *Creating Church Online: Ritual, Community, and New Media*. New York: Routledge, 2017.

Internal Revenue Service, Department of the Treasury. "Charities, Churches and Politics." updated June 5, 2020, https://www.irs.gov/newsroom/charities-churches-and-politics.

Itkowitz, Colby, Emily Davies, and Hailey Fuchs. "Latest Sexual Assault Allegation against Trump Draws Muted Political Reaction." *Washington Post*, June 25, 2019.

Jiminez, Paul. "Culture, Politics and the Church, Week 2." Sermon, November 6, 2016. Taylors First Baptist Church, Taylors, SC.

Johnston, Ray. "Separation of Church and Hate." Sermon, November 6, 2016. Bayside Church, Granite Bay, CA.

Jones, Robert P. *The End of White Christian America*. New York: Simon & Schuster, 2016.

Jordan, Miriam, and Ron Nixon. "Trump Administration Threatens Jail and Separating Children from Parents for Those Who Illegally Cross Southwest Border." *New York Times*, May 7, 2018.

"Kaepernick Explains His Protest." Reuters, September 13, 2016.

Katz, Michael. *In the Shadow of the Poorhouse: A Social History of Welfare in America.* Rev. ed. New York: Basic Books, 1996.

Keith, William M., and Christian O. Lundberg. *The Essential Guide to Rhetoric*. New York: St. Martin's Press, 2008.

Kellogg, Dan. "How Would Jesus Vote." Sermon, September 11, 2016. Gold Creek Community Church, Mill Creek, WA.

Kellstedt, Lyman A., and John C. Green. "The Politics of the Willow Creek Association Pastors." *Journal for the Scientific Study of Religion* 42, no. 4 (2003): 548.

Ketterling, Rob. "None of the Above: Part One." Sermon, October 23, 2016. River Valley Church, Burnsville, MN.

King, Elizabeth. "Stressed? Blame the 2016 Election." *Time,* April 26, 2016. https://time.com/4299527/election-mental-health/.

Kintz, Linda. *Between Jesus and the Market: The Emotions That Matter in Right-Wing America*. Durham, NC: Duke University Press, 1997.

Kuruvilla, Carol. "A Megachurch Reels after Learning Pastor Let His Professed Pedophile Son Work with Kids." Huffington Post, July 14, 2020. https://www.huffpost.com/entry/john-ortberg-menlo-church_n_5f04e820c5b67a80bbffcdc4.

———. "Pastor Steps Down after Megachurch Learns He Let Pedophile Son Work with Kids," Huffington Post, July 30, 2020, https://www.huffpost.com/entry/john-ortberg-resignation_n_5f22d01ec5b68fbfc87fc983.

———. "Preacher Speaks Up about the Misogyny She's Faced in Evangelical Circles." Huffington Post, May 4, 2018. https://www.huffingtonpost.com/entry/female-preacher-speaks-up-about-misogyny-shes-faced-in-evangelical-circles_us_5aeb7f33e4b0c4f193207bb2.

Lakoff, George. "Understanding Trump." *University of Chicago Press* (blog). August 2016, https://www.press.uchicago.edu/books/excerpt/2016/lakoff_trump.html.

Lebron, Christopher J. *The Making of Black Lives Matter: A Brief History of an Idea.* New York: Oxford University Press, 2017.

Lee, Bruce Y. "Why People Vote against Their Own Interests." Forbes.com, November 8, 2016. https://www.forbes.com/sites/brucelee/2016/11/08/heres-why-you-may-vote-against-yourself/#3ca55bab25fa.

Lee, Michael. *Creating Conservatism: Postwar Words That Made a Movement*. East Lansing: Michigan State University Press, 2014.

Lee, Michelle Ye Hee. "Donald Trump's False Comments Connecting Mexican Immigrants and Crime." *Washington Post*, July 8, 2015. https://www.washingtonpost.com/news/fact-checker/wp/2015/07/08/donald-trumps-false-comments-connecting-mexican-immigrants-and-crime/?utm_term=.967220e8ebe7.

Lee, Morgan. "Mark Driscoll Steps Down While Mars Hill Investigates Charges."

Christianity Today, August 24, 2014. http://www.christianitytoday.com/news/2014/august/mark-driscoll-steps-down-while-mars-hill-investigates-charg.html.

Leff, Michael. "Dimensions of Temporality in Lincoln's Second Inaugural." *Communication Reports* 1, no. 1 (1988): 26–31.

Leff, Michael C., and Gerald P. Mohrmann. "Lincoln at Cooper Union: A Rhetorical Analysis of the Text." *Quarterly Journal of Speech* 60, no. 3 (1974): 346–58.

Lewis, C. S. *Mere Christianity*. New York: Harper Collins, 2015.

Lewis, William F. "Telling America's Story: Narrative Form and the Reagan Presidency." *Quarterly Journal of Speech* 73, no. 3 (1987): 280–302.

Lipset, Seymour Martin. *American Exceptionalism: A Double-edged Sword*. New York: W. W. Norton, 1996.

Lockerman, Allan. "How to Choose a President." Sermon, November 6, 2016. First Baptist Cleveland, Cleveland, TN.

Lodge, Milton, and Charles S. Tabor. *The Rationalizing Voter*. Cambridge, UK: Cambridge University Press, 2013.

Loveland, Anne C., and Otis B. Wheeler. *From Meetinghouse to Megachurch: A Material and Cultural History*. Columbia: University of Missouri Press, 2003.

Lucaites, John Louis, and Celeste M. Condit. "Re-Constructing Narrative Theory: A Functional Perspective." *Journal of Communication* 35 (1985): 90–108.

Lynerd, Benjamin T. *Republican Theology: The Civil Religion of American Evangelicals*. New York: Oxford University Press, 2014.

Madsen, Deborah L. *American Exceptionalism*. Edinburgh: Edinburgh University Press, 1998.

Maher, Bill. *Religulous*. Documentary film, dir. Larry Charles. Santa Monica, CA: Lionsgate, 2009.

Mannon, Bethany. "Xvangelical: The Rhetorical Work of Personal Narratives in Contemporary Religious Discourse." *Rhetoric Society Quarterly* 49, no. 2 (2019): 142–62.

Markham, Annette N. *Life Online: Researching Real Experience in Virtual Space*. Walnut Creek, CA: Altamira Press, 1998.

Marsden, George M. *Fundamentalism and American Culture*. 2d ed. New York: Oxford University Press, 2006.

Martin, Stephanie A. "Money and the Electronic Church: Decoding Dave Ramsey's Debt-Free Gospel." In *The Electronic Church in the Digital Age: Cultural Impacts of Evangelical Mass Media*, ed. Mark Ward. Santa Barbara, CA: Praeger, 2015.

———. "Recession Resonance: How Evangelical Megachurch Pastors Promoted Fiscal Conservatism in the Aftermath of the 2008 Financial Crash." *Rhetoric & Public Affairs* 18, no. 1 (2015): 39–78.

———. "Transformational Presidents, New Media Strategies, and the Necessity of a Universal Audience." In *Columns to Characters: The Press and the Presidency Enter the Digital Age,* ed. Stephanie A. Martin. College Station: Texas A&M Press, 2017.

Martin, Wallace. *Recent Theories of Narrative*. Ithaca, NY: Cornell University Press, 1986.

Martin, William. *With God on Our Side: The Rise of the Religious Right in America*. New York: Broadway Books, 1997.

Martin, William C. *A Prophet with Honor: The Billy Graham Story*. Updated ed. Grand Rapids, MI: Zondervan, 2018.

Mason, Lilliana. *Uncivil Agreement: How Politics Became Our Identity*. Kindle ed. Chicago: University of Chicago Press, 2018.

Mason, Paul. *Meltdown: The End of the Age of Greed*. Brooklyn: Verso, 2009.

McCammon, Sarah. "Trump's Vision: Uniting 'under One God' vs. Religious Freedom." *NPR News: Weekend Edition Saturday,* September 17, 2016. https://www.npr.org/2016/09/17/494360236/trumps-vision-of-uniting-under-one-god-versus-religious-freedom.

McDermott, Kevin. "Conservative Icon Schlafly Faces Revolt over Trump Support; Ed Martin Possibly Removed." *St. Louis Post Dispatch,* April 11, 2016. https://www.stltoday.com/news/local/govt-and-politics/conservative-icon-schlafly-faces-revolt-over-trump-support-ed-martin/article_8268e112–4f2f-560c-9e7d-f445078fc5a8.html.

McGee, Michael Calvin, and John S. Nelson. "Narrative Reason in Public Argument." *Journal of Communication* 35, no. 4 (December 1985): 139–55.

McKinnon, Sara L., Robert Asen, Karma R. Chávez, and Robert Glenn Howard. *Text + Field: Innovations in Rhetorical Method*. University Park: Penn State University Press, 2016.

McLoughlin, William G. *The American Evangelicals, 1800–1900: An Anthology*. Gloucester, MA: Peter Smith, 1976.

Meacham, Jon. "The End of Christian America." *Newsweek*, April 3, 2009. https://www.newsweek.com/meacham-end-christian-america-77125.

Micklethwait, John, and Adrian Woolridge. *The Right Nation: Conservative Power in America*. New York: Penguin, 2004.

Mill, John Stuart. *On Liberty*. New York: Compass Circle, 2019.

Moll, Rob. "Dave Ramsey Goes Beyond Credit Card Shredding." *Christianity Today*, August 2011. https://www.christianitytoday.com/ct/2011/august/dave-ramsey-money-church.html.

Montesquieu (Charles-Louis de Secondat, Baron de La Brède et de Montesquieu). *Selected Political Writings*. Ed. Melvin Richter. Indianapolis: Hackett, 1990.

Moore, Beth. "Wake up, Sleepers." Tweet, October 9, 2016. https://twitter.com/bethmoorelpm/status/785119502769852418.

———. "A Letter to My Brothers." *The LPM [Living Proof Ministries] Blog* (blog), May 3, 2018. https://blog.lproof.org/2018/05/a-letter-to-my-brothers.html.

———. "A letter to my brothers." Tweet, May 3, 2018. https://twitter.com/BethMooreLPM/status/992035713079267328.

———. "I'm pro marriage." Tweet, April 28, 2018. https://twitter.com/BethMooreLPM/status/990417498607468544.

Moore, Russell. "Why This Election Makes Me Hate the Word Evangelical." *Washington Post*, February 29, 2016.

Mountford, Roxanne. *The Gendered Pulpit: Preaching in American Protestant Spaces*. Carbondale: Southern Illinois University Press, 2003.

Mullins, Todd. "Decision 2016." Sermon, November 6, 2016. Christ Fellowship Church, Palm Beach Gardens, FL.

Muravchik, Stephanie. *American Protestantism in the Age of Psychology*. Cambridge, UK: Cambridge University Press, 2011.

Murphy, Nancy. *Reasoning and Rhetoric in Religion*. Valley Forge, PA: Trinity Press International, 1994.

Myers, Kevin. "Faith. Politics. Church." Sermon, October 23, 2016. 12Stone Church, Lawrenceville, GA.

———. "Faith. Politics. Freedom." Sermon, September 11, 2016. 12Stone Church, Lawrenceville, GA.

———. "How We Work." Sermon, February 19, 2012. 12Stone Church, Lawrenceville, GA.

"NBC News Exit Poll: White Evangelical Women Stand Squarely with the Republicans." *NBC News,* November 6, 2018. https://www.nbcnews.com/card/nbc-news-exit-poll-white-evangelical-women-stand-squarely-republicans-n933236.

Needtobreathe. "Wasteland." From *Rivers in the Wasteland*. Music recording. Atlantic Records, 2014.

Noble, O. Alan. "Evangelical Views of the 2016 Election: Not the Lesser of Two Evils, Choose Candidate Evan McMullin Instead." *The Exchange with Ed Stetzer* (blog). *Chrristianity Today,* October 3, 2016. https://www.christianitytoday.com/edstetzer/2016/october/evangelical-views-of-2016-election-in-support-of-third-part.html.

"No Clear Choice: Three Perspectives on the 2016 Election." *Christianity Today* 60, no. 8 (2016): 52.

Noden, Kirk. "Why Do White Working-Class People Vote against Their Interests? They Don't." *The Nation,* November 17, 2016. https://www.thenation.com/article/why-do-white-working-class-people-vote-against-their-interests-they-dont/.

Noll, Mark A. *The Civil War as a Theological Crisis*. Chapel Hill: University of North Carolina Press, 2006.

Norris, Kristopher, and Sam Speers. *Kingdom Politics: In Search of a New Political Imagination for Today's Church*. Eugene, OR: Cascade Books, 2015.

Northrop, Dary. "Politics." Sermon, October 16, 2016. Timberline Church, Fort Collins, CO.

Onishi, Bradley. "The Rise of #Exvangelical." *Religion & Politics,* April 9, 2019. https://religionandpolitics.org/2019/04/09/the-rise-of-exvangelical/.

"Opinion: I Was Assaulted. He Was Applauded." *New York Times,* March 9, 2018. https://www.nytimes.com/2018/03/09/opinion/jules-woodson-andy-savage-assault.html. Accessed July 27, 2020.

Osnos, Evan. "Donald Trump and the Ku Klux Klan: A History." *New Yorker,* February 29, 2016.

Ortberg, John. "Greatest Political Decision Ever Made." Sermon, November 6, 2016. Menlo Church, Menlo Park, CA.

———. "How Not to Be Anxious during an Election." Sermon, October 30, 2016. Menlo Church, Menlo Park, CA.

———. "How Not to Fall Apart." Sermon, November 13, 2016. Menlo Church, Menlo Park, CA.

Paulson, Michael. "A Brash Style That Filled Pews, Until Followers Had Their Fill: Mark Driscoll Is Being Urged to Leave Mars Hill Church." *New York Times,* August 22, 2014.

Peck, Reece. *Fox Populism: Branding Conservatism as Working Class.* Cambridge, UK: Cambridge University Press, 2019.

Perelman, Chaïm, and Lucie Olbrechts-Tyteca. *The New Rhetoric: A Treatise in Argumentation*. Notre Dame, IN: University of Notre Dame Press, 2010.

Perkins, Miriam Yvonne. "Preaching and Rhetorical Responses to Terror: American Evangelical Sermons Delivered in Reaction to September 11, 2001." PhD diss., Catholic University of America, 2008.

Perlstein, Rick. *Before the Storm: Barry Goldwater and the Unmaking of the American Consensus*. New York: Nation Books, 2009.

Peters, Jeremy W., and Elizabeth Dias. "Evangelical Leaders Are Frustrated at G.O.P. Caution on Kavanaugh Allegation." *New York Times*, September 20, 2018.

Pew Research Center. "Religious Landscape Study." http://www.pewforum.org/religious-landscape-study/.

Pezzullo, Phaedra C. "Resisting 'National Breast Cancer Awareness Month': The Rhetoric of Counterpublics and Their Cultural Performances." *Quarterly Journal of Speech* 89, no. 4 (2003): 345–65.

———. "Touring 'Cancer Alley,' Louisiana: Performances of Community and Memory for Environmental Justice." *Text and Performance Quarterly* 23, no. 3 (2003): 226–52.

Phillips-Fein, Kim. *Invisible Hands: The Making of the Conservative Movement from the New Deal to Reagan*. New York: W. W. Norton, 2009.

Piper, John. "What's the Recession For." Sermon, February 1, 2009. Bethlehem Baptist Church, Minneapolis. MP3 audio file.

Pitney, John. "The Tocqueville Fraud." *Weekly Standard,* November 12, 1995. https://www.weeklystandard.com/john-j-pitney/the-tocqueville-fraud.

Pokluda, Jonathan. "Anxiety: A Perspective Problem." Sermon, December 1, 2015. Watermark Community Church, Dallas.

———. "How to Spot Fake Christianity." Sermon, July 21, 2015. Watermark Community Church, Dallas.

———. "Sex and Government." Sermon, October 25, 2016. Watermark Community Church, Dallas.

Prindle, David F. *The Paradox of Democratic Capitalism: Politics and Economics in American Thought*. Baltimore: Johns Hopkins University Press, 2006.

Putnam, Robert D., and David. E. Campbell. *American Grace: How Religion Divides and Unites Us*. New York: Simon & Schuster, 2010.

Raburn, Garrett. "How to Choose a Leader." Sermon, November 1, 2016. Watermark Community Church, Dallas.

———. "Sex & Purity." Sermon, September 13, 2016. Watermark Community Church, Dallas.

Rai, Candice. *Democracy's Lot: Rhetoric, Publics, and the Places of Invention*. Tuscaloosa: University of Alabama Press, 2016.

Rainer, Thom. LifeWay press release, April 30, 2018.

Ramsey, Dave. "Enough." Sermon, March 9, 2009. Willow Creek Community Church, South Barrington, IL.

Ratcliffe, Krista. *Anglo-American Feminist Challenges to the Rhetorical Traditions: Virginia Woolf, Mary Daly, Adrienne Rich*. Carbondale: Southern Illinois University Press, 1996.

———. *Rhetorical Listening: Identification, Gender, Whiteness*. Carbondale: Southern Illinois University Press, 2005.

Redick, Kip, and Lori Underwood. "Rationality and Narrative: A Relationship of Priority." *Philosophy & Rhetoric* 40, no. 4 (2007): 394–405.

Reich, Robert. "Fear Is Why Workers in Red States Vote against Their Economic Self-Interest." *Berkeley Blog* (blog), January 16, 2014. https://blogs.berkeley.edu/2014/01/16/fear-is-why-workers-in-red-states-vote-against-their-economic-self-interest/.

Reichley, A. James. "The Evangelical and Fundamentalist Revolt." In *Piety & Politics: Evangelicals and Fundamentalists Confront the World*, ed. Richard John Neuhaus and Michael Cromartie. Lanham, MD: University Press of America, 1987.

Ricci, David. *Politics without Stories: The Liberal Predicament*. New York: Cambridge University Press, 2016.

Ricoeur, Paul. *Time and Narrative*. Vol. 1. Chicago: University of Chicago Press, 1990.

Robin, Corey. *The Reactionary Mind: Conservatism from Edmund Burke to Sarah Palin*. New York: Oxford University Press, 2011.

Ross, Nate. "Who Are You Voting For." Sermon, October 28, 2016. Northside Christian Church, New Albany, IN.

Rowland, Robert. "The Narrative Perspective." In *Rhetorical Criticism: Perspectives in Action*, ed. Jim A Kuypers. New York: Rowman & Littlefield, 2016.

Rueckert, William H. *Encounters with Kenneth Burke*. Urbana: University of Illinois Press, 1994.

San Clemente Presbyterian Church (San Clemente, CA). Website. https://www.scpres.org/.

Schmidt, Samantha, and Michelle Boorstein. "For Religious Conservative Women, the Kavanaugh-Ford Hearing Was Particularly Disorienting." *Washington Post,* September 28, 2018.

Sciupac, Elizabeth Podrebarac, and Gregory A. Smith. "How Religious Groups Voted in the Midterm Elections." Pew Research Center, November 7, 2018. http://www.pewresearch.org/fact-tank/2018/11/07/how-religious-groups-voted-in-the-midterm-elections/.

Scott, Eugene. "Trump Believes in God, But Hasn't Sought Forgiveness." *CNN Politics,* July 18, 2015. https://www.cnn.com/2015/07/18/politics/trump-has-never-sought-forgiveness/index.html.

The Scrapbook. "Fake Tocqueville Lives!" *Weekly Standard,* October 13, 1997. https://www.washingtonexaminer.com/weekly-standard/fake-tocqueville-lives.

Sears, Waylon. "Who Do I Vote For." Sermon, October 9, 2016. Victory Worship Center, Tucson, AZ.

Shellnut, Kate. "LifeWay Stops Selling Jen Hatmaker Books over LGBT Beliefs." *Christianity Today,* October 27, 2016. https://www.christianitytoday.com/news/2016/october/lifeway-stops-selling-jen-hatmaker-books-lgbt-beliefs-chris.html.

———. "Women's March Sets Out to Exclude 40 Percent of American Women:What Pro-Life Feminists Actually Have in Common with Their Pro-Choice Counterparts." *Christianity Today,* January 18, 2017. https://www.christianitytoday.com/women/2017/january/womens-march-sets-out-to-exclude-40-percent-of-american-wom.html.

Sider, Ron, James Dobson, and Sho Baraka. "Clinton, Trump, or Neither? 3 Views on the 2016 Presidential Election." *Christianity Today* (Special Section), September 23, 2016. https://www.christianitytoday.com/ct/2016/october/clinton-trump-or-neither-3-views-on-2016-presidential-elect.html

#SilenceisnotSpiritual. Statement. https://www.silenceisnotspiritual.org/statement.

Silver, Nate. "Election Update: Are Trump's Polls Getting Worse?" Fivethirtyeight, October 7, 2016. https://fivethirtyeight.com/features/election-update-are-trumps-polls-getting-worse/.

Skocpol, Theda, and Vanessa Williamson. *The Tea Party and the Remaking of Republican Conservatism*. New York: Oxford University Press, 2012.

Skowronek, Stephen. *The Politics Presidents Make: Leadership from John Adams to Bill Clinton*. Rev. ed. Cambridge, MA: Harvard University Press, 1997.

Smidt, Corwin E. *American Evangelicals Today*. Lanham, MD: Rowman & Littlefield, 2013.

Smietana, Bob. "2016 Election Exposes Evangelical Divides." LifeWay Research, October 14, 2016. https://lifewayresearch.com/2016/10/14/2016-election-exposes-evangelical-divide/.

Smith, Christian. *Christian America? What Evangelicals Really Want*. Berkeley: University of California Press, 2000.

Smith, Christian, and Michael Emerson. *American Evangelicalism: Embattled and Thriving*. Chicago: University of Chicago Press, 1998.

Smith, Gregory A., and Jessica Martinez. "How the Faithful Voted: A Preliminary 2016 Analysis." Pew Research, November 9, 2016. http://www.pewresearch.org/fact-tank/2016/11/09/how-the-faithful-voted-a-preliminary-2016-analysis/.

Smith, Mark A. *The Right Talk: How Conservatives Transformed the Great Society into the Economic Society*. Princeton, NJ: Princeton University Press, 2007.

Snowball, David. *Continuity and Change in the Rhetoric of the Moral Majority*. New York: Praeger, 1991.

Solomon, Lon. "The Lying Prophets of America." Sermon, July 4, 2012. McLean Bible Church, Vienna, VA.

Stanback, Marsha Houston, and W. Barnett Pearce. "Talking to 'the Man': Some Communication Strategies Used by Members of 'Subordinate' Social Groups." *Quarterly Journal of Speech* 67, no. 1 (1981): 21–30.

Stanfill, Kristian. "Jesus Paid It All." Music recording. Sixstepsrecords, Nashville, 2006.

Stanley, Andy. "In God We Trust—Part One." Sermon, February 14, 2010. Willow Creek Community Church, South Barrington, IL. MP3 audio file.

———. "Recovery Road, Recession Lessons." Sermon, August 21, 2011. North Point Community Church, Alpharetta, GA. MP3 audio file.

———. "We the People: Recovery Road, Recession Lessons." Sermon, August 21, 2011. North Point Community Church, Alpharetta, GA. MP3 audio file.

Stein, Judith. *Pivotal Decade: How the United States Traded Factories for Finance in the Seventies*. New Haven, CT: Yale University Press, 2010.

Stetzer, Ed. "Why Evangelicals Dislike and Distrust Hillary Clinton So Much." *The Exchange with Ed Stetzer* (blog). *Christianity Today,* October 31, 2016. http://www.christianitytoday.com/edstetzer/2016/october/why-evangelicals-dislike-and-distrust-hillary-clinton-so-mu.html.

Stone, Dave. "Cliffhanger: The Family, the Foundation of a Nation, the Story of Us." Sermon, July 4, 2010. Southeast Christian Church, Louisville, KY. MP3 audio file.

Strachan, Owen. *Awakening the Evangelical Mind: An Intellectual History of the Neo-Evangelical Movement*. Grand Rapids, MI: Zondervan, 2015.

Subsplash. "Subsplash: The Ultimate Engagement Platform." http://www.subsplash.com/.

Tarnow, Adam. "Everybody Plays But Nobody Wins." Sermon, April 26, 2016. Watermark Community Church, Dallas.

Tavernise, Sabrina, and Katherine Q. Seelye. "Political Divide Splits Relationships—and Thanksgiving, Too." *New York Times*, November 15, 2016.

Taylor, Charles. *Modern Social Imaginaries*. Durham, NC: Duke University Press, 2004.

———. *Sources of the Self: The Making of the Modern Identity*. Cambridge, MA: Harvard University Press, 1989.

Taylor, Jessica. "Citing 'Two Corinthians,' Trump Struggles to Make the Sale to Evangelicals." *NPR News: All Things Considered,* January 18, 2016. https://www.npr.org/2016/01/18/463528847/citing-two-corinthians-trump-struggles-to-make-the-sale-to-evangelicals.

———. "Cruz: Opposition to Same-Sex Marriage Will Be 'Front and Center' in 2016 Campaign." *NPR News: Morning Edition,* June 29, 2015. https://www.npr.org/sections/itsallpolitics/2015/06/29/418398912/cruz-opposition-to-gay-marriage-will-be-front-and-center-in-2016-campaign.

Thumma, Scott, and Dave Travis. *Beyond Megachurch Myths: What We Can Learn from America's Largest Churches.* San Francisco: Jossey-Bass, 2007.

Tocqueville, Alexis de. *Democracy in America.* New York: Alfred A. Knopf, 1948.

Tompkins, Paula S. *Practicing Communication Ethics: Development, Discernment, and Decision Making.* 2d ed. New York: Routledge, 2019.

Troy, Gil. *The Reagan Revolution: A Very Short Introduction.* New York: Oxford University Press, 2009.

Trump, Donald. "Address Accepting the Presidential Nomination at the Republican National Convention in Cleveland, Ohio." July 21, 2016. American Presidency Project, University of California—Santa Barbara. https://www.presidency.ucsb.edu/documents/address-accepting-the-presidential-nomination-the-republican-national-convention-cleveland.

———. "Remarks to the 11th Annual Values Voter Summit in Washington, DC, Omni Shoreham Hotel, Washington, DC." September 9, 2016. American Presidency Project, University of California—Santa Barbara. https://www.presidency.ucsb.edu/documents/remarks-the-11th-annual-values-voter-summit-washington-dc-omni-shoreham-hotel-washington.

12Stone Church. "About 12Stone." https://12stone.com/about/.

Utter, Glenn H., and James L. True. *Conservative Christians and Political Participation: A Reference Handbook.* Santa Barbara, CA: ABC-CLIO, 2004.

Waldron, Stephen. "Evangelical Views of the 2016 Election: 'Jill Stein Is My Imperfect Candidate.'" *The Exchange with Ed Stetzer* (blog). *Christianity Today,* October 6, 2016. https://www.christianitytoday.com/edstetzer/2016/october/evangelical-views-of-2016-election-jill-stein-is-my-imperfe.html.

Wallbuilders. "About Us." https://wallbuilders.com/about-us/.

Wan, William, Tanya Sichynsky, and Sandhya Somashekhar. "After Trump's Election: 'There Are Two Americas Now.'" *Washington Post,* November 21, 2016.

Warnick, Barbara. "The Narrative Paradigm: Another Story." *Quarterly Journal of Speech* 73, no. 2 (1987): 172–82.

Warren, Rick. "The Five Foundations of Financial Freedom." Seminar, June 4, 2010. Saddleback Church, Lake Forest, CA. Video file.

Warren, Tish Harrison. "I Overlooked the Rural Poor—Then Trump Came Along," *Christianity Today* August 22, 2016. https://www.christianitytoday.com/ct/2016/september/i-overlooked-rural-poor-then-trump-came-along.html.

Wear, Michael. "Why Democrats Must Regain the Trust of Religious Voters." *Atlantic,* November 21, 2018. https://www.theatlantic.com/politics/archive/2017/11/why-democrats-must-regain-faith-among-religious-voters/546434/.

Weber, Max. *The Sociology of Religion.* Boston: Beacon Press, 1993.

Weiner, Greg. "Of Prudence and Principle: Reflections on Lincoln's Second Inaugural at 150." *Society* 52, no. 6 (2015): 604–10.

Weiser, M. Elizabeth. "Burke and War: Rhetoricizing the Theory of Dramatism." *Rhetoric Review* 26, no. 3 (2007): 286–302.

Wellford, Rachel. "Here's the List of GOP Responses to Trump's Vulgar Comments about Groping Women." *PBS Newshour,* October 7, 2016. https://www.pbs.org/newshour/politics/headline-republicans-react-trump-comments-objectifying-women.

West, Thomas G. *The Political Theory of the American Founding: Natural Rights, Public Policy, and the Moral Conditions of Freedom*. New York: Cambridge University Press, 2017.

White, James Boyd. "Law as Rhetoric, Rhetoric as Law: The Arts of Cultural and Communal Life." *University of Chicago Law Review* 52 (1985): 684–1146.

White, Ronald C. *Lincoln's Greatest Speech: The Second Inaugural.* New York: Simon & Schuster, 2002.

Wilcox, Clyde. *Onward Christian Soldiers: The Religious Right in American Politics*. 2d ed. Boulder, CO: Westview Press, 2000.

Wilhite, Jud. "Hope beyond Politics." Sermon, November 6, 2016. Central Church, Henderson, NV.

Wilkerson, Bryan. "Good Work, Good People Are Hard to Find." Sermon, June 6, 2010. Grace Chapel, Lexington, MA. MP3 audio file.

Wilkin, Jen. "Where Kids Get Their Political Views." *Christianity Today*, September 23, 2016. https://www.christianitytoday.com/ct/2016/october/where-kids-get-their-political-views.html.

Williams, Raymond. *Keywords: A Vocabulary of Culture and Society*. New York: Oxford University Press, 1976.

Willow Creek Community Church. "Statement of Faith." http://www.willowcreek.com/about/statement_faith.asp.

Wilsey, John D. *American Exceptionalism and Civil Religion: Reassessing the History of an Idea*. Kindle ed. Downers Grove, IL: IVP Academic, 2015.

Wilson, Don. "Freedom." Sermon, July 4, 2010. Christ's Church of the Valley, Peoria, AZ.

———. "Rehoboam." Sermon, November 6, 2016. Christ's Church of the Valley, Peoria, AZ.

Wolf, Jay. "Be Wise with Wealth." Sermon, February 6, 2011. First Baptist Church, Montgomery, AL. MP3 audio file.

Woodbridge, John D., Mark A. Noll, and Nathan O. Hatch. "'Holy Bible, Book Divine': Evangelicals and the Bible." In *The Gospel in America: Themes in the Story of America's Evangelicals*, ed. Mark A. Noll. Grand Rapids, MI: Zondervan, 1979.

Young, Ed. "How to Pick a President: A Christ Follower's Responsibility in the Election." Sermon, November 6, 2016. Fellowship Church, Grapevine, TX.

Young, Neil J. "White Evangelicals Win White House for Trump, But Lose Big."

Religion Dispatches, November 9, 2016. http://religiondispatches.org/white-evangelicals-win-white-house-for-trump-but-lose-big/.

Zarefsky, David. "Knowledge Claims in Rhetorical Criticism." *Journal of Communication* 58, no. 4 (2008): 629–40.

Index

abolition, 30, 205n25. *See also* slavery
abortion, 2, 3, 10, 11, 21, 24, 35, 46, 63, 73, 77, 79, 87, 96, 98, 100, 112, 126, 135, 136, 139, 141, 143, 144, 150, 160, 163–64, 165, 171, 194n10, 198–99nn33–34, 208n48. See also *Roe v. Wade*
Access Hollywood tape, 21, 80, 147–52, 155, 229n18
active-passivism (rhetoric of), 9, 11, 12, 20, 21, 51, 53, 77–80, 87, 101, 103, 108, 109, 111, 133, 137, 144, 148, 160, 166, 168, 169, 171, 173, 174, 234n8
Adams, John, 61, 62
agency (political), 233–34n5
agency (rhetorical), 164, 168–71; defined, 169, 229n18
Aleppo, Syria, 173, 174
"A Letter to My Brothers," 154, 155
Alexander, Michelle, 225n37
Althusser, Louis, 45
ambiguity (rhetorical), 21, 152, 153, 159, 163, 164
American Council of Christian Churches (ACCC), 33
American Dream, 26, 36, 57, 65, 67, 71, 80, 97
American exceptionalism, 5, 7, 15, 18, 19, 28, 36, 37, 39, 46, 48, 55, 57, 59–60, 66, 67, 68, 71, 78, 84, 89, 101, 115, 135, 144, 152, 166, 168. *See also* narrative(s)
American Family Association (AFA), 35
American flag, 89, 121, 127, 173
American Grace, 51
American Left, 20, 34, 74, 112, 165
American Revolution, 25
Anderson, Benedict, 5, 203n10
Anyabwile, Thabiti, 158
Apple corporation, 64, 126
Arbury, Ahmaud, 226n43
Arendt, Hannah, 233–34n5
argument (in rhetoric), 47
Aristotle, 7, 16, 61, 215n23
Armageddon, 31, 84
Atlantic, 151
audience, 2, 10, 11, 20, 23, 25, 33, 38, 41, 53, 56, 63, 64–65, 67, 69, 70, 71, 81, 84, 89, 93, 113, 114, 115, 117, 121, 123, 126, 127, 130, 134, 137, 139, 142, 148, 150, 162, 169, 170, 171, 173; and creation of audiences in speaking or writing 143, 155–56, 157, 161; and digital rhetorical ethnography 6, 40, 45, 107; and rhetorical practice 8, 14, 16–17, 27, 49–50, 60–61, 72, 75–76,

96, 97, 98, 99, 106, 108, 110, 111, 112, 124, 125, 128, 129, 131, 132, 140, 145, 146, 174. *See also* founders' rhetoric; Moore, Beth; rhetoric: rhetorical identification
Augustine, Saint, ix, 48, 101

Bakhtinian dialogism, 28
Balmer, Randall, 24, 28, 195–96n14, 204n19, 208n45
Baltimore Sun, 32
Baptist Blogger, 153
Barthes, Roland, 16, 202n51
Barton, David, 62, 215n25
Barzun, Jacques, 47, 48
Bayside Church, 87
Beatles, 80
Beckstrom, Rod, 42
Bellah, Robert, 94
Berger, Peter, 206n33
Berry, Jason, 133–134
Bethlehem Baptist Church, 66
Beyond Megachurch Myths, 195n12, 209n1
Bible, 17, 42, 51, 58, 61, 75, 110, 111, 119, 137, 143, 154, 161; and scripture authority 29, 49, 51, 81, 124
Billy Graham Center, 151, 160
Bizzell, Patricia, 44
Black Lives Matter (BLM), 23, 128–33, 145, 173, 175, 225–26n38. *See also* Kaepernick, Colin; race/racism/racial justice
Boise, Idaho, 18
Bolsinger, Tod, 41, 42, 69, 210–11nn11–12
Bonhoeffer, Dietrich, 100–101
Borowitz, Andy, 76
Brafman, Ori, 42
breast cancer awareness, 14, 44
Brown, Michael, 127
Brown v. Board of Education, 129
Bryan, William Jennings, 206n32
Buchanan, Pat, 88
Burgen, Jim, 70
Burke, Edmund, 100, 106, 108, 117
Burke, Kenneth, 49, 57, 72, 152, 153, 199n35, 201n45, 203–4n10
Bush, George H. W., 36
Bush, George W., 9, 24

Calvary Chapel, Albuquerque, New Mexico, 60, 99
Campbell, David, 51
Campbell, Karlyn Kohrs, 169, 229n18
capitalism, 19, 31, 36, 56, 152; and industrial slums 30, 31
Central Church, 40, 108, 109
Charland, Maurice, 203–4n10
Charles, Prince of Wales, 76
Chauvin, Derek, 133
Chicago Cubs, 76, 80, 111
Chicago Declaration of Evangelical Social Concern, 34, 207n42
Christ Church of the Valley, 61
Christ Fellowship Church, 81, 84, 97, 148
Christian Coalition of America, 35, 149, 208n47
Christian Defense Fund, 88
Christian Left, 34
Christian Right, 34, 35
Christian Nationalism, 84, 93, 94, 98, 109, 144. *See also* narrative(s)
Christianity Today, 33–34, 197n29, 215–16n31
Cho, David Yonggi, 210n7
Cho, Eugene, 160
Church by the Glades, 84
church online. *See* digital church
#ChurchToo, 153, 157, 158, 160, 229n18
citizenship, 57, 67, 68, 69, 118, 123, 138; and dual citizenship, 19–20, 82, 91, 94, 101, 112, 174; and heavenly citizenship 79, 110; and primary citizenship 5, 81; and true (real) citizenship, 18, 78, 113, 117

"city on the hill" (America as), 9, 36, 57, 72
Civic Hope, 197n24
Civil War, 30, 62, 129, 205n25
Clarke, Tess, 163–64
Cleveland Indians, 80, 111
climate change, 112
Clinton, Bill, 21, 88, 148, 149, 226n40
Clinton, Hillary, 1, 3, 5, 8, 10, 11, 15, 20, 23, 45, 76, 78, 79, 80, 82, 85, 86, 87, 88, 95, 96–102, 108, 118, 124, 125, 126, 137, 139, 144, 147, 148, 149, 151, 166, 168, 170, 173, 19, 197n29, 198n32, 199n35
Clinton-Lewinsky scandal, 149
CNN, 75
Collins, Jim, 42
community of minds. See *The New Rhetoric*
complementarian gender roles, 151, 154, 158, 216n36, 228n14, 231n32
Concerned Women for America, 35, 208n47
conservative social movements, 165
Constitution, 35, 61, 62, 75, 88, 123, 166, 205n25, 215n25. *See also* founding documents
Conquergood, Dwight, 44, 52, 201n46
constitutive rhetoric, 5–6, 203–4n10
consumer credit. *See* credit
consumer goods, 32
consumer model of Christianity, 67
Continental Congress, 62
convenience sample, 43
copresence, 44, 211n18
Corrigan, Lisa, 225n37
counterculture, 24
COVID-19 pandemic, 226n43
credit, 32, 65
critical rhetorical ethnography, 46
Crossing Church, 80
Crowley, Sharon, 46
Cruz, Ted, 75, 163–64
cultural studies, 44, 211n15
culture wars, 11, 19, 20, 57, 58, 63, 73, 74, 79, 84, 85, 100, 113, 194, 199n34. *See also* rhetoric: and culture wars
Culture Wars, 58
Curtice, Kaitlin, 159

Dallas, Texas, 18, 105, 109, 149, 163, 164, 170, 214n14
Daniel in the lions' den, 91–94
Darby, John Nelson, 31
darkness (as metaphor), 161–62, 232n46
Darrow, Clarence, 206n32
Democrats/Democratic Party, 3, 10, 21, 24, 82, 226n40; and voting demographics, 224n28; and 2010 midterm election, 12. *See also* Reagan, Ronald; Reagan, Ronald: and Reagan Democrats
democratic participation, 169
Dias, Elizabeth, 163, 164
digital church, 4, 17, 18, 40, 43, 45, 46, 47, 77, 105, 106, 174
digital community, 40. *See also* virtual community
digital ethnography, 41, 43
digital Jesus, 15
digital rhetorical ethnography, 17, 28, 29, 51–52, 80; experience of, 39, 52; explained, 4, 41–48; as hybrid methodology, 43, 44, 48; as practiced by author, 56, 135, 144, 166, 168; as research methodology, 18, 48, 172. *See also* narrative(s); sermons; story/stories
dissenting Protestantism, 94
Dobson, James, 35, 75
Dowling, William, 168
Down Syndrome, 150
Driscoll, Mark 67, 69–70, 161, 216n37
du Plessis, Pierre, 76
Durkheim, Emile, 214n17

Eagle Forum, 75, 218n8

economics, 39
Edman Chapel, 160
Edwards, Jonathan, 52, 198n33
Eisenhower, Dwight, 34
election day, 38
Elevation Church, 83
Elisha, Omri 52, 209n56
Elizabeth II, Queen, 76
Ellingson, Stephen, 222–23n7
emplotment 16, 167–68, 171
Engel v. Vitale (1961) 34, 62. *See also* school prayer
Enlightenment/post-Enlightenment, 13, 94
esprit de finesse 27, 47, 48, 49, 52, 86, 90, 91, 95, 98, 101, 111, 115, 125, 129, 133, 135, 136, 141, 144, 142, 143, 146, 158, 166, 175, 212n27. *See also* narrative(s); story/stories
esprit de géométrie, 47, 86
ethnographer(s) 44, 45, 174
ethnography 14, 27, 39, 43, 46, 172. *See also* digital ethnography, internet ethnography
evangelical Protestantism, 28
evangelical Republicanism, 73
evangelicals: and author's own experience with, 2; and conservative worldview, 48; defined, 5, 28–29, 58–59; demographics 12, 73;as electorally transactional, 4, 77, 84, 87, 101; identity, 197n26; and individualism of message and movement, 105; and megachurch attendance, 12; and movement leaders, 21; and political narratives, 13, 15, 25, 36–37; and political worldview, 10, 39, 43, 48; portrayals in media, extreme, 15, 201n49; and self-identification, 5; and support for Republican party, 35, 41, 71, 78, 79, 84–85, 87, 102, 106, 118, 170; and the Tea Party, 12; and truth, 4; and white (demographic), 6. *See also* active-passivism (rhetoric of); American exceptionalism; personal responsibility; Protestant work ethic
Evans, John, 42
Evans, Rachel Held, 150, 151, 153, 229n17
"exvangelical," 158, 230n23

Facebook, 2, 7, 83, 113, 121, 133, 150, 158, 224n20
Falwell, Jerry, Jr., 75, 218n7
Falwell, Jerry, Sr., 14, 30, 34, 35, 196n18, 198n33
Family Research Council, 108
family separation policy (Trump administration), 163–64
Fargo, North Dakota, 18
The Father's House, 76
Fea, John, 89, 90–91, 205n25, 232n47
Federal Communication Commission, 36
Federal Council of Churches (FCC), 33
federal deficit, 21
Fellowship Church, 91, 108, 137–44
feminism, 7, 10, 26, 44, 73, 91, 171, 194n11
feminist scholarship, 44, 202n51
financial crisis (2008). *See* Great Recession
Finney, Charles, 30
First Baptist Church, 149
First Baptist Cleveland, 149
Fisher, Walter, 13, 26, 27, 28, 49, 50, 204n10, 212–13n36; and good reasons, 13, 27, 140, 145. *See also* narrative paradigm
FitzGerald, Frances, 29, 33, 206n32
Flatirons Community Church, 70
Floyd, George, 119, 133, 225–26n38, 226n43
Focus on the Family, 35, 75, 108, 208n47
Ford, Christine Blasey, 159–60
founders (American), 25, 37, 61–64, 88, 144, 166

founders' rhetoric, 4, 25, 51, 60, 169
founding documents, 25. *See also* Constitution
Frank, Thomas, 3, 4, 5, 12, 24, 25, 136, 170
Freedom Riders, 132
Friedman, Milton, 106
Fuller, Charles, 33
Fuller Theological Seminary, 33, 210n11
Furtick, Steven, 83

Gallup poll, 5, 208n44
Gardner, Christine, 9, 52, 231n31, 234n8
Gary, Ron, 128–33
gay marriage. *See* marriage equality
gay rights, 10. *See also* LGBTQ rights
Geertz, Clifford, 13, 14, 17, 28, 201n46
Geiger, T. J., 232n45
Gelsinger, Carly, 160
Germany, 57
Gilens, Martin, 225n37
Glasper, Cameron, 128–33
God's sovereignty, 48
God's will, 46
Gold Creek Community Church, 23, 25
Goldwater, Barry, 132
Goodstein, Laurie, 74
Google, 42, 220n37
GOP. *See* Republicans
Gordon-Conwell Theological Seminary, 33
government spending, 143, 144
Graham, Billy, 33, 34, 36, 149, 205–6n31
Graham, Franklin, 149
Gramling, Troy, 85, 147–49
Gramm, Phil, 88
Gray, Freddie, 127, 225–26n38
Great Awakening, 99
Great Commission 5, 28
Great Depression, 24, 33, 205–6n31
Great Recession, 3, 12, 15, 19, 29, 39, 41, 55–58, 57, 59, 73, 93, 136, 215n29. *See also* pastors, sermon topics of: Great Recession
Green, Emma, 151
Greek (language), 16, 61
Griffith, R. Marie, 52
gun control, 143, 144
Gwinnett County, 131

Harding, Susan 48, 52, 196n18
hard work (necessity of), 26, 36, 50, 56, 64, 66, 67, 69, 71, 136, 141, 227n54
Harlow, Tim, 76
Harris, Joshua, 65, 215n25, 215n30
Hartford Institute for Religious Research, 43, 109, 137
Hartouni, Valerie, 165
Harvard College, 62
Harvard Divinity School, 33
Hatmaker, Jen, 150, 151–52, 159, 229n17
Hayek, Friedrich von, 106
Hays, Sharon, 225n37
Hebrew (language) 16, 61
Heitzig, Skip, 60, 81, 82, 99–101
Henry, Carl, 33, 34
Hess, Aaron, 44, 46, 52
Hewitt, Hugh, 54–55, 56, 66
hierarchy in argument, 49, 122, 123
Highpoint Church, 159
historically Black colleges, 129
Hitler, Adolf, 57, 100, 101
Hochschild, Arlie Russell, 25, 26, 170, 204n10
Hofstadter, Richard, 143, 227–28n55
Holder, Greg, 80–81, 86, 101
Hollywood, 3, 10, 23, 24, 90, 126, 136, 153
Horwitz, Robert, 205–6n31
Howard, Robert Glenn, 52
Huffington Post, 160
Hughes, David, 84
human rights, 101, 168
Hummel, Dale, 88–89, 91
Hunter, James Davidson, 58, 205–6n31, 214n10

Hurricane Matthew, 173
Hybels, Bill, 159, 198n33, 213n37

imagined community (communities), 6, 45, 105
immigrant rights, 171
immigration, 91, 98, 164, 226n39
Independence Day sermons, 60–64, 215nn22–23
inequality, 118
information economy, 129
International Congress on World Evangelization, 207n42
iPod, 42, 165
Instagram, 6, 133, 150, 151
internet ethnography, 40
IRS, 36, 122, 194n10
Israel, 36, 101

Jazzercize, 118
Jeffress, Robert, 149
Jerusalem, 101, 222n61
Jim Crow, 130
Jiminez, Paul, 38, 39, 52, 53
Johnson, Gary, 9, 197n29
Johnson, Lyndon B., 226n40; the "Johnson Amendment," 194n10
Johnson, Torrey, 33
Johnston, Ray, 87, 90–91, 220n41
Jones, Robert P., 232n47
Joy, Emily, 153, 161, 230n23

Kaepernick, Colin, 120–23, 129, 134, 145, 224n31. *See also* Black Lives Matter (BLM); race/racism/racial justice
Katz, Michael, 31
Kavanaugh, Brett, 159–60
Kayongo, Derreck, 128–33
Keillor, Garrison, 153
Kellogg, Dan, 23, 25
Kennedy, Anthony, 159
Kennedy, John F., 137
Kerry, John, 24
Ketterling, Rob, 91–95, 102
Keynesian economic policies, 24
King, Martin Luther, Jr., 132
Kintz, Linda, 41, 194n11, 212n27
Ku Klux Klan (KKK), 132

LaHaye Beverly, 35
laissez-faire economics. *See* capitalism
Lauer, Matt, 153
Lausanne Covenant, 34, 207n42
Lean In, 153
Lee, Michael, 223n9, 227n49
Lewis, C. S., 9, 11, 13, 14, 27, 90
Lewis, William, 13, 14, 27, 90
LGBTQ rights, 35, 141, 150, 211n15; *See also* marriage equality; *Obergefell v. Hodges*
Liberty University, 75, 218n7
LifeWay Christian Resources, 154, 229n17
Lincoln, Abraham, 8, 61, 62, 63
Livingproof Ministries, 154
Lockerman, Allan, 149
lynching, 130
Lynerd, Benjamin, 108

mainline Protestantism, 18, 30, 133, 196n18, 210n11
Make America Great Again (2016 campaign slogan), 36, 73, 80, 152
Mannon, Bethany, 230n19
Markham, Annette, 40
marriage equality, 2, 11, 19, 21, 46, 73, 74–75, 77, 87, 100, 112, 136, 139, 140, 143, 163, 165, 171. *See also* LGBTQ rights; *Obergefell v. Hodges*
marriage and family issues. *See* marriage equality
Marsden, George, 30, 205–6n31
Mars Hill Church, 67, 161, 216n37
Martin, Trayvon, 225–26n38
Massachusetts Bay Colony, 37

Mason, Paul, 12
McConnell, Mitch, 147
McIntire, Carl, 205–6n31, 207n40
McLean Bible Church, 51, 67, 216–17n38
McLoughlin, William, 29
McKinnon, Sara L., 14
Meacham, Jon, 54
Medicare, 136, 142, 227n53
megachurches, 3, 19, 20, 21, 38, 49, 50, 53, 56, 59, 61, 65 105, 73, 75, 76, 78, 79, 87, 93, 98, 101, 107, 109, 110, 116, 118, 133, 137, 148, 166, 168, 169, 171, 172, 193n1, 210n7, 215–16n31, 220n32; and adaptive methods, 209n1; and consumer model of Christianity, 67; demographics, 200n38; and external architecture, 80; membership, 12, 195n12; and misogyny, 216n36; and personalization of messages, 104–5, 222–23n7, 223n8; and Republican party, 108; and seeker-friendly, 102, 159, 198–99n33 216n36; as sites for research, 2, 3–4, 15, 17, 39–47, 51, 52, 209n5, 211nn13–14, 222n1; and video montages, 87, 88, 120, 137, 173; and web architecture, 195n13. *See also* pastors; pastors: sermon topics of; sermons
Mein Kampf, 57
Mencken, H. L., 32, 206n32
Menlo Church, 1, 8, 193n1
#MeToo, 153, 156, 157
Mill, John Stuart, 233–34n5
Mohler, Albert Jr., 54–55, 72
Montesquieu, 61, 215n23
Moore, Beth, 21, 151–52, 153–60, 161–63, 229nn17–18, 231n34, 232nn45–46
Moore, Russell, 9, 158
moral arguments, 27
moral imagination, 27
Moral Majority, 30, 34, 35, 208n44, 208n47, 220n32
moral relativism, 139
motivated reasoning, 27
Mountford, Roxanne, 43, 44, 52, 202n51, 211n15
MP3, 43
Mullins, Todd, 81, 82, 84, 97, 98, 148
multiculturalism, 54, 213n3
Murphy, Nancy, 81
Myer, Danny, 42
Myers, Kevin, 4, 21, 66, 67, 78, 108, 118–35, 136, 137, 141, 144, 145, 224n32, 225n35
Myers, Marcia, 118

narrative(s), 13, 15, 24, 26, 53, 73, 86, 110, 143, 174, 210–11n12, 222n1, 227n54; and active-passivism, 21, 148, 166, 167, 172; ambiguity, 153, 163; American, 15, 24–25, 54, 56, 62, 65, 67, 142; and American abundance, 70–71; and American exceptionalism, 57, 72, 78, 86; and Black Lives Matter, 131–32; and Christian Nationalism, 98; and culture, 20, 63; defined ,16, 211–12n26; and digital rhetorical ethnography, 2, 3, 17–18, 39, 41, 43, 46, 47, 52, 172, 173; and Donald Trump, 57, 139, 163; and *esprit de finesse*, 27–28, 47–48, 90–91, 141, 143; and evangelicalism in the U.S., 17, 18–19, 28, 29, 48; and evangelical political worldview, 22, 56, 79–80, 99, 134, 140, 167; founding narrative, 25, 60–61, 66, 152; hardship, 65–66; lived, 26; political narrative, 27, 77, 79, 83, 108, 113; and megachurches, 43, 87; and nostalgia, 113–14, 145; and pastoral rhetoric, 7–8, 11–12, 14, 19–20, 37, 50, 79, 81, 84–85, 91, 99–100, 109–10, 135–36, 166; and rhetoric (theory), 27–28, 50, 130, 165, 167–68, 203–4n10; and women, 151, 158–59, 161, 163–64, 229n17, 230n19

narrative paradigm, 13, 212–13n36. *See also* Fisher, Walter
National Association of Evangelicals (NAE), 33, 34
national debt, 21
National Public Radio (NPR), 74, 75
NBC News, 163
Needtobreathe, 173
negative partisanship, 20, 48, 77, 96
neo-evangelicalism, 33, 35
neoliberalism, 12
Nero, Roman Emperor, 114–15
Netflix, 104
New Deal 24, 205–6n31
The New Rhetoric, 49, 212n32, 224n20; and "community of minds" 10, 50, 111, 158, 231n34
Newsweek, 54
New York City, 120
New York Times, 74, 163–64, 200–21n41
New Yorker, 76
Nixon, Richard, 132
Noll, Mark, 205n25
North Point Community Church 59, 112
Northrop, Dary, 82
Northside Christian Church, 173

Obama administration. *See* Obama, Barack
Obama, Barack 12, 15, 19, 34, 41, 54, 55, 56, 73, 137, 149, 165, 199–200n36, 213n3, 221–22n54
Obamas (Barack and Michele), 26
Obergefell v. Hodges, 74. *See also* LGBTQ rights; marriage equality
obligation, 106, 108, 109, 117, 118, 134–35, 143, 146
Ockenga, Harold, 33
oil embargo, 24
Olbrechts-Tyteca, Lucie, 49, 50, 60, 127, 212n32, 224n20, 231n34
One Nation under God, 88
Orange County, California, 41, 54
Oreos (cookies), 113–14, 145, 224n20
O'Rourke, Beto, 163
Ortberg, John 1, 2, 3, 8, 193n1, 197n21
Outreach (magazine), 118

Paasch, Hannah, 153, 154, 161, 230n23
parable of the talents, 50, 212n34
Parkview Christian Church, 76
partisan identity 12
party platform, 3, 56, 79, 98, 107, 126, 139, 140, 143
Pascal, Blaise 27, 47, 48, 49, 86, 166. See also *esprit de finesse*; *esprit de géométrie*
pastors: 6, 23, 25, 48, 49, 51, 53, 74, 199, 146, 149, 153, 160, 163, 170, 195n12, 195–96n14, 201n49, 222n1; and active-passivism, 168, 169, 174; and 2016 campaign, 75–80; and conservative worldview (personal), 96; and digital rhetorical ethnography, 3, 10–11, 14, 15, 16–18, 29, 39–48, 102, 104, 105–6, 136, 147, 148, 172, 196n18; and formal rhetoric, 196–97n20, 198n32, 198–99n33; and Great Recession, 56; and storytelling, 2, 7–8, 28, 50, 56, 116, 107, 152, 166, 169, 171; 203–4n10. *See also* active-passivism (rhetoric of); digital rhetorical ethnography; Great Recession; story/stories; 2016 campaign
pastors, sermon topics of: active-passivism and "dual citizenship," 4–5, 11,19–21, 80–87, 101; 109–18; active-passivism plus Christian nationalism, 19, 87–94; American affluence and the rhetoric of "true" suffering, 67–71; American exceptionalism, 59–64, 87; the American nation and American founding, 37, 46, 61–64; Great Recession, 57–58, 64–67, 72–73; joining the Republican Party's *esprit*

de finesse, 94–101, 102–3; 107–8, 123–27, 136, 137–44; race, 120–23, 127–34; the use of dubious history, 61, 62–63, 89, 90, 142, 196–97n20. *See also* active-passivism (rhetoric of); American exceptionalism; citizenship: and dual citizenship; founders' rhetoric; Great Recession; megachurches; narrative(s); pastors; sermons; story/stories; 2016 campaign
patriotism, 8, 37, 138, 166, 167, 205n31, 212n26, 230n23. *See also* Kaepernick, Colin
Patterson, Paige, 154, 155
Paul, Apostle, 83, 115, 142, 154, 158, 231n32
Peck, Reece, 227n54
Pence, Mike, 147
Perelman, Chaïm, 49, 50, 60, 127, 212n32, 224n20, 231n34
personal responsibility, 7–8, 31, 36, 46, 48, 64, 70, 129, 135, 141, 145
Peter (Apostle), 114, 115
Pew Research Center, 5, 6, 163, 200n38
Pezzullo, Phaedra, 44, 46, 52, 211n18
Piper, John, 68, 93, 216n33
Pledge of Allegiance 62, 122, 123, 127, 224n32
pluralism (religious), 95
police brutality, 129–30, 133–34
political correctness, 62, 63
political identity, 48, 77, 96, 119, 140
political rights, 168–69
Politics without Stories, 47, 211–12n26
postmodernity, 170
Potential Church, 85, 147
poverty, 68, 71, 129, 141. *See also* pastors, sermon topics of: American affluence and the rhetoric of "true" suffering
pregnancy, 105
Prohibition, 33
Proposition 8 (California), 165
Protestant work ethic, 7, 32, 35, 64, 152
public school board deliberations, 14
Puritans, 37
purity culture. *See* sexual purity/purity pledges
Putin, Vladimir, 88
Putnam, Robert, 51

Quest Church, 160–61

Raburn, Garrett, 105, 106
race/racism/racial justice, 98, 108, 124, 127, 166, 224n31, 225n37–38, 226n43. *See also* Black Lives Matter (BLM); Kaepernick, Colin
Rai, Candace, 52
Rainer, Thom, 154
Ramsey, Dave, 65, 215–16n31
Reagan, Ronald, 9, 13, 35, 36, 88, 102, 106, 137, 200n36; and Reagan Democrats, 24, 208n45
Reed, Ralph, 35, 149
"Reflections: A GC2 Summit on Responding to Sexual Violence," 160
religious freedom, 94, 97, 98, 100, 143
religious plurality, 170
Religious Right, 35
Religious Roundtable, 35
religious schools, 36
reproductive freedom. *See* abortion
Republican theology, 108
Republicans, 1, 3, 10, 24, 35, 49, 56, 58, 108, 118, 226n40; and voting demographics 224n28
rhetoric, 15; and active-passivism, 77, 78–79, 80–87, 98, 101, 102, 103, 107–9, 112, 133, 134, 136, 137, 144, 145, 148, 160, 166, 167–74, 220n32, 234n8; and American evangelicalism, 2; and culture wars, 11, 20, 57, 63, 85; defined, 16; and evangelical worldview, 6; and power, 16; and rhetorical identification, 40, 49, 174, 203–4n10; and rhetorical resonance, 4, 41, 42, 43, 47,

210–11n12, 212n27. *See also* active-passivism (rhetoric of); constitutive rhetoric; founders' rhetoric
rhetorical criticism, 41, 172
rhetorical resonance. *See* rhetoric: and rhetorical resonance
Ricci, David, 47, 48, 211–12n26
Ricoeur, Paul, 16, 167–68
River Valley Church, 91
Robertson, Pat, 35, 149
Roe v. Wade, 34, 208n48. *See also* abortion
Rome, 114–15
Romney, Mitt, 221–22n54
Roosevelt, Franklin D., 24, 137, 200n36
Roosevelt, Theodore, 62, 63
Rose, Charlie, 153
Ross, Nate, 173–75
Ryan, Paul, 147

Saddleback Church, 51, 54, 65, 195n13, 210n7, 215–16n31
salvation (personal). *See* evangelicals: defined
Salvation Army, 30
San Clemente, California, 18
San Clemente Presbyterian Church (SC Pres), 18, 210n11
sanctity of life. *See* abortion
Sandburg, Sheryl, 153
Sanders, Bernie, 227–28n55
Savage, Andy, 159
saving (necessity of), 56. *See also* credit
Schlafly, Phyllis, 75
school prayer, 35. See also *Engel v. Vitale*
Scofield, Cyrus I., 31
Scofield Reference Bible, 31
Scopes Trial, 30, 32, 33, 205–6nn31–32
scripture, authority of. *See* Bible
Sears, Waylon, 97
second coming (of Jesus), 31
Second Great Awakening, 30, 32
secular humanism, 34, 171
secularism/secular world, 30, 55, 57, 137
Seneca, 114
September 11 attacks, 119–20
sermons: and American moral decline, 124–26; and Christian Nationalism, 71; and claims to basic identity, 81, 119; and digital rhetorical ethnography, 42; and the importance of unity, 118–23, 124–25; locations, 214n14; and main themes of 2016 campaign 78–79; and the problem of racism in the U.S., 127–35; and reliance on active-passivism, 80–87; as rhetoric, narratives, or stories, 50, 222n1. *See also* megachurches; pastors; pastors, sermon topics of; story/stories
sexual purity/purity pledges, 14, 105, 106, 153, 154, 160, 161, 162, 231n31, 234n8
sexually transmitted infections, 105, 106, 234n8
#SilenceIsNotSpiritual, 153
Silicon Valley, 42
Sivers, Derek, 210–11n12
Skocpol, Theda, 12
Skowronek, Stephen, 199–200n36; 203n6
slavery, 130
Smith, Christian, 29, 204n19, 210–11n12
social facts, 214n17
Social Gospel, 31
social safety net, 36
Social Security, 136
Solomon, Lon, 51, 67, 216–17n38
Southeast Christian Church, 51, 61
Southern Baptist Convention Ethics and Religious Liberty Commission, 158, 229n17
Southern Baptist Theological Seminary, 54
Southwestern Baptist Seminary, 154
Spacey, Kevin, 153
Spicer, Sean, 88

Spotlight, 161
stagflation, 24
Stanfill, Krstian, 219n17
Stanley, Andy (Charles Andrew), 59–60, 64, 68–69, 71, 112, 214n17
The Starfish and the Spider: The Unstoppable Power of Leaderless Organizations, 42
statement(s) of Faith, 5, 6, 40, 45
Stein, Jill, 9, 197n29
Stetzer, Ed, 151
Stone, Dave, 51, 61–64
story/stories, 15, 171, 172; based in nostalgia, 109–10; defined, 17, 26–27; deep story, 26; and digital rhetorical ethnography, 26, 28–29, 39–47, 47–53, 63, 169, 174; and *esprit de finesse*, 27–28, 90–91; and evangelical political worldview, 22, 25, 28, 36–37, 79–80, 106–7; and founders' rhetoric, 60–61; and "good reasons," 140; and the Great Recession, 56–58, 65–66, 67–71; and personal responsibility, 19, 105–6, 142; and politics, 211–12n26; and rhetoric, 12–15, 72, 165–66, 167–68, 203–4n10; and sermons, 196n18; and sexual abuse in the church, 151, 153, 157, 159; and truth in American culture, 18; and 2016 election, 76–77; and 2018 midterms, 163–64; and women, 230n19
Strangers in Their Own Land, 25
Supreme Court, 19, 34, 74, 87, 96, 97, 101, 129, 135, 159, 208n48
Syrian refugees, 88

tax/taxes, 3, 14, 58, 81, 112, 142, 145; tax policy, 165, 194n10
Taylor, Breonna, 226n43
Taylor, Charles, 6, 196n16
Taylor, Jessica, 75
Taylors First Baptist Church, 38–39, 52–53, 209n1
Tea Party, 12, 13, 15, 26, 41, 56, 165
temperance, 30
terrorism, 101
terrorist attacks, 120
Thomas Road Baptist Church, 14, 196n18, 198n33
Thumma, Scott, 195n12, 209n1
Timberline Church, 82
Tijuana, Mexico, 56
Time (magazine), 8
time shifting, 45
tithe, tithing, 15, 141
Tocqueville, Alexis de, 21–22, 72, 88, 220n37, 233–34n5
tolerance, 140–41
traditional values, 46, 89, 90, 135, 143, 146
transcripts, 44
Travis, Dave, 195n12, 209n1
true citizenship. *See* citizenship: and dual citizenship; citizenship: and true (real) citizenship
Trump, Donald, 1–2, 5, 8, 9, 10–12, 15, 19, 21, 23, 28, 29, 36, 45, 49, 57, 73, 85, 87, 88, 96, 98,99–100, 101, 102–3, 107, 108, 117, 118, 124, 125–27, 132, 136, 137, 139, 146, 153, 156, 159, 163, 166, 168, 171, 173, 192, 197n29, 198–99n32–35, 207n39, 208n48, 220n32, 224n28; and *Access Hollywood* tape, 147–52, 155; as candidate, 76, 78, 80, 82, 94–95, 144, 226n39; and character flaws, 3, 20, 34, 75, 77, 84, 86, 95–96; and language use, 170; and law and order rhetoric, 131; and "make America great again," 79–80, 90, 91; as president, 165; and primary campaign, 75; and women, 9, 147, 152, 164. *See also* 2016 campaign
truth, 4, 13–14, 17, 18, 25, 26, 27, 49, 58, 67, 82, 89–90, 109, 110, 111, 115, 124, 125, 131, 133, 138, 139–41, 142–43, 170, 201n46

12Stone Church, 4, 21, 78, 108, 109, 110, 118–34, 141, 195n13
2010 midterm election. *See* Democrats/ Democratic Party
2016 campaign, 8, 9, 15, 19, 23–24, 25, 36, 38, 39, 45, 52–53, 73, 75, 91, 99, 100, 101, 102, 107, 110, 124, 136, 144, 145, 148, 153, 168. *See also* sermons; Trump, Donald
2018 midterm election, 163
Twin Towers, 120
Twitter, 6, 76, 113, 133, 150, 151, 153, 154, 158–60, 224n20

The Uneasy Conscience of Modern Fundamentalism, 34
unemployment, 24, 225n37
Union Theological Seminary, 33
University of California, San Diego, 42

Values Voter Summit, 95
Victory Worship Center, 97
Vietnam War, 24
Vietnam War Memorial, 14
virtual community, 40, 47. *See also* digital community

Walker, Andrew, 158, 229n17
WallBuilders, 62, 215n25
Wall Street, 90, 220–21n41
Wall Street Journal, 220–21n41
Warren, Rick, 51, 54–56, 65, 66, 72, 210n7
Warren, Tish Harrison, 207n39
Warner, Michael, 211n18
Washington, George, 61, 62, 63, 215n25
Washington Monument, 173
Washington Post, 1–2, 147, 160, 220–21n41
Watergate, 24
Watermark Community Church, 105
weak parties-strong partisanship, 48
Weber, Max, 48
Weinstein, Harvey, 153
welfare, 36, 142
What's the Matter with Kansas, 3, 24, 136
Wheaton College, 151, 160
White House, 5, 54, 82, 84, 88, 165
White, James Boyd, 5
white privilege, 128–29
#WhyIDidntReport, 159
Wikileaks, 80, 148
Wilhite, Jud, 40, 108, 109–18, 119, 120, 144, 145, 224n20, 224n24
William, Prince, 76
Williams, Raymond, 91
Williamson, Vanessa, 12
Willow Creek Community Church, 64, 65, 159, 213n37, 215–16n31
Wilson, Don, 61, 66, 70–71, 95–97, 98
Winthrop, John, 36–37
wisdom, 142–43
Women's March on Washington (2017), 153
Wooddale Church, 88
World Series, 76, 80
World War II, 33, 205–6n31
Wright, J. Elwin, 33
Wynn, Steve, 153

Yale, 62
Yoido Full Gospel Church, 210n7
Young, Ed, 91, 108, 109, 137–44
Youth for Christ, 33

Zimmerman, George, 225–26n38